US-Egypt Diplomacy under Johnson

US-Egypt Diplomacy under Johnson

Nasser, Komer, and the Limits of Personal Diplomacy

Gabriel Glickman

I.B.TAURIS

LONDON • NEW YORK • OXFORD • NEW DELHI • SYDNEY

I.B. TAURIS
Bloomsbury Publishing Plc
50 Bedford Square, London, WC1B 3DP, UK
1385 Broadway, New York, NY 10018, USA
29 Earlsfort Terrace, Dublin 2, Ireland

BLOOMSBURY, I.B. TAURIS and the I.B. Tauris logo are trademarks
of Bloomsbury Publishing Plc

First published in Great Britain 2021
This paperback edition published in 2022

Series design by Adriana Brioso
Cover image © Tango Images / Alamy Stock Photo

A catalogue record for this book is available from the British Library.

A catalog record for this book is available from the Library of Congress.

ISBN: HB: 978-0-7556-3402-6
PB: 978-0-7556-3994-6
ePDF: 978-0-7556-3403-3
eBook: 978-0-7556-3404-0

Typeset by Newgen KnowledgeWorks Pvt. Ltd., Chennai, India

To find out more about our authors and books visit www.bloomsbury.com
and sign up for our newsletters.

For Lexie, Darien, and Sebastian

Contents

Acknowledgments

Thank you to everyone who has opened up doors for me—whether a crack or wide open. First and foremost, Efraim Karsh, who took me on as one of his final PhD students at King's College London. His advice and support over the years, especially during difficult times, was invaluable. He is a mensch. And without his faith in me, so many years ago, I would not be in a position today to be able to write about history and international relations. I cannot thank him enough.

I am grateful to the Made by History section at the *Washington Post*—especially Nicole Hemmer, Kathryn Brownell, and Brian Rosenwald. They are phenomenal editors (I live in a state of anxiety when waiting for their track-changed Word documents), and their helpful feedback on my 2018 article about the value of personal diplomacy with difficult leaders very much shaped my completion of this book. Material from that article, "Has Trump Figured Out a Winning Strategy on North Korea?" is reproduced in the introduction and conclusion chapters with their kind permission.

I also want to thank Alan Johnson of *Fathom* for publishing my article, "How Nasser's Vendetta against America Led the Six-Day War," on the fiftieth anniversary of the 1967 Arab-Israeli War. Material from that article is reproduced in Part 3 with his kind permission. The Association for the Study of the Middle East and Africa (ASMEA) was also kind enough to invite me to share material from the unfinished manuscript for a panel in 2017, where I received helpful feedback and, most importantly, words of encouragement.

I owe a debt of gratitude to Niall Ferguson for the most important words of encouragement I received about the manuscript: to stop fine-tuning it and send it off to the publisher. It is because of his advice that my manuscript was turned into a book.

I also want to thank early reviewers of the manuscript, whether in its entirety or in excerpted papers, for their feedback and encouragement—Michael Sharnoff, Simon Waldman, David Tal, Neill Lochery, Gideon Remez, Isabella Ginor, Doug Feith, Efraim Karsh, and William Quandt—as well as the anonymous reviewers provided by Bloomsbury. All of them helped to shape this book, though I alone am responsible for any of its errors.

Special thanks to Rory Gormley and his team at the I.B. Tauris imprint of Bloomsbury—especially Yasmin Garcha. They opened another door for me by greenlighting this book, and their shepherding of it during a pandemic is nothing short of impressive.

Finally, I want to thank my family. My parents, Richard and Marilyn Glickman, taught me history at a young age. Some of my earliest memories are my mother reading me history in the car while listening to the daily "8 o'clock morning march" on the radio. My father, though he doesn't realize it, is my intellectual hero. It is because of him—his example—that I pursued a PhD in Middle Eastern Studies.

Most importantly, this book is dedicated to my wife, Lexie, and our two sons, Darien and Sebastian. Without Lexie's unwavering support, in particular, this book never would have been written. The three of them remind me on a daily basis that there is more to life than books and documents.

Abbreviations

ADST	Association for Diplomatic Studies and Training
AID	Agency for International Development
ASU	Arab Socialist Union
BOB	Bureau of the Budget
CCC	Commodity Credit Corporation
CIA	Central Intelligence Agency
CINCSTRIKE	Commander in Chief, United States Strike Forces
CREST	CIA Records Search Tool (College Park, Maryland)
DOD	Department of Defense (America)
EXIM	Export-Import Bank
FBIS	Foreign Broadcast Information Service
FCO	Foreign and Commonwealth Office (Britain)
FOIA	Freedom of Information Act
FRUS	Foreign Relations of the United States
FYI	For your information
GAO	Government Accounting Office (America)
GPO	Government Printing Office (America)
IAEA	International Atomic Energy Agency
IMF	International Monetary Fund
JCS	Joint Chiefs of Staff
JFK	President John F. Kennedy
JFKL	John F. Kennedy Presidential Library
LBJ	President Lyndon Baines Johnson
LBJL	Lyndon Baines Johnson Presidential Library
NEA	Bureau of Near Eastern and South Asian Affairs (Department of State)
NSAM	National Security Action Memorandum
NSF	National Security File
NSC	National Security Council
OH	Oral History (Interview)
PL 480	Public Law 480
S/S	Executive Secretariat, Department of State
SSM	Surface-to-surface missile
State	State Department
UAR	United Arab Republic (Egypt)
UARG	United Arab Republic Government
UKNA	The British National Archives (Kew, London)
UN	United Nations

UNYOM   United Nations Yemen Observer Mission
USAID   United States Agency for International Development
USG   United States Government
USNA   United States National Archives (College Park, Maryland)
YAR   Yemen Arab Republic

Note to the Reader

From 1958 to 1971, Egypt was referred to as the United Arab Republic (UAR). This was symbolic of a political union between Egypt and Syria that dissolved in 1961. Egypt carried on the UAR name for a further decade. However, since the events in this book took place after the collapse of the merger, the name "Egypt" is used in the narrative, while passages from documents referring to the "UAR" are left in their original form.

Prologue: The Swerve

On July 21, 1962, amid a celebration in Cairo for the tenth anniversary of the coup that toppled Egypt's last monarch, President Gamal Abdel Nasser oversaw the testing of four rockets in a secluded patch of desert: the long-range "al-Qahir" (The Conqueror) and the shorter-range "Zafir" (The Victorious). Intended for international consumption, the event was attended by numerous Egyptian officials and fifty journalists. It was the first time Nasser held a "press conference" in three years, and the president even stopped his car along the road, where the journalists were gathered, to take questions. Nasser jubilantly claimed Egypt's largest rocket could travel 400 miles, which meant it was within striking distance of Israel. Asked why Egypt needed the rockets, Nasser jokingly retorted, "What is the purpose of a rocket?" On a more serious note he made sure to emphasize that neither rocket was equipped to carry a nuclear payload. "No, we are against that," he insisted.[1]

Despite the military bluster from Cairo and its close association with Moscow, US-Egypt relations were remarkably good at the time. Returning to Washington from a quick visit to Cairo, the Egyptian Ambassador to the United States, Mustafa Kamel, informed his hosts that Nasser felt the United States and Egypt now had "good" relations as opposed to just "normal" relations.[2] This upbeat prognosis was echoed in a Department of State (State) memorandum to Robert Komer, the main Middle East adviser in the National Security Council (NSC), which emphasized the steady improvement in bilateral relations since the resumption of US economic assistance programs in 1959, noting in particular "the progressively increasing disposition of United Arab Republic leaders from President Nasser down the line to consult and be consulted, to be more forthright in discussing issues and exploring solution to problems . . . Whereas formally we faced a wall of suspicion and reserve, we are gradually working into a position of being able to get sympathetic hearings for our views and to elicit reasonably frank and genuine responses."

The note ended with a warning that relations could deteriorate at any point over hot button issues. "We recognize that this is still a very fragile and uncertain relationship," State's memorandum read, "which might easily be broken by a hasty or ill-considered action, whether on the United Arab Republic's part or on ours."[3]

John F. Kennedy, however, hoped good relations would continue. Writing to Nasser a month after the rocket test, he informed him that the US ambassador to Egypt, John Badeau, would soon pay him a visit to discuss the sale of Hawk (surface-to-air) missiles to Israel.[4] The president wanted to get in front of the situation to ensure that Nasser did not use the missile sale as an excuse to sabotage the improving relations between the United States and Egypt. "I am confident that in your reflections you will find these matters, difficult as they are, to be within the limits not to be exceeded," he wrote Nasser. "I can assure you that there is involved no change in United States policy toward the United Arab Republic or the Near East in general; nor is there intended any alteration in the basis of our cordial and expanding relationship." Kennedy had a personal touch with Nasser. Over the years their relationship had been built upon it and maintained through carefully worded letters ghost-written by Komer.[5]

Nonetheless, that all changed on November 22, 1963, when gunshots rang out in front of the Texas School Book Depository in Dallas, killing the young president. Kennedy's death was mourned by the country. However, as condolences from world leaders began to pour into the White House, it soon became clear that the loss was also felt throughout the world.[6] A president with a particular set of values was about to be replaced by another, who would have his own set of values. Lyndon B. Johnson took his place in the oval office the same day Kennedy died. And, at that moment, the axis of American policy toward Egypt swung in a different direction.

Under Kennedy, Nasser had indicated through his Washington ambassador that he thought US-Egypt relations were good. Under Johnson, however, the relationship very clearly deteriorated way before the June 1967 Arab-Israeli War (1967 War)—the point at which Nasser formally severed diplomatic relations.

Preface: The Argument and Themes of the Book

It will come as a surprise to readers that the main figure of this book is Robert Komer—a mid-level foreign policy adviser with a wicked sense of humor (indeed a gift for pithy one-liners in his memos) and a larger personality than his superiors. But Komer was an American Machiavelli: he used strategy and realpolitik to have an outsized influence over American foreign policy. Komer was not a student of strategy; he did not always align his ends with his means or accurately read the political environment in which he operated. He used his Machiavellian skills to pursue big ideas and uncertain gambles—things that Machiavelli looked down upon—and this sometimes led to him losing control over the policies and strategies he spearheaded. Nevertheless, Komer's influence over US-Egypt relations was so significant that relations between the two countries quickly crumbled after he left Middle East policy to work on the Vietnam War in March 1966. Thus, the central argument of this book is that Komer's efforts to engage Nasser, which at times became Herculean and came at a great cost to his standing in Washington, kept diplomatic relations afloat for over five years. In short, Komer's story demonstrates the power of an individual to shape policy as well as how policy can fall apart when a key individual exits the scene.

Komer was not an Arabist, but he certainly was the most important advocate for Nasser in Washington DC from 1961 to 1966. "Komer you're a God-damned Nasser lover," said Johnson to Komer, according to the latter. Johnson assumed that Komer was an Arabist because of his policy prescriptions and that Komer's sympathies clouded his judgment when it came to the Middle East. But what Johnson never understood was that Komer was Jewish—an identity that Komer reportedly kept well hidden.[1] Advocating for good relations with Nasser, an adversary of the only Jewish state in the world, was an exercise in prudent policy for Komer; a matter of choosing national interest over a possible implicit bias.

Some readers will see US efforts at diplomacy with Nasser as a measure of hegemonic pressure—a superpower badgering a small state into doing its bidding in a faraway region or, worse yet, coming under its sphere of influence. Others will see a misguided foreign policy of accommodation (or, perhaps, even appeasement) that demonstrates the perils of working with leaders like Nasser who openly criticize the United States. Recent debates about the nature of US foreign policy during the Cold War raise important questions about the use of aid as a form of coercive power. But rarely do these accounts produce accompanying micro-histories to truly understand the factors that shaped these policies.

Only micro-histories can get to this level of understanding. But this type of history-writing should also be related to concepts or theories that can explain the connections between limited events and the age in which they occur. According to the political scientist Alexander Wendt, a leading proponent of the constructivist theory of international relations, "States are people too." They are "purposive actors with a sense of Self."[2] The story of US-Egypt relations under Johnson not only demonstrates this component of Wendt's theory but also challenges other more deterministic theories of international relations that would explain away relations solely under the rubric of material power; not least because the dominant power in this story, the United States, treats its weaker interlocutor, Egypt, as a formidable rival capable of inflicting significant damage. Wendt's approach, though not religiously applied in this history, allows for viewing international relations in accordance with socially constructed national identities—and, significantly for this story, ideas—that change over time. While Wendt's work did not explicitly allow for the socially constructed identities of individuals in shaping international relations, instead focusing on larger forces and processes, his research no doubt leaves room for this possibility.

In addition to the nature of relations between the United States and Egypt changing from Kennedy to Johnson, coinciding with three transitional phases in which policymakers sympathetic to Kennedy's approach departed from the Johnson administration (Komer being the last), the American "sense of Self," relative to Nasser, certainly underwent a radical change. As described by another international relations scholar, Kori Schake, Wendt's theory posits that "what might have caused war between, say, Britain and Germany in one epoch would not in another because how those states view their interests and each other's behaviour would have changed."[3] The way America defined its interests radically transformed between Kennedy's death and Komer's exit from the Middle East portfolio, thereby contributing to Johnson's negative reception of Nasser's behavior in the international arena. In the center of that transformation was Komer. During his time dealing with Middle East policy under Johnson he behaved like a reactionary, seeking to hold onto his perception of a better past under Kennedy. The larger structural change that coincided with Komer's efforts to swim against the current was America's cultural sense of hegemonic invincibility being shattered by its inability to quickly solve the Vietnam quagmire. The resulting pressure of this critical realization impacted the Johnson administration's interactions with Nasser insofar that it could not handle "another Vietnam," this time in the Middle East, nor could it tolerate the leader of a smaller state so openly challenging its regional interests while its global image was being impugned in Asia.

The culmination of this constantly second-guessing US self-perception was the abandonment of a confident policy of engaging Nasser through personal diplomacy—the art of making a foreign leader feel comfortable through a close and hands-on relationship. Arguably, the limits of a personal diplomacy approach are demonstrated in the story of US-Egypt relations under Johnson; particularly the role of individuals and the feasibility of maintaining a delicate relationship without the guiding hands of those individuals. In short, personal diplomacy may not be a viable long-term strategy for democracies like the United States, where there is a constant changeover in leadership and accompanying staff.

The narrative in this book begins in 1963, starting with the transition from Kennedy to Johnson, and ends at the beginning of the 1967 War. This story of US-Egypt relations should be included in the story of the 1967 War, not least because it represents the very war the United States had hoped to prevent in the Middle East by engaging Nasser through personal diplomacy, but also because the state of relations with America was a concern for Nasser on the eve of that war, and his preoccupation with the collapse of those relations is apparent in speeches he gave in February 1967 denouncing the United States and Israel as one and the same—a message that increased in velocity during the run-up to war and suddenly dovetailed with his moves against Israel in May after years of promising the United States that the Arab-Israeli conflict was contained in an "icebox." This reversal of Nasser's policy toward Israel is given new meaning when viewed in the context of his sudden estrangement from the Johnson administration— which, according to observers at the time, left Nasser seething in the months leading up to the war. The 1967 War is an event that could be viewed as the conclusion to the US-Egypt diplomacy narrative of the 1960s—a tragic end.

The story in this book has themes that resonate on a broad level: the idealism vs. realism debate in US foreign policy (in this case, the merit of working with a difficult leader like Nasser); the role of individuals in crafting and shepherding policy; and the ramifications of inconsistent policy. Thus, in addition to being a micro-history, this book is a study of how foreign policy is constituted and why it must be shepherded in order not to fail. The intention is to produce "applied history"—a set of lessons that can be turned to in future situations with difficult leaders.

A motif in this book that underlies the themes identified above is American grand strategy in the Middle East. This was a strategy that changed from administration to administration. Presidents and their advisers had different ways of approaching the issues of a region that traditionally had little importance in American foreign policy— that is, until the British pulled out of the Persian Gulf at the end of the 1960s, and America came to see itself as the sole power responsible for upholding the former empire's security obligations in the region.

Middle East policy under Kennedy and Johnson was secondary to the more important struggle against the Soviet Union. America's Cold War strategy was to contain the communist superpower until it reached a point where its internal contradictions—the struggle for political power and nationalist ambitions under an ideology that eschewed such things—would lead to its fatal combustion.[4] Sometimes this meant Middle East strategy was approached under the rubric of the larger containment strategy. Since Nasser led arguably the most powerful nation in the Middle East and held unmatched influence on the Arab street, he was seen as a likely bridgehead for Soviet incursion into the region. A redirection strategy was crafted under Kennedy that was intended to guide Nasser away from the Soviets. It consisted of giving Nasser generous amounts of economic assistance in order to develop Egypt's economy. Nasser was aware of this strategy and, as will be seen, played on American fears of a Soviet-Egypt alliance in order to get substantial economic assistance out of the United States without having to moderate his stances that ran counter to America's interests. Ultimately, this tactic failed to move Johnson, who was more reluctant to give aid than Kennedy, thus leading to the diplomatic break in 1967. Johnson, arguably, let his personal feelings about Nasser override his sense of strategy.

Since this book provides a look at American grand strategy in the Middle Eastern context, a brief overview of strategy is in order. Isaiah Berlin, the perspicacious British historian of ideas, wrote a book in 1953 that unwittingly explains the underpinnings of strategy—it is called *The Hedgehog and the Fox*. The philosophical focus of Berlin's book, which was a literary analysis of Tolstoy's *War and Peace*, was a line from the ancient Greek poet Archilochus: "The fox knows many things, but the hedgehog knows one big thing." As explained by Berlin, there are thinkers who see endless possibilities, but are hesitant to commit to any one action (foxes); and there are thinkers who act according to one "central vision," but without regard for the various possible outcomes (hedgehogs). Berlin did not know at the time that the parable he resurrected was the most apt description for grand strategy. Rather, he believed it was a way to classify thinkers and applied it to "human beings in general."[5]

This parable and Berlin's book were recently resurrected by the American Cold War historian, John Lewis Gaddis. The latter writes in his book, *On Grand Strategy*, that "intelligence requires ... the coexistence of opposites within a space" and, most importantly, that an individual must simultaneously possess these opposites "while retaining the ability to function"—in other words, being both fox and hedgehog at the same time.[6]

Grand strategy, as it applied toward Nasser, meant that the Johnson administration was required to work with him, in spite of ideological and personal differences, because the alternative scenario meant undermining the Cold War containment strategy by allowing the Soviets to expand their influence in another part of the world. Komer understood this. Many in Washington, including Johnson, did not.

Finally, while this book is primarily a history and an international relations case study, it also falls under the genre of tragedy. Alongside Komer, the other central figure in the story is Nasser, because either he is the one driving events or others make their decisions based on what they think Nasser will say or do. In Greek tragedy, a main character often falls at the height of their power. At the beginning of this story Nasser is courted by the Kennedy administration. By the end, he is shunned by Johnson. This shift in Nasser's relationship with the United States concludes with him going to war against Israel—the catastrophic results of which leave Nasser a shell of his former self until his death in 1970.

Ironically, Nasser is also a deuteragonist in the narrative, a secondary character unwittingly supporting or spoiling Komer's efforts in Washington; and Komer, at times, plays a similar role for Nasser. Although the two characters' stories are entwined, Nasser's motivations and decision-making procedures are mostly shrouded in mystery since the relevant Egyptian archives are not widely accessible. And while there is a plethora of scholarship seeking to account for these gaps in information about Nasser's life, many of them rely upon conjecture or interviews with personalities who were invested in portraying Nasser in a positive light.[7] Therefore, while this book illuminates many aspects of Nasser's story not found in previous studies, sadly it is not possible to fully account for Nasser's agency in the same way as Komer and his cohort. This book portrays Nasser from the American perspective at the time, from which he was constantly second-guessed as an inscrutable and mercurial character. In this way, the primary focus is on the motivations of American policymakers and their perceptions of Nasser rather than the other way around.

Nevertheless, given that Nasser is an important character in this story and is primarily portrayed through Westerners trying to make sense of him, a short context of his background is in order.

The son of a postal worker, Nasser was a simple person in spite of his stature as Egypt's postcolonial modernizer. His favorite food was white cheese. He denied his children the luxury of meat at least once a week. And until the day he died, he maintained a private residence in the modest Manshiet al-Bakr neighborhood of Cairo. To be sure, it was a step-up from the mud-brick house in Alexandria where he grew up, but it was still a far cry from the shimmering golden palaces occupied by future leaders in the Middle East, many of whom would proclaim themselves as Nasser's heir. At first the villa was one-story tall. Nasser later expanded it by one floor in order to entertain foreign guests. The Egyptian leader wanted his "palace" to retain the illusion of a private residence.[8] He was known to be a heartfelt and personable man—a quality that would make and break his relations with the United States from the warmer days of Kennedy to the standoffishness of Johnson.

Brown eyes, tanned skin, and a pearly smile made up the portrait of Nasser's charming physical appearance. He had a neatly kept moustache that followed the curve of his upper lip. And he wore an always trimmed haircut that implied experience with swathes of matching silver above the ears. If Nasser hadn't been a politician, he might well have been a movie star.

In many ways, Nasser's charm offset his ambition. Without his magnetic smile and seemingly warm embrace of potential foes, he would have been left exposed with an ideology that envisioned himself in control of a vast Middle Eastern empire. However, his dreaming earned him a nickname in Washington DC: "Hitler on the Nile."

In the nineteenth century, Egyptians were chanting "Egypt for Egyptians" to the annoyance of their Ottoman masters in Istanbul.[9] Nasser had bigger plans for Egypt in the twentieth century. As a military man who overthrew his country's monarchy in 1952—a monarchy that was viewed by the Egyptian people as a ruse for British colonial rule—he followed a consistent dogma from the beginning of his rule over Egypt. His ambitious agenda was to modernize Egypt and establish it as the hub, even center, of the Arab, African, and Muslim Worlds.[10]

Nasser promised a gradual, yet consistent, revolution for his country.[11] He proposed to "increase agricultural output by 50 percent," "increase national production by $450,000,000 a year" and "add an annual government revenue of $60,000,000."[12] He also proposed to reclaim "cultivated land" through an ambitious public works project which would also be "for the benefit of the Palestine refugees." There would be an "Agrarian Reform Program" that would "increase agricultural production per acre." Peasants would become "owners of their land."[13] New factories would be built and goods produced.[14] There would be "measures to help private industry," "new outlets in foreign markets," and most importantly, a reduction of "our imports of foodstuffs and manufactured goods . . . chiefly wheat, oil, and household articles." In the end, he said, "These savings will not only improve Egypt's trade balance, but also preserve precious earnings in hard currency."[15]

This was Nasser's revolutionary mandate, but it would take time to achieve such lofty and ambitious social and political aims. Herodotus described Egypt as a "land that was deposited by the river," adding that the land was the "gift of the river to the Egyptians."[16] In Nasser's time, that gift was spoiled by famine and economic mismanagement, which made achieving his revolutionary mandate unrealistic.

Nasser employed the language of socialism, but he was not a communist. This made him an enigma to American policymakers who were used to seeing the global chessboard in black-and-white. So too did his presence in the nonaligned movement (countries that claimed neutrality in the Soviet-American competition). For American policymakers, it was unclear whether this made Nasser more or less of a threat to America's Cold War strategy.

The foundation of America's policy toward Nasser was an acute awareness that the Egyptian leader wielded considerable power and influence within the Arab world and beyond. This observation had been made early on in his rise to power.[17] However, there was a certain paradox to the viewpoint: no matter how anti-Western Nasser appeared, America believed that it could have good relations with him. Oscillations between this belief and moments of genuine contempt for Nasser among policymakers and members of Congress translated into uneven policy.

In a study of Soviet policy in the Middle East, Mohamed Heikal, a close confidante of and adviser to Nasser, noted that Nasser had a written system for "how to deal with the Soviets."[18] Nasser, however, no doubt also had a system for dealing with America. He would often present himself as an influential figure who could either help American interests in the Middle East or make trouble for them.[19] Under Johnson, that strategy finally fell apart.

Part One

After Kennedy
(November 1963–June 1964)

1

Introduction: Kennedy's Men

John F. Kennedy was not the first president of the United States to have lofty goals—but he was certainly one of the most uplifting when articulating them. He said at his acceptance speech at the Democratic National Convention in 1960 that he was going to create a "new frontier" for the United States. Like the frontier of the bygone American West, this new frontier represented "unknown opportunities and perils." However, rather than it being an exercise in grabbing land for the United States—as frontiers typically are—this new frontier was about revitalizing America's influence in the world. Among other things, Kennedy sought to tackle the "unsolved problems of peace and war." He also wanted to match the revolutionary zeal of the Soviet Union, whose appeal for a new universal truth for humanity under the rubric of socialism threatened America and the spread of liberal democracy. Unlike his predecessors Woodrow Wilson and Franklin Roosevelt, whose respective and equally lofty promises to find "New Freedom" and a "New Deal" for the American public were intended to provide comfort for the American people at home, Kennedy admitted he was asking Americans to be his "pioneers" abroad. Americans would have to roll up their shirtsleeves and work longer hours. The country was on the precipice of a turning point in history, Kennedy argued. His prospective presidency was a matter of achieving "national greatness" or entering "national decline."[1]

Once he secured the presidency in November 1960, Kennedy immediately went to work to turn his idealism into reality. He began by recruiting bright and energetic Ivy League scholars who shared his idealism. David Halberstam famously described them as "the best and the brightest" and the "whiz kids."[2] These scholars-turned-activists were the intellectual vanguard of Kennedy's new America. There were no ideas too big for his administration. The dreamy atmosphere usually afforded to the ivory tower at Harvard was seemingly transported to the bureaucratic hustle and bustle of Washington DC.

When Kennedy was assassinated three years later, in November 1963, his administration suddenly became Johnson's. Along with it, Johnson inherited a policy paradigm that began under Kennedy.[3]

Johnson did not share the idealism of his predecessor. Neither did he particularly trust the previous administration's officials. He deeply disliked Attorney General Bobby Kennedy, whom he viewed as a political competitor. And he dismissed the rest of the personnel, both staffers and officials, as "Harvard men." This put Johnson at odds with his predecessor's taste for "intellect and culture."[4] The high culture of the Kennedy administration was replaced with the hard pragmatism of a man who had worked as a schoolteacher to put himself through college.

Hailing from Stonewall, Texas, a Hill Country town, Johnson was the grandson of a cattle speculator and the son of a Texas politician. Both men left their mark on the thirty-sixth president of the United States. His grandfather, Samuel Ealy Johnson Sr., was the first in the family to dabble in politics. Lyndon Johnson won his first elected office at age 28—the same age as his grandfather. His father, Samuel Ealy Johnson Jr., won his first office at age 27. Fathers often have high expectations for their sons, which can lead to paternal disappointment. But Lyndon Johnson was the disappointed one in the relationship. A bad investment by his father when he was 13 put the family at "the bottom of the heap," according to Johnson. The son vowed to do better than his father.[5]

Johnson had an old face even when he was a young man. The wrinkles on his forehead, the pulled cheeks, and a small southern smile suggested a friendly, but take-no-nonsense, attitude. At 6 feet 4 inches, Johnson was taller than most. He was tied with Abraham Lincoln, a calm and steady giant, for being the tallest president. Johnson used his elevation to intimidate others. He was famous for giving the "Johnson treatment," in which he would lean over his interlocutor: legs straight, hands in pockets, and the upper torso uncomfortably occupying the boundaries of the other person's space. Johnson liked to use this technique on staffers, members of Congress, and even a Supreme Court justice.

Robert Komer, the top Middle East adviser in the White House, liked Johnson very much. The two men first met in 1962 on a trip to the Middle East. Komer was one of the few "Kennedy men" Johnson came to trust. Komer spoke plainly—like Johnson. And the two men had a shared dislike of the "Eastern establishment." Although Komer was a Harvard graduate, he considered himself a "Missouri boy" at heart, and attributed his affinity for Johnson to that aspect of his identity.[6]

Johnson, for his part, valued Komer's ability to take on difficult tasks and see them through to completion. Komer was skilled at blustering his way through bureaucratic red tape. He received the nickname "Blowtorch Bob" because of his later role as Johnson's peace czar in South Vietnam. The moniker referred to his aggressiveness when pursuing any given policy. Quite simply, Komer never gave up. As described by Henry Cabot Lodge II, the American ambassador to South Vietnam, arguing with Komer was like someone taking a flamethrower to the seat of your pants. [7] Even Komer was willing to admit, "I'm a much more activist guy . . . I was always saying 'Hey, let's do this, let's do that.'"[8]

Before Komer switched full-time to the war in Vietnam in March 1966, he was the top Middle East adviser in the National Security Council (NSC) under Kennedy and Johnson. It was in this role that Komer came to have a large impact on US foreign policy in the Middle East—and, crucially, on diplomatic relations with Egypt, arguably the largest power wielder in the region.

A former colleague of Komer's, John Jernegan, later described him as a Middle East policy coordinator situated between State and the White House. This was unusual because the NSC traditionally had no authority over State—which was the main body for running foreign policy. Komer managed to build up a strong personal relationship with Kennedy, even occasionally pushing him to make certain interventions in the Middle East:

> Bob Komer is such a live wire and was strategically placed in the White House staff with easy access to Mac Bundy [National Security Adviser] and relatively easy access to the President personally . . . While some people complained about this arrangement (claiming the White House staff under Bundy was duplicating or overriding the State Department), our experience in the Near Eastern Bureau was not bad . . . Komer was very knowledgeable, very bright, as I said, full of ideas, full of energy, and usually could get the ear of Bundy and/or the President at least to put a problem or something requiring decision before them quickly.[9]

As a result of Komer's high access (not to mention high stock) within the White House, State officials would often send him drafts of interdepartmental telegrams (between State and US embassies in the Middle East) for input. State relied on Komer to gage Kennedy's and later Johnson's thinking on Middle East policy—most situations did not warrant directly bothering the president. But, in reality, Komer was often the one driving policy. This was a working relationship that began under Kennedy and was continued under Johnson for the first few years of his presidency until the Vietnam War overtook his foreign policy in 1966.[10]

Komer did not work alone. He relied on close allies to support whatever policy he was driving at the time. His most important ally was Phillips Talbot, the assistant secretary of state for Middle Eastern and Asian affairs. According to Komer, the secretary of state, Dean Rusk, had "great confidence" in Talbot. Komer also earned the confidence of his superior, McGeorge Bundy, the national security adviser to the president, who, in turn, had the ear of Kennedy and Johnson. "I could probably sell [Bundy]   unless we were suggesting something really wild," Komer later recalled. Indeed, he was aware that he and Talbot had an atypical amount of influence for their positions. "In essence we were in an unusual sideshow area where the second level or third level guys were really running the show as long as their bosses had confidence in them," he later said.[11] According to Komer, this arrangement was tolerated because "it was an unusually competent group," and the Middle East was considered a "secondary problem area" by both presidents and Rusk.[12]

Bundy had another reason for empowering Komer. According to him:

> I was fortunate in having for most of the countries of the third world that most unlikely soft-liner, Mr. Robert Komer, who got himself almost perfectly attuned to the Kennedy mind, and was an extremely valuable staff officer in very large areas of the world where he came to know what the President was going to want, and where the President came to know that what Komer recommended coincided with his own temperamental approach to the matter, and really my only usefulness was in knowing that it was better to stand out of the way.[13]

Komer was brought into the NSC at the beginning of the Kennedy administration. His hiring was part of an evolution of the NSC's role in foreign policy-making. Bundy angled to run a more efficient and leaner version of State from the NSC. This vision became a concrete reality during the botched Bay of Pigs invasion in 1961, when Kennedy had the NSC moved into the White House basement from across the street. Thereafter, in the words of one scholar, Bundy effectively turned the role of national security adviser "to that of a cabinet secretary."[14]

The NSC, under Bundy's watch, became a place for foreign policy-making rather than its traditional role as the president's personal think tank on international affairs. All information that was considered important for conducting foreign policy flowed through Bundy to Kennedy, and later Johnson when he came into office. The NSC also became a clearinghouse for vital communication going abroad.[15] To pull off this new approach, Bundy required staffers capable of quick decision-making and bureaucratic leveraging. Komer fit this description.

In one interview, Komer told the story of how he got his job because he wrote to Bundy that he ought to abolish the NSC's "papermill." Under Eisenhower the NSC gained a reputation for writing academic papers without regard for tangible policy decisions. When Bundy called in Komer for a meeting, Komer spoke his mind. Bundy asked, "What do you think about the NSC structure? Is the NSC as big a papermill as we think it is?" According to Komer, "I said, 'absolutely. I think you are very much on the right track. Having an NSC meeting over a single operative word in the 34th paragraph of a twenty-five-page booklet on France is no way to make policy.'"[16]

Another reason Komer was brought into Kennedy's NSC was because he understood how Washington worked. Komer had been the CIA's liaison to the NSC under Eisenhower and had attended every meeting. As Komer later said: "Bill Bundy [McGeorge Bundy's brother] told me that brother Mac [Bundy] had asked him to suggest a couple of bright middle-level doers inside the Eisenhower Administration whom he should pick up because they'd know where the bodies are buried and who plugs into whom ... So I was hired partly as an inside man who knew how the machine had worked."[17]

Komer was an ideal fit for Kennedy's bold new vision. One radical idea he had coming into the NSC was to hit the reset button on US relations with Nasser. He later recalled:

> So as my valedictory I sat down and wrote a four page, double-spaced memo to Bundy and Rostow [Deputy National Security Adviser] saying, "I have been three years in the NSC policy business, and in my view here are a dozen unfamiliar issues which the New Frontier is going to have to tackle because the last frontier didn't. These are not the great big issues that you fellows already know about, like arms control or re-examination of NATO strategy." They were like: Can we establish a workable relationship with Nasser?[18]

From the White House, Komer was in a position to steer the president's approach to Nasser. However, he also desired a counterpart in Cairo to interact with and guide Nasser in person. That role fell to John Badeau, whose name was placed on a so-called talent list and handed to Kennedy. Badeau was chosen for his expertise on Egypt. He spoke fluent Arabic and had previously been the president of the American University in Cairo. According to Badeau, Kennedy "had identified certain countries where he felt our policies were distanced or we had unusual problems, and he wanted to appoint these people who had a particular background of experience or knowledge or competency in that country."[19]

Undersecretary of State Chester Bowles, the man who recruited Badeau, later described how Kennedy restructured State and brought in new people to better fit his foreign policy vision: "In a sense, I think it is fair to say that Kennedy during this period looked on the State Department as a huge bureaucratic roadblock to all the things he would like to do. He saw foreign policy making [as] a personal basis—moving from problem to problem or area to area." As a result, Kennedy sought out experts like Badeau and empowered them. According to Bowles, "Most of the new people were from the universities or from foundations—individuals who knew foreign affairs, had experience in it, were professionals, had been abroad, and were a kind of new element in foreign affairs. Kennedy backed this change very fully by ordering a directive to all the ambassadors to really take charge of the embassies and run the whole mission. I think this constituted a kind of a revolution in the operation of embassies and the choice of ambassadors."[20]

In line with Kennedy's shake-up of the foreign policy establishment, Komer staged his own intervention in American Middle East policy. Specifically, he sought to mold Badeau to fulfill the role of a guide for Nasser; to gently redirect him when he came into conflict with the United States. Komer later recalled that Badeau initially came into State skeptical of his push to build a new relationship with Nasser. A few months later, however, Komer and Talbot sat down with him when he was home for consultations and convinced him that Nasser was capable of becoming a strategic partner. According to Komer, Badeau thereafter became the "strongest advocate" for his pro-Nasser policy and a key component of the redirection strategy.[21]

Badeau himself later recalled that it was Komer who ran Middle East policy in the White House. "No. not with Bundy. My most steady contact was with Bob Komer because Komer really appeared to be the person chiefly responsible in the White House staff. He more or less rode herd on the [State] department, on Phil Talbot."[22] Komer agreed with this type of description of his role in and influence on Kennedy and Johnson's foreign policy-making. "I do not think this organization undermines morale, by and large, within the State Department," he later recalled. "Let's just take the area I know best, the Middle East and Africa. Those guys were pathetically grateful—this went right on down to the desk officers—that they had their man at the White House. I was regarded as much as their man at the White House as Kennedy and Johnson's man at screwing them."[23]

While Komer was initially brought into Kennedy's NSC to control State's handling of Middle Eastern policy,[24] his influence increased under Johnson because of the new president's initial hands-off approach to foreign policy-making. Komer later recalled that Johnson "was less knowledgeable in foreign policy." Eventually, Johnson came to rely more on State because he thought foreign policy should not be run from the White House. However, State more or less continued to rely on Komer until his departure for Vietnam in 1966. As Komer observed, "by that time everybody had been working so much in this informal pattern that it continued."[25]

In part, Komer's unusual role as an NSC staffer was due to Bundy's hands-off corporate management style of the president's "foreign policy shop."[26] Bundy ran the

NSC like a business CEO and delegated to senior officials whom he essentially treated as corporate vice presidents. This allowed Bundy to be highly organized, efficient, and quick to make decisions based on the recommendations of his trusted staff. Bundy "generally ruled the way I hoped," Komer later recalled.[27]

Indeed, Bundy empowered his staff. They did not just come up with policy, they also actively pursued its implementation. For example, Komer described the unusually close working relationship between Bundy's NSC and the Bureau of Budget (BOB): "Money dictates policy . . . there was not much point in our coming up with a brave new policy toward Latin America, Nasser, or anybody else if the requisite appropriations or adjustments could not be made . . . frequently Budget knew ways to get money that we didn't, so we worked extremely close with Budget."[28]

Nonetheless, although Komer was well situated in the White House by the time Johnson became president, the two had fundamentally different ideas about how to approach and practice foreign policy. Johnson viewed the world according to the norms of nineteenth-century European imperialism. As described by one historian, "Johnson subscribed to the doctrine of credibility, which dictates that a great power must be consistent in its direction, even when it discovers it is wrong, in order to husband its credibility and maintain the trust of other nations." The problem was: great power nations, like the United States, were no longer seen as infallible in the twentieth century. Nationalism had taken root since World War I, and every nation (both small and large) was equally jealous to guard its independence from would-be empires.[29]

Komer, however, was a pragmatist who believed in the necessity of a fluid response mechanism in American foreign policy. In his eyes, a twentieth-century superpower nation like the United States needed to be adaptable, and capable of mounting a rapid response to the crises sometimes injected into the global arena by much smaller nations. Komer did not view the Cold War in terms of two competing ideologies, that is, the Western "free world" or the "communist world." Instead, he saw the benefit of maintaining good relations with so-called neutralists—the proud nationalist leaders of smaller countries that refused to take sides in the Cold War—like Nasser.[30]

Komer and Kennedy had shared this view that it was better to deal with neutralist leaders as individuals rather than as potential customers of the two competing Cold War ideologies. According to Bundy, "[Kennedy] had a very clear sense that Nasser was Nasser and not a Soviet stooge."[31] Indeed, if Nasser was not an American nor Soviet stooge, then at least his supposed neutralism helped to check Soviet incursion into the Middle East. It was this philosophy that Komer admired the most about Kennedy. And he would later attempt to emulate it under Johnson. "[Kennedy] was the first American President who really understood the nationalist revolution and the revolution of modernization in the underdeveloped areas," Komer later said, "and the necessity of both adjusting to it and feeding it in order to guide it in directions that served our interests."[32]

Komer applied Kennedy's philosophy to Nasser—who rose to power in 1952, by overthrowing Egypt's British-installed constitutional monarchy, and was jealous to guard his nationalist revolution from outside powers. For the most part, the Eisenhower administration had labeled developing countries like Egypt in terms of friend or enemy. Nasser was originally a friend. However, after the 1956 Suez Crisis, when Nasser seized the Suez Canal from its British and French owners and then accepted Soviet aid, Eisenhower came to view Nasser's ideology of Arab nationalism with suspicion, and later as a potential communist threat that needed to be contained. Eisenhower eventually cut off American aid to Egypt, and said American soldiers would deploy to the Middle East if Nasser ever attempted to expand territorially under the banner of his self-proclaimed empire, the United Arab Republic (UAR).[33]

Komer described Eisenhower's thinking as "rigid and moralistic," and incompatible "with the realities of life in the third [i.e., neutralist] areas."[34] He believed leaders like Nasser could be encouraged to adopt pro-Western policies if they could be convinced that a relationship with the United States would be genuine and stable. Indeed, Komer subscribed to a school of thought that partly blamed the Suez Crisis on the United States and Britain for withdrawing funding for Nasser's ambitious construction of the Aswan High Dam. Komer believed that economic aid was the most efficient vehicle for demonstrating authenticity and fostering a relationship. The lesson of Aswan was that Nasser could inflict damage upon the United States if he wasn't engaged. Moreover, if backed in to a corner, he would turn to the Soviets for help—which is what he did for Aswan. Therefore, under Komer's urging, the United States brokered an unprecedented three-year aid agreement with Egypt in 1962 under a foreign assistance program commonly known as PL 480 (Public Law 480) or Food for Peace. The deal gave Nasser a level of comfort knowing that Egypt's food requirements (which were subject to regular shortages due to its outdated agricultural system and frequent ecological disasters) would be taken care of—especially wheat, a low-cost staple of the Egyptian diet. At the same time, the United States accepted that Egypt was to be an independent, nonaligned nation. Nasser had to repay some of the aid in Egyptian currency. However, in return, the United States would spend a portion of it on development projects in Egypt, which would build up the country's infrastructure.[35]

The Soviet Union, however, also realized the value of personal diplomacy. And, as Komer observed, they too began to give economic aid (as opposed to just military aid) to "bourgeois nationalist regimes" like Nasser's, so long as those regimes remained reasonably neutral. Thus, by the mid-1960s, foreign aid in the Middle East turned into another Cold War stalemate, with both superpowers supplying aid to block each other's advances in the region.[36]

This development meant that Johnson needed a fluid approach to foreign aid in order to compete with the Soviets. However, he did not share Kennedy's interest in the third world. As his advisers later recalled, Johnson cared more about reacting to crises than preventing them.[37] Thus, responsibility for ensuring smooth relations with Nasser fell to the remaining optimistic officials like Komer, Talbot, and Badeau—with Komer being the lead, and the one who would work on Middle East policy the longest under Johnson.

The United States was faced with several potential crises in the Middle East that happened to boil over as Johnson took office. Komer and State reacted to these crises with a strategy to present the Johnson administration as a continuation of the Kennedy administration. Thus, for the first six months, the policy was to continue interacting with Nasser as much as possible—as Kennedy had done—in order to redirect his decision-making on issues that affected America's interests in the Middle East. Most importantly, however, Komer did his best to convince the new president that Kennedy's approach to Nasser was worth preserving.

2

Komer's War

Under Kennedy, the most important issue Komer had worked on was a civil war in Yemen. The war began in September 1962 when the head of state, Imam Ahmad bin Yahya, died and left the throne to his son, Muhammad al-Badr. Capitalizing on the uncertainty surrounding the political transition, the commander of the palace guard, Abdullah Sallal, seized power with the help of the military and proclaimed a new state, which he called the Yemen Arab Republic. Meanwhile, Badr fled to the northern mountains of Yemen from where he launched a resistance. Sallal's republican government (Sallal's new Yemeni state was "republican" insofar as the new leader sought to portray himself as a man of the people and not another monarch) was left in control of two-thirds of Yemen, while Badr's royalist forces—comprising Yemeni pastoral tribes—controlled a mountainous region to the north and northeast.[1]

Sallal was ostensibly a Nasserist: a true believer in the Egyptian leader's call for a union between Arab nationalist states. So, when Sallal learned Badr had managed to flee the capital on foot during the coup, he asked for Nasser's help stamping out any would-be resistance from the deposed monarch. Eager to resurrect his image after the short-lived merger of Egypt and Syria under the so-called United Arab Republic (Nasser was effectively deposed in Syria by the then-emergent socialist Ba'ath Party), Nasser responded to the call. He sent troops to Yemen and set his sights on Badr's mountainous stronghold which fatefully (or perhaps strategically) happened to be alongside Saudi Arabia's southern border. Saudi Arabia was deeply concerned about having Nasser on its doorstep. Not surprising, it immediately opened a supply line to Badr's forces to keep the Egyptian leader at bay. Rather than remaining a local conflict, Yemen's civil war became a proxy war between the two most powerful Arab nations.[2]

The likelihood of the situation turning into a direct clash between Egypt and Saudi Arabia—which would have been the Middle Eastern equivalent of Europe's 1914 nightmare of entangled alliances—increased when Egypt initiated an aerial bombing campaign that crossed into Saudi Arabia's territory.

At Komer's urging, the Kennedy administration did not publicly choose a side in this conflict. But the brewing conflict's relevance to America's Cold War grand strategy was well understood in Washington: two recipients of American aid were on the verge of war; if that happened, the Soviet Union was likely to increase its military aid to Nasser in a bid to win his allegiance. From the Americans' perspective, they did not want regional instability to provide another opportunity for further Soviet encroachment in that part of the world.

Not surprising, Kennedy resorted to diplomacy to pull the two Arab adversaries apart. In March 1963, he sent Ellsworth Bunker, a former US ambassador to Argentina and Italy, to mediate between Saudi Arabia and Egypt. In return for Riyadh's agreement to a ceasefire in Yemen, Bunker promised Crown Prince Faisal (the real authority figure in Saudi Arabia, much to the dismay of his brother, King Saud) a squadron of noncombatant American planes as a demonstration of America's commitment to the Arab Kingdom. To demonstrate his own commitment to resolving the conflict, Faisal was asked to stop the flow of supplies to Badr's royalists. Faisal only partly followed through: he decreased the amount of supplies but did not completely stop it. Nevertheless, Kennedy sent the squadron. It soon became apparent that Kennedy had made a mistake.

Sending the squadron, despite Riyadh only making a half-hearted effort on the supplies flow, gave Nasser the impression he had been betrayed by Kennedy. Moreover, Nasser saw it as a breach of the so-called Bunker Agreement, which provided him with an excuse to undermine the US-led negotiations even further. He subsequently resisted reducing Egypt's troop levels in Yemen, which was his obligation per the agreement.[3]

Komer oversaw America's response to the Yemen conflict. At his suggestion, the United States had granted diplomatic recognition to the Nasserite Yemen Arab Republic—a controversial move, to be sure, that was intended to make Nasser more comfortable negotiating his exit from the country. Komer's strategy for Yemen was to get Nasser to accept America's security commitment to Saudi Arabia. Komer believed this would lead Nasser to give up Yemen because, "he doesn't want to jeopardize our aid." This strategy required time and constant redirection of the two sides, Egypt and Saudi Arabia, in order to keep the situation from escalating.

As a believer in Kennedy's "new frontier," Komer did not seem to mind the challenge. He seemed to possess a natural inclination for unconventional strategy and was a frequent proponent of unpopular approaches for dealing with Nasser. Indeed, it was he who devised the plan to contain the Yemen conflict by sending American planes to Saudi Arabia, which he hoped would send a strong message to Nasser. Komer later recalled his thinking at the time: "Maybe, instead of using the carrot, we ought to shift a little while to using the stick. I recall that at the time I was advocating the stick a little more strongly than the President or Bundy were and certainly more stronger than the State Department. The State people were very much opposed to pushing Nasser too hard because they thought it would be counterproductive."[4]

To be sure, Komer was behaving like Gaddis's ideal strategist: he was willing take whatever approach he thought was best—no matter how contradictory or controversial it seemed in the moment—as long as it served a long-term purpose. On Yemen, he believed it was necessary to redouble "efforts to end the war" to prevent Kennedy from having to send American troops. Failure meant being forced to choose a side, which would lead to alienating the opposing side and its allies. Kennedy's entire Middle East policy of neutrality was at stake. "Komer's war" was on the cusp of becoming a wider regional war.[5]

The officials at State were coming up with their own strategies for ending the Yemen conflict. But most of their proposals were more cautious than Komer's. Badeau later recalled his opposition to Komer's handling of Yemen at the time. "Komer professed to be urging much stronger tactics," he said, "possibly, letting American planes patrol the border [and] any Egyptian plane that got out of line, shoot them down. By this time Yemen was called 'Komer's War.' I set myself very strongly in opposition to that course of policy."[6]

This struggle over strategy between Komer and State became typical of Komer's pattern of operation. It was not so much a disagreement over policy as it was figuring out the best means to an end. In the case of Yemen, the goal was to contain the war without having to choose one side over the other. Komer did not actually want to shoot down Egyptian planes. Rather, he hoped the presence of American planes would send a strong enough message to Nasser that he needed to back down over Yemen. Thus, the potential aerial operation was given an appropriate title: Operation Hard Surface.

Secretary of State Dean Rusk, however, was the opposite of Komer: cautious, conventional, and slow-moving. Indeed, Rusk never had truly fit in with Kennedy's "new frontiersman." He resented how much foreign policy was being run from the White House and that it was increasingly run at Bundy's discretion instead of his. Rusk dragged his feet on Middle East strategy. Sometimes, it seemed he was doing so in order to protest the administration's entire foreign policy operation. Because of this, Komer often got frustrated with Rusk to no end. And, by extension, he would become at odds with State whenever Talbot failed to win support for their shared agenda vis-à-vis Nasser.[7]

It was Kennedy himself who coined the phrase, "Komer's War." He intended it as a joke about Komer's frequent briefings at the White House about Yemen. This joke was taken a step further by Bundy, who once said to a reporter, "When it goes well, we call it Komer's war, and when it goes poorly, we call it Talbot's war."[8] In the summer of 1963, Komer's war was increasingly becoming Talbot's war.

Specifically, Saudi Arabia and Egypt were no closer to meeting their obligations under the Bunker Agreement for a ceasefire. And, to make matters worse, the UN Yemen Observer Mission (UNYOM), an impartial, international security force that was necessary to have in place in Yemen if there was even to be a ceasefire, was in danger of falling apart because Yugoslavia and Canada wanted to pull their troops out. These significant obstacles led Komer to admit the failure of his strategy to Kennedy a little over a month before the president's untimely death. On October 7, Komer wrote, "Our Yemen enterprise is in danger of coming unstuck." Komer thought it was time for Kennedy to use personal diplomacy on Faisal and Nasser.

Komer advised Kennedy that the first step to salvaging Yemen was to strengthen the UNYOM—it was the only security mechanism capable of establishing a neutral zone between the belligerents, short of sending in US troops. As it will be recalled, although Faisal and Nasser failed to keep their mutual promises to de-escalate in Yemen (though Faisal did significantly reduce the supply line), the United States sent a squadron of planes to Saudi Arabia. Komer began to worry that Egypt might actually attack Saudi Arabia while the planes were there, and that the United States would then be forced to respond. His solution was to reduce the tension between Faisal and Nasser by getting Nasser to *immediately* reduce his troop levels in Yemen.[9]

The first step in the new strategy, according to Komer, was "to go back hard at Nasser" in a personal message from Kennedy. Komer believed that a message from the president, whom Nasser highly respected, would carry significant weight in Cairo. Indeed, in the past, their correspondence had succeeded in de-escalating tensions between the two countries. Nasser had even once said that he considered the correspondence to be symbolic of a special relationship between him and Kennedy.

There was no way for Komer to know at the time, but his approach was a surefire misstep: pegging Nasser's behavior on his relationship with Kennedy meant that the latter's death one month later would be viewed by Nasser as a release from any of his obligations vis-à-vis Yemen. Before that fateful November 1963 trip to Texas, however, Komer was trying everything in his power to avoid the outbreak of a direct war between Egypt and Saudi Arabia. He wrote to Bundy, "We're moving forward on preventing [a] Yemen crisis, on which I'm spending all [my] necessary time."[10]

Kennedy, for his part, liked Komer's new approach. He was happy to get more involved with the Yemen conflict because it was an opportunity to demonstrate the power of personal diplomacy to head off a developing crisis. On October 19, two messages from Kennedy, which were actually written by Komer, were sent to the US embassies in Saudi Arabia and Egypt. Each US ambassador met with their respective hosts and read to them their separate messages from Kennedy.

The message to Faisal was brief. Mostly, it was intended to reassure him about America's security commitment to the Arab Kingdom. Komer wanted to keep the Saudis in a holding pattern while he worked on Nasser. The key line of the message to Faisal went, "We intend to exert strong pressure on President Nasser and expect to be able to see the results shortly."[11]

In the message to Nasser, Komer made sure to play up the personal relationship between the Egyptian leader and Kennedy. The scolding message that Komer ultimately wanted to convey to Nasser had to follow warmer opening words. Thus, the message began, "In the spirit of frank exchange which I believe we have both come to value I must tell you of my own personal concern over the UAR's failure to date to carry out its part of the Yemen disengagement agreement." With that affirmation of friendship, designed to keep Nasser reading, the message then admonished the Egyptian leader for not following through with his end of the Bunker Agreement. The United States had no "leverage" with Faisal without proof that Nasser actually planned to disengage from Yemen, went the message from Kennedy via Komer's hand.

Then came the threat of punishment for Nasser. While still attempting to appeal to Nasser's emotions by framing Kennedy as a friend out on the limb of a tree, the message framed Yemen as a fork in the road that would impact the future of US-Egypt relations. The Bunker Agreement had been "underwritten" by Kennedy, went the message, and therefore the president would look bad if Nasser did not honor it. "Because of my own personal role in the matter," went the message from Kennedy, "I think you will understand why I feel involved when the US is criticized both at home and abroad. This issue is inevitably complicating, not least in the Congress, my own effort to carry forward our policy of friendly collaboration in areas of mutual interest with the UAR."

The next few lines in the message then conditioned future American aid to Egypt on Nasser making tangible progress pulling out of Yemen.

There could be no mistaking this message as a carrot; it was all stick. Indeed, Komer hoped Nasser would take the threat seriously enough to consider withdrawing at least a portion of his troops as a gesture of goodwill toward Kennedy. The message from Kennedy concluded by framing the situation as nothing short of US-Egypt relations speeding toward a train wreck. It was Nasser's choice on how to proceed—he could do so with caution or recklessness. "I continue to believe in this policy," went Kennedy's message. "If we should let Yemen affect our larger interests in this manner, we would have lost our ability to shape events and have permitted events to dominate us."[12]

On October 20, Nasser received Kennedy's message from Badeau. He then sat down for a supplemental presentation from the ambassador. The Egyptian leader listened carefully. However, he did not mince words nor hide his feelings when he replied to Badeau that Kennedy must not be aware of Saudi Arabia's continued trickle of supplies to the royalists (indeed, both Komer and Kennedy were aware). Nasser continued to respond to Kennedy's message with an air of defiance: Egypt would not unilaterally disengage from Yemen, he said. Moreover, he added, the Bunker Agreement had a built-in understanding that Egypt was under no obligation to reduce its troop levels in Yemen until three months after Saudi Arabia completely stopped its supply line to the royalists. And Faisal had not yet done that, Nasser said.[13]

In this way, Komer had inadvertently made a small, but significant mistake when writing Kennedy's message: by failing to recognize Nasser's legitimate grievance about Faisal's half-hearted follow-through on the supply flow, the Kennedy administration had somewhat damaged its credibility in the eyes of Nasser. The Egyptian leader now had the impression that the United States was working against him in Yemen for Faisal's benefit.

Although Nasser agreed to withdraw six thousand troops from Yemen immediately, and to withdraw another five thousand before the end of 1963, these were to be no more than empty promises to keep up the pretence of an eventual disengagement. Some US officials began to think Nasser was stalling and waiting for Faisal to fully open the supply line so that he could justify maintaining his high troop levels in Yemen. Komer, for his part, did not subscribe to the rumor. He appeared unwavering in his belief that Nasser could become a good faith partner to the United States.[14]

Komer continued to hold onto this optimism about Nasser even when the Yemen disengagement scheme came unglued almost completely a few weeks later. Specifically, the Secretary General of the UN, U Thant, declared he had no choice but to dismantle the UNYOM due to a lack of funding. In order to stay afloat, the UNYOM required Saudi Arabia and Egypt each make a payment of $200,000 every two months. Faisal refused to pay anymore citing Nasser's failure to make any movement toward disengagement. Komer began to wonder whether Faisal planned to abandon the disengagement scheme altogether and fully reopen the supply line to the royalists. He lamented the likelihood of his failure to Bundy by writing, "Mac, I am most concerned lest Komer's war is well on the way to becoming Talbot's war again."

The only immediate solution to this urgent problem, believed Komer, was to go to the UN Security Council and demand a broader mandate for the UNYOM; one that would grant the peacekeeping body the ability to closely monitor the military situation on the ground in Yemen and, more importantly, empower it to keep either side from escalating.

Unfortunately for Komer, he required Rusk's approval to put this plan into motion because the entire US mission at the UN was reluctant to go to the Security Council. Instead, they preferred to wait for another flare-up between Egypt and Saudi Arabia before making any moves at the international body.

As a result, Komer was exasperated. He wanted to stop a crisis from occurring, not react to one after it had occurred. "Can you tell Rusk he ought to grab hold of this one before it is too late?" he asked Bundy. Komer's main concern was that any sudden escalation in Yemen could lead to Saudi Arabia requesting commencement of Operation Hard Surface. Komer's careful, tightrope-like strategy on Yemen was wearing dangerously thin.[15]

Miraculously, on November 4, Faisal suddenly changed his mind and paid his portion of the UNYOM maintenance fees. The next move fell to Nasser: he had to make the promised troop withdrawals or risk scuttling US mediation efforts in Yemen altogether.[16]

On November 20, two days before Kennedy's fateful trip to Dallas, State sent a telegram to the US embassy in Cairo: Nasser had not upheld his agreement to reduce Egypt's troop levels in Yemen. He had promised to withdraw to 26,000 troops by November 1; instead, he had kept in an additional 4,000 troops. Meanwhile, Egypt's air force continued to bomb the royalists' bases and, more significantly, resumed bombing Saudi territory.[17]

The prospects of a mutual Saudi-Egyptian disengagement from Yemen were looking increasingly bleak. Thus, the United States was in a difficult position with Nasser just as Johnson—an untested and unfamiliar figure in the situation—was about to take office. US-Egypt relations had entered a period of indefinite uncertainty at the worst possible time.

The defining feature of Kennedy's Middle East policy was an attempt to court relations with everyone in the region at the same time—hence the reason why the administration avoided taking sides in the Yemen conflict.[18] This was, inherently, a difficult policy to maintain because it often meant that the United States was simultaneously acting on behalf of and against the many countries it had relations with. For example, selling American missiles to Israel was not seen favorably by the Arab monarchies; nor was giving economic aid to Nasser since Israel and the Arab monarchies were united in their perception that Nasser was a threat to the region's status quo. Conversely, Nasser disliked America's relationship with the Arab monarchies because he viewed them as a collective reactionary roadblock to his brand of Arab progressivism. In Nasser's eyes, the Arab monarchies were yesterday's news, clinging to the vestiges of a decaying old-world nobility. He, on the other hand, represented the future of the Middle East.

At Komer's urging, Kennedy had chosen to pursue good relations with Nasser because he seemingly wielded unmatched power in the Middle East and his appeal to Arabs beyond his own borders was significant. Moreover, the threat Nasser posed as a potential springboard for Soviet incursion into the Middle East—should he decide ever to fully commit to Moscow—was too great to be overlooked from Komer's point of view. Nevertheless, neither Kennedy nor Komer wanted the United States to be accused of choosing Nasser over everyone else in the Middle East. There had to be balance in America's Middle East relations.

This careful and deliberate policy began to fall apart shortly before Kennedy's death, in large part due to Nasser's unwillingness to compromise on Yemen. After the fateful trip to Texas, Kennedy's officials—now Johnson's officials—tried to continue with Kennedy's approach to foreign policy-making. However, there had always been criticism of the old policy; especially about the decision to constructively engage Nasser. Therefore, with a new president coming into the White House, some officials saw an opportunity to change that policy. For these officials, Yemen became a focal point for trying out a different approach on Nasser. Komer and his allies, however, attempted to maintain the approach they had spearheaded under Kennedy. Komer's camp worried about continuity during a period of uncertainty. They wanted to get Nasser to see Johnson as Kennedy in order to preserve the achievements of the latter.

Indeed, the day after Kennedy's death, Talbot laid the Middle East situation out on the table for Rusk, writing, "I know of no problems in the NEA [State's Bureau of Near Eastern and South Asian Affairs] that will require the immediate attention of the President." However, as far as the policy implications of Kennedy's death, Talbot suspected that Nasser would require some reassurance that Johnson would not be "harder to get along with." Indeed, he thought it was important to immediately send "signs to the contrary." After all, Johnson was an unknown to Nasser.[19]

As a starting point to show Nasser how the Johnson administration planned to proceed with diplomatic relations, Talbot had to look no further than a list of six recommendations (dubbed "Talbot's list") he had given to Ambassador Kamel on ways Egypt could improve its relations with the United States. The list included: softening anti-American propaganda, taking steps to install a more inclusive government in Yemen; cooperating with the UNYOM; reducing troop levels in Yemen; avoiding the UN's proposed demilitarized zone between Yemen and Saudi Arabia; and, most importantly, no more aerial bombing campaigns over Yemen. By focusing on this list, Talbot hoped Egypt and the United States, under Johnson, could pick up where Kennedy had left off.[20]

However, Talbot's desire to maintain the status quo in US policy toward Egypt was not a universally shared sentiment in Washington. Indeed, uncertainty in the wake of Kennedy's death led others at State and the Department of Defense (DOD) to question the effectiveness of Kennedy's approach. Indeed, this camp proposed a reset of American policy in the Middle East and, specifically, a re-examination of the benefits of a continued relationship with Nasser.[21] This rift over the best approach to take with Nasser suddenly widened when Saudi Arabia complained that Egyptian planes had flown into their territory and bombed civilians.[22]

A telegram from the US embassy in Saudi Arabia got straight to the point: "Disengagement [from Yemen] is not succeeding. UAR troops not only are not being withdrawn but [the] process is now reversed and according [to] most estimates [the] UAR has as many troops in Yemen as [it did] at any time previously." To make matters worse, Anwar Sadat (President of Egypt's National Assembly) apparently told British officials that Egypt intended to keep troops in Yemen "for years," thus contradicting the considerable US efforts to negotiate a settlement. In short, redirecting Nasser on Yemen did not appear to be working.

The ambassador to Saudi Arabia, Parker T. Hart, was extremely frustrated about the situation and joined the opposite camp in defiance of Komer. Hart claimed his credibility in Saudi Arabia had been eroded because of Nasser's violation of the Yemen disengagement scheme. In a missive to State, he criticized Kennedy's "quiet diplomacy" as not being effective on a demagogue like Nasser, who aired his grievances about the United States publicly. Indeed, Nasser often blasted US policy in his speeches. But Komer, for his part, dismissed these speeches as political posturing that was intended for the ears of the common person rather than being a reflection of Nasser's true policy.

Hart also argued that Nasser was placing a soon-to-be irreversible strain on US-Egypt relations and on the administration's other relationships in the Middle East. He concluded that Nasser was more of a nuisance than an asset. It was time for a re-examination of the current policy toward Nasser, he argued. "It has been said that [the] US should not place US-UAR relations on [the] line because of Yemen," Hart wrote to State. "In fact, it is Nasir . . . who has placed those relations on the line, not over Yemen but over Saudi Arabia."

Hart wanted incoming President Johnson to hand over to the UN all of America's responsibilities in the Yemen conflict, essentially calling for the abandonment of America's role as a mediator between the two duelling Arab powers. He argued that the UN could more effectively pressure both sides to disengage by expanding the role of the UNYOM and demanding a complete withdrawal of the Egyptian army.[23] Prima facie, Hart's recommendation was not so different than Komer's earlier plan to go to the Security Council for assistance on Yemen. Komer, however, had wanted to *partner* with the UN on Yemen, not force Nasser into a box on the global stage.

Thus, from the onset, the newly minted Johnson administration was in a difficult position with its policy toward Egypt. Could the United States still pretend that courting Nasser was more beneficial to its Cold War containment strategy of keeping the Soviets out of the Middle East than the potential damage it was doing to its long-term diplomatic relations in the region? Komer and Talbot still did think in these terms. And they planned to convince Johnson and Rusk of the policy's merits. But first, they intended to put pressure on Faisal and Nasser in order to head off a presumably more serious escalation of the Yemen conflict that could potentially force Johnson's hand from the get-go.

On December 1, State (with Komer's input) sent a response to Hart (also copying in the US embassy in Cairo). It was titled, "Next Steps in Yemen." Operation Hard Surface was not enough of a deterrent to keep Egypt from bombing Saudi territory, State wrote. Therefore, it was imperative that Hart get Faisal to pull his "chestnuts out of [a] fire which he appears [to] intend [to] rekindle in Yemen." Cleared by Komer, the purpose of the directive was to keep Faisal from completely reopening the royalist supply line, which Komer feared would lead to Nasser sending additional troops to Yemen. At the same time, Badeau, for his part, was instructed to explain to Nasser that if he wanted good relations with the new US president, then he needed to take a meaningful step toward disengagement from Yemen.[24]

With the two embassies aware of the next steps to take on Yemen, per Komer and State's instructions, it was time to stress the gravity of the Yemen situation to Johnson himself.

To be sure, Johnson was actually well acquainted with the growing problem in Yemen. By December 2, a little over a week after Kennedy's death, the Director of the CIA, John McCone, had already met with him and Bundy no less than two times to address "the seriousness of the Yemen problem." According to McCone, "I extended the discussion to express my worries over the entire Middle East because of the Yemen conflict."[25] Thus, the CIA's concern about Yemen, now made clear to Johnson, was a perfect opportunity for Komer to exploit.

Indeed, the next day, he wrote to Bundy that he needed a "Presidential stamp" to move forward with redirecting Nasser. "We're probably in for real trouble here, as no one now thinks [the] UAR will pull enough [troops] out by 4 January [the new deadline for Nasser to reduce troop numbers] to permit us to get disengagement extended once again," Komer wrote. "Nasser has the bear by the tail and the fool can't let go. So we face some tough decisions." The decisions were (1) whether to cancel Operation Hard Surface should Faisal reopen the supply line; and (2) "what next steps to prevent [an] explosion" of the Yemen conflict. Komer wanted to be patient with Nasser and, in the meantime, keep Faisal from overreacting. "At my urging NEA . . . is ready with anti-Saudi proposals," Komer wrote to Bundy. In other words, Komer wanted to maintain the existing strategy of trying to redirect Nasser on Yemen, even though Kennedy no longer was in the picture. Komer reasoned that things could quickly spiral in the Middle East over Yemen, and that Johnson would then get pressured into siding against Nasser.[26]

Later that day, he sent another memo to Bundy to further explain his concerns: "Adding to the impact of the last ten days [since Kennedy's assassination] is my increasingly grim feeling that we're in for a time of trouble throughout the Middle East." Specifically, Komer worried about the undoing of the foreign policy he had spearheaded under Kennedy:

> I raise Yemen last among these problems, because it is intrinsically not very important. But the way the Saudis . . . are playing it, the UAR's failure to perform in Yemen will be used as a club to try and force us to do what we have so far avoided—*coming down on one side against the other.*

Interestingly, Komer appeared more concerned about Faisal forcing Johnson's hands via diplomatic pressure than he was about Nasser's actions themselves forcing the president.

But Komer was also worried about the shortsightedness of a group of American congressmen and senators who insisted on cutting off aid to Egypt as a way of sending a strong warning to Nasser about his actions in Yemen. "Nasser won't get out of Yemen just because we cut off aid; we'd have to push him out," Komer wrote to Bundy. "And if we try, you know where he'll go for support [the Soviet Union]." Komer did not see any upside to cutting off Egypt's aid. He thought aid was a useful tool for preventing crises, not for creating one. After all, the three-year PL 480 agreement that had been signed by Kennedy in 1962, at Komer's urging, was still the foundation of US-Egypt relations when Johnson unexpectedly came into office. Aid was what had allowed relations to bloom under Kennedy after the colder Eisenhower years.

In part, Komer blamed State and specifically, Rusk, for the potential storm on the horizon if the Yemen conflict got out of hand and forced Johnson to choose between Faisal or Nasser. He wrote to Bundy, "this is a product of circumstances beyond our control, though I find State and others terribly slow to practice preventive diplomacy instead of reacting to events." Indeed, Komer and Rusk had never seen eye-to-eye on how to handle Nasser. And Komer particularly worried about Rusk attempting to take a more pronounced role in Middle East policy now that Johnson was president. Komer felt that he alone knew best how to handle Nasser. And what he most strongly believed was that the continuation of the redirection strategy could lead Nasser toward a resolution of the Yemen conflict.

Yet Komer still had to make his case directly to the new president, and he had to make it convincing. His solution, made apparent in his memo to Bundy, was to link Yemen to domestic affairs: problems in the Middle East could potentially become problems for Johnson's election campaign, argued Komer. Indeed, Johnson was not an elected president. He was even referred to by some journalists as the "accidental President." Johnson had less than twelve months to campaign and win the presidential election in November 1964.

Komer wrote to Bundy: "the important thing is that, if I'm even half right, President Johnson will be faced with a series of tough policy problems in my area . . . at a time when he'd prefer tranquillity—if not a few successes—as [the] 1964 election draws near." He followed with a call for continuing Kennedy's flexible approach to diplomacy:

> This memo is mood music to communicate my sense of foreboding. What we can do [in the Middle East] varies in each case; in some we have real leverage, in others little. But one problem in most cases is that the short term argues with the longer run. I suspect it would be domestically popular, for example, to revert to a tougher line on impossible neutralists like Nasser . . . though I fear this would merely give new openings to the Soviets and Chinese (as did our policy in the '50's).[27]

Perfectly playing his role as a strategist, Komer was keeping his eyes trained on the larger objective (shaping Nasser), but adjusting his arguments in order to align with the new realities at Johnson's White House.

While Komer worked to convince Bundy and, more importantly, Johnson not to give up on Nasser, State, on Talbot's instructions, attempted to convince Nasser via diplomatic channels that it was in his interest to leave Yemen as soon as possible. On December 2, Talbot's assistant, John Jernegan, deputy assistant secretary for Near Eastern Affairs, met with Kamel. The purpose of the meeting was to bring up the administration's concerns with Kamel before he met with Egypt's foreign minister on December 5, who would in turn meet with Nasser himself.

In the time that had passed since Kennedy's death, the officials at State struggled to effectively communicate with Nasser. Ambassador Badeau had received "inconclusive results" from a meeting with Nasser's "no. 2," Prime Minister Ali Sabri. And Talbot felt that he never had received a proper response to his list of six points. The administration needed to understand how Nasser planned to proceed on Yemen. Specifically, was he willing to ignore the disengagement scheme to the point of risking a war with Faisal? If so, he needed to understand that he would be starting off relations with Johnson on the wrong foot.

Thus, Jernegan began the meeting by explaining to Kamel how the situation in Yemen threatened to undo the two countries' years of hard work to improve their diplomatic relations. The United States was beginning to think that Nasser sought to damage the relationship, Jernegan said. There were even reports of Egyptian officials discouraging prominent Yemenis from voicing their support for a speedy resolution of the civil war. Jernegan wanted to know if Nasser did in fact want the civil war to go on indefinitely.

Kamel replied that he was surprised by "all this tension about Yemen." Of course, Nasser wanted good relations with the United States. The ambassador then read aloud a list of the ways in which, he thought, the United States had benefitted over the years from having good relations with Egypt: "Communism controlled, US oil interests not harmed, Arab-Israel issue dampened down, anti-West feelings in UAR wiped out, and US again playing influential role, and Egyptian economic development moving forward." Kamel added that the conflict in Yemen had been greatly "exaggerated" by "irrational quarters" seeking to undermine Egypt's good relations with the United States. If anything, he said, Egypt sought to decrease tension in the region and to normalize relations with Saudi Arabia.

Kamel compared Egypt's involvement in Yemen to America's covert war in Vietnam. According to the memorandum of their conversation, he described Yemen as a quagmire: "[The] UAR wants [to] settle [the] Yemen problem and there is no dispute in principle with the US. However, like [the] US in Vietnam, [the] UAR cannot leave Yemen in [a] state of anarchy and ripe for Communists . . . [The] Yemenis [are] unable [to] agree among [them]selves what [they] want." It was an indication that Nasser felt he had a legacy to protect in Yemen. He did not want to leave the country in ruins, so he would not be leaving anytime soon. The argument was an appeal to what the Egyptians perceived as America's reasons for staying involved in Vietnam.

Jernegan, however, rejected Kamel's argument out of hand, saying that he had overstated it. Egypt's military presence was not bringing stability to Yemen. In fact, according to American intelligence, the situation on the ground was actually getting much worse. He reminded Kamel that Nasser had entered into a diplomatic agreement (the Bunker Agreement) with the Kennedy administration. As such, he was obligated to reduce Egypt's troop levels to 21,000 by January 4. This was a much more appropriate number of troops for a peacekeeping mission, Jernegan said, which was how Kamel, a few minutes prior, had described Egypt's intervention in Yemen. Jernegan added that contrary to reducing its troop levels, Egypt now had an excess of 33,000 troops in Yemen. How could the Johnson administration justify relations with Egypt "if [the] US public gets [the] image [that the] UAR [is] predatory and aggressive?" he asked. Kamel did not respond.

The mood at the meeting was reportedly tense. The two men were uneasy in general, as it was their first meeting since Johnson took office. At Komer's urging, Jernegan made sure to compare Johnson to Kennedy in order to address any concerns in Cairo about a possible change in US foreign policy. He also made sure to stress that Johnson was ready to pick up the disengagement scheme where Kennedy had left off. However, most Egyptian officials did not know Johnson; it was impossible to know whether he would be their friend. As Jernegan later reported, Kamel was "visibly upset [about me] having raise[d] the issue [of Yemen] so soon after [the] change [in] US leadership."[28] Indeed, with Kennedy gone, uncertainty had entered into the US-Egypt relationship. Nasser still had to get to know Johnson. It was risky pushing him on Yemen before he even had a chance to do so.

One reason why Komer was so anxious to get Nasser to leave Yemen right away, however, was Congress. Specifically, legislation had been proposed that would limit the administration's ability to continue giving aid to Egypt under the existing PL 480 agreement if the Yemen conflict escalated any further. Shortly before Kennedy's death, Senator Ernest Gruening (D. Alaska) added an amendment to the 1964 appropriations bill that blocked aid to any country "engaging in or preparing for aggressive military efforts directed" at the United States or "any country receiving assistance under [PL 480] . . . or any other act." Before passing the amendment, the Senate had exclusively discussed Nasser's intervention in Yemen, and the threat it posed to Saudi Arabia, as an appropriate example of the amendment's application.[29] The Gruening Amendment meant that Nasser's refusal to disengage from Yemen and his brazen attacks against the Saudis were likely to cause domestic problems for Johnson.

Talbot worried about the future of US-Egypt relations if Nasser did not agree to back down on Yemen. His concern moved him to write a personal letter about it to Badeau. Yemen had always been a hot button issue between the United States and Egypt, Talbot wrote, but now it threatened to be the relationship's undoing. He asked: What does the word "aggression" even mean? Did it apply when Egypt bombed Saudi territory or flew into their airspace? Would it apply if Egypt refused to withdraw from the demilitarized zone (after one was officially designated by the UN)?

These were not hypothetical questions. The Gruening Amendment meant that the Johnson administration would at some point likely be forced to argue in front of Congress the definition of the word "aggression." More importantly, Johnson would quickly have to decide how far he was willing to stick his neck out for Nasser in order to maintain the diplomatic relationship he inherited from Kennedy. The situation was potentially explosive, with ramifications for Johnson both at home and abroad. Talbot instructed Badeau not to discuss the amendment with anyone in Egypt until Johnson took a position on it.[30]

Johnson certainly needed time to formulate his own policy toward Nasser. However, the clock was ticking. A strategy was needed to redirect Nasser on Yemen and to contain the conflict before Johnson was forced to choose between Faisal or Nasser. Failure to contain Yemen would mean the immediate unraveling of Kennedy's neutralist policy.

As Johnson continued to settle into the Oval Office, US officials continued to worry about the outbreak of a direct war between Egypt and Saudi Arabia. The US embassy in Cairo wrote to State that both Egypt and Saudi Arabia saw the Bunker Agreement in terms that were mutually exclusive. Saudi Arabia was implying it would bring a friendly government into power in Yemen once Nasser withdrew his troops. Egypt, however, apparently viewed America's efforts to strengthen the UNYOM as a sign of its "acceptance" of Sallal's regime. The embassy staff felt that short of shooting Nasser out of Yemen—a scenario that would lead to the unraveling of years of careful diplomacy with the Egyptian leader—the United States had no choice but to play the role of "honest power-broker." In other words, the United States had to continue to avoid taking sides as it had done under Kennedy.[31]

Komer and Talbot fully agreed with this assessment. They still believed the best course of action was strengthening the UNYOM so that Nasser would eventually get frustrated and decide to leave Yemen on his own.

In Washington, Talbot met with the executives of American oil companies on December 6 to explain the proposed strategy. The oil companies were concerned that if the United States took sides in Yemen it would become unpopular in the Middle East—where countries were being divided into camps that supported Faisal or Nasser. The executives asked Talbot what Johnson planned to do if Nasser did not withdraw his troops by the January 4 deadline. Talbot reassured the nervous executives that the administration was not going to take any drastic action in Yemen that could hurt them in the region. However, he also noted that the United States could not simply abandon Yemen and hand it over to Nasser. Instead, the administration would stay the course, and work to increase the role of the UNYOM. Talbot added that Nasser's Yemen intervention was not widely supported in Egypt. Its excessive financial cost was putting a noticeable strain on the Egyptian economy. Moreover, Talbot said, the Johnson administration had already hinted to Nasser that it would withhold aid if he did not soon take steps to disengage. It was hoped that Nasser and his economic advisers would heed the threat and realize the unnecessary burden that Yemen was placing on Egyptian shoulders.[32]

Now that Talbot had pacified the oil companies, it was time to get Johnson on board for the strategy that Komer and Talbot had already sold to their respective superiors, Bundy and Rusk.

On December 11, Komer sent his first memo about Nasser to Johnson. He explained that while Faisal had upheld his end of the Bunker Agreement by more or less halting the royalist supply line, Nasser had not made any effort to meet his end of the agreement, which threatened to derail the opportunity for peace in Yemen. "But we doubt that further US pressure would get Nasser to play ball; more likely it would have the opposite effect," he wrote. "So State recommends that we keep trying to make disengagement work, keep the Saudis and UAR apart, and promote a compromise regime in Yemen acceptable to both." This was Komer's way of telling Johnson that both he and State wanted an opportunity to redirect Nasser. But like Komer's previous strategies on Yemen, he required some presidential muscle. As an incentive for Faisal to be patient a while longer, Komer wanted to extend Operation Hard Surface for an additional month.[33]

This was no small request. Indeed, Komer's proposal met resistance from the Joint Chiefs of Staff (JCS), who argued that the force was "operationally incomplete" and "incapable of effective self-defense against" Egypt's "forces available in Yemen." It had all been for show, claimed the military chiefs. The entire force consisted of eight F-100s and three KB-50s—a total of eleven planes. And the original operation had been set up under the ruse of a routine training program for Saudi pilots. This particular cover story was no longer plausible.

The Saudis themselves no longer seemed to view the operation as a temporary affair. Indeed, the government in Riyadh was behaving as if American planes were there to provide permanent "air defense of their nation, including the villages on the Yemen border." If the planes remained in Saudi Arabia, there was a significant risk that the Yemen conflict could boil over and the Saudis would drag the United States into a Middle East conflagration.

The Chairman of the JCS wrote to Johnson's secretary of defense, Robert McNamara: "With Hard Surface in place, the United States will be forced to respond militarily or risk loss of credibility of its military power, not only in the Middle East, but world-wide." Instead, the military chiefs proposed periodic aerial exercises in or nearby Saudi Arabia by a much larger, combat-ready force.

In the end, the JCS reluctantly agreed to extend Operation Hard Surface until January 31—the date Komer wanted. But they strongly advised there be no further extensions.[34]

Komer's call for the continuation of the strategy he spearheaded under Kennedy was successful. But the clock was ticking for the redirection strategy to work.

As a result, responsibility fell to State to accomplish three things in a timely manner: (1) convince Secretary General U Thant to extend the UNYOM; (2) get Faisal to promise not to pour any gasoline on the Yemen fire by resuming aid to the royalists; and (3) convince Nasser it was in his best interest to work with the United States on a disengagement plan.

On December 18, State went to work on the first goal by sending a directive to its mission at the UN. In November, U Thant had sent Pier Spinelli, a UN Special Representative, to Yemen. His mission had been to lay groundwork for a representative government that could be agreed upon by Saudi Arabia and Egypt. This was the international community's political solution to the civil war. In December, Spinelli was due to submit to U Thant a report of his travels through the conflict zones. Since it was likely he would report that Nasser had made no significant effort to disengage from the conflict, Talbot and Komer were concerned that U Thant would unilaterally decide to dismantle the UNYOM, thus leaving the United States with sole responsibility for finding a solution to the conflict. State instructed its diplomats at the UN to speak to U Thant in a hurry—framing was everything in order to spin Spinelli's report in a more positive light.[35]

However, around the same time that State was directing its representatives at the UN, Badeau miraculously ran into Spinelli in Cairo, where he learned that the UN investigator had an inaccurate perception of the situation in Yemen: Spinelli drastically underestimated that the number of Egyptian troops in Yemen was 20,000—an erroneous figure that Badeau made no effort to correct.

Moreover, Spinelli seemingly misunderstood the nature of the conflict itself. "As to [Egyptian] bombings within Yemen territory," wrote Badeau to State, "Spinelli stated these [are] primarily directed against recalcitrant tribes and had often been successful in forcing or reinstating [a] truce." Thus, Spinelli's warped perception of Egypt's operations in Yemen was helpful to the Americans' strategy because it put him in favor of extending the UNYOM's mandate.[36]

The next step in containing the Yemen conflict was to reach out to Faisal. Komer wrote a message in Johnson's name, which was sent to the US embassy in Saudi Arabia. "I know your concern for our policy toward Yemen," went the message. "We have only one purpose in regard to Yemen: to protect Saudi Arabia's integrity . . . You have kept your disengagement agreements. The UAR's performance has been far less satisfactory."

The purpose of the message was to restrain Faisal a little longer while Badeau worked on Nasser. It warned that Yemen was a "trap for those who would seek to dominate it." Faisal was told he could emerge unscathed if only he heeded Johnson's advice. "Let me add," went Johnson's message, "I would be concerned that Saudi aid to Yemeni royalists now most likely would provide Nasser with provocation for resuming bombing attacks, relying even more on Soviet assistance, and attempting to shift to you the burden of responsibility which he now must bear . . . the UAR is gaining little, losing much in Yemen . . . On the other hand, your course for Saudi Arabia is steadily increasing world stature and respect for yourself and your country."[37]

It was an overt attempt to flatter the Saudi leader. But Faisal was a different case: he needed to be wooed, not pushed like Nasser.

The third, and most important, step to making progress on Yemen was getting through to Nasser. Again, Komer wrote Johnson's message. As it was the first instance of any form of contact between Johnson and the Egyptian leader, it is worthy of reproduction in its entirety:

Mr. President,

Being aware of the scope and the candor that characterized the dialogue between you and President Kennedy, I hope this dialogue may be continued. I also intend to continue the policy of seeking to expand the cooperation between our two countries.

But the continued instability in Yemen confronts our two governments with a serious challenge. I know your often expressed repugnance to Arab fighting Arab, and we too look forward to the creation of circumstances whereby the conflict can be terminated and disengagement carried out. Only through measures to set an independent Yemen Government squarely on its feet can we reaffirm our common support for the principle of self-determination.

I urge you to accept the sincerity of our counsels, as expressed by us to your Ambassador in Washington, and to you by our Ambassador in Cairo. Let us work together to see if we can continue the closer cooperation which has marked our relations over the past few years.

Lyndon B. Johnson

The intent of the message was to link Johnson to Kennedy. Indeed, it not only asked to "continue" the relationship as it had been under Kennedy, it also asked Nasser to demonstrate his interest in such a relationship by making progress on leaving

Yemen. There was an underlying theme in the letter: only by following through on Yemen, could Nasser demonstrate his interest in moving forward in the spirit of the Kennedy era.[38]

Alongside Johnson's message to Nasser, State sent careful instructions to the US embassy in Cairo. Badeau was asked to make it clear to Nasser that the United States was dissatisfied with his lack of progress on leaving Yemen. His reneging on the Bunker Agreement had made it difficult for the United States to have any leverage with Faisal. Therefore, he was advised to withdraw a portion of his troops by the January 4 deadline in order to alleviate the growing tension in the region.

Badeau was instructed to make sure that Nasser understood the United States "would not stand idly by if [the] UAR should attack Saudi Arabia—whether or not [the] UAR considers it has adequate provocation." Nasser was invited to immediately contact the Johnson administration if he had any evidence of Faisal resuming supplies to the royalists. The purpose of the invitation was to preclude Nasser's habit of acting unilaterally and then later excusing his actions on the basis that Faisal was not acting in the spirit of the Bunker Agreement.

The goal of this carefully managed diplomatic outreach was to maintain the United States as a neutral entity between the two dueling Arab states. Not only would this give the United States the sole credit for finding a diplomatic solution to the conflict but it would also mean the United States would not have to take sides in the Middle East.

State and Komer were working together to paint Yemen as a calamity for Nasser; one that only a country like the United States could provide the solution for. Indeed, Badeau was instructed to tell Nasser that he "should not let this golden opportunity pass."[39]

The United States might have been taking the lead on solving the Yemen problem for everyone's benefit. But Nasser was beginning to show renewed interest in the Soviet Union and China, which indicated that pushing him too hard on Yemen might drive him into the welcoming arms of the two communist powers.

Specifically, the CIA learned in December that the Soviet premier, Nikita Khrushchev, was planning to visit Egypt in January 1964. The visit was reportedly planned as a response to an announcement by the Chinese premier, Chou En Lai, that he would visit Egypt at the end of December. If the introduction of a new American president seemed like an unexpected roadblock in US-Egypt relations, Nasser's courting of the two communist powers signaled significant mechanical troubles. There could now be little doubt in Washington that US-Egypt relations had been significantly weakened in the wake of Kennedy's death.[40]

Despite the sudden arrival of the Chinese premier at the same time as the renewed push on Yemen, Badeau did his best to get an immediate meeting with Nasser. He told Egyptian officials that there needed to be a much needed "review" of US-Egypt relations to date.[41] Yet this failed to provoke the intended response. Badeau was told that Nasser was taking vacation time. Nasser also delayed seeing Spinelli until January 2, which was only two days before the disengagement deadline. Reacting to these political games, Badeau believed it was better for him to meet with Nasser after the Spinelli meeting. He became concerned that meeting beforehand might preempt

Spinelli and make Nasser believe the UN representative was acting in concert with the United States.

In the interim, however, Badeau took it upon himself to recommend that the White House rewrite the message from Johnson to Nasser. He felt that the already-approved message (written by Komer) was too short and too cold to give Nasser a good first impression of Johnson. His request, however, went unheeded. Yet, when Badeau finally did meet with Nasser in January, he broke up Johnson's message into sections as he delivered it orally, and thus made it appear longer than it really was. He also inserted Johnson's name into the conversation as much as possible in order to positively associate the new president in Nasser's eyes—these little tricks were the mark of a savvy diplomat.[42]

On January 6, Badeau was received by Nasser. Their meeting started at 7 o'clock in the evening and lasted for over an hour. The two of them had not met for over two months. Therefore, it was an important meeting because it was the first time a representative from the Johnson administration had sat down with the Egyptian leader.

Badeau began by expressing gratitude for the well-wishes the United States had received from Nasser and the rest of Egypt in the wake of Kennedy's death. "President Nasser responded by reiterating [a] deep sense of shock and admitted his own surprise at [the] extent to which the butcher, the baker, [and] the candlestick maker in [the] Nile Valley had been moved by President Kennedy's loss," Badeau reported. Nasser then asked whether Johnson would continue with Kennedy's tradition of sending him personal letters. He also said that he had always appreciated them.

Badeau did his best to reassure Nasser that American foreign policy under Johnson would be no different than how it had been under Kennedy. "I then turned to resume of the opening weeks of President Johnson's leadership," according to his report to State, "emphasizing [a] general continuity of foreign policy."

Badeau moved on to point out the positive developments in US-Egypt relations since the two men had last met. Among other things, he expressed gratitude that the claims of American businessmen were being "adjudicated" by the Egyptian government "with reasonable speed." And he noted that the United States, in turn, was responding with "significant business interests" in Egypt. Badeau also applauded an upcoming summit in Cairo for Arab leaders. Indeed, both Komer and State saw it as a sign that Nasser possibly planned a reconciliation with Faisal, which would make it easier to get Johnson interested in having good relations with him. Badeau said to Nasser: "[The] shut-down of [the] UAR propaganda mill against [the] surrounding Arab world [is] encouraging and, if continued, [it] could be a permanent element [in] easing relations with [the] US."[43]

At that point, however, Nasser interrupted Badeau. He did not want the Americans to think that the upcoming Arab summit had anything to do with American pressure. He made decisions regardless of Washington's position, he said. He claimed that the relaxation of propaganda against his Arab enemies was the result of external factors. Specifically, the collapse of the Ba'ath party—Nasser's main political rival in the Arab world—in Iraq, led him to conclude that his rivals were now too weak to reject an invitation for Arab unity.

Quickly recovering from Nasser's interruption, Badeau transitioned to a discussion about ongoing problems in US-Egypt relations, and how Johnson was eager to see them get resolved. "I resumed [my] presentation by stating that while I had listed certain favorable developments over [the] recent months, problems still remained. Change in American Presidents had not altered concern for these problems and [the] US reaction to them continued." Badeau told Nasser that Johnson was "following" Yemen in the "same detail and concern as had President Kennedy." "I expressed personal and official dismay [that the] level of UAR troops in Yemen remained so high," Badeau later reported. Nasser asked Badeau how many troops he thought there were in Yemen. Badeau replied, "at least 30,000." Nasser did not deny the figure. His only response was that "for a short time" there had been as many as 40,000.

The main purpose of the meeting had been to express dissatisfaction with the pace of Nasser's disengagement from Yemen. To that end, Badeau noted that the Johnson administration understood Yemen's nascent government was unstable. Nonetheless, the situation would not improve until Egyptian troops left the country—only then could Yemen heal. In some ways, the comment was a hint that the administration was willing to recognize that Nasser had a legacy to protect in Yemen, and that the country would not be left in ruins as Nasser purportedly feared.

Nasser, however, did not want to go into detail on Yemen. "His only comment was [the] problem of broadening" the popular "base" of Yemen's new republican government was "proving very difficult," Badeau reported. The recent "resignation of [the] Presidential Council resulted from that body being unwieldy in size and beset by in-fighting. In interests of efficiency he [Nasser] had therefore abolished it and was instituting [a] 3-man supreme council in its place."

This revelation did not give the impression that Nasser was going to leave Yemen any time soon—he was enmeshed in reshaping its system of government. Thus, Badeau delivered his most important message of the evening: Yemen had led to the Gruening Amendment. Nasser's continued involvement in Yemen's civil war and his meddling in its politics posed a serious threat to US-Egypt relations.

Nasser agreed that US-Egypt relations seemed to have entered a more difficult period because of Yemen. However, he told Badeau that from his perspective, the only useful policy between the two countries was one that provided maximum cooperation and friendship. To be sure, this was the most positive sign the United States had received from Nasser since the death of Kennedy. And it implied that Nasser was open to further dialogue on Yemen or any other issues that affected US-Egypt relations.[44]

Badeau reported to State that he found Nasser at ease during the meeting. The Egyptian leader said that "it had been too long" since the two men last met. He "appeared genuinely glad to see me," Badeau wrote.

For the time being, personal diplomacy still appeared to work. Nasser communicated to Badeau that he would not go to war with Faisal over Yemen. Thus, Badeau walked away from the meeting with renewed hope that Nasser was open to having a constructive relationship with Johnson. He urged State to have Johnson reach out to Nasser again as soon as possible. "In view of his direct expression of [the] value he set upon correspondence with President Kennedy," Badeau wrote, "I urge [that] in [the] near future [a] written letter from President Johnson be transmitted."[45]

Komer's war had been contained to a sufficient level to keep it from becoming an immediate problem for Johnson in the opening months of his first term in office. As Operation Hard Surface was withdrawn at the end of January, Komer proudly reported to Johnson, "our best guess is that the Yemen flap is about over . . . I think we can keep this messy little problem off your list of trouble spots." No doubt, it was a major victory for Komer.[46]

3

Nasser's New Frontier

As the Yemen conflict momentarily settled down, offering the possibility of a respite between the two countries for the time since Kennedy's death, a new problem came to the fore: Israel was on the verge of completing construction of its National Water Carrier. It was an ambitious project to pipe in water from the Jordan River to the arid southern deserts of Israel. The Arab states planned to take drastic action to stop it; they felt the water did not belong to Israel. And they feared it would lead to Israel exponentially increasing its population size. The Kennedy administration had supported Israel's water project in spite of the Arabs' opposition. One of Johnson's first acts after assuming office was to write a letter to the Israeli prime minister, Levi Eshkol, confirming America's continued support of the project. He wrote, "we stand behind you in your right of withdrawal in accordance with the Unified Plan."[1]

Therefore, when Badeau met with Nasser in early January to talk about Yemen, he also explained that the Johnson administration shared Kennedy's firm position on downstream water rights for all riparian states. He asked Nasser how Egypt could be against such a policy when its own Nile waters originated upstream.

Nasser turned the question back around on Badeau and asked what he thought about the situation, "not as ambassador but as [a] long-time student of Middle Eastern affairs." Badeau answered that no one wanted to see the water issue become another source of conflict in the Middle East. That being said, he insisted that Israel had a right to protect its water. Any potential problems (e.g., Israel taking more than its allotment) could be dealt with at the UN—where both Israel and the Arab states were members. Nasser replied, "Do you mean if we were to divert [the] headwaters of Jordan, we would be subject to Israeli aggression?" Badeau asserted that water was equally valuable to all countries. Therefore, no country's legitimate rights to it could accurately be described as "aggression." Nasser did not like Badeau's response. "This means we must remain strong," he said, "and prepared."[2]

What Nasser exactly meant by his promise to remain "prepared" wasn't revealed right away. But his steadfastness about the water issue foreshadowed what was to come at the Arab summit he later hosted in Cairo from January 13 to 17. Until then, US officials remained cautiously optimistic that the summit would bring an end to the often-destructive rivalries between the Arab states.

US officials in Cairo and back in Washington hoped to guide Nasser toward a moderate summit that would bring the Arabs closer together and foster peace in the region. But they failed to read the signs showing it was going to be anything but that. On December 30, a week before Badeau's meeting with Nasser, a US embassy official in Cairo met with Nasser's confidante (and editor of Egyptian daily *Al-Ahram*), Mohamed Heikal, who was bristling with excitement. Heikal claimed that Nasser was poised to alter the course of Middle Eastern politics at the upcoming Arab summit. He noted that the recent revolution in Iraq had swept the Ba'ath party out of power. The Ba'ath party was Nasser's only other ideological competitor in the battle to win hearts and minds on the Arab street—the Saudis could hardly hope to have the same populist appeal as these two progressive entities. So for the first time, said Heikal, Nasser was in a strategic position to unite the Arab world under his leadership.

Badeau, for his part, was skeptical about the premise behind the Arab summit. He shrewdly questioned whether Nasser would truly reconcile his differences with his enemies, or whether he was just making a play for more power, which would in turn make him a more dangerous adversary in the region. Badeau wrote to State:

> Heykal was at [the] peak of ebullience throughout [our] discussion. Realism impels us [to] discount prospects of [a] new heaven and new earth in [the] UAR outlook towards relations with other Arab states. At [the] same time, there have been [a] number [of] indications of pressures within [the] regime to forsake past fruitless and wasteful UAR policies of activism for activism's sake of Arab world . . . Things are moving fast out here and [the] Egyptians have previously demonstrated [their] ability [to] shrewdly and pragmatically exploit trends as they see them.[3]

British officials were even more pessimistic about the summit than Badeau. One official from the Foreign Office told the American ambassador to Britain that the summit was a "ruse" by Nasser "to demonstrate continued leadership in [the] Arab community." It would ultimately play out with Nasser feeling emboldened and perhaps becoming more hostile to the West, predicted the Foreign Service officer. He also expected the Arab states to collectively announce a plan to divert the Jordan River, which would deprive Israel of water. And he predicted that Arab guerrilla fighters would increase their sabotage attacks against Israel's National Water Carrier (the attacks were increasingly becoming a national crisis for Israel); perhaps because the fighters too would feel emboldened by the summit proceedings and its demonstration of Arab power.[4]

Not all observers, however, were pessimistic about Nasser's summit. Indeed, an unlikely source, the Saudi ambassador to the UK, was more focused on the prospect of peace between his nation and Egypt. He hoped the summit would provide an opportunity for Nasser and Faisal to finally have a face-to-face meeting about Yemen. His speculation was met with approval from his American interlocutors. Any potential for Nasser to embrace his Arab enemies and give up a prolonged struggle over Yemen was seen in Washington as nothing short of a diplomatic miracle—if it indeed were to happen.[5]

There is little doubt that ginning up speculation about the summit was Nasser's intention. He masterfully controlled the summit proceedings from beginning to end. There was no mistaking the fact that Nasser wanted to restrict information about the summit; possibly in order to avoid any embarrassments from leaking. But, more likely, Nasser wanted to be viewed as an all-powerful political broker. His strategy worked: foreign officials, including American ones, were frustrated to no end that they had little-to-none awareness of what Nasser was really up to.

During the summit itself, Nasser took extreme precautions to maintain this level of secrecy—which only added to the fantastical quality the summit came to hold. The delegates were housed at the Hotel Nile Hilton, with their meetings taking place in an adjoining building formerly used by the Arab League. And the visiting Arab dignitaries were separated from the rest of Cairo by a series of barriers alongside the hotel. Diplomatic access was completely restricted. One US embassy representative was told point-blank that the summit was solely an "Arab" affair.

Badeau, for his part, attempted to glean as much information as possible about the summit's proceedings from other foreign diplomats. He hoped to continue doing so at his annual "stag dinner," which was coincidentally scheduled for the same week as the summit.[6]

State, however, strongly warned the ambassador against showing too much interest in the conference, lest it give the wrong impression that the United States was attempting to influence its outcome. Badeau and his staff were instructed not to secretly meet with any of the Arab delegates. Instead, it was deemed preferable for US embassies located in Arab states to inform their hosts of America's well-documented stance on Israel's right to water from the Jordan River—and then wait and see how things went at the summit.[7]

The United States was not the only outside country eager to see the results of the summit. The Chinese premier, Chou En-Lai, made sure to send a message to the Arab leaders on the opening day. In stark contrast to America's official stance, he wrote, "The Chinese government sincerely supports the stand of the Arab states on the question of changing the course of the Jordan river [sic] by Israel." Chou expressed his country's desire to see the summit become a rallying point for the Arab states to "combat imperialist plots for aggression" in the Middle East.[8]

At that point, China was at odds with the Soviet Union. The message was Chou's way of stepping on Moscow's toes. Nevertheless, the global importance of the summit was clear, even if it was not clear which direction Nasser would take at it. Things could go for or against America's interests.

On the opening day of the summit, the Arab leaders ceremoniously took their seats in the conference hall. The Arab League's secretary general, Abd al-Khaliq Hassunah, thanked "the almighty" and Nasser for making the summit possible.[9] The Arab League had been formed in 1945. It was the most prominent forum for Arab affairs—yet this was the first time it had held a summit. Nasser was immediately invited up to the microphone before any other Arab leader. He spoke only for three minutes before Hassunah dramatically interrupted with an announcement: the meeting was moving into "secret" session. All non-delegation members (i.e., the press) were asked to leave the room.[10]

The three minutes of Nasser's speech that was recorded by Western observers was a history of the Arab response to Israel's water project. It went like this: In 1960, the Arab League discussed the problem of Israel withdrawing water from the Jordan River, which would increase immigration to its southern territories. In 1961, a meeting of Arab foreign ministers asked Arab military chiefs to come up with a comprehensive strategy to thwart Israel's water project. Finally, in 1961, a study was presented by the Arab military chiefs that called for unified military action against Israel. Nasser claimed that none of these steps had amounted to anything concrete that could demonstrate to Israel the folly of its water project. This was an unfortunate oversight that he now planned to rectify.[11]

Nasser proceeded by reading aloud the Arab League's original decree from 1960. In his paraphrased words, it declared: "Israel's venture to divert the water of the Jordan River is an act of aggression against the Arabs which justifies the legitimate action of self-defence in which the Arab states will collectively participate."[12] According to Nasser, it was the lack of preparations for this "self-defence" that had led him to organize the current summit. In his opinion, the preparations had been sidelined for too long. Thus, he proposed that he take over the Arab response to Israel's water project. And he also proposed establishing a framework for the liberation of Palestine:

> Last December ... I called for an Arab summit meeting. The reason for this meeting
> was what I read in the minutes of the meetings of the Arab chiefs of staff. The Arab
> League political committee had passed a resolution calling for the establishment
> of a unified Arab command and the establishment of a Palestinian entity. But in
> the course of two years none of these resolutions was implemented. Moreover, at
> the meetings of the Arab Chiefs of Staff it transpired that the political committee's
> resolutions could not be implemented. The most important of these resolutions
> was the diversion of the Jordan River tributaries.[13]

Of course, over the years Nasser himself had remained absent from the Arab League's meetings concerning Israel's water project. He too had been sidetracked—especially with the conflict in Yemen.[14] However, in the new year, 1964, he now apparently intended to assert himself in a novel manner. Indeed, according to one scholar, Nasser's inauguration of an Arab summitry was a way to unify the Arab ranks and to present himself as their undisputed regional leader.[15]

Right before the summit went into its "secret" session, Nasser spoke briefly about the future. He said he wanted to fix a date for the Arab states to begin diverting the Jordan River in order to ensure that the water never reached Israel. In three minutes Nasser managed to do something that Kennedy's officials had worked hard to avoid: he once again made Israel a hot button issue in the Arab world. For three years he had promised the Kennedy administration—and later the Johnson administration—that he would keep the Arab-Israeli conflict contained in an "ice-box." It had been one of the hallmark concessions for him getting the three-year PL 480 agreement from Kennedy in 1962. Prima facie, that promise was now broken.[16]

The international image coming out of the summit was that Nasser had unified the Arab world. Indeed, it was a massive propaganda victory for Nasser. On the morning of the summit's opening day, a small number of Egyptian troops returned from Yemen. They were greeted on the airport tarmac by a reception of senior army officers and a celebration. As the soldiers began to disembark from the plane, everyone cheered Nasser's name. This was his summit through and through; a staged event to show off his unrivalled leadership and popularity in the Arab world.[17]

To be sure, the summit paid off handsomely for Nasser. On the third day, Egypt and Jordan restored diplomatic relations – which had been severed since 1961. A joint communiqué warmly described the two countries now as "sisterly states."[18] The next day, Jordan officially recognized Sallal's Yemen Arab Republic.[19] To be sure, this was an affirmation of Nasser, and a slap in the face to Faisal—who had always been a key ally to Jordan. Moreover, at the summit, Nasser was invited by King Hassan II (another of Faisal's allies) to visit Morocco over the summer. Relations between the two countries had been strained since 1963, when Nasser sent troops to Algeria to support its border dispute with Morocco (the Sand War).[20]

The summit ostensibly led to three major decisions: (1) the Arab states were going to generate a detailed plan to divert water from Israel—though, for the time being, the exact details of that plan would remain secret; (2) the formation of a unified military bloc (officially designated as the "United Arab Command") to fight Israel, with the Egyptian chief of staff, General Ali Amer, placed in charge, thus giving Nasser considerable control over the combined Arab military operations; and (3) plans to establish an official Palestinian organization to spearhead Palestinian involvement in "liberating" their homeland from Israel.

There was no mistaking it, the summit was all about Israel. On the final day, Hassunah spoke to the press. "In the conference we came to an understanding," he said, "on all the steps regarding Israel and on every future possibility." Nasser had managed to rally the Arab states. For all intents and purposes, they now had a unified voice through him.[21]

Of course, Nasser had masterminded the whole affair even before it had started—right down to the reproach with King Hussein. A CIA cable written on January 9, but based on intelligence received between January 5 and 7, reveals a portion of his plans. Nasser had coordinated with Hassunah ahead of time to ensure he was invited up to the stage as the first speaker. He told a confidential informant that he would call for there to be no further speeches in order to avoid his enemies coming up to the podium and attacking him in front of the press. The CIA's source noted that Nasser desperately wanted to appear to the world as a "conciliator of Arab problems and as an advocate of Arab peace and non-interference." To that end, he wanted a six-month truce between the Arab states, during which they would refrain from propaganda attacks "or interfering in each other's affairs."

Nasser's main goal for the summit was to unify as many of the Arab states as possible under his leadership. When he received word that King Idris of Libya was too sick to come, he dared not let word slip lest the other monarchs also find an excuse not to attend.[22]

At the summit, Nasser effectively created his own version of Kennedy's new frontier. The *Arab street* was enthusiastic about Nasser, and this placed significant pressure on the other heads of state to bow before him.

But it was to be no more than a pyrrhic victory for Nasser. For though the summit brought certain recognition to his hegemony over the region, the ambiguous threats against Israel did not sit well with American observers—particularly those in Congress. At a time when Nasser was supposed to be building ties with Johnson, he was instead building up tension with Israel (vis-à-vis the water issue) on a global stage. The Arabs' rejection of Israel's water rights was also a rejection of America's long-standing support for them.

To be sure, the euphoria in Cairo was high in the aftermath of the summit, but an unexpected high-level incident soon dashed some of the jubilance and, in the process, reminded Nasser of the loftiness of his mass campaign against Israel. On the morning of January 19, two days after the summit had concluded, an Egyptian pilot defected to Israel. The Egyptian press covered the incident as a plane crash. "An official source has stated that a military training plane was lost yesterday due to bad weather," reported Radio Cairo. "The plane was from one of the Sinai bases. A search was made for this plane but it has not been found."[23]

What actually happened was a major in Egypt's air force, Mahmud Hilmi Abbas, took off unannounced and then outran the Egyptian air force. Egyptian planes chased him all the way to Israel's border until the Israeli air force safely intercepted him. The major brought with him a Soviet Yakovlev Yak-11 trainer aircraft and earned himself a hero's welcome in Israel.[24]

Nasser attempted to downplay the embarrassing story by blasting propaganda over Israeli airwaves about an American senator named Kenneth Keating (R. New York). Specifically, a message was broadcasted in Hebrew calling him a "mouthpiece of Tel Aviv." The broadcast went on to claim that Keating was pressuring the US government to thwart Arab plans for diverting the Jordan River. However, the recording noted, "reasonable departments in Washington" did not subscribe to such "illogical talk." It was no doubt a petty response to Israel's welcoming of the Egyptian defector.[25]

The target of the propaganda attack, however, was likely symbolic to Nasser. In 1962, Keating had proposed legislation that resembled what later materialized as the Gruening Amendment—the only difference being that Keating had called for cutting off aid to Egypt immediately due to Nasser's "military and propaganda" attacks against other recipients of US aid.[26]

Ironically for Nasser, Keating, a Republican, was also an enemy of the Democratic Party (the same party of Kennedy and Johnson). As the story goes, he had embarrassed the Kennedy administration in 1961 by publicly exposing the existence of Soviet missiles in Cuba. This forced Kennedy's hand, thus leading to the botched Bay of Pigs invasion. It had been a politically inconvenient time for a crisis, with a special congressional election in Texas (to replace Johnson's Senate seat) only a month away.[27]

Since the senator was certainly no friend of the White House's, the propaganda attack perhaps reflected Nasser's fears and misconceptions about the future of US-Egypt relations under Johnson. Nasser tended to let congressional figures like Keating or Gruening get into his head. However, the Keatings and Gruenings of Washington DC were merely politicians, not policymakers. They were the type to subscribe to the "simple-minded," inflexible Cold War ideology that Komer, an actual policymaker, so greatly detested. Nasser appeared to be misreading the climate in Washington.

Nevertheless, after the Arab summit, there was considerable reason for the United States to reconsider its relationship with Nasser, which is perhaps what Nasser was (wittingly or unwittingly) picking up on: With a new president in the White House and Nasser having won far-reaching influence in the Middle East, how should the traditional aid relationship be defined moving forward? Did Nasser need a generous hand or a firm hand? Komer, who had been the chief architect of Kennedy's generous aid policy toward Egypt, was asking these types of questions. But he had no desire to cut off aid to Nasser. Toward the end of the Kennedy era, he began to think it might be necessary to restrict aid to Egypt and start getting tougher on Nasser in light of the Yemen crisis. Yet, like all of Komer's strategies, his thinking on this issue was nuanced.

It's summer 1963, a few short months before Kennedy's assassination: Nasser asks Kennedy for a $30 million loan. Komer is against it; but only on principle. He wants to stimulate economic reform in Egypt, not continue to throw money at Nasser. Nasser is running Egypt's economy into the ground. And, to make matters worse, he has taken out numerous short-term bank loans that he could not afford to pay back. Harold Saunders, Komer's junior partner in the NSC, writes to Komer on September 10, "The current payments crisis gives us considerable leverage. Each one has been more serious than the last because Cairo has steadily drawn down its foreign exchange reserves to almost nothing."[28] Komer thinks it should be a soft no to the $30 million. "We won't say 'nem nem soha,'" he writes to Bundy, using a Hungarian phrase that meant "no, no, never."[29] Instead, he wants to use the situation as an opportunity to nudge Nasser toward economic reform.

Komer had his work cut out for him. The problem was this: Egypt's population continued to grow, but wasteful agricultural development projects and ecological disasters routinely kept Nasser from being able to feed his people without the crutch of American aid. Moreover, Egypt was on the verge of running out of money. Its only liquid asset was $174 million in gold reserves, which Nasser could not actually spend because it was the only asset that still gave Egypt a decent credit rating and, more importantly, gave foreign banks some measure of confidence that Egypt ultimately could afford to repay its debts. What Nasser really needed was help getting out of Yemen—which was costing him $3–$5 million per month in foreign currency—and America's help to kick-start a responsible fiscal spending plan. This was the best way for the United States to position itself as a useful ally to Nasser. As Saunders pointed out, "the [Soviet] Bloc probably doesn't have this kind of money." However, not everyone in Washington saw the value in using American aid to "turn Nasser inwards."[30]

Indeed, Komer needed to demonstrate that Nasser was a worthy investment—not just another dictator on the US dole. In order to steer the situation, Komer began to exert authority over all aid decisions concerning Egypt. In early December 1963, while officials were waiting for Johnson to decide on how he wanted to proceed with aid to Egypt in light of the Gruening Amendment, Talbot and William Gaud, an administrator at the Agency for International Development (AID), were awaiting Komer's approval of two pending "aid actions" for Egypt—one of which was a small loan for cardboard. On December 3, Komer wrote to Bundy that he was "holding back." Komer struggled with the decision. But his reason was straightforward: he believed there should be no new loans for Egypt until Nasser made progress on Yemen. He wrote to Bundy, "My thought is to treat [the] UAR like Indonesia."[31]

American aid to Indonesia had been a corollary of Kennedy's plan to contain the spread of communism in Southeast Asia. Indonesia's president, Sukarno, was an ardent nationalist. He was also a leader of the Nonaligned Movement, thus a self-styled neutralist like Nasser. Sukarno, however, caused trouble for the United States and Britain by opposing independence for Malaysia—whose nationhood was seen by the two Western allies as essential for bolstering the British commonwealth in the region in an attempt to stop the spread of communism. Under Kennedy, the United States began to give aid to Sukarno under the premise he drop his opposition to Malaysia's independence and refrain from becoming an agent of Moscow. For a period of time the strategy worked—though Sukarno continued to build up Indonesia as a formidable military power using Soviet weapons.

Komer evidently believed that the United States should stop giving blind aid to Egypt. Like Sukarno, Nasser would have to take concrete steps to show he was listening. Of course, Komer did not foresee that one year later, in 1965, US relations with Indonesia would eventually fall apart and Sukarno would angrily declare, "Go to hell with your aid!"[32] In 1963, Komer thought (or at least hoped) that Nasser was malleable under a reasonable amount of economic pressure—which, at the time, he still believed was a fruitful strategy in Indonesia that could be applied elsewhere.

In the aftermath of Kennedy's death in November 1963, and a few short weeks before the Arab summit in January, Komer dedicated his time to "catching up on back reading" of embassy reports and telegrams in order to gain a better sense of Nasser's economic situation. If he was going to apply the Sukarno strategy on Nasser, he needed to be well informed on Egypt's economy. At one point, he wrote to Talbot and chided him for missing an opportunity to study the effectiveness of Soviet military aid to Egypt. He asked with a hint of passive aggressiveness, "What do you think of asking the Embassy to tackle that one?"[33]

In order to increase his control over US aid to Egypt, Komer restricted the Cairo embassy's autonomy in handling economic agreements. He wrote to Bundy that he was going to "insist on WH [White House] clearance" on all economic matters. Indeed, as he wrote to Bundy in reference to one pending agreement, "As soon as I saw Cairo 1234 that [the] US and UAR plans on signing [a] cotton textile agreement for December, I checked by with State and Aid. It turns out that is no sweat . . . State and AID say it has much in our interests."[34]

Komer was certain that Nasser could be a key partner for the United States. And he wanted to prove to Johnson that Nasser was worthy of America's aid. To that end, he continued to obsess over State's correspondence, one day coming across a report of the Canadian ambassador's conversation with Nasser, which gave him renewed confidence about continuing to work with Nasser. Komer sent the report to Bundy and excitedly wrote, "What comes through again and again is how Nasser is by far the most savvy of the Arab leaders. He sees things from his own room with a view but he's a guy with whom we can talk."

However, the difficulty of dealing with Nasser was the *extent* to which the administration could have any actual measure of control over him; a problem Komer readily admitted. Bribing Nasser was necessary in order to get him to modify certain positions that ran contrary to American interests. Komer understood this—it was the basis for the redirection strategy he crafted. In his eyes, the potential of good relations with Nasser, who was undoubtedly the most powerful Arab leader after the summit, justified a morally questionable road getting there. "If we get through '64 with Nasser in fact having restrained [the] Arabs over Jordan Water (however much noise he makes)," he wrote to Bundy, "it will amply justify our whole Nasser policy."[35]

Arguably, this was strategy at its finest. As John Lewis Gaddis points out in his book, sometimes rules (and, by extension, morals) must be bent in order to reach a positive outcome that outweighs the pitfalls of bending those rules and morals. Komer clearly believed this approach was appropriate for dealing with Nasser. Directing Nasser through aid, however much his values were at odds with America's, was worth it in the long run if it meant avoiding a conflagration between the Arabs and Israel—at least, so Komer thought.

However, since the strategy relied on using aid to redirect Nasser on issues that were important to the United States, Komer needed to be able to justify Nasser's abysmal economics record—which would help prove to naysayers he was worth helping in the first place. There were a few steps Nasser could immediately take to improve his economy. Notwithstanding the need for an immediate cash infusion, he could cut back on overly ambitious development programs that he called "5-year plans," and temporarily reduce imports to repair the damage incurred from years of wasteful spending. This was the type of rational decision-making that Komer hoped to see from Nasser. In December 1963, Nasser had several payments due from short-term bank loans. A restriction on spending was just what he needed in order to get his affairs in order and meet his financial obligations.[36] Thus, coming into the Arab summit in early January 1964, implementing a pragmatic fiscal policy for Nasser was Komer's main goal.

Instead, Nasser had luck on his side. In December 1963, Egypt's cotton and rice yields were better than expected, which brought in an unexpected cash flow for the Egyptian leader. Exports also suddenly improved (more than likely due to the high crop yields). Therefore, rather miraculously, Nasser was able to avoid the projected shortfalls he was supposed to suffer going into 1964. Moreover, he was able to pay back all of Egypt's short-term loans in full.

To be sure, this was good for Nasser in the short run. But lingering doubts about his long-term fiscal responsibility remained. The International Monetary Fund (IMF) was concerned that Nasser was not taking economic reform seriously enough; this was an issue since the IMF was getting ready to make a loan to Egypt in the spring. According to the IMF's bylaws, developing countries like Egypt were required to make certain reforms recommended by the IMF in order to maintain their eligibility to withdraw from the fund. John Gunter, acting Director of the IMF's Middle East division, had paid a visit to Cairo in December to discuss these recommended reforms with Egyptian officials. Before leaving Cairo, Gunter left behind an "informal memo," which was a list of the reforms Egypt needed. Gunter, however, reportedly left Cairo feeling exasperated. Nasser's longtime finance minister, Abdel Moneim Kaissouni, appeared to be opposed to any type of economic reform. Gunter feared it was an indication that Nasser felt the same way.[37]

This was troubling news to US officials. Komer, however, was still optimistic about Nasser. He wrote a New Year's message to Bundy about the prospects of getting along with the Egyptian leader. "The Near East will be quite a test of our policy (and nerves) in '64," he observed. Nonetheless, Komer strongly felt that Johnson should not allow the Gruening Amendment, the Yemen conflict, or the potential conflict over Israel's water project stand in the way of reaching out to Nasser. Nasser needed money, and the United States needed him. There was no reason Kennedy's policy of flexible outreach could not be made to work under Johnson, Komer argued. Fortunately for Komer, he still had allies in Washington who shared this point of view.[38]

Indeed, in early January, Badeau took it upon himself to write a lengthy letter to Johnson to convince him of the merits of working with Nasser. He started off with an explanation of just how much US-Egypt relations had improved since Kennedy took office in 1961:

> I was told that Egypt represented both an indispensable element and a continuing problem in formulating United States policy towards the Near East . . . Slowly but surely, the West in general and United States in particular is becoming urgently needed for the development and well-being of Egypt . . . I believe that Egypt now recognizes that its Soviet connection, no matter what its size or character, is no substitute for good ties with the Western world.

Badeau strongly recommended to Johnson that he continue in the vein of Kennedy's "quiet diplomacy" approach to foreign policy—at least, in Egypt. There is "no alternative" he wrote, "except to maintain as good relations with Egypt as circumstances permit and by this continue to press for moderation and redirection of Egyptian action." He warned Johnson against "dramatic and publicized reductions of aid." And noted that such action "would only prevail in the loss of any American influence in Egypt." His closing words for Johnson were almost prophetic of the mistakes that would occur a little over two years later under Johnson's watch. "In my opinion," Badeau wrote, "such a guillotine operation [cutting off aid to Nasser] should only be used when direct American interests of overwhelming importance are at stake."[39]

Badeau's letter received significant attention in Washington. Rusk sent a copy of it to Johnson and included a cover letter urging him to read it in its entirety. Bundy forwarded the letter to Komer with a handwritten note, "Speak to me on this." Bundy hardly ever brought matters before Komer; usually, it was the other way around.[40]

Komer immediately got in touch with Johnson's unofficial chief of staff, Bill Moyers, to ensure Badeau's letter was seen by the president. A one-page summary of it had been prepared by State in case Johnson thought the letter was too long. Komer facetiously asked, "Why can't our ambassadors be brief?" However, he only had good things to say about Badeau. "Badeau is one of our best non-career ambassadors," he wrote. "He's past 60 and has long planned to retire this year . . . the President may want to urge him to stay on during the ticklish period in US-UAR relations which are sure to develop over the Jordan waters." Komer believed this was no ordinary letter. He seemed concerned that Badeau was on the verge of leaving his post in Cairo—especially, perhaps, if there was to be a disagreement with Johnson over policy.

Once again, Komer, ever the foreign policy activist, offered to draft a reply to Badeau on behalf of Johnson. Bundy wrote on the bottom of the memo: "Bill: I agree. Badeau has been good. I can arrange his staying-on if [the] President wishes." Both Komer and Bundy strongly felt that Badeau should remain in Cairo for the time being; particularly since relations were still uncertain in the wake of Kennedy's passing.[41]

Johnson approved reaching out to Badeau on his behalf. Moyers wrote a response to the executive secretary of the NSC, Bromley Smith. On top of the note it said "hold for Bundy," who was away on a trip. The note stated, "The President saw this. McB should talk to him when he returns about asking Badeau to stay on."[42] The letter, and the reception it received in Washington, was an inadvertent affirmation of Komer's strategy vis-à-vis Nasser. Any semblance of optimism about Nasser in Washington, however, quickly changed after the Arab summit.

Following the summit, Nasser appeared to feel more emboldened than ever. "Cairo is [a] mountain in [the] heart of Arab world to which all Mohammads must come," Badeau observed in the aftermath of Nasser's political triumph. Indeed, Nasser had pulled off an improbable victory in spite of the unpopularity of his war in Yemen. As Badeau noted, "Improbable [that a] conference call from any other city or leader would have resulted in such universal attendance."[43]

After the summit, Badeau continued to reiterate that dealing with Nasser was vital for ensuring America's success in the Middle East. The results of the summit negated Ambassador Hart's earlier argument that Nasser was dividing the Arab world over Yemen. Instead, Nasser had brilliantly shifted the Arabs' focus onto Israel's water project. True, the threat of a war between Egypt and Saudi Arabia had passed. Now, however, the United States needed to shift its focus to keeping Nasser from turning the water issue into another Arab-Israeli war. Badeau wrote, "On [the] wider horizon, it must be clear that to protect US interests in Arab world at [the] present time involves us in maintaining good relations with [the] UAR and continuing to exert maximum influence in Cairo." He was hopeful that Nasser's decision not to openly criticize the United States at the summit was a sign of his interest in having a constructive dialogue with Johnson.

Badeau believed the United States could harness Nasser's newfound success in the Arab world to its benefit. He told of a "number of western and Arab diplomats" who had approached him since the summit and had paid compliments about the "wisdom of [the US in] recognizing [the] indispensable role Nasser plays in the Arab world." It appeared that playing along with Nasser before the summit (or at least giving the appearance of doing so) was helping America's image in the region. The United States had "no alternative" but to continue dealing with Nasser, Badeau wrote. Nasser was now, more than ever, a "keystone in . . . Arab world policy."[44]

Crucially, however, while Komer and Badeau were busy giving a hard sell to Johnson about the merits of working with Nasser, Nasser was apparently harboring his own doubts about the merit of working with Johnson. At the end of January 1964, one of

Nasser's closest advisers, Hassan Sabri al-Khouli, approached an American diplomatic officer in Cairo, saying he was concerned about the Johnson administration's rhetoric about Israel. Badeau reported to State, "Khouli opined to [the] Embassy officer that US-UAR relations were in for [a] fairly rough period in so far as public statements emanating from both countries were concerned."[45]

It was clear exactly which "public statements" Nasser's adviser was referring to. A few days after the summit, the deputy undersecretary of state for political affairs, Alexis Johnson, had given a major foreign policy speech. He said that the United States would not "stand idly by if aggression is committed . . . we would support appropriate course of action in the United Nations or on our own to prevent or put a stop to such aggression. Any victim of a would-be-aggressor can count on our support." The undersecretary, a junior level official, was merely reiterating America's long-standing stance on Israel's right to draw water from the Jordan River. The Arab states, however, read into the speech that the president was going to be anti-Arab. Nasser himself took it as a sign that Lyndon Johnson was personally against him.[46]

Khouli warned the US embassy officer that Egyptian officials would soon be responding to the undersecretary's speech with propaganda in the press and with "speeches . . . in our new national assembly." He explained that while Nasser was aware it was an important election year in the United States, which meant there would be more pro-Israel speeches than usual from politicians who were looking to court Jewish voters, there was little choice besides responding to such tough talk in kind.

Khouli made it clear to the US embassy officer that Israel's water project was a serious problem between the United States and Egypt. He turned to the officer and asked whether Israel could be persuaded to "postpone" its scheduled water withdrawals from the Jordan River. Surprised by the request, the US official was placed in the awkward situation of having to review the long-standing US policy on the Jordan River issue. Khouli left the room understanding that it was a firm "no" to the request.

Badeau interpreted the episode as a possible indication that Nasser planned to "take [a] firmer public line re US support of Israel."[47] Indeed, this was *Nasser's* new frontier: he was actively using Israel as a hot button issue to rally the Arab states behind him.

With Israel coming between the United States and Egypt so early in Johnson's presidency, the success of Komer's strategy to court Nasser through personal diplomacy à la Kennedy depended on cooling the rising rhetoric between the two nations. Thus, it was unfortunate that on February 6, Lyndon Johnson himself gave a speech at the eighteenth annual gala for Israel's Weizmann Institute of Science, which was misinterpreted as being anti-Arab.

Speaking in the ornately decorated Grand Ballroom of the Waldorf-Astoria in New York City, Johnson made an extraordinary offer to help Israel desalinate water using American nuclear technology. "We will pool the intellectual resources of Israel and America, and all mankind, for the benefit of all the world," he said. He then praised Israel as a country that "knows well the importance of science." That statement alone would have made the Arab states suspicious about a pro-Israel bias in Johnson. But it was what he said next, as an indirect reference to the Arab summit, that really upset the Arab states. "Water should never be a cause of war," declared Johnson, "it should always be a force for peace." Throughout the speech, the president had many accolades for Israel, which did not sit well with Arab observers. At one point, he said, "I speak to you with affection and share with you pride in Israel's achievements."[48]

Not surprising, the Arab press responded to Johnson's speech with a flurry of criticism. On February 8, Egypt's most popular newspaper, *Al-Ahram*, published an article that it attributed to its "New York correspondent" in "discussion with a leading US scientist." The article quoted a fictitious American scientist who claimed the United States was giving Israel a nuclear power plant for desalinizing water, and that the plant would have the capability to produce the material that Israel needed to make its own atomic bomb. The article also claimed that the United States was going to provide advanced nuclear training for Israeli scientists.

A source later told the CIA that the article had been made up by Nasser himself, and that he had dictated it to a writer after learning about Johnson's speech. "Nasir has repeated this theme so often that he believes it," claimed the source. "He seems genuinely convinced that President Johnson intends to help Israel develop atomic weapons." Moreover, the source warned the CIA that Nasser was planning to attack Johnson in his February 22 speech marking the anniversary of the formation of the UAR. Nasser reportedly planned to say that Johnson was "treating the Arabs unfairly and unjustly favouring Israel." [49]

On February 11, Badeau reacted to the rise in tension with Nasser by sending an urgent telegram to Talbot. It was now his turn to be concerned about the future of US-Egypt relations. Specifically, Badeau stressed that time was of the essence for Johnson to write a personal letter to Nasser since a planned letter for after the summit had already been put off for several weeks. Badeau stressed that the letter had to be sent immediately after an Egyptian holiday that was occurring the following week: "I believe now is time to begin what can be a useful exchange of correspondence, which can have some effect in shaping and moderating [the] UAR response to developments in the United States during [the] difficult election year period which lies ahead."[50]

Talbot immediately consulted Komer. He showed him a preliminary draft of a letter for Nasser from Johnson that had been written at the State Department. Komer did not like State's draft. It didn't strike the right tone. So, he took it upon himself to write a new version. He wrote to Talbot that he believed his version was "closer to what the President would like to say, and Nasser to hear."[51]

Indeed, Komer's version was reflective of everything he had been telling his superiors for months: that Johnson needed to be warm and persistent with Nasser despite their rising differences. Since 1964 was expected to be a difficult political year for Johnson—given he had to run for president only months into the job—Komer believed it was important to make Nasser aware. It was all part of redirecting Nasser.

"Dear President Nasser, I am writing to you, in the same spirit of candor as my predecessor, because of my deep concern over the signs of discord between the US and Arab world," went Komer's version of the letter. "In part such discord is inevitable, because of our long-standing policy toward Israel and our necessary stand on principle in the Jordan Waters issue." Komer wanted to communicate to Nasser that US policy was not suddenly going to change under Johnson. He wanted Nasser to see Johnson as the continuation of Kennedy, not as the start of something new. The letter's reference to

Kennedy (the "predecessor") was intended to invite the same level of personal relations between the two leaders that Nasser previously had enjoyed.

As it will be recalled, Komer favored Kennedy's "quiet diplomacy" approach to foreign policy as a way to head off crises. To that end, the letter he wrote in Johnson's name welcomed Nasser to always air his grievances directly with the administration rather than in public. "I have asked John Badeau, in whom I have the same full confidence as my predecessor," went Komer's draft, "to take up with you certain facets of our policy which again risk being misconstrued. I know you will not hesitate to comment on them to him or directly to me. The next few years will be a strain on both of us."[52]

The above-noted elements of Komer's draft made it into State's second draft the following day.[53] Meanwhile, Komer took it upon himself to write to Johnson directly. He stressed the need to continue dealing with Nasser. Now was the time to offer economic aid to Nasser in order to prove to him that the relationship had not perished along with Kennedy. "Our Arab policy is in deep trouble," Komer wrote. "So State urges a series of moves . . . to minimize the risk of a real falling out. Our chief item is our willingness to go ahead with a loan [i.e. the $30 million] to the UAR if it meets our previous conditions. Second is a letter to Nasser which in effect tells him we are not changing our policy."[54]

In the opening weeks of Johnson's presidency a plethora of issues between the United States and Egypt—Yemen, aid, and Israel's water project—had simultaneously converged. But Johnson still had not formulated his own policy on Egypt. It was now time for him to make a decision on how he wanted to proceed with Nasser; especially since the Egyptian leader now had elevated status in the Arab world.

But there was still one remaining shoe left to drop in US-Egypt relations: the arms race in the Middle East. And once again, Israel would become the main issue between the two countries.

4

Weapons and Bases

Apart from a long-standing contention over Soviet arms sales to Nasser, there were two immediate concerns about Egypt's involvement in the Middle East arms race: (1) the United States thought Egypt would respond to Israel's nuclear facility at Dimona by mass producing missiles; and (2) Egypt's production of ballistic missiles was driving Israel to seek more sophisticated weaponry. The latter concern, in particular, came to the fore for the Johnson administration when Israel claimed that it needed to buy American tanks in order to protect itself from Egyptian missiles.[1]

Egypt's missile production had been a problem for Kennedy's administration too, culminating in a secret mission by John McCloy, the former assistant secretary of war under Roosevelt and Truman and an arms proliferation adviser to Kennedy, in the summer of 1963. McCloy's mission had been to convince Nasser to drop his missile program in order to eliminate the arms race with Israel. Nasser had gently rebuffed the request. Correspondence relating to this mission had been marked "CANE," and was restricted to a small number of officials to keep it secret that the United States was conducting an arms probe in the Middle East.[2] The optics of an arms probe risked lending credence to Soviet claims about American interference in the affairs of other nations.

Nonetheless, in February 1964, Komer and Talbot once again marked their correspondence with "CANE," and revisited the issue of arms control. Specifically, there was disagreement among NSC staffers on how to respond to Israel's request for tanks. It had been over four months since Israel's prime minister, Levi Eshkol, had made the request. Meanwhile, there also had been concern over reports that Israel was developing an interest in procuring its own missiles from France; possibly even nuclear ones.

Myer Feldman, White House Counsel, was in favor of selling the tanks to Israel. However, as Komer wrote to Johnson on February 18, "State, Bundy, and I are vigorously opposed." Komer proposed that Johnson maintain flexibility on the matter. "[We] believe we should first attempt to dissuade Israel from taking the highly risky missile road," he wrote. Moreover, Komer wanted permission to tell Nasser that the latest inspection of Dimona showed that the program was "strictly for peaceful purposes." He added, "We see this as essential to prevent the Arabs from going off half-cocked when they're already violent about the Jordan waters."[3] The report on Dimona was somewhat of a fabrication. Komer's notes reveal that Israel's nuclear reactor at

Dimona had just gone "critical," which he worried might "trigger irrational Arab moves" alongside news of Israel's attempts to procure French missiles.[4]

As a way of staying ahead of these spiraling developments, Komer wanted to restart McCloy's arms mission. The best place to start was in Cairo, believed Komer. The United States already had assurances from Israel that it would not produce nuclear weapons. Now it needed assurance from Nasser that he would not mass produce missiles. Komer wrote in one of his CANE memos, "The only symmetrical deal would be for the UAR to deny itself something that Israel fears [missiles], in return for Israel denying itself what worries the UAR most [nuclear weapons]."[5]

The problem, however, was timing: it had taken Komer months to convince Kennedy of the value of linking Israel's nuclear program to Nasser's missile program as a way to mutually de-escalate the capabilities of the two adversaries. However, Israel expected an answer about the tanks soon, and Komer once again had to initiate the lengthy process of convincing the president—this time Johnson—to sign off on an arms probe.

On February 21, Komer aired his concerns in a memo to Talbot. "While thoroughly in favor of another CANE probe," he wrote, "I question whether we should try to sign the President on to this exercise until we have a clearer view of just what we want to accomplish and how." Komer added, "I doubt whether we should tell Nasser now that we are under pressure to sell Israel 'tanks' . . . tanks are not terribly germane to our arms limitations proposals."

Indeed, Komer was worried about the probe being too "transparent"; that it would give Nasser the impression Israel was preparing for war. His solution was a sophisticated dual track process to gently feel out Nasser's response to reducing Egypt's armaments. The United States would: (1) ask Nasser to accept International Atomic Energy Agency (IAEA) safeguards (i.e., international oversight) should Egypt eventually develop a nuclear program—the request would be prefaced with the fact that the United States was also going to ask Israel to accept IAEA safeguard at Dimona; and (2), ask Nasser to sign a pledge not to produce more than 100 surface-to-surface missiles (SSMs). The second request was to be prefaced with an explanation that such assurances would absolve Israel's fear that Nasser intended to produce "1,000 missiles," and therefore deter Israel from creating a far "superior" missile program of its own.

Nonetheless, Komer still feared that Johnson would ultimately give in to the Israeli request for tanks. And he saw this as problematic since Johnson was already being painted by Nasser as anti-Arab in the wake of the Weizmann speech. Thus, Komer faced considerable pressure to get the US-Egypt relationship back on track before the administration would be capable of pulling off nothing short of a diplomatic miracle with selling tanks to Israel. If Komer failed, it would spell the end of the promising diplomatic relations that had been built under Kennedy.[6]

On top of it being a complicated multistep process potentially to both reduce Egyptian arms and sell tanks to Israel, Komer had to act quickly. An opportunity fell into place to use aid as an incentive for Nasser on the arms issue. And Talbot had an upcoming annual visit to Cairo in early March, which presented an opportunity to sound out Nasser's reaction to a new arms probe.

First, Kaissouni was in Washington at the end of February to discuss the $30 million loan request—which remained unanswered. Rusk had been given the difficult task of telling Kaissouni that the administration was only willing to consider a $20 million loan; it was felt that anything more would enable Nasser to be fiscally wasteful. However, in order even to be eligible for the reduced loan, Egypt first had to meet certain obligations, which Komer later summarized in a memo as "acceptance of IMF terms" and progress "on Yemen."

Komer, for his part, was certain that Egypt's fulfillment of these terms would soften some of the inevitable controversy that would arise when the public learned Johnson had given money to Nasser—congressional dislike of the Egyptian leader was something to seriously consider during an election year. However, the decision to dole out more aid to Egypt was ultimately Johnson's, as it was his political career on the line. "These [loan clauses] give us an out," wrote Komer to Bundy, "but political sensitivity of a UAR loan in '64 is so high that I've urged we put this before LBJ."[7]

However, while Komer was sensitive to the restraints of domestic politics, he also felt pressure to make an immediate deal with Nasser. Therefore, on February 24, he pressed Bundy for a response on the $20 million loan. Kaissouni was returning to Egypt that day, and Komer wanted him to be able to deliver good news to Nasser upon his return. He also asked Bundy about the status of Johnson's letter to Nasser—which once again had been placed on hold.[8]

The request for a quick decision on the loan was denied. But Komer was still given a path to sell the president.

On February 26, Komer sent Johnson a memorandum with four attachments. Included was some reassurance for the president. "All these moves were worked out with Bundy and myself; they entail minimum risk of adverse repercussions," he wrote. "We recommend you approve."[9] In reality, Komer had done the thinking entirely on his own, and had merely written to Bundy earlier in the day to get his approval.

First, Komer again revised the proposed letter from Johnson to Nasser. "[I] think it strikes just [the] right touch," he told Bundy in a memo earlier in the day. He stressed to Bundy the importance of sending the letter no less than two times, noting that Ali Sabri, "UAR No. 2," had recently inquired whether Johnson would be continuing Kennedy's approach of personal letter writing. Sabri noted that the correspondence had been special; he encouraged the Johnson administration to pick it up again. Komer agreed. "Nasser letter is long overdue for optimum impact," he wrote Bundy.[10]

Once Komer got Bundy on board, he turned to Johnson. He wrote in a memorandum for the president: "The good relations we've built up with the Arabs are in increasing jeopardy, primarily because in their frustration over their inability to stop Israel's water diversion, they're lashing out at all [of] Israel's friends." He added with emphasis, "This is why they reacted adversely to your Weizmann speech; it will color their reaction to *anything* we say or do this year."

Komer explained to Johnson his solution to the problem of the administration appearing anti-Arab: it was an Arab-Israeli aid package "designed to compensate for the pro-Israeli stand we'll have to take this year." It included, among other things, dual loans to Egypt (the $20 million loan) and Israel. However, Komer assured Johnson "[there are] loopholes for us to renege [with Egypt] if the going gets too rough."

Finally, Komer asked Johnson to authorize the new arms probe with Nasser. "To show that the probe has the same high auspices as before," he wrote, "Talbot should have your blessing."[11]

All of Komer's requests were approved. It was a promising indication that Johnson was leaning toward continuing along the lines of Kennedy's Middle East policy. The letter to Nasser was sent out to the US embassy in Cairo on February 27. Among other things, it called for better relations "rather than letting our two nations drift apart." It still referred to the coming "strain" between the two countries, as Komer originally had phrased it. However, the final draft of the letter also identified specific areas where the United States hoped to see a positive outcome. "We welcome the prospect of normalization in Yemen, of temperance in the Arab-Israeli problem, and of increasing the Arab League's potential for constructive cooperation." Ironically, it was a list of rhetorical promises that had been given to US officials by various Egyptian officials since the Arab summit. Now, Komer was attempting to use their very own words to get Nasser to show results.[12]

With the personal letter from Johnson now approved and ready to hand to Nasser, it was time for Talbot to feel out Nasser on the arms probe.

On February 29, State prepared detailed instructions for Talbot. They were spread over three telegrams and sent to the US embassy in Cairo ahead of his arrival. The first telegram was to let him know that Johnson approved him renewing dialogue with Nasser on the arms issue. It was marked CANE.[13]

The second telegram contained a warning. Evidently, Komer had been right to push for giving Kaissouni a firm commitment on the $20 million loan. Kamel, Nasser's ambassador to the United States, told State that Kaissouni's failure to secure any commitment during his Washington trip had caused officials in Cairo to wonder whether the Johnson administration intended to renege. State told Talbot to make it clear to Nasser that the loan would indeed go through so long as the conditions were met.[14]

The third and final telegram touched upon the other issues that had affected US-Egypt relations in the preceding weeks: the Arab summit, economic aid, and Johnson's speech at the Weizmann Institute gala. However, there was a new issue to discuss. One that had come up at the last minute. In his February 22 speech to celebrate the anniversary of the UAR's formation, Nasser had called for eradicating America's Wheelus Air Base in Libya—even though he knew it was an important tactical base for the Americans in the event of a hot war against the Soviet Union. Back in Washington, officials were wondering whether it had been Nasser's way of making a small demonstration of his ability to inflict harm upon America's interests; particularly in the wake of the Weizmann speech.[15]

Thus, in the evening of March 3, Nasser, Talbot, and Badeau had much to discuss. The three men talked for over two hours. It was the most constructive dialogue between the two countries since the failure of the disengagement scheme in Yemen. Talbot later reported that Nasser was "cordial, quiet-voiced, and apparently relaxed" throughout the meeting. It was an encouraging sign.

Talbot started off the conversation by handing Nasser two letters. One was from Johnson. The other was from Jackie Kennedy—with the intention of linking Johnson to

Kennedy in Nasser's mind as much as possible. Nasser was more interested in reading the letter from Johnson. He put aside Jackie Kennedy's letter, promising to read it later. According to Talbot, Nasser read through Johnson's letter on the spot, very "slowly and carefully." It was the first formal letter he had received since Johnson took office.

After Nasser finished reading the letter and put it down, Talbot began his presentation. He said Johnson had carefully studied Kennedy's policies, and that he wanted to continue the close relationship that had developed under Kennedy. To that end, discussions between the two countries had to occur often and be frank in order to avoid the pitfalls of miscommunication.

Talbot identified the positive aspects of the current state of US-Egypt relations. He said, for example, that the United States was glad some of its cereal companies recently had been able to contribute food to help Egypt meet its "consumption requirements." Johnson was happy to invest in Egypt's future, said Talbot. Then, moving into a discussion about the $20 million loan request, Talbot said that the talks with Kaissouni in Washington had been a demonstration of Johnson's willingness to continue lending to Egypt. As his final positive remark, Talbot congratulated Nasser on the success of the Arab summit. He said the administration had been "impressed by [the] moderate and statesmanlike management of [the] meeting." It was a compliment that was intended to smooth over Nasser's impression that Johnson had overlooked the summit's significance.

Talbot then switched to discussing recent problems between the two countries. He started off by saying the positive developments coming out of the Arab summit had encouraged the United States to speak plainly with Nasser about "several issues which would probably face us in [the] course [of] this year." First, he brought up the issue of Palestinian refugees displaced by the 1948 Arab-Israeli War—which was an issue that had been brought up by the Arabs leaders at the summit. He told Nasser that a solution to the problem would not be forthcoming. Israel could not feasibly take in all the refugees. And without knowing what the Arab states planned to do vis-à-vis Israel (i.e., to "liberate" Palestine as it was phrased at the summit), it was difficult for the administration to take sides on the issue.[16]

Nasser began to speak. According to Talbot, "Nasser responded that, as he had said before, we have few problems in our direct relations. Troubles arise out of third party issues." Specifically, Nasser identified Israel as the number one issue between the two countries. "As he had said in [a] recent speech, [the] US had always supported Israel and had supported [the] status quo. [The] Arabs could not accept this." The Arab states were unified in their desire for the United States to change its position, and to work toward a permanent solution of the Palestinian refugee problem. Talbot replied that such things take time. Therefore, a solution was unlikely to happen under Johnson. Nasser said nothing in return. He apparently just smiled.

After a moment of silence, Nasser brought up Israel again. He said that while Kennedy had worked for peace in the region, the Arab leaders felt that Johnson was taking a different approach. "After . . . [Kennedy's] death, had come new policy statements by Alexis Johnson and President Johnson which troubled [the] Arabs," said Nasser. Talbot immediately countered. He assured Nasser that the Weizmann speech was merely an expression of Johnson's personal interest in desalting, and that Israel was deemed a suitable test case for the research. Badeau chimed in to note that American desalting specialists were also working on several ongoing projects in Egypt. Nasser did not respond.

Instead, the conversation shifted to Yemen. Talbot asked Nasser why he did not get out of Yemen so that he could instead focus on Egypt's economic development. Nasser replied that he had initially accepted the Bunker Agreement, "only to find [that] implementation [was] so delayed that [the] Saudis had time put in what he described as 70,000 pieces of weaponry." Nasser insisted that Egypt's problem in Yemen was not a military one, "but political and economic." Yemen was mostly comprised of independent tribes, said Nasser. And "they could be paid by Saudis or by [the] UAR, sometimes by both." Therefore, the country was impossible to govern. Nasser claimed that he had used Egyptian pounds to pay the salaries of Yemeni civil servants, who had gone three months without pay. "Now he was thinking [the] UAR might have to move in and take over [the] political situation itself," reported Talbot.[17]

Although Nasser was justifying his continued intervention in Yemen on political grounds, he also claimed that security issues required his strong military presence in the country. He said that certain tribes had recently blocked key roads, which led to the cutting of communication between several major cities. Only Egyptian troops—not Sallal—had been able to rectify the situation. As a result, "He was sending in fresh troops on rotation but had decided to leave other troops there." Nasser, however, surprisingly admitted that his troop levels in Yemen were at an all-time high. Badeau interrupted and said there were 35,000 Egyptian troops in the country by America's count. Nasser avoided confirming the figure. He only replied that he personally did not keep count.

The conversation shifted to its penultimate topic. Nasser recently had become involved in Cyprus. Talbot wanted to know why he was beginning to send arms to the nationalist leader, Makarios III, who was interfering with Britain's efforts to negotiate a peace settlement between the Greek and Turkish inhabitants of the island. Nasser said he was involved because he supported the country's independence. It also bothered him that Cyprus had been used by the British to launch an attack against Egypt in the 1956 Suez War.

Talbot pointed out that Britain's position in the Middle East had greatly diminished since then. Why did Nasser want to create a problem where one did not exist? Furthermore, in his February 22 speech, Nasser had extended his criticism of British bases in the Middle East to America's Wheelus base in Libya. Why? Nasser was dismissive in his response. He asked how he could give a speech about foreign bases in the Middle East and not mention the American ones? "As we well know he doesn't like system of bases anywhere in world," reported Talbot. "He had been thinking primarily of our support of Israel, and this was a connected question."

Nasser clearly had Israel on his mind. And the meeting represented a fundamental shift in dialogue between the two countries. It was not just a meeting with Egypt's president, Nasser presented himself as speaking for the entire Arab world on Israel. As Talbot wrote, "At several points in [the] conversation Nasser found ways to reinforce [the] impression he obviously sought to convey that what we are doing for Israel is on his mind in this election year."[18]

Thus, with the conversation having repeatedly moved onto the topic of Israel, Talbot then went into a "long" presentation, for what was essentially a second meeting for the night: Israel's nuclear program and Nasser's missiles. With permission from Israel obtained prior to the meeting, Talbot informed Nasser about the results of the recent inspection at Dimona, which had confirmed that Israel was not looking to produce nuclear weapons. Nonetheless, Talbot said that the United States remained concerned about a Middle East arms race. "In particular, [the] UAR['s] development of surface-to-surface missiles" is "having [a] clearly unsettling effect," he said. "It . . . [is] seen by Israel and by other nations including [the] US as [the] next step in [an] arms race":

In our people's judgement, UAR surface-to-surface missiles . . . might be [a] considerable psychological threat but would not have great military importance so long as numbers were kept low. This was London's experience under V2 attack in World War II. However, Israel is uncertain and fearful of UAR['s] missile plans and our intelligence indicates [the] Israelis [are] taking steps to redress [the] situation. If [the] numbers of missiles [are] kept low on both sides, [the] problem might be largely psychological. However, should [the] UAR develop [a] large missile force and Israel follow suit [the] two forces would obviously be self-defeating as we assume Nasser would recognize.

Talbot explained to Nasser that the United States was looking to take concrete steps to reduce the chances of a "chain reaction" that could lead to both countries increasing their arms capabilities. Therefore, the Johnson administration wanted both Nasser and Israel to sign a pledge to limit their number of missiles. And they wanted Nasser to agree to implement nuclear safeguards for "any large reactor" Egypt "might build in [the] future."

Nasser responded to the surprise presentation with resentment. "He started by observing that once again [the] heart of [the] problem between [the] US and [the] UAR was Israel," wrote Talbot. "It seemed always this way." Nasser said that he did not trust Israel. "None of them [Nasser nor his advisors] could forget those days of 1956," he said, making reference to the Suez War, when Israel, France, and Britain launched a surprise attack against Egypt in retaliation for the latter's nationalization of the Suez Canal. In fact, he claimed that the only reason he pursued missiles was to have an element of deterrence that could dissuade Israel from attacking again. Therefore, he would not divulge how many missiles he ultimately intended to produce. "Returning to [the] question of [the] number of SSMs contemplated by [the] UAR, I again got no answer," reported Talbot.

However, Nasser said that in principle he was willing to accept nuclear safeguards when Egypt advanced its nuclear program, and that he would not pursue nuclear weapons. "Nasser said point is [that the] UAR feels [it] must get into [the] nuclear age in good time," wrote Talbot. Thus, Talbot and Badeau walked away from the meeting feeling slightly optimistic. "Ambassador [Badeau] and I believe there may be some significance in Nasser's indication he may be prepared [to] write [a] letter to President [Johnson] stating [the] UAR['s] intention not to develop or acquire nuclear weapons," wrote Talbot. "This was the clearest indication we got that he did not consider CANE exercise necessarily closed with President Kennedy's death." Talbot added, "[However] his repeated references to Israel arms suggests his willingness [to] proceed along these lines could be withheld if he comes to believe [the] US [is] changing its restraint on arms provided [to] Israel." Therefore, the administration needed to proceed cautiously, if it proceeded at all, with the tank sale to Israel, lest word get out and cause Nasser to lash out at the United States.[19]

The meeting had been revealing. Nasser seemed willing to work with the United States on a variety of issues—arms control being one of them. For a brief moment, relations between the two countries suddenly looked warmer.

However, unknown to Talbot and Badeau, who enthusiastically reported to Washington about their positive impressions of the meeting, was that Nasser most certainly did not trust Johnson. According to a CIA report the day after the meeting, "UAR President Jamal Abd Al Nasir said that he could not accept Assistant Secretary Talbot's presentation that US Middle East policy had not changed since the death of President Kennedy." Specifically, Nasser complained to a CIA informant that the United States had asked him for years to stop propaganda attacks against the other Arab states. But now that he had unified the Arab states at the summit, the United States was getting closer to Israel. While Nasser welcomed Johnson's letter, he felt deceived by what appeared to be a fundamental shift in US foreign policy. In other words, Nasser felt that unlike Kennedy, Johnson was choosing sides in the Middle East.[20]

Therefore, it is not surprising that shortly after the meeting with Talbot and Badeau, Nasser began to secretly lobby against continued US access to Wheelus—even going so far as to speak in person with Libya's King Idris about the matter. Nasser believed he was doing this in secret. But the CIA listened in on Nasser's conversations, meaning US officials were well aware of what he was doing behind their backs. According to one report from March 8, "Nasir said that he was continuing to exert pressure on Libya . . . Nasir said that he was pressing the Libyans by every available means and commented that he knew which parliamentarians would attack the bases even before they spoke." The base issue subsequently became the dominant obstacle standing in the way of US-Egypt relations. From the American perspective, the issue needed to be dealt with before things got out of hand.[21]

On March 17, State sent a telegram to Badeau (and a copy to Talbot who was in Ankara). "We must make plain to Nasser that should US rights at Wheelus or Kagnew [a US base in Eritrea] be substantially impaired as [to] result [in] any further UAR fomenting [of the] base issue," wrote State, "USG will lack [the] congressional and public support necessary [to] carry forward existing policies toward UAR." The telegram went on, "On other hand Nasser's forbearance or, hopefully, positive assistance toward mitigating [the] situation re[garding] Wheelus would be welcome evidence [of the] fruitlessness [of] our policy toward him."

Badeau was instructed to meet with Nasser right away, and to make it clear to him that meddling with US strategic installations in the region "threatens seriously to overload [an] already strained circuit." State wondered whether Nasser's campaign against Wheelus was part of a tactic to limit US military movements in the Middle East; possibly even to provide an opportunity for himself to invade Libya. After all, he was presumably aware of the strategic importance of Wheelus to America's Cold War strategy. Even Kamel, Nasser's ambassador to the United States, claimed to have sent a letter to Nasser by special channel, warning him not to interfere with America's rights to the base.[22]

Badeau, however, was reluctant to press Nasser about the base. He felt that Nasser's response would be predictable. The ambassador played devil's advocate in a telegram to State, asking: "Why talk to UAR? Air base is in Libya . . . British appear acquiescent to their base removal. Why does USG take different view? What specific evidence [is there] that [the] UAR [is] responsible for maintaining and accelerating [the] issue in Libya?" Badeau wanted his presentation on the matter "to go beyond hand-wringing and finger-pointing." He asked for clarification on a number of questions. "Is [the] US now convinced that [the] retention [of] Wheelus rights [is a] top defense priority? Is [the] retention [of] Wheelus base such [a] vital US interest that [we are] prepared to go all the way in its protection? Does US in fact see no alternative between complete possession and complete relinquishment of Wheelus rights?"[23]

It was unclear from the telegram whether Badeau agreed with Nasser or just strongly felt that the base was not important enough to risk upsetting an already fragile US-Egypt relationship.

Back in Washington, Bundy wrote down a joke on Badeau's telegram: "The headline could be Badeau Bites Back."[24] He later wrote to Komer, "saw Badeau's Nasserite answer. Will you help him to the mark?"[25]

Badeau's resistance to the idea of confronting Nasser over the base was rooted in his concern that Johnson's seemingly preferential treatment for Israel was putting the entire Middle East policy at risk. But Badeau was not the only Middle East ambassador to feel this way.

Indeed, Talbot was told as much when he had his annual meeting with the Middle East ambassadors in Beirut at the end of March. What he heard there moved him to write a telegram for Rusk's "eyes only." According to Talbot, the ambassadors all felt that Israel's water project was causing the United States to lose the gains it had made with the Arabs under Kennedy. The speeches by Alexis Johnson and the president in the wake of the Arab summit had spoiled Arab "euphoria." The Arabs "had persuaded themselves that they could be masters in their homes," wrote Talbot to Rusk. "It is obvious that [an] accident of timing shortly after [the] Cairo conference [i.e., Alexis Johnson and the President's speeches] plus super acute anxieties about [the] policies of a new President reinforced [these] Arab reactions."

Among the group of ambassadors, the one based in Syria had the most extreme view about the state of America's position in the Middle East. He told Talbot that the United States may need to evacuate the embassy staff's dependents out of fear there would be retribution for Johnson's support for Israel. The other ambassadors agreed with him that the relationship with Israel was increasingly coming into conflict with the administration's policy toward the rest of the Middle East. The ambassador to Kuwait, for example, noted that Kuwaitis were so anxious to be seen as "good Arabs," that they were adopting an unusually "strong line on Israel and US-Israeli relations."

The ambassadors collectively emphasized that Johnson's speeches had to be toned down when he spoke about the Middle East. They argued that friendly speeches about Israel threatened to do more harm than good for him in the region. Talbot wrote, "I would describe their mood not as critical of our policy but as disquieted by [the] thought [that] this is likely to be [an] even more difficult year than they had anticipated."[26]

But the pressure from the ambassadors didn't stop there. A few days later, Badeau sent a telegram to State, writing that his entire embassy staff in Cairo advised against the tank sale to Israel. They too believed that Johnson was putting Israel ahead of Nasser. And that continuing to do so by selling tanks to Israel would lead to Nasser getting more weapons from the Soviet Union, "heating up the Arab-Israeli cold war," and retaliating "against US material interests in other Arab states." According to Badeau, the embassy staff believed that Nasser's campaign against Wheelus had been a demonstration of his ability to interfere with US interests in the region, and they were worried that he would escalate if Israel became an even bigger issue between the two countries. Thus, Badeau wrote, "Our over-all estimate is that [the] UAR retains [the] capability [to] impair and organize opposition to US material interests in other Arab states such as Libya, Jordan and Kuwait and would not hesitate use such capability if [the] US departs from traditional policies and becomes [a] major arms supplier to Israel." Badeau ended with advice, which held the collective weight of the embassy staff, that the administration should walk away from the tank sale to Israel.[27]

Surprisingly, Rusk disagreed with his diplomats. He personally did not have any patience for Nasser's pressure tactics—even though he too was against the tank sale. At an NSC meeting on April 2, he announced that State was putting together a detailed study of US relations with Egypt. Nasser had scuttled any chance for peace in Yemen, said Rusk. And, more importantly, Nasser had revealed his true colors when he interfered with US access to Wheelus. In short, Rusk saw no benefit to continuing relations with Nasser, and he informed the NSC at a joint meeting that the rest of State agreed with him—which, as seen above, was quite an inaccurate statement.[28]

Nasser's verbal attacks on America's foreign bases could not have come at a worse time. Some officials—like Rusk and others in the DOD and the CIA—had patiently been waiting to see the relationship fall through in the wake of the Arab summit. Nasser was stepping on America's toes in the Middle East. It fell to Badeau to redirect him in Cairo in order to prove that the Kennedy approach still worked.

On April 4, Badeau had a meeting with Nasser that was watched carefully from Washington as a litmus test for continuing the Kennedy approach. Nasser began by apologizing to Badeau for putting off their meeting for several weeks. Badeau observed that he looked tired. Nasser replied he had been away for a short stay at his house in the desert. It was a respite after taking care of his sick father. The truth, however, was that it had been a very difficult month for Egyptian military forces in Yemen—which Nasser dared not mention to Badeau.

Badeau began his presentation by pointing out that the Johnson administration had maintained Kennedy's friendly policy toward Egypt. The three-year PL 480 deal was ongoing until mid-1965, a potential $20 million loan was on the table, and the United States continued to recognize the Arab Republic of Yemen. Badeau attempted to turn the table on Nasser. He asked whether Nasser's policy toward the United States had changed. Badeau added that it was Nasser who had brought the United States and Egypt into conflict over Wheelus. Moreover, Nasser had stirred up the negative reaction in the Arab press to Alexis Johnson and the president's speeches. According to Badeau's memorandum of the conversation: "Personal attacks against President Johnson had been highly disturbing, in support of which I read verbatim phrases from [the] March 17 Voice of Arab Nation."[29]

Nasser replied that he had already put a stop to radio attacks against Johnson like the one Badeau brought up. Such propaganda was "undignified and unworthy," he said. He even claimed that the radio station was now solely dedicated to reading from the Koran. Badeau interrupted. It was not enough to change the future tone of the broadcast, he said. "Severe damage had already been done that could not be fully obliterated even by future restraint." Nasser, however, was dismissive, and moved on to comment about the foreign bases issue.

"President [Nasser] then said that [the] UAR['s] resistance to foreign bases was not [a] new policy and had been consistently reiterated in [the] past," reported Badeau. Nasser said that the Arab states had reason to be nervous about an American base in their midst; particularly in light of their perception from the Weizmann speech that Johnson was pro-Israel. Nasser pointed out that he also had been critical of Britain's bases in Aden (located in a part of the Arabian Peninsula adjacent to Yemen).

"At this point I interjected [with a] review of USG policy on [the] Arab-Israeli dispute," reported Badeau. "As president [Nasser] himself knew by experience, [a] non-aligned position [is] most difficult to obtain sympathy for. [The] USG [is] striving to be non-aligned between Arabs and Israel." Badeau posed a question to Nasser: As a self-proclaimed neutralist, could he not sympathize with the difficulties of striking a balance between opposing sides? Besides, Badeau pointed out, America's foreign military bases were strategically located to defend the "free world" from Soviet advancement. Surprisingly, Nasser backed down on the issue. He said that he could not suddenly reverse himself on his long-standing opposition to foreign military bases; however, he could refrain from specifically referring to American ones in his speeches.[30]

"I responded that this was his problem and that it needed to be most soberly considered in light of my presentation," reported Badeau. "A breakdown in USA-UAR relations could only lead to a campaign of mutual hurtfulness." Nasser asked Badeau what measures the United States would consider taking against him if he did not drop his attacks on Wheelus. "I responded that whatever measures would be taken would be appropriate to the situation," reported Badeau. Nasser could help the situation by remaining silent about the bases, Badeau added. Propaganda itself was a "form of pressure" which threatened to bring the United States and Egypt into confrontation. Nasser simply repeated that he would not mention American bases by name when speaking about the issue.

In spite of tension between the two countries, the two men kept their composure throughout the meeting. "The interview was exceedingly relaxed and calm," reported Badeau. However, Badeau had a warning for Washington: "I am strongly of the opinion that Nasser believes something new is in the making between the United States and Israel." He added:

> I am convinced, that he suspects something is afoot. Therefore it well may be that USG must decide which is the more important to its national interests— negotiating [the] position of Wheelus in [a] relatively calm atmosphere or some new gesture of support for Israel such as providing tanks or other weapons. I do not believe we can accomplish both . . . I hope this fact will be read, marked, learned, and inwardly digested before any final decision on Israel is reached.[31]

Indeed, Nasser's threat to American interests in the Middle East continued to cause considerable doubt among Johnson's officials about the merits of selling tanks to Israel.

Nonetheless, Nasser had somewhat passed the litmus test. By "mitigating" his stance on the foreign bases issue, he had demonstrated the "fruitfulness" of the current policy. Therefore, after the meeting with Badeau, the United States met a special request from Egyptian officials to increase corn shipments in 1964. The administration was able to do so by making early withdrawals from the 1965 allotment. It was an easy solution to a potentially larger problem, and was seen as an opportunity to make a friendly gesture toward Nasser. As Harold Saunders observed when he wrote to Komer, "Badeau tried to get a little mileage out of [the] special request in his latest talk with Nasser." More importantly, however, it was a sign that the administration could perhaps return to offering Nasser carrots in order to guide him, rather than prodding him with sticks.

Nasser certainly did not see Johnson as Kennedy. But, perhaps, the old strategy of redirection could still work—so long as the right person was in Cairo to redirect Nasser. For now, Komer's approach was still winning out.[32]

5

Enter Britain

Badeau had played the pivotal role in smoothing over the base issue. So it was ironic that as soon as one problem had been solved, another should appear: Badeau was adamant about leaving the Foreign Service in June, which was only two months away. This was a major blow to Komer's approach. On the ground in Cairo, the Johnson administration would soon be deprived of its most important remaining link to Kennedy, and at a time when relations between the two countries were starting to heat up over Britain's military presence in Southern Arabia—something which Nasser viewed as a serious threat to his interests in Yemen. Indeed, Britain did its best to damage US-Egypt relations as much as possible in the wake of its own problems with Nasser.

Komer thought Badeau's announcement could not have come at a worse time. It is the "year of the Jordan Waters," he pointed out to Badeau, reminding the ambassador about the still unresolved conflict over Israel's National Water Carrier. In particular, Komer was worried about continuity. His main strategy for 1964 had been to convince Nasser that things would be no different between the United States and Egypt under Johnson than they had been under Kennedy. Now he needed to find a new ambassador who could share his vision of better relations between the two countries. And he had to find a replacement capable of redirecting Nasser as well as Badeau had. Otherwise, the continuity of policy could also be broken.[1]

On April 1, Komer wrote to Ralph Dungan—the administration's de facto appointments chief. Komer did not think it was possible to convince Badeau to stay on in Cairo for an additional period of time. In January, Rusk had written to the ambassador and asked him to stay on, adding that Johnson was also making the request. Badeau, however, had been noncommittal. Now he was insisting that his wife wanted to return to the United States. Komer was worried about having enough time to find Badeau's replacement. He wrote to Dungan, "I hate to see [the] key Cairo spot uncovered or in green hands at what might be a crucial time." Talbot wanted to immediately appoint Parker T. Hart, who was still serving as ambassador to Saudi Arabia. Komer, however, worried that Hart's previous position in the Eisenhower administration associated him too closely with its "anti-Nasser policy." Also, as it will be recalled, Hart had been critical in the past about the merit of using preventive diplomacy on Nasser.

"Let's not signal [to] Cairo [that] we're fed up by assigning a non-simpatico guy," wrote Komer to Dungan. "When we want to be tough we can do it from here." If it had to be a career diplomat, Komer preferred Charles Yost, who had been in the Foreign Service since 1931, and was currently serving as deputy assistant representative to the UN. Nonetheless, Komer was anxious to fill the position, lest an extended vacancy damage the already fragile US-Egypt relationship. "Ralph, Talbot doesn't know Ted Harris, but he agrees with me that Gyppos [archaic slang word for Egyptians] would be skittish as hell," wrote Komer, with his usual blunt tone, about the possibility of an extended vacancy. "They're quite color-conscious on this score."[2]

Walt Rostow, the counselor and chairman of the Policy Planning Council at State, suggested another name to Komer: Bill Polk. Polk also was on the Policy Planning Council. And he was a well-known Middle East studies scholar, who used to teach at Harvard University. In other words, he was like Badeau. The Near East and South Asian Bureau (NEA) officials at State, however, saw Polk as too much of an "activist"— someone like Komer who thought outside of the box. Of course, this meant Komer saw Polk as the perfect ally to redirect Nasser on the ground.

Komer wanted an ambassador who would be capable of winning Nasser's trust. In Komer's eyes, it was a bonus that State saw Polk as an activist. Komer wanted somebody who would be keen to practice preventive diplomacy despite the occasional pushback from State. He joked to Bundy, "as a fellow poker of needles, I'll join Walt in saying [the] gadfly role [a person who provokes others into action] makes this [State's reluctance] inevitable." Now set on Polk as ambassador, Komer pushed Bundy to take action. "WH [White House] would have to seize the ball and rush with it," he wrote. He added for good measure, do "not let State bureaucracy take its course."[3]

To entice Dungan, Komer promoted Polk as a potential political asset for Johnson's presidential campaign. "NEA would no doubt oppose," wrote Komer, "but [an] extra plus in Polk would be that he's a Texan, and I gather [he] could also bring some sizable oil money into [the] party coffers." The other bonus was that Nasser already knew Polk. Indeed, the two men had met in Cairo in 1962 to talk about the Yemen conflict. Komer pointed out that Polk was "well-regarded by [the] UAR hierarchy from Nasser on down." His appointment would give the administration the ability to be simultaneously tough and friendly with Nasser—which now, more than ever, seemed like a sensible strategy in light of Nasser's backing down on the base issue. "We can be tough as we want from here," wrote Komer to Bundy, "while sending Bill would signal that at least we want to be friends if [the] Arabs will let us."[4]

Bundy gave his approval to Komer about Polk and advised him to "privately" take care of the matter.[5] The next day, Dungan wrote to Bundy and Komer that he trusted their judgment on Polk since he personally did not know him. He also let them know that State wrote a letter in Johnson's name asking Badeau to stay on until autumn. None of the three men, however, thought that Badeau would agree to it.[6]

The three of them contemplated the best way to convince Johnson to appoint Polk. "I gather he also has power political credentials from Texas," Komer wrote. "His family is in oil and he apparently has pull with Clint Murchison, Gordon McLendon, and Bill Buller [wealthy businessmen and political operatives in Texas]." Komer wanted to be strategic. He asked Bundy to be the one to sell Polk's appointment to Johnson since Dungan did not know Polk.[7]

Komer was clearly concerned. There was an entire Middle East policy to protect. And constant communication with Nasser, in order to redirect him on important issues, was imperative to the preservation of that policy.

Fatefully, at the same time that Badeau announced his imminent departure from the administration, Komer's policy of redirecting Nasser came under serious review: Rusk's study on the merit of the current approach to Egypt was coming due. On April 11, the US embassy in Cairo completed its portion.[8] Badeau included a separate summary with his own thoughts. He noted there was substantial concern within the administration about the current policy toward Egypt. And he noted, as well, that Nasser was skeptical about Johnson's sincerity. In spite of all this, Badeau still believed it was possible to improve relations between the two countries. "[The] Egyptian [is] probably persuadable over [the] long run that Soviet communism constitutes the major threat to UAR independence," he wrote. "Aside from weapons and [funding for the Aswan] high dam, [the] Egyptian [is] already convinced [that] Western culture, technology, and agriculture offer preferable alternatives to Soviet aid."[9] Badeau added that while US-Egypt interests "remain small . . . their enlargement will require much time, patient effort, and common experience." In other words, he was once again reiterating the importance of sticking with Kennedy's policy.

Ironically, Badeau saw Israel as one potential area of common interest between the United States and Egypt. He believed both the United States and Egypt wanted to avoid another Arab-Israeli war. And he argued that Nasser was only bluffing when he talked tough about Israel. A "vital US national interest is restricted to [the] prevention [of] large-scale hostilities between [the] Arabs and Israelis," Badeau wrote:

> UAR policy, despite occasional public statements to the contrary, is aimed at containment of Israel rather than liberation of Palestine . . . This congruence of US and UAR interests . . . provided ample area of maneuver on such issues as support for UNTSO, maintenance of UNEF on Egyptian territory and concomitant use of [the] Gulf of Aqaba by Israeli shipping.[10]

Back in Washington, Talbot echoed Badeau's arguments, and asked Rusk to trust the current approach to Nasser. "You asked me to take a hard look at our UAR policy," he wrote to his superior. "Toward this end a good many months of effort have already gone into the National Policy Paper on the UAR, the current draft of which substantially supports our policy approach"—which, in a nutshell, was to have Johnson follow in Kennedy's footsteps. Talbot reminded Rusk that "Ambassador Badeau addressed himself to this same subject in a recent letter to the President [Badeau's letter in January]." No doubt Talbot was encouraging Rusk to remain patient with Nasser.

Indeed, Talbot had a warning for Rusk. "Advocates of the 'get tough with Nasser' policy," he wrote, "fail to realize that we already appear to the UAR to have embarked on this course." He noted that Kennedy's assassination and the Gruening Amendment had already significantly altered the course of US-Egypt relations in a short amount of time. If the United States got even tougher, by immediately cutting off aid to Nasser as advocates of the "get tough with Nasser" policy wanted, it was liable to push the relationship to its brink, wrote Talbot.

He added to his warning that it was important to take stock of Nasser's ability to inflict considerable damage upon American interests in the Middle East. This had already been demonstrated vis-à-vis the base issue. Talbot wrote, "With all its weaknesses . . . [Egypt] remains the most populous, most powerful, and most influential of the Arab states, with a capability not only to move but to lead other Arab states against Western interests." He aimed to make Rusk see that the United States needed Nasser more than Nasser needed them. "We are not concerned merely with U.A.R.'s capacity to do grave damage to our interests in 1964," he wrote. "To my mind, the most compelling objection to jettisoning our present policy is that it offers the best prospect for building a durable position for the United States in the Near East in the years to come." In other words, redirecting Nasser and enticing him with aid was still the best policy for bringing about a more constructive relationship between the two countries. Nasser was just too popular in the Middle East and therefore too powerful to avoid, reasoned Talbot.[11]

Talbot was doing his best in Washington to provide a strong defense of Badeau's analysis from Cairo. Nevertheless, problems between the two countries continued to pile up, giving further cause to the advocates of the "get tough with Nasser" policy.

In late March, after weeks of Sallal's republican forces repeatedly making incursions into the British territory of Aden, British forces responded by attacking the republican fort of Harib in Yemen. Not surprising, the Arab states were less than pleased about Britain exercising its power in the region. As a result, anti-British protests quickly spread across the Middle East. Egypt joined in with a propaganda attack against the United States too.[12]

One Egyptian newspaper called *Al Haq'iq*, published a pamphlet titled, "American Intelligence—This Is Your Enemy." It claimed that the CIA was looking to undermine Arab authority in the Middle East. Earlier in the month, Egypt's minister of Information and National Guidance (popularly known as the censor) privately told an American informant that he would not approve the pamphlet's publication. But since it ultimately was published, CIA analysts surmised that the about-face must have come from a "higher authority." According to Egyptian law, a publishing company risked the government seizing its assets if it disobeyed a direct ruling from the censorship office. This meant that only Nasser or someone from his inner circle could have overridden the censor and approved the propaganda.[13]

With this new round of problems building up between the two countries, Komer wrote a secret telegram to Badeau on April 17, marked "eyes only for ambassador." Mimicking the earlier Talbot-Badeau correspondence, it was now Komer's turn to express concern about the future of US-Egypt relations. To begin with, he expressed regret that Badeau had to retire in such an "unusually ticklish" year. But he made sure to note that the ambassador had "done a great job" during his tenure. Komer added, "[however,] now it behooves you and those of us who have fought for a more sensible long-range Arab policy to consider how to preserve and expand it."

Komer asked Badeau, "in confidence," for advice on the right candidate to succeed him. He stressed the importance of quickly finding someone who could come across in

Nasser's eyes as a link of continuity between Kennedy and Johnson. Referring to State's shortlist for the position—which was Parker Hart, Charles Yost, and now Lewis Jones (a former ambassador to Tunisia)—Komer wrote, "I'm a bit concerned that reverting to a career ambassador, following on an ambassador so obviously selected for the job, may be a bad noise." He explained to Badeau his preference for an outsider (i.e., Bill Polk), with a strong background in Middle Eastern studies like Badeau, and asked Badeau if he had any suggestions.

He also asked Badeau to commit himself in his final months as ambassador to leaving Nasser as optimistic as possible about the new ambassador (whomever it was to be) and, more importantly, to plant seeds with Nasser for a more positive outlook about Johnson himself. Komer added for good measure, "It is vital that Nasser not rock the boat unduly."

Komer was obviously on the defensive to preserve the policy he had spearheaded under Kennedy, which was under continuous attack in the wake of the base issue. But he recommitted himself to the policy in his letter to Badeau: "many . . . are beginning to question again whether we can do business with Nasser. But we have invested three years in a constructive policy and we mustn't let it slide away without the old college try."[14] Komer was not planning to give up without a fight.

In addition to the growing anti-British protests in the Middle East, which threatened to pull the United States into a bitter propaganda fight, Komer's other main area of concern was congressional opposition to the administration contributing to a small UNESCO project that sought to preserve a set of ancient Nubian temples in Egypt called Abu Simbel. Nasser's construction of the Aswan Dam in the 1950s had unexpectedly caused the water levels of the Nile River to rise. As a result, the temples were now in danger of flooding. The "Abu Simbel monument project is a cultural matter," wrote Komer to Johnson back in March, "which feelers indicate would not create any political problems here." Johnson had no objection to the project.[15]

Indeed, America's contribution would be going directly to UNESCO, not Nasser. Komer had arranged for a contribution of $12 million to come from the government's surplus holdings of Egyptian pounds it received as payment for the PL 480 loans. In fact, the United States received $25–$30 million a year from these payments, so Treasury officials felt that there was no budgetary obstacle to making the donation.[16]

However, Congressman John Rooney (D. New York, chair of the House Appropriations Committee) was against the project and threatened to scuttle it. Komer asked Johnson to intervene and change the congressman's mind. "The problem is Rooney," he wrote to Johnson. "Rooney reportedly made at least a half promise to President Kennedy on this, but has since seemed to be getting cold feet (Brooklyn constituency?). He suggests the Senate take the rap for initiating an Abu Simbel request, but this means more delay at best." Komer was worried that Rooney's stalling would give Nasser the impression of a "political cold shoulder."[17]

Now concerned by the added effect the holdup on Abu Simbel would have on Nasser's opinion of Johnson, Komer redoubled his efforts to secure Polk's appointment. He wanted to ensure there would still be a friendly face to represent the United States in Cairo after Badeau left.

On April 21, Komer sent Bundy a list of politicians who could expedite Polk's appointment. Because these men agreed with Komer's line of thinking when it came to Nasser, many of them "jumped the gun" by immediately lobbying Walter Jenkins and Jack Valenti (two close advisers to Johnson) for a speedy appointment. "Ball's in your court," wrote Komer to Bundy.[18] Komer assumed Polk's appointment was now a sure thing.

Now that Komer felt he had dealt with the ambassadorship issue, he focused all of his attention on heading off a British threat to his Egypt policy.

Britain wanted the United States to stop giving aid to Nasser in light of the propaganda attacks against British and US bases in the Middle East. In fact, the British foreign secretary, R. A. Butler, was coming to Washington at the end of April to personally convince Rusk and Johnson. Komer strongly felt that the United States should separate itself from Britain's Middle Eastern policy. He recalled to Bundy that the United States withdrew funding for Nasser's Aswan Dam in 1956, which in turn caused Nasser to nationalize the Suez Canal and turn to Moscow for aid. Komer wanted to avoid Nasser once again closing himself off to the United States. "We've spent some years digging out of that hole; why get into it again?" he asked.

Komer argued that aid was the most effective tool for getting close to Nasser. He believed it was the only thing standing in the way of the United States being shut out of the Middle East entirely. "The key point is that our support to him (which goes directly into the bellies of the fellahin) constrains him from pushing too hard . . . He knows he has something to lose if he makes too many speeches about Libyan bases (one was bad enough)," wrote Komer to Bundy. The United States could not "lick" Nasser while he remained the symbol of Arab nationalism, Komer argued. The only alternative was to "string . . . [Nasser] along, [and] not give him a bloody nose." But this is not what advocates of the "get tough with Nasser" policy wanted to do. They wanted to give Nasser a "bloody nose" in order to give him a reality check about who held the power in the US-Egypt relationship.[19]

Evidently, Komer's approach won out. When Rusk met with Butler on April 27, he repeated many of the same arguments that Komer had given to Bundy ahead of Johnson's weekly Tuesday lunch-meeting with senior advisers. According to the memorandum of their conversation, Butler pressed the administration to get tough on Nasser. "Clearly he is our enemy," Butler said. "Therefore, we must frame a joint Anglo-American policy to cope with him. The British Cabinet doubts that continuing Western aid to Nasser is . . . [in America's] interests." Rusk replied that the United States was committed to preserving Kennedy's policy toward Egypt. "The USG . . . [is] concerned over its relations with the UAR," he told Butler. "If we start actions which will annoy and antagonize Nasser, we have not helped our situation but have hindered it by closing a channel of communication to him and losing what little influence we have in Cairo."[20]

At Komer's urging, the Johnson administration was now doubling down on Nasser—even at the cost of a potential rift with Britain.

Meanwhile, word got out in Cairo that Badeau was planning to resign over the summer. On April 18, he paid a personal visit to the governor of Cairo. After being "closely" questioned, Badeau felt pressured to confide in the governor, whom he considered "an old friend and a person of integrity." He wrote to State, "While I am prepared to dissemble to the brink of prevarication, I cannot go beyond that." Badeau was anxious for the administration to find his replacement. As Komer had wanted, he applied pressure on Talbot and William Crockett (deputy under secretary of state for management) to find a suitable candidate for his replacement as soon as possible. Badeau agreed with Komer that there had to be a smooth transition to the new ambassador.[21]

However, Badeau's final month as ambassador proved to be a difficult one, with Britain continuing to be a source of conflict between the United States and Egypt. The new tensions threatened to undermine Komer's attempt to continue with Kennedy's friendly and flexible approach to Nasser.

On April 30, Badeau casually told Khouli that Nasser's criticism of the British base in Aden was putting the United States in a difficult spot; not least because the United States had a "subsidiary naval interest" in the base. The next day, Nasser gave his annual May Day speech, which contained a new propaganda attack about the British base: specifically, he claimed that the United States directly profited from the base.

Badeau was concerned that his talk with Khouli had somehow influenced Nasser's speech. "How could the United States possibly express interest in other countries' foreign military bases without it seen within the 'colonialist' context?" he asked State with an air of exasperation. Badeau pointed out that Nasser had remained silent about Wheelus since their meeting earlier in the month. Since at that meeting Badeau had clearly explained the base's importance within the larger structure of America's Cold War strategy, Badeau came to a promising realization: Nasser responded well if the administration came to him with a specific problem, not with a principled stance. He excitedly wrote to State asking, "Is [Aden] base actually available [for the] US [to] use: how much is [the] base relevant to our position in [the] Far East (e.g. in moving units from 6th to 7th fleet)?" In other words, Badeau was hopeful that Nasser could be redirected on the British/Aden issue too if the United States could give him some reasonable explanation for why it mattered so much to them.[22]

In his May Day speech, Nasser had criticized British policy in the Middle East. He cast Britain as a villain and tied its presence in Aden (which he called a "counterfeit state") to the United States. He said, "[the] British take 500 million and [the] Americans [take] 900 million from oil of the Arab world." Next he tied British and US policy to Israel:

Israel buys rockets and obtains aid from [the] United States of America. Israel also obtains aid and buys from Britain. It is therefore our money that helps Israel to arm itself and it is with our money that Israel buys armaments to kill Arabs and to raise an army to stand equal to all Arab armies.

Nasser also read deeply into Butler's visit to the United States. While it was public knowledge that Butler had attempted to persuade Rusk and Johnson not to continue giving aid to Egypt, Nasser reacted as though the United States had actually cut off its aid. "If they apply economic sanctions against us we are willing to face them," he said. "Each one of us is willing to eat half a loaf instead of a full loaf."[23]

Nasser's speech provoked a flurry of analysis from Badeau and the rest of the embassy staff as they searched for a deeper meaning behind his aggressiveness. Badeau observed, "We have not heard his tone of voice and manner of delivery reflect so much anger in several years." He considered it a reflection of the difficulties Nasser was experiencing in Yemen, compounded by Britain's pressure on the United States to discontinue aid. He believed that Nasser was invoking the "ghost of 1956" in order to warn the United States against the "fatal step" of cutting off his economic pipeline.[24]

Indeed, Nasser had substantial reasons for being upset about Yemen. British mercenaries had joined the royalist forces. And the tribes continued to be unruly and would not submit to Sallal. Nasser had achieved some success in stemming the flow of arms across the Saudi border into northern Yemen. However, a new supply line opened in the south from Beihan, which was part of Britain's Aden Protectorate—a vast territory in Aden's hinterland under British control. Badeau surmised that Nasser's propaganda blitz against the British was part of a strategy to deal with these setbacks in Yemen. He wrote, "With his usual sharp eye for tactical advantages, but not necessarily thinking out full strategic implications, Nasser hit on [a] plan to launch [an] all-out campaign against [the] British."[25] But in the midst of his frustration with Britain, Nasser had momentarily forgot that he was supposed to be on good terms with the United States. Badeau described an interesting mistake that Nasser had made during his speech:

> At one point, in [the] midst of [his] harangue about those who support Israel, he started to say 'Britain and US' but choked it off before 'US' uttered and ended up saying lamely 'Britain and England . . .'[26]

Badeau argued that in the short run, the United States needed to keep Nasser and Britain apart in order to avoid a direct confrontation between the two foes. However, he also pointed out that Yemen still threatened to be a powder keg for the entire region. Badeau predicted that if Nasser was unable to break the current impasse in Yemen in a year's time, he would probably lash out at the West and rally the other Arab states to his side. "Past has shown that when Nasser is unable make political headway by any other means, he is prepared [to] cause free-for-all trusting to his own talent . . . to emerge on top of [the] heap." Indeed, in 1956, Nasser managed to seize the Suez Canal from the French and British and, in the process, damaged the international stature of the two European powers. Badeau believed that Nasser was prepared to "play for equally high stakes again."[27]

Thus, Badeau advised that the Johnson administration stay out of the Nasser-British conflict altogether, arguing that "Nasser's actions do not yet appear to have involved direct US interests." Badeau believed that the best response to Nasser's rhetoric was to remain silent. He wrote there was "no question" that Nasser had the ability to reignite the conflict over Wheelus. Therefore, if the United States made an issue of Aden (where it did not have facilities), it meant risking its direct interests in Libya. However, cautioned Badeau, silence did not necessarily mean acceptance. The United States had to warn Nasser about the dangers of escalation in general. (Indeed, Jernegan had already met with Ambassador Kamel to warn him about the potential costs of Nasser's recent speeches.)

Badeau wanted to use his upcoming farewell visit with Nasser to "smoke out" the Egyptian leader's intentions vis-à-vis Yemen and Britain. It was important to find out whether Nasser was going to take a more hostile position against the West. But Badeau did not want Nasser to know ahead of time what the conversation would be about because he believed Nasser might prepare talking points, which would then exclude the potential for a more open conversation. "After this initial exploration," wrote Badeau, "we can begin if need be to take [a] hard line on points where we wish to make US interests unmistakably clear." It was the perfect opportunity for redirecting Nasser on matters of US strategic importance, argued Badeau.[28] It was a very Kennedy-esque approach.

Of course, Yemen was not the only problem driving Nasser, which complicated Badeau's plan for a one-dimensional, soft approach. Nasser was also panicking about Egypt's economic outlook. Due to the continued delay over the $20 million loan from the United States, Nasser began to suspect that Johnson was going to overturn Kennedy's aid policy. Thus, in his May Day speech, Nasser prepared Egypt for the possibility of heavy cutbacks to government subsidized commodities. Responding to this added factor, Badeau proposed untangling the two economic instruments of US policy. Nasser was dependent on PL 480 aid to feed Egypt. However, the administration could dangle the additional $20 million loan ("if we wish to use [the] loan in this way," warned Badeau), and entice him to back down on the British base in Aden. Badeau wanted to use the money to redirect Nasser. He needed something to offer Nasser as a carrot since the administration had not authorized any new aid since before the death of Kennedy. Badeau reiterated his earlier argument that Nasser had shown restrain in situations where the United States had pointed out its direct interests. As a way of showing a direct interest in Aden, Badeau proposed, why not send a naval squadron to the British base?[29]

To be sure, Badeau's understanding of and approach to Nasser was based on a friendship that had been built up over time.[30] And his personal relationship with him, at times, even preempted the diplomatic one between the two countries—even more so after Johnson took office. Therefore, Badeau felt strongly that the administration could improve relations with Nasser only if it was a little softer on him. He wrote to State:

> One of [the] factors I believe is important [to] consider in direct dealings with Nasser and [his] immediate entourage, is their demonstrated willingness [to] listen, and modify [their] actions, when [a] clear and convincing case [is] made [that] they have, or are about to, tread on direct US interests. We are less effective when we protest on principle or appear to be intervening purely on behalf [of the] interests of others.[31]

Badeau's suggestions did not fall on deaf ears in Washington. On May 5, State presented the ambassador with talking points on Yemen and Aden that were specific about how the two issues affected US interests—something that Badeau could use in his redirection strategy with Nasser. The first point was that a British evacuation from Aden threatened security in the region and threatened to drag the United States into a new unilateral role to restore peace. The argument was intended to show Nasser that he was being shortsighted by pressuring the British to abandon Aden. "[Nasser] has been operating on [the] basis [of] tactical rather than strategic considerations," wrote State. Badeau was instructed to make clear to him the importance of a British base in Aden as a strategic position between Southern Arabia and the Persian Gulf. Without a suitable base in the area, Britain would be incapable of policing the Persian Gulf—a region where British security kept the local forces from fighting. "In [the] short run[,] and at this stage of primitive political development of most [of the] Persian Gulf principalities[,] [the] problem is who is to replace [the] British in [the] Gulf and occupy [the] vacuum created by [an] abrupt withdrawal?" State rhetorically asked.

To ask the question was to answer it. Nasser was incapable of providing stability in the Persian Gulf, and the United States was looking to get out of wars, not get into new ones. "Result would be [a] build-up of tensions, chaos and perhaps local war," wrote State. "Only [the] USSR would ultimately benefit therefrom."

State wanted Badeau to remind Nasser about his difficulty controlling the tribes in Yemen. State wrote, it "must be admitted [that the] British administrative and security umbrella there tends to keep [a] lid on." Without the administrative stability provided by British forces, Yemen would be overrun by tribes from the Aden protectorates. How would Nasser maintain the loyalty of local tribes if their forces suddenly multiplied? He already found it difficult to control them in their current, more limited state.

State also wanted to show Nasser that he needed to be patient and more realistic about Southern Arabia's gradual independence from Britain. "While [the] case could perhaps be made that [the] path toward self-government [is] too slow ... [there is] no denying that [the] British [are] on [the] right track," State wrote.

The directive ended with a warning for Badeau: his meeting with Nasser was important, because all of Britain's problems could suddenly become America's problems should the British be pushed out of Aden. "FYI," State wrote to Badeau, "Our hope [is] that [the] combination of diplomacy, British restraint and acceleration of [the] process of Adeni 'constitutional advance' (which British officials here last week hinted at) will check [the] current trend toward [an] erosion of [the] British position."[32]

On May 4, Harold Saunders wrote to Bundy about Nasser's May Day speech, letting him know that "Badeau and State favor keeping our shirts on with Nasser." Badeau's plan, wrote Saunders, was "to make a stab at finding out what's on Nasser's mind" by giving a general review of relations. Only once Badeau was aware of Nasser's outlook would the administration respond with light pressure. "But a hard reaction now, he feels, could push Nasser overboard," Saunders wrote. He reminded Bundy that the administration was getting ready to make the $20 million loan to Egypt. Indeed, State and AID were already processing the paperwork, which could be signed in as little as "2–3 weeks" after Nasser had worked things out with the IMF.[33]

US-Egypt relations were at a pivotal point: Nasser had much to lose or gain depending on how he proceeded with his latest diatribe against Britain.

Unfortunately, at that point things quickly began to fall apart in a way that made it difficult for the Johnson administration to have any leverage with Nasser moving forward. To begin with, on May 5, Congressman Rooney unexpectedly denied the $12 million appropriations request for Abu Simbel. Rooney said he considered the project a waste of money. He reportedly had given private assurances to Kennedy that he would not stand in the way of the contribution since it had originated as Jackie Kennedy's pet project. However, Rooney was now reneging, which meant the appropriations request would move into the Senate. The congressional advisers at State counseled waiting for the Senate vote before fighting the decision. "They don't want to antagonize Rooney by provoking a House floor fight," wrote Saunders to Bundy. Indeed, State did not want to pick a fight with Rooney because he controlled their funding.[34]

The next day brought even more bad news for the administration. As it will be recalled, one of the conditions of the $20 million loan was that Egypt had to sign a new Stand-By Arrangement—otherwise known as a "stabilization loan"—with the IMF. On May 6, the IMF board of directors postponed a vote on the loan because seven countries purportedly planned to abstain. "The abstainers argue on economic grounds that the agreement isn't stiff enough," wrote Saunders. Indeed, it was going to be the fourth time that Egypt made a withdrawal from the fund. And each time the conditions of the loan were supposed to get stricter. Saunders informed Bundy that while the abstainers were technically correct, State saw "the fine hand of the British Foreign Office behind all this." Evidently, Butler was resorting to economic pressure against Nasser after having been rebuffed by Rusk in Washington.

British pressure was beginning to make the current approach to Nasser stumble in Washington as well as in Cairo. The Agency for International Development was willing to see both the stabilization loan and the $20 million loan fall apart. "AID never has been keen on the loan," wrote Saunders to Bundy, "and wouldn't be sorry to see it delayed now."[35]

"Neither would I, if it works this way," Bundy surprisingly wrote back. Evidently, even he was beginning to have doubts about Komer's line of policy toward Nasser. Bundy insisted that no one from the administration (i.e., Komer) should press the IMF for Nasser's sake. He stressed, "I certainly *don't* think we should override or use pressure to reverse the economists."[36]

The administration could not afford any additional controversy because Johnson was in the middle of a political crisis. In an effort to appease a racially divided voting bloc, southern senators from his own party were filibustering against his groundbreaking civil rights legislation (the 1964 Civil Rights Act) and, in the process, blocking its passage on the Senate floor. Johnson was also facing the possibility of a contested convention in August, which meant he might get passed over for the party's nomination. It was a serious threat that was to consume the majority of his time and attention in the coming months.[37]

Nonetheless, on May 6, Komer comprehensively prepared Johnson for a press conference in case he was asked any questions about Nasser. Komer wrote, "Press stories about Butler pushing us to cut off aid have made Nasser very nervous. We need some signal that we aren't following the British lead." Komer instructed Johnson to say that Abu Simbel was part of UNESCO's mandate "to preserve monuments." He added, "which after all are part of all mankind's cultural heritage." On the issue of economic aid, Komer wanted Johnson to focus on humanitarian grounds for providing it. "We have aided the UAR for sound humanitarian and economic reasons," Komer wrote. "(75% of our aid over the years and 93% today is in the form of food, which helps improve the diet of the Egyptian people. When we have made loans, we have done so for soundly conceived projects or in connection with IMF stabilization programs)." Komer was worried that the press would bring public light to the $20 million loan to Egypt. Neither he nor Johnson could afford for that to happen, lest it lead to the undoing of Komer's policy and negatively impact Johnson's presidential campaign. Nasser was a deeply unpopular figure in American politics.[38]

Komer's fear of an inconvenient backlash against the current policy turned out to be grounded. While the IMF eventually approved the stabilization loan in late May, a short time later it became the object of a *New York Times* article called, "US Allies Irked On Loan To UAR." In short, a journalist spun a story that the Johnson administration was recklessly assisting Nasser despite the concerns of its "European allies." As set out in the article: "The United States, over the objections of its Western European allies, has virtually forced through the international Monetary Fund a $40 million loan to the United Arab Republic that sets precedents in its liberal terms." According to the article, the European countries resented the Johnson administration for its "political use of the monetary fund."[39]

Fortunately, the day before the article's publication, Saunders received enough notice to be able to warn Komer, writing, "FYI, tomorrow may be UAR day." Specifically, he informed Komer that the article revealed there had been a split vote on the IMF board. The journalist, however, spun a story that the administration had bought the tie breaking vote from the IMF's director. Saunders dismissed the article's relevancy: "Point is: This [split vote] is what happens when you make loans to politically important LDC's [Least Developed Countries]." Nonetheless, he too worried that enough people in Washington knew about the administration's connected $20 million loan that it could potentially turn it into a political crisis and lead to the loan being scuttled altogether.

To make matters worse, Saunders also informed Komer that the IMF suspected Egypt had failed to meet some of the preconditions for receiving the loan. As a result, the IMF was sending an investigator to Cairo. "If the Egyptians try to cover up too obviously," he observed, "the Fund management will have trouble going ahead in the face of an obvious fudge."[40] Fortunately for Komer (thanks to Saunders), he was prepared to defend himself and his policy in front of Bundy.

The next day, after the story broke, Komer assured Bundy that the journalist's claims were fabricated. "Far from making economics bow to politics, [the] shoe is in fact on [the] other foot," he wrote. Komer confirmed to Bundy that it was Britain that originally had attempted to delay the IMF vote, and that it had done so for "political reasons." Komer attributed it to their "distaste for [the] UAR."

Komer also informed Bundy that the IMF vote had been Managing Director Pierre-Paul Schweitzer's "first big test of strength." Komer stressed that "*he* decided to go ahead," not anyone from the administration. In other words, it was not Komer's doing. He wrote that Schweitzer had disagreed with Britain's attempt to link the Aden issue to Egypt's economic crisis. He added that the "IMF felt politics and economics should not be mixed up."

Thus, Komer recommended backgrounding the affair—when a government official anonymously speaks to the press—in order to make it clear there had been no meddling on the administration's part. In reality, however, there was very little the White House could do. A journalist had taken advantage of the public's distaste for Nasser. Before the story's publication, Treasury officials had even sat down with the journalist to clear up some of the inconsistencies in his reporting. However, he chose not to include their accounts in the published draft.

The journalist had succeeded in casting negative light on a policy that Johnson already was unsure of. But Komer continued to assure Bundy that the terms of the stabilization loan were strict enough. "In fact [the] terms [are] strict enough," Komer wrote, "that we hear [the] UAR is failing to observe them."[41]

The additional strain on US-Egypt relations—at a time when they were already weak from the prolonged period of uncertainty following Kennedy's death—promised to break everything Komer had built under Kennedy. It was up to Badeau to make everything right before he left.

6

Badeau's Final Mission

On April 30, a final meeting about the Israeli tank request took place in the "Situation Room" at the White House. At the meeting Johnson decided that the administration could not afford to sell tanks to Israel at the cost of damaging relations with the Arab states. Instead, the United States would help Israel buy the tanks it needed from West Germany. At the same time, it was decided the administration would need to take immediate steps to curb Nasser's missile program as a way to soften the news to Israel about the tank request and to keep it from pursuing French missiles. Moreover, in order to keep Israel from pursuing nuclear weapons at Dimona, the administration decided to get Nasser to commit to IAEA safeguards on record so that Israel would feel pressure to do the same. Thus, attention was suddenly shifted to getting Nasser to make a number of concessions in order to keep Israel from taking steps that could significantly escalate the Arab-Israeli crisis—which was already heightened due to the Jordan waters issue.[1]

Nasser's May Day speech had thrust Aden and Yemen into the spotlight. However, once Johnson's approval of the new arms probe reached State, they had to quickly back down from heading off these other crises. On May 6, State wrote to Badeau that it was now imperative for him to get Nasser's response to the new arms probe. Johnson was scheduled to meet with Israel's prime minister at the beginning of June. Therefore, Badeau needed to get a "favorable" response from Nasser on the probe so that Johnson would feel comfortable throwing "his weight behind [the] new approach to Israel."[2]

The next day, when Badeau met with Nasser for forty-five minutes (an extra meeting before his official farewell call), the two men principally spoke about the arms race in the Middle East. Badeau encouraged Nasser to consider signing a pledge not to pursue nuclear weapons. He read to Nasser a letter from Johnson which called for both Egypt and Israel to limit their arms purchases. Nasser realized that he was being asked to agree to a new arms probe. Unlike his previous talks with McCloy though, he agreed to seriously consider the request; particularly, he said, since it was coming from Johnson himself. Badeau, however, was skeptical of Nasser's response. He wondered whether the Egyptian leader being sick had anything to do with it. "He looked grey and drawn," Badeau reported, "and told me that ever since his return from Yemen he had been ill and was still taking heavy doses of antibiotics." Indeed, it was unexpected to hear that Nasser was still open to working with Johnson.[3]

Badeau also used the meeting to officially inform Nasser of his resignation. He emphasized that the decision had been made for personal reasons, not due to a change in US policy. He explained to Nasser that officials in Washington were worried the resignation would get misconstrued as a change in policy. Nasser replied, "Of course, I do not completely control the newspapers but I recognize that your departure is not connected with United States policy." Badeau told Nasser that he was going to be meeting Johnson for the first time when he got back to Washington. He encouraged Nasser to be prepared to discuss beforehand "whatever was on his mind vis-à-vis the USA and its relations to Egypt and the Arab world." That way, Nasser could have his concerns directly relayed to Johnson by Badeau.[4]

Nasser accepted Badeau's resignation at face value. However, he warned that others in his inner circle would not. Indeed, on May 12, Talbot met with Kamel in Washington to discuss the matter. Talbot stressed that, "the Departure would have no policy implications whatsoever." Kamel replied that the resignation of a diplomat who had been so committed to US-Egypt cooperation cast considerable doubt about the continuation of that policy. Kamel also warned about the timing. It was not strategic, he said, to announce Badeau's resignation in the middle of a visit to Cairo by the Soviet Premiere, Nikita Khrushchev, who had arrived on May 9 and was not due to leave until the 25th. Kamel asked whether the announcement could be delayed until after Khrushchev left the country. Talbot politely, but firmly, replied "no." Badeau was pressuring State to make the announcement as soon as possible so that he could return home and take up a teaching position at Columbia University.[5]

As Kamel had warned, Egyptian officials did not respond well to the news of Badeau's departure. Some publications even suggested that the poorly timed announcement was an off-the-cuff response to Nasser's warm welcoming of Khrushchev.[6]

Indeed, the Soviet-Egyptian summit had been productive. In fact, on his final day in Cairo, Khrushchev announced a $282 million credit line for Egypt, which the Egyptian press subsequently portrayed as a sign of America's waning influence in the region. Back in Washington, officials temporarily paused to determine whether a new crisis was forming just as Badeau was set to depart. However, the ambassador to Moscow, Foy Kohler, argued that the announcement was not as threatening as it appeared. "Sov-Egyptian communique on [the] conclusion [of the] Khrushchev visit [is] noteworthy more for economic than for political content," he wrote. "In addition to the atmospherics, which were as helpful to Nasser as they were to Khrushchev, [the] UAR leader gained 252 million rubles from [the] visit." In other words, it was just money that Nasser had gained, nothing more.[7]

Komer agreed that the announcement did not indicate a potential shift in Nasser's allegiance to neutrality. He wrote to Bundy, "Mac: Interesting that even a hard-liner like Foy Kohler sees little new in Krush/Nasser communique except that Gamal squeezed out some more aid." Bundy replied, "I agree with you." In spite of the fact that American newspapers had given the story, in Komer's word, a "sober appraisal," neither of them viewed Moscow's sudden generosity as a sign that Nasser was turning his cheek on Johnson. Thus, everybody quickly resumed putting together a comprehensive strategy for renewing the arms probe with Nasser in order to manage Israel's response to the aborted tank deal.[8]

In the May 7 meeting with Badeau, Nasser had agreed in principle that nuclear weapons would destabilize the Middle East. However, he had yet to commit to signing a public statement of intent not to go nuclear. More importantly, Badeau still needed to probe Nasser on Egypt's missile production. As it will be recalled, the threat of Egypt producing a high number of SSMs had prompted Israel to look into obtaining its own missiles from France. Now that Johnson had cancelled the tank deal with Israel, the administration felt it was more important than ever to receive concrete assurances from Nasser that could be used to reassure Israel.

On May 15, Komer drafted a letter in Johnson's name and sent it to Myer Feldman, who was instructed to officially inform Israel that the tank deal had been cancelled. "Our restraining influence on issues like the Jordan diversion would be thrown away just when it is needed most," went the letter. "Arab frustration over their inability to do much about it could easily be catalyzed by a tank deal into a violent reaction against us."[9] On May 16, Feldman left for Israel under a cover story that he was discussing PL 480 aid.[10]

Meanwhile, State had been studying the notes of Badeau and Nasser's meeting from May 7, with a view to develop a comprehensive strategy for the farewell call. During the meeting Nasser had asked Badeau for a written presentation of his points. State decided it would be worthwhile to give him one. On May 14, they asked Badeau to write up a memorandum for Nasser, but on one condition: "In light [of the] implications [a] written presentation could have for subsequent arms control efforts with Nasser and other states concerned[, we] believe it would be useful for [the State] Department to consult on phraseology."[11] Unknown by State, however, was that Badeau had already produced such a memorandum and that it had been submitted to Nasser's office two days prior. Badeau replied to State that the memorandum had been marked, "unofficial and personal," and he suggested having Johnson write an "official" document for him to give to Nasser instead.[12]

While Badeau had overstepped his authority by issuing the unofficial memorandum to Nasser, Komer liked the idea of producing an official one. He immediately wrote to Johnson that a letter would be useful to "smoke out Nasser." If it was phrased carefully, argued Komer, it could potentially convince Nasser to sign a pledge not to go nuclear. Komer, however, was mindful that Johnson could not afford to get publicly rebuffed by Nasser at a time when he was already hurting from his rift with the southern democrats—who were still filibustering on the Senate floor against his civil rights legislation. Thus, Komer wrote to him, "your letter is carefully couched to avoid any possible kickback if this probe fails."[13]

Komer was optimistic about the strategy. Obtaining concrete assurances from Nasser about his missile program would be helpful for mitigating Israel's response to the cancellation of the tank deal and for mollifying Jewish-American criticism of the policy that Komer wanted Johnson to take with Nasser. Indeed, Komer was still worried about a possible public backlash against the proposed $20 million loan. He wrote to Bundy, "wouldn't it be nice if Gamal were smart enough to come through in time . . . Also, whenever Nasser came through (if he did) we'd have a powerful lever to persuade Israel against going nuclear."[14]

Komer and State spent considerable time preparing for Badeau's final meeting with Nasser in Cairo. Johnson's letter to Nasser was carefully written by Komer. It asked Nasser to sign a pledge not to be the first leader to introduce nuclear weapons in the Middle East. But Komer wrote it in a way that prodded Nasser without putting Johnson on the hook:

> Since assuming the Presidency, I have had an opportunity to review the statements made by you and your representatives on the need for disarmament . . . I find in your statements assurances that the United Arab Republic views nuclear warfare as the greatest danger to mankind and that your Government regards itself as committed, in a broader sense, not to develop nuclear weapons or introduce them into your defense program. Your confirmation that this understanding is correct would represent a step which others might follow to ensure that the threat of nuclear warfare is further contained.[15]

The letter's purpose was to find out, once-and-for-all, whether Nasser was willing to officially commit himself to scaling back the arms race in the Middle East. More than that, it was a litmus test on whether Nasser would be responsive to Johnson on major issues that concerned the United States. While Nasser had already told Badeau he would publicly declare his lack of interest in producing nuclear weapons, Komer pointed out that it was not yet clear "whether Nasser would do so publicly or privately, or in what form."[16]

Alongside the important letter, State prepared a series of talking points for Badeau to use during the meeting. After reviewing Badeau's "unofficial" memorandum of the May 7 conversation, State admonished him for committing the United States to factually incorrect positions on paper. Evidently, Badeau had misspoke. "While [it is] true we rely to [a] certain extent on intelligence capabilities, it [is] not accurate that each country has sufficient intelligence capacity [to] keep informed about other's activities," wrote State, "any implication [that the] production [of] fissionable material can be monitored unilaterally [is] not only factually incorrect but tends also [to] undercut our position on IAEA safeguards for [the] UAR and Israel." It was important that Badeau not undermine the ongoing operation to get Israel to commit to similar safeguards at Dimona.[17]

State diligently prepared Badeau for his final meeting with Nasser in order to ensure the arms probe did not transpire into yet another crisis. The plan was to hand Nasser a hard copy of Johnson's letter before it was entered into the public record. In doing so, State hoped that Nasser would privately share his response before making it public. "We would hope [to] thereby preclude his preparing [a] response with conditions that would emasculate assurances we seek from him," wrote State. Most importantly, Badeau was told to ensure that his final meeting with Nasser ended on a positive note. "If Nasser's general attitude [is] negative and [the] discussion proves unproductive, we would hope you nevertheless could keep [the] door open and obtain his agreement

[to] reconsider various aspects at some later date," wrote State. "In so doing, [we] suggest you say our concern over arms rivalry has received and will continue to receive attention [from the] highest levels of [the] USG."[18]

On May 30, a second telegram with further instructions was sent to Badeau. This one concerned Egypt's missile program. State was nervous about the farewell call having the appearance of a campaign on behalf of Israel to dismantle Nasser's weapons program. "We recognize of course [the] thin line between insuring Nasser understands and appreciates [the] nature of this escalation," wrote State, "and on [the] other hand giving him [the] impression [that] Israel [is] about to go nuclear with our understanding and tacit support." State wanted it to be clear that the United States did not want Israel or Egypt having weapons that could lead to either side's destruction.

Middle East arms control was to be the last issue that Badeau handled as ambassador to Egypt. And he was being carefully guided from Washington in order to secure a major diplomatic victory for Johnson.[19]

To be sure, Nasser partially came through for the Johnson administration. However, it was not in time for Johnson's meeting with Israel's prime minister. On June 8, Badeau and Nasser talked about US-Egypt relations for seventy-five minutes. The topic of arms control came up at the beginning of their conversation.

Nasser agreed to sign a declaration of non-intent to pursue nuclear weapons. He added that he thought it was ridiculous to accept IAEA safeguards—although he still agreed to do so—when Egypt did not yet have a nuclear plant. Nonetheless, Badeau scored a victory for Johnson on the nuclear issue, which could now be taken to Israel.

On the issue of non-nuclear missile production, however, Nasser was unwilling to capitulate. He pointed out that Kennedy had sold Hawk missiles to Israel in 1962. He asked how Egypt could protect itself if Israel used them? Badeau wrote to State: "Although no concrete progress [was] made in general [on] arms control, I believe Nasser is certainly open to further and more specific approaches in this field. I doubt if much will be gained by continuing to urge that he 'put his ideas forward.' Here as elsewhere Nasser usually reacts rather than acts." If the Johnson administration wanted progress on the missile issue, it had to continue coming to Nasser rather than waiting for him to come to them.

Badeau added that the administration needed to come up with a more specific plan if it wanted to curtail the arms race in the Middle East. Nasser was only receptive to carefully laid-out arguments and gentle redirection efforts, observed Badeau.

It was a good suggestion from Badeau. A problem, however, was that Johnson had just lost the best person to take up the task. It had taken Badeau several years to build up a rapport with Nasser. Johnson himself did not yet have a strong enough relationship with Nasser to be able to redirect him from Washington.

Nasser ended the farewell call with Badeau on a positive note. He walked Badeau to his car and remarked that they had met 43 times in 35 months. It was a bittersweet moment between two friends and, more importantly, the last time Nasser would ostensibly show so much affection and respect toward an American official.[20] Indeed, without the important link that Badeau served as the only visibly remaining representation of the Kennedy administration, the US-Egypt relationship quickly took a turn for the worse; particularly since Badeau's successor would not arrive in Cairo for three months. With no one in Cairo to guide Nasser, Komer's policy was in jeopardy. Moreover, with Badeau having overstepped his bounds, he had demonstrated to Johnson and Rusk the danger of having too many activists in the driver's seat of foreign policy.

After Badeau, Komer would become more vocal than before in guiding US-Egypt relations. Johnson, however, was privately frustrated with Nasser. He did not truly understand Komer's desire to form closer relations with the Egyptian leader. Indeed, he seemed to be in agreement with Rusk, when the latter said over the phone: "He [Nasser] has not performed in Yemen, he is undermining us in the Wheelus Base and he's pitching this arms race into the Near East . . . I think it's important for Nasser to know that . . . he just mustn't take us for granted on these things . . . we're . . . coming close to the end of the trail on this business."[21]

Part Two

After Badeau
(June 1964–March 1966)

7

Starting Over with/in Cairo

Without an ambassador in Cairo, the Johnson administration was missing its most direct line of communication to Nasser. This was particularly problematic since the Kennedy policy had relied on constant communication with Nasser in order to redirect him on issues that intersected with American interests. Without this direct form of communication, Nasser and the United States came into new conflict in the summer of 1964. The relationship was no longer about seeing Johnson as Kennedy, it was now about finding new common ground that made sense to both sides.

On May 22, just as Badeau was about to leave the US embassy and drive over to Egypt's Foreign Ministry to deliver an "agrément" on behalf of his successor—a formal request to the host country to accept an individual as ambassador—State called over the telephone and told him to turn around: the Senate was temporarily blocking the confirmation of Johnson's nominee for the ambassadorship to Egypt, Lucius Battle.[1] The objection over his appointment was a political maneuver by Senator William Fulbright (D. Arkansas), who was then chairman of the Foreign Relations Committee, and happened to be "a very good friend" of Battle's.

Before his nomination, Battle had served as State's assistant secretary for cultural affairs, which put him in charge of securing congressional approval for cultural projects like Abu Simbel. Over the years, Battle had built up strong relations with senators and congressmen. Fulbright came to see Battle's leadership on cultural matters as "an integral part of the [State] department," and told him that he was holding up the appointment in order to put pressure on Johnson to continue with Battle's approach.[2] Fulbright was also one of the southern democrats who challenged Johnson's attack on racial segregation—he had taken part in the filibuster of the 1964 Civil Rights Act. Thus, in part, the holdup seemed related to the ongoing dissent over the civil rights issue that would continue to plague Johnson's political party through the Democratic National Convention in August. More importantly, however, it was symbolic of the many conflicts that the Johnson administration would come to have with Congress over the next eighteen months while attempting to uphold a relationship with Nasser.

To be sure, Johnson's choice for the ambassadorship was unusual: Battle had no formal experience with the Middle East. Moreover, after Kennedy's death, he—like many others from the Kennedy administration—questioned Johnson's seemingly detached approach to foreign policy. "I found it very difficult to relate to President

Johnson's White House and that included the President himself," Battle later recalled. "I always felt a little uncertain." However, instead of appointing William Polk—who, as it will be recalled, had been Komer's choice for the position—Johnson ultimately chose Battle, in part, to capitalize on his good relations on Capitol Hill. Indeed, Polk's appointment was derailed shortly after he and Komer lobbied for congressional support, with many of the politicians they approached also knowing Battle. "He approached good friends of mine on the Hill," Battle later recalled. "It might have worked at some other time, but it wasn't the proper strategy for this particular time and position. He was trying to knife me in the back . . . But it didn't work."[3]

Thus, while Battle's nomination was intended as a conciliatory response to Johnson's domestic political troubles, the plan backfired by leading to a delayed confirmation. This left the Johnson administration without representation on the ground in Egypt until the end of the summer. Consequently, relations between the United States and Egypt suffered.

Komer had argued for many months that it was important to have the new ambassador made known to Cairo as soon as possible in order to pick up where Badeau left off. Komer was also concerned because mutual frustrations continued to linger between the two countries in the wake of the rocky transition from Kennedy to Johnson. In spite of these valid concerns, Nasser was not even made aware of Battle's appointment until after it was confirmed by the Senate in August. Therefore, what should have been a simple switchover to a new ambassador turned instead into another dividing wedge between the two countries, leaving Nasser with the impression that he was being overlooked by Johnson.

This did not bode well for Komer's strategy to win over Nasser. Nasser strongly believed Egypt should be treated as an important state. The United States should come to him because he was a political broker not only for the Arab world but for Africa and the nonaligned states as well.

Indeed, Nasser arranged for Cairo to host an African states summit in July 1964 and a summit for nonaligned states in October. There also was a second Arab summit planned for September—this time in Alexandria. Nasser was setting himself up to be a powerful statesman in the region, and the United States did not even have a representative for him to communicate with.

Both Western and Eastern world leaders should visit Egypt, Nasser told the visiting Italian foreign minister in April 1964. However, it was only ever leaders from China and the Soviet Union that came—which left the West at a disadvantage, Nasser said. Nasser wanted the world to see Egypt as moving away from the junta that seized power in 1952, and instead see it as a developing nation worthy of respect. He insisted to the Italian foreign minister that he was steering Egypt toward democracy.[4]

Without effective communication from Cairo, due to the unfilled ambassadorship, it became increasingly difficult for officials in Washington to see the virtue of continuing to deal with Nasser. This soon led to a bitter war over aid that suddenly became the main focus of US-Egypt relations. It also marked the beginning of the end for the Johnson administration's relationship with Nasser. As a result of this scuffle over aid, Komer began to have a more pronounced role than before in keeping US-Egypt relations from completely falling apart. Instead of focusing on getting Johnson to see the value of continuing with Kennedy's approach, Komer attempted to get Johnson to see strong relations with Nasser as his own policy—separate from Kennedy's and worthy of pursuing for the preservation of America's position in the Middle East.

In the summer of 1964, while Battle waited to get his appointment confirmed in the Senate, the administration temporarily drifted away from dealing with Nasser, which was opposite of the constant contact it had had with him in the months preceding Badeau's departure. Nasser once again started to take hostile actions that undercut US interests in the region. Komer and State took notice, and attempted to quietly steer another outreach to Egypt with renewed discussions about giving aid.

The discussions started with cotton, which American farmers had produced too much of that year. Instead of a federal mandate to cut down on acreage—which brought the risk of upsetting the farmers during an election year—the government was going to export the surplus cotton at a competitive rate. "Does LBJ need any more political support? And are the financial gains enough to justify?" Komer asked. He and State worried about upsetting Nasser, because Egypt was a major cotton exporter. In fact, it was one of the few profitable commodities that Egypt produced. "A shrill scream on long staple cotton, which I just heard about from State (I do wish Francis [Bator] would clue the rest of us on the things with political hooks attached)," wrote Komer to Bundy on June 10. Incidentally, Bundy had already been made aware of the decision a week earlier. But, for some reason, he had failed to inform Komer. "NEA is terrified that our doing something we've never done before will be taken by Cairo as a clear signal that we've changed our policy." Komer worried about the optics of this perceived change in policy "coming just after Eshkol['s] visit."[5]

So far, Arab reaction in the wake of the Israeli prime minister's visit to the United States to discuss the aborted tank deal with Johnson—which was now being secretly processed via West Germany—had been "most restrained," Komer observed in a memorandum to Johnson. Komer believed it was important to keep that positive momentum moving forward. And, more importantly, to use the momentum to head off the possibility of a clash between Israel and the Arab states over the Jordan waters in 1965. Johnson managed to convince Israel to consider IAEA safeguards at Dimona. And Eshkol had consented to the administration telling Nasser that Israel's nuclear program was only for peaceful purposes—which Badeau subsequently did in his final talk with Nasser. "We also managed to steer [the] press successfully (so far) away from [the] sensitive arms issue," remarked Komer to Johnson. Indeed, the political environment was looking ideal for taking further preventive diplomacy steps with Nasser.[6]

To that end, in June, Talbot held a "think-session" at State on "The Palestine Problem, 1964–1965." The officials at the gathering concluded that the Arab-Israeli dispute could benefit from a major arms control initiative; a conclusion that was based on the positive results received from the preliminary arms probes with Israel and Nasser. "This effort with Nasser should be the early business of our new Ambassador, and perhaps of a special Presidential emissary," wrote Talbot to Rusk. "After the election, it might call for a visit to Egypt by the Secretary of State or the Vice-President, followed perhaps by a Nasser visit to the US." Talbot, however, added, "Hope of success in this effort would rest on [the] maintenance of effective political and economic relations with Nasser."[7]

Komer, for his part, set his sights on ensuring that Johnson remained interested in dealing with Nasser; especially during the undefined period of transition between ambassadors. On June 17, Komer and Bundy wrote to Johnson, urging him to meet with Badeau in Washington—even if it was only for fifteen minutes. "Badeau—a non-career man—turned in quite a performance," wrote Komer. "A chat with him would be both pleasant and profitable."[8]

For Komer, it was an important meeting, because he saw it as an opportunity to provide a lesson for Johnson on how US-Egypt relations had evolved under Kennedy—and how relations could potentially continue to grow and prosper under Johnson himself. Komer even had Saunders write up a chronology "geared specifically to [the] evolving JFK-Nasser relationship," in order to provide a model for Johnson on how to formulate his own approach to Nasser. The long list showed the results of a generous and patient policy toward Nasser, which, as Komer noted, had succeeded in repairing the damaged relationship that Kennedy inherited from Eisenhower.[9]

There was also another reason for the meeting, which was perhaps a more important one. "The primary reasons for your seeing Badeau are to thank him for his outstanding job in Cairo," Komer wrote to Johnson, "and also to signal that his resignation does not mean a change in our Arab policy." Komer was getting more and more nervous. Battle's appointment was indefinitely delayed in the Senate, and the administration had not yet approved any additional aid to Egypt outside of the regularly scheduled shipments of PL 480 aid. Without an ambassador to represent the administration in Cairo, it was important to send a message to Nasser that Johnson (at the very least) still cared. Komer was also transparent with Johnson about his intention to soften him up on Nasser. "This is also a good chance to get a feel for what you can realistically expect to accomplish by building a personal relationship with Nasser," he wrote. "Badeau watched the Kennedy-Nasser relationship grow and appreciates its advantages as well as its limits."[10]

On June 29, Johnson met with Badeau. He started off the meeting by thanking Badeau for his service. The retired ambassador replied that while he regretted his resignation, pressing personal reasons had called him home. Badeau noted how much he had enjoyed his time in Cairo. He felt that "significant progress had been made in furthering American interests in the Arab world as these relate to the United Arab Republic." Badeau also noted that State and the White House had been instrumental in that progress.

Badeau presented a brief history of US-Egypt relations to point out the many ways in which relations had improved over the years. After this positive overview, Badeau leveled with Johnson. He told the president that Egyptians remained suspicious of him. "The pressures of an election year and the fact of a new Administration . . . [make] policy-making circles in Egypt unusually sensitive to American actions," he said. However, he added that it was his belief both countries were unwilling to hurt each other. Indeed, he pointed out that just as Nasser could raise trouble for the United States in the Middle East, as he had done vis-à-vis the bases issue in the spring, so too could the United States to Egypt if it wanted to. Thus, inherent in the two countries' relationship was an element of mutually assured destruction, Badeau observed—which made the relationship more special, but also complicated. According to a report of what Badeau said:

> It was this fact that had prevented a major confrontation in the past. The Ambassador believed that it would continue to make a major confrontation unlikely in the future unless the UAR should threaten an American interest of so basic a character that the United States would be willing to risk imperilling its position in adjacent Arab lands. This was to say that American-Egyptian relations might well continue to fluctuate between cordiality and opposition, but always avoiding the final step of major confrontation.

Badeau insisted there had to be "room" for disagreement between the two countries. Disagreement should always be encouraged, he said, but never allowed to actually damage the relationship itself:

> It was inevitable that both the United States and the UAR would find it necessary to oppose specific policies adopted by the other. Egypt had long opposed American policy toward Israel, while in recent months the United States had been in opposition to UAR policy on foreign policy bases and the British position in South Arabia. But opposition on specific issues need not continuously call into question the basic mutual and continuing interests on which a lasting American-Egyptian policy could be built.

Johnson seemed skeptical about what Badeau was saying. He asked whether Nasser "would understand such a sophisticated policy." Badeau responded affirmatively. He referred to his final talk with Nasser, noting that the Egyptian leader had privately agreed this was "the only possible policy between the two countries." Badeau, however, warned Johnson that many in the United States and Egypt would never understand such a policy. He noted that it was these people who were likely to stand in the way of what could possibly be a long-lasting and fruitful relationship rather than the "off-again, on-again, gone-again" relationship between the two countries since Nasser first came into power in the 1950s.[11]

Badeau's presentation was nothing new; it was merely the culmination of the views he had been expressing from Cairo since Kennedy, and reflective of the policy that Komer and a few others, like Talbot, had been pursuing for quite some time. According to this view, Nasser was to be encouraged through economic aid, and tolerated for his occasional outbursts. Because, ultimately, his cooperation was vital to securing America's interests in the Middle East.

There was no question that the Kennedy administration had been generous to Nasser. The United States gave Egypt $146 million between 1946 and 1961. Once Kennedy came into office, $663 million was given, alone, between 1961 and 1964. For comparison purposes, the next highest recipient of US aid in the Near East was Iran. It received $389 million between 1961 and 1964. However, the majority of Kennedy's generosity toward Nasser had been under the three-year PL 480 agreement, which some US officials were beginning to believe was too generous of a program to keep

Nasser from feeling like he could occasionally challenge the United States and still receive aid. This was a fair assessment. Nasser himself later reportedly said to a CIA informant that "the USA is afraid to cut off aid to Egypt because the USA knows that Egypt will react by sabotaging all American efforts in the area."[12]

However, the United States had nothing new to offer Nasser since Johnson had taken office. And during the summer of 1964, without an ambassador in Cairo, Johnson was giving Nasser the impression that he was steering a different course than Kennedy. This had to change if Johnson was actually going to follow Badeau's advice about working with Nasser.

Short of approving the $20 million loan request, which still was not possible due to Nasser's failure to disengage from Yemen, there were two cultural/developmental projects on the table, which Komer and State vigorously pursued as a means to an end in order to change Johnson's seeming reluctance to engage on Middle East policy. First, there was the restoration of the temples of Abu Simbel, which was a project that received lobbying from influential American business and community leaders. Komer drafted a letter in Bundy's name to one Ward M. Canaday, chairman of the Board of the Overland Corporation, who was widely considered the "father of the Jeep." Canaday was concerned that the Abu Simbel project was no longer moving forward under Johnson. Komer, picking up Bundy's pen, wrote to reassure Canaday: "The request for appropriations of the equivalent of $12 million in surplus Egyptian pounds to help save the Abu Simbel monument is now before the Senate Appropriations Committee which will probably consider it next week."[13] Komer must have thought that support for the project from influential businessmen like Canaday would play into his goal to get Johnson himself more interested in Nasser.

At the same time, there was another, more ambitious, developmental project, which was being spearheaded by former US treasury secretary, Robert Anderson. Specifically, Anderson wanted to put together a consortium to oversee the irrigation and reclamation of land in the Nile Delta. The project (officially referred to as "Salhia") intended to develop 321,000 acres of Egyptian desert in order to build business and residential communities. It was expected to take eight years to complete, with a total cost of $212 million. However, the main obstacle was funding. Anderson was hoping to get it off the ground with money from the federal government. Nasser took interest and was apparently watching Anderson's efforts from afar—perhaps to read the mood about himself in Washington. "Nasser reportedly rates this project second only to Aswan," Saunders wrote to Bundy on July 1. He was referring to the Aswan dam that the United State promised Nasser it would fund in 1955, only to pull out after Nasser bought weapons from the Soviet Union. "Some US papers have billed it as our 'second chance to participate in the high dam project,' [irrigation water was slated to come from Aswan] so it has more political potential than usual," observed Saunders.

The Anderson consortium scheduled a meeting with Bundy for the middle of the summer. However, the group had already met with officials from AID, which informed them that the agency could only produce a "study" of the subject, since funding was out of the question for the time being—mainly due to the bad politics of associating with Nasser. State, on the other hand, was considering taking the $20 million loan— which was essentially a blank check to Egypt—and applying it to Salhia instead. "Key question," wrote Saunders, "is what we want to do for the UAR. If anything, a project like this might be a good substitute for a stabilization loan that looks like money down a rathole."[14]

Some US officials were still opposed to giving any aid to Nasser. Thus, the cultural projects began to take on life as litmus tests for doing any additional business with Egypt outside of the ongoing three-year PL 480 deal.

When Polk led a study in the Policy Planning Council, outlining future US objectives vis-à-vis Egypt, hard-liner DOD officials in his group dissented on the grounds that any form of aid over a long period of time was likely to preclude the chances of Nasser moderating his anti-American policies. Instead, they argued for taking a different approach: giving Nasser smaller amounts of aid at a time in return for him doing something that the United States wanted—in other words, a quid pro quo relationship.

On July 17, Saunders wrote to Komer, "Bill Polk's UAR policy paper is a good job. Its main contribution is to establish the line that we get further with Nasser by working with him than by threatening him." Saunders, however, worried that Johnson was not getting a full picture of the "consequences of the harder line" proposed by the dissenters. He wrote, "The President's choice lies between these two approaches [i.e. a soft or hard line], and he should have a clearer view of the second."

Indeed, Saunders wondered how a hard-line approach would work with a project like Salhia. "Its thrust seems to preclude our financing such a big project over an extended period," he wrote, "unless Nasser concedes us an unexpected say in his overall development planning." Such a transformation in US policy would fundamentally change the relationship from gifting Nasser in order to "turn him inwards," which was still the official policy at the time, to constantly pressuring him with both the carrot and stick.[15]

Ironically, these discussions about the future of aid to Egypt occurred around the same time that Abu Simbel was once again being scuttled in Congress; this time, by the Senate Appropriations Committee. Dispensing congressional funds for Nasser's benefit was seen as too politically controversial for an election year. Members of the committee secretly proposed that Johnson use "Cooley loan money" instead—which was an earmarked account of Egyptian pounds from PL 480 Title I sales. These funds were eligible to give out as loans for commercial development projects in Egypt. The recommendation was made with an outside-the-box argument that Abu Simbel was a development project to increase tourism to Egypt.

It was a creative solution. But Saunders and State worried it would be shot down by Congressman Rooney, who ultimately had the power to block it; and would probably do so since it would set a precedent of the president funding archaeological works in countries where the United States did Title I sales. Congressional pressure was becoming a deeper thorn in the side of the Johnson administration's ability to offer any kind of economic incentive to Nasser. Indeed, over the summer, several influential senators had put an even further strain on US–Egyptian relations by proposing legislation that called for immediately cutting off aid to Egypt. Nasser had never been so unpopular on Capitol Hill. Saunders wrote to Komer, "State is afraid to talk to Rooney but feels someone should assure his assent."[16]

The apprehension in Washington about Nasser was not entirely unfounded. Over the summer, Nasser took a number of steps that did not sit well with American observers: (1) he continued to send arms to Makarios III, the orthodox Greek President of the Republic of Cyprus, who refused to partition Cyprus in spite of the threat of a war breaking out between Greece and Turkey over ownership of the island (this left US officials worried that a war would soon bring disaster to what was essentially NATO's southern flank); (2) Nasser was caught red-handed trying to convince King Hussein of Jordan to accept Soviet military equipment (Komer called it "the UAR attempt to suborn Jordan"); (3) Nasser sought a rapprochement with Iraq (much to the dismay of the Shah of Iran, who did not get along with Nasser, and asked for America's protection); (4) Nasser continued to secretly stir up controversy over Wheelus Air Base (thus seemingly abandoning his agreement with Badeau to refrain from such attacks); (5) Nasser proposed an Arab boycott of the Chase Manhattan Bank if it continued to accept Israeli business ("which the UAR must know is an annoyance," commented Komer); and (6) Nasser continued to show no intention of disengaging from Yemen.

On July 28, Komer wrote to Talbot, "As I follow the traffic these days, I'm stuck by the increasing number of points at which UAR policies are coming into conflict with ours. Such conflict is nothing new, of course, but the number of such instances may be of significance." But Komer still did not see the rise of so many difficulties at once as a reason to cut off ties with Nasser. Instead, from Komer's vantage point, it only further supported Badeau's thesis that the two countries needed to be capable of airing their disagreements in private. Thus, Komer wrote to Talbot, "their cumulative impact is sufficient to suggest that we need to re-open dialogue with Nasser on a broad front." He worried that remaining silent about the cumulative issues would send a message to Nasser that the United States no longer cared about him. He proposed having John McCloy, who Komer and Talbot had already asked to visit Cairo for further talks with Nasser on arms limitations, also address the political issues in lieu of an ambassador. "Whatever the reasons," Komer wrote, "the time may be at hand to let Nasser know he's treading on our toes in all these respects."

The main obstacle, still, was getting Nasser's attention without possessing any leverage. As Komer wrote, "The UAR may have concluded that we're no longer pushing our previous policy (our lack of movement on Abu Simbel, the $20 million commodity loan, or much else recently may have contributed to this view)."[17] What Komer needed was an opening.

In the midst of these rising tensions in the Middle East, America's ongoing military engagement in Vietnam took an unexpected turn when North Vietnamese torpedo boats attacked the USS *Maddox* off the coast of southern China in a body of water called the Gulf of Tonkin. Johnson asked Congress for special powers to send US regular combat troops to Vietnam in order to commence an open war against the North. "I have today met with the leaders of both parties in the Congress of the United States," Johnson declared on August 4, "and I have informed them that I shall immediately request the Congress to pass a resolution making it clear that our Government is united in its determination to take all necessary measures in support of freedom and in defense of peace in southeast Asia."[18]

In the following days, Johnson extensively met with his closest advisers. There was some question whether the *Maddox* actually had been attacked. It was unclear whether the situation warranted escalation of what had mostly been a covert war in Southeast Asia. "For all I know, our Navy was shooting at whales out there," Johnson later claimed.[19] The Asian affairs specialist at the NSC asked Komer what their roles would be in the coming conflict. Komer responded with his characteristic humor, "What we do is go to lunch. In situations like this the big boys take over."[20]

What Komer really meant was that the sudden distraction of Vietnam was a perfect opportunity for him to spearhead a major shift in the administration's dealings with Nasser. Indeed, in the midst of large-scale and worrisome developments in Vietnam, an unexpected opportunity presented itself to reconnect with Nasser. Komer planned to act quickly.[21]

Specifically, Komer received word that Nasser wanted his ambassador to the United States, Kamel, to personally deliver a letter to Johnson; it was his official reply to the nuclear proliferation agreement that Badeau had secured in June. To be sure, it was an important olive branch. And the timing suggested that Nasser, like Komer, was looking for an opportunity to reconnect. Of course, Johnson was now consumed by Vietnam. Komer suggested that Johnson only needed to meet briefly with Kamel. "It need only take five minutes *off-the-record*," he stressed. "When you saw Kamel on May 25, you invited him to come in whenever he had a problem."[22] Komer asked Bundy—who was the next logical senior official in the administration that could make a meeting with Kamel meaningful—to have a more comprehensive follow-up meeting with Kamel to discuss the recent strains on US-Egypt relations. "I'd like to see you express some considerable discouragement with UAR policy—citing Libya, Cyprus, Jordan, Yemen, and Aden," Komer wrote to Bundy. "Value of such noises is that as we approach [the second] Arab Summit (5 Sept.) and then 2nd Neutralist Conference in October, we want to put Gamal on his good behavior." In other words, without an ambassador in Cairo, Komer was looking to redirect Nasser from Washington.[23]

Both Johnson and Bundy approved Komer's proposals. The two meetings with Kamel were scheduled for August 10. On the morning of the meeting, Komer sent a briefing to Johnson. Now that the United States had Nasser's pledge not to go nuclear, Komer thought it was time to confront Nasser about his missiles. Komer wrote: "FYI (Kamel is *not* witting) we plan another quiet probe by John McCloy in a week or so to hit Nasser on the UAR missile buildup as well. If you approve, he'll go as your personal envoy and carry a letter thanking Nasser for his nuclear self-denial."

The two issues—meeting Kamel to show Nasser that Johnson still cared about US-Egypt relations and arms limitations—might have seemed unrelated, but Komer was working on multiple levels at once. If McCloy was to get anywhere with Nasser in Cairo, then the meeting between Kamel and Johnson in Washington had to go well.

To that end, Komer wanted to keep Johnson's meeting with Kamel brief. Indeed, it was the only reason Johnson had agreed to take the meeting in the first place. Therefore, Komer instructed Johnson to gracefully dodge any attempt by Kamel to engage him on substantive issues. Even a brief meeting was enough of a signal to send Nasser that Johnson cared. "You'd hoped to resume your useful talk with Kamel last 25 May, but can't just now, so [you] have asked Bundy to talk with Kamel," Komer wrote as instructions for Johnson on how to gracefully bow out of the meeting without offending Kamel. "NOTE: Kamel may try to argue for new US aid to improve US/UAR relations. If so, we urge you simply [to] tell him to talk it over with Bundy."[24]

In a separate memo to Bundy, Komer warned him that Kamel was likely going to make a request for aid. "His favorite theme—which he plugs a lot harder than Cairo," Komer wrote. State wanted Bundy to tell Kamel that the administration wanted to continue the "US/UAR economic relationship," but that "recent frictions may make it hard to justify." Komer disagreed with the approach. He thought Nasser could use a stick in this instance. "I'd argue for being a bit less forthcoming," he wrote to Bundy. "While we don't want to get [the] UAR sore at us just before [the] September Arab summit and October's Belgrade II in Cairo [nonaligned nations summit], we do want to put [the] UAR on good behavior by stressing how it is putting strains on our relationship rather than the reverse." Komer suggested that Bundy attempt to place responsibility on Nasser to fix the strains on US-Egypt relations. "After saying how we've tried every way to signal Nasser that LBJ wants to continue the Kennedy policy, I'd like to see you express *discouragement* over the load that [the] relationship currently has to bear. More in sorrow than in anger, we wonder whether *Nasser* is as interested in good relations as he used to be." Komer instructed Bundy to then list the specific problems between the two countries. "So those in USG who want good relations with UAR (and this includes President [Johnson]) hope [that the] UAR won't make [the] freight too heavy to carry. Both sides must exercise restraint and keep [the] dialogue going. We know Kamel feels this way, and hope he's making [a similar] point in Cairo."

Komer reminded Bundy to put in a good word for Battle at the end of the conversation. In order for the redirection strategy to work it required Nasser to see the new ambassador as a friend. Komer wrote, "Do stick in a good buildup for Luke Battle as [the] personal choice of LBJ and a man deliberately chosen because he'll come with [an] open mind and no preconceptions."[25]

On August 10, Johnson sat down with Kamel for what amounted to a 10-minute discussion. Kamel opened the conversation with well-wishes from Nasser. He then remarked on how successful the relationship between the United States and Egypt had been to date. According to a memorandum of their conversation:

> The Ambassador lavishly praised the State Department, and especially Secretary Rusk and Assistant Secretary Talbot, for their great accomplishments in US policy toward the Middle East . . . Kamel thought good relations between the UAR and US were essential for the stability of the Middle East . . . stability was the great "friend" of the US in the Middle East.

Kamel then "pled" for keeping Arab-Israeli issues separate from US-Egypt relations. He used the phrase "ice-box," specifically, in reference to an agreement that Nasser had with Kennedy not to stir up trouble with Israel while being a recipient of US aid. According to the memorandum of conversation, Kamel said, "Some problems . . . [can] not be quickly solved; the Arab-Israeli issue, for example . . . [will] probably exist long after both the President and . . . [I have] gone." It was Kamel's way of stressing that the

Cairo summit notwithstanding, Nasser still had no intention of stirring up trouble with Israel. Nasser wanted Johnson to understand that.

As expected, Kamel asked Johnson to consider giving more aid to Egypt. He proposed that Johnson increase the amount of the ongoing three-year PL 480 agreement, issue a stabilization loan, and drum up business for Egypt with American companies. With more aid, Kamel said, Johnson could "activate" US-Egypt relations. Evidently, Komer's earlier thesis had been correct: Nasser was fishing through Kamel to see whether the administration was going to carry forward Kennedy's approach to aid.

Johnson followed Komer's script word-for-word. He thanked Kamel for coming to see him. And he extended his best wishes for Nasser. Then he excused himself from the conversation—but not before putting in a quick good word for Battle. "[He's] one of our better men," Johnson said. Having accomplished the symbolic gesture of a meeting with the president, it was now Bundy's turn to directly address the more substantive issues with Kamel. And more importantly, Bundy's turn to try out the novel approach of privately airing grievances.[26]

A few minutes passed before Bundy entered the room. When he did he asked Kamel to summarize his meeting with the president. Kamel recapped the conversation, but with one addition. According to the memorandum of conversation, "The Ambassador's advice was that the US should now go back to the UAR with a specific program to build on the nuclear assurances received." Bundy replied that, like Kennedy, Johnson hoped to build up a good personal relationship with Nasser. Johnson "took a direct personal interest in finding a suitable successor to Badeau," Bundy said. "Luke Battle's appointment would help to keep up the tradition of effective communication which had been built up over the past few years." Finally, Bundy said the administration would be happy to consider the "next steps" to take on the nuclear issue—it was, after-all, a good excuse for sending McCloy to Cairo, as Komer and Talbot wanted.

After hearing what Bundy had to say, Kamel brought up the upcoming summits in Egypt. Specifically, he wanted to know what the administration had to say about Nasser hosting them. Evidently, Nasser wanted to understand where he stood in light of the backlash he received after the first Arab summit. Bundy did not want to get mousetrapped by Kamel into sanctioning the summits. His reply was, "conferences are as conferences do." The administration did not object to conferences per se, he said. But it could not be forthcoming without knowing what the Arabs and nonaligned states planned to say at these conferences.

Bundy added that what would negatively impact Nasser's image in Washington, for certain, was his continued involvement in hot spot conflicts across the Middle East. According to the memorandum, Bundy said, "what concerned us [the Johnson administration] was giving even more concern in the country as a whole and to the Congress in particular, especially in an election year. Not everybody was as sophisticated in their view of US/UAR relations as those who dealt with them regularly."

Kamel's response was that he hoped the administration could still see the long-term benefit of good relations between the two countries, and not worry too much about temporary issues like Yemen. The lesser issues "should not be permitted to stand in the way of good US/UAR relations," he said. Kamel observed that it was more important that communism had not taken root in the Middle East, that the United States was able to continue drilling for oil in the region, and that "Israel was for all intents and purposes still in the 'ice-box.'"

Kamel then launched into an impassioned speech. Time was of the essence, he said. "For eight months the US hadn't done any real business with the UAR. He—Kamel—understood this matter but the 'impatient young men' who ran the government in Cairo were beginning to wonder." He followed this with a request for a firm commitment to renew the three-year PL 480 agreement when it expired on June 30, 1965. According to the memorandum of conversation, "Kamel recommended that we begin negotiations on renewal to show our good intentions." He also wanted the administration to immediately follow through with the $20 million loan as a gesture of goodwill toward Nasser.

Bundy replied that Egypt had not yet fulfilled its preconditions for receiving the loan. Kamel replied that he personally understood the reason for the hesitation in Washington; however, officials in Cairo saw the loan as something more important. To them, it was "proof of whether the US would continue to engage Nasser and give aid to Egypt," Kamel said.

Toward the end of the meeting, Kamel said he had one final request to make. He added that he was acting alone in this request. He wanted to form a Western consortium to oversee economic development in Egypt. Bundy replied that Britain would heavily object to such a venture given its recent difficulty with Nasser over Aden. Kamel asked why the Johnson administration couldn't take the matter up with Britain after its upcoming parliamentary election. Kamel believed the new liberal government that was expected to take power would be more likely to change its outlook toward Nasser. And he hoped the United States could use its good office to convince Britain to recognize the Yemen Arab Republic. It would help reduce some of the tensions in the Arabian Peninsula, Kamel said. Komer later wrote, "In Kamel's view, US policy toward Yemen was far wiser than that of the UK."

Bundy, who was caught off guard by Kamel's extreme request, deflected. US-Egypt relations had to be a "two-way street," he said. "It was just as important that the UAR not give disquieting signals to us as that the US make economic signals to Cairo."

The two men were on the verge of an argument. Kamel interjected that the only reason the Johnson administration was "upset," was because Nasser had not withdrawn his troops from Yemen. Kamel blamed Britain for its "machinations" in Yemen and implored for Johnson not to allow himself to be so easily swayed. Despite the outburst, Bundy was honest with Kamel. "It was not just a matter of troop withdrawal per se," he said, "but of the damage to the UAR reputation from having agreed to disengagement and not performing." What had so far been a fairly pleasant meeting, now truly was an airing of grievances.

The meeting ended abruptly when Komer suddenly interrupted. He said that the two men were in no way capable of resolving the Yemen conflict in one evening. Indeed, the purpose of the meeting had been to reestablish common ground for the relationship, not to get tough on Nasser. When Komer produced a memorandum of the conversation for the record, Bundy gratefully wrote: "Approved con amore. You make me sound so much smarter than I am."[27]

The meetings with Kamel were somewhat of a success. With the door now ajar for a follow-up on arms control directly with Nasser, Komer turned his effort to getting Johnson to sign off on McCloy's visit to Cairo—which Komer had taken the unusual step of planning before receiving Johnson's approval. On August 11, Komer wrote to Johnson, "Actually Nasser's nuclear self-denial is of more symbolic value than real. Our real target is Nasser's missiles." Komer wanted Johnson to briefly chat with McCloy. He wrote, "This would let him tell Nasser of your personal interest."[28]

Komer now was ready to move to phase II of his plan for "tacit Arab/Israeli arms control." And, to that end, he wrote a letter in Johnson's name for McCloy to hand to Nasser. It went: "It is most gratifying to have your personal assurance that the United Arab Republic does not intend to devote its efforts or resources to acquiring weapons of total destruction. Your interest in developing the well-being of your people and the peace of the world is attested by your statement that United Arab Republic has no thought of introducing the danger of nuclear conflict into the region of which it is a part." It was intended as a conversation starter on a topic that was important to Johnson: arms control.[29]

At that point, Johnson was holding regular Tuesday lunch-meetings with Bundy, Secretary of State Rusk, and Defense Secretary Robert McNamara, which were primarily used as an opportunity to discuss Vietnam. Komer, playing the gadfly role, suggested that Bundy "clue everybody" in at lunch about the new McCloy mission. And, more importantly, get Johnson to approve the trip. McCloy was coming to Washington two days later, and Komer did not yet have Johnson's backing for the imminent trip to Cairo.[30]

The next day, Komer wrote again to Johnson. "Since McCloy should go off on his arms control probe as a Presidential envoy, we suggest you let him be the bearer of your reply to Nasser's letter of nuclear assurances." He asked Johnson to sign the letter for Nasser. Fortunately, for Komer, Johnson did.[31]

On August 13, Komer wrote to Talbot. The latter was concerned that McCloy's visit was getting confused with the duties of an ambassador. "I quite agree that we shouldn't lightly risk dimming Nasser's receptivity to Mr. McCloy's mission, or diluting its impact, by asking Mr. McCloy to take up political matters," Komer wrote. "Nonetheless, the fact remains that Mr. McCloy is the only American of stature who will be seeing Nasser himself before the crucial Arab Summit. He'll be a Presidential envoy. So he's really the only direct high level channel open to us at the moment."

Komer was counting on McCloy to make the type of progress with Nasser that an ambassador normally would. Not surprising, Komer proposed an "added chore" for McCloy to "gently" press Nasser on the issues that Bundy had raised in his meeting with Kamel. Komer suggested that McCloy take the following approach: "Speaking quite unofficially, McCloy found in Washington a firm sense that President Johnson and his advisors wanted to continue the repair job on US/UAR relations begun by President Kennedy. However, there is a mood of some discouragement in Washington that divergent US and UAR attitudes on a whole series of issues . . . keep getting in the way."[32]

To be sure, Komer was counting on McCloy to get some mileage for the United States in Cairo. But, as it turned out, McCloy's trip to Cairo had to be postponed. He could no longer visit Cairo until after the Arab summit in September. This would not work—Komer had to get US-Egypt relations back on track before the summit in order to avoid further diplomatic hiccups from the Arab leaders' anticipated inflammatory rhetoric.

Reacting to the postponement of McCloy's trip, State sent three telegrams to the US embassy in Cairo, encouraging them to do their best to get in touch with Nasser via non-traditional channels. State wrote, "Prior [to the] convocation [of the] Second Arab Summit we wish [to] express USG concerns that developments flowing from [the] first Arab Summit meeting could affect profoundly [the] balance of political and military forces in Near East if they should continue along [the] present course." The directive was in line with Komer's thinking. He desperately wanted to get word to Nasser ahead of the summit that the threat of a renewed arms race in the Middle East (Jordan was now lobbying to buy planes from the United States and threatening to buy weapons from the Soviet Union if the United States did not agree to a sale) and additional threats against Israel would add too much tension into the region. "To sum up," State wrote to the embassy, "USG hopes [the] Second Arab Summit will not foreclose our efforts to preserve area calm and US-Arab cooperation."[33]

Fortunately, the embassy staff were granted a reprieve from this monumental task. A few days later, Battle made it through the confirmation hearings. Both Rusk and Komer advised Johnson to meet briefly with Battle before his departure to Cairo. "It would be most useful to our Arab policy if you could see Luke Battle on the record for even a moment just before he leaves for Cairo," Komer wrote to Johnson. "It would be a partial antidote for what we fear will be a strong Arab reaction to the platform Arab/Israeli statement [at the Democratic Party Convention], which once again came just before an Arab summit meeting."[34]

Indeed, the Democratic Party's platform referred to Palestinian refugees, and implied they should be resettled outside of Palestine—which was contrary to the official stance of the Arab League. The Arabs wanted an internationally sanctioned plan to impose a resettlement of the refugees in Israel. The Democrats also referred to Israel's territorial integrity in a statement that could be perceived as a rejection of the Arabs' plans to divert the Jordan River. The full statement went:

> Work for the attainment of peace in the Near East as an urgent goal, using our best efforts to prevent a military unbalance, to encourage arms reductions and the use of national resources for internal development and to encourage the resettlement of Arab refugees in lands where there is room and opportunity. The problems of political adjustment between Israel and the Arab countries can and must be peacefully resolved and the territorial integrity of every nation respected.[35]

Johnson was too busy to meet with Battle. He had no "more than a minute" to spare for the newly confirmed ambassador. The African-American civil rights activist, Martin Luther King Jr., was leading a protest outside the Democratic Convention, and the press was giving it significant coverage—Johnson was spread thin between Vietnam and his domestic woes.

A minute, however, was more than enough time from the president. Indeed, once again, it was the symbolism of the meeting that mattered most, not the substance itself. "Luke Battle is in for a moment on the record primarily so the UAR and other Arabs will know he's your ambassador," Komer wrote to Johnson. "This is useful because he'll have to carry quite a burden in convincing Nasser not to cause trouble for us during our election campaign." Komer wanted to give Battle the best chance possible for starting off on the right foot with Nasser.[36]

Meanwhile, Komer received good news about Abu Simbel, which promised to make it easier for Battle to get on Nasser's good side ahead of the upcoming summits. Congressman Rooney came through, after all, and assured the administration he would not stand in the way of Johnson using Cooley loan money to make the contribution. Nonetheless, Johnson had to immediately approve the loan because the new aid bill for 1965 included an amendment requiring all grants to be approved by Congress. "We're trying to get this knocked out," wrote Komer to Johnson, "but [we] may fail." He added for good measure, "Meeting this long-standing commitment of ours will cost us literally nothing yet be a positive gesture toward the UAR at a very useful time just before the new Arab summit." He recommended that Johnson make a public statement about the contribution in order to make it clear to Nasser that the money was coming from the president himself.[37]

However, a few days later, Komer changed his mind about the statement. Instead, he suggested having Battle personally deliver the good news to Nasser. "After all," Komer wrote to Bundy, "it's in [the] UAR that we need the favorable play, not here. OK?"[38]

Unfortunately, Battle did not end up meeting Nasser until after the two summits—which was too late for the two men to build any relationship before US-Egypt relations entered their most challenging period to date. Indeed, it was a period that Battle would later call, "a little series of horrors."[39]

8

Two Summits

Nasser hosted two summits in the autumn of 1964. One was for the Arab states to discuss diverting Israel's water. The other was for nonaligned states—countries that did not align themselves with either the United States or the Soviet Union. These two summits, which brought hot button issues to the forefront, complicated Komer's efforts to get Johnson interested in having good relations with Nasser.

The second Arab summit was held in Alexandria from September 5 to 11. While it once again highlighted Nasser's control over Arab affairs, a British official observed that the summit also heralded "the beginning of a breakdown in cooperation rather than a movement towards unity of action." Indeed, Syria wanted to launch an immediate war against Israel. Nasser, however, did not yet want war. Thus, he blocked Syria's attempt to hijack the proceedings, declaring that the Arab states needed to possess a certain standard of armaments before they would be ready to fight Israel. The unexpected openness of Syria and Nasser's disagreement made it clear to international observers that there was a rift between the Arab world's two most populist nations. Nonetheless, at the summit, the Arab states commissioned the creation of the Palestinian Liberation Organization (PLO)—a movement to spearhead Palestinian nationalism—and renewed their pledge to stop Israel's water project. Expanding on the resolutions from the first summit, they announced the imminent construction of dams to divert the tributaries of the Jordan River.[1]

The summit also addressed the issue of foreign bases in the region. Of significance, however, was the fact that the final communiqué refrained from mentioning American bases by name. A portion of the summit's final communiqué went: "The conference stressed the necessity to liquidate imperialist bases which threaten the security and peace of the Arab area, particularly in Cyprus and Aden." It was a small indication that the understanding reached between Badeau and Nasser was not entirely abrogated—notwithstanding the difficulties over the summer.[2]

In Washington, officials wondered about how Nasser truly felt about America. It was never easy to tell. Kamel was the only channel the United States had to the Egyptian leader at the moment. At a meeting before the summit to discuss the state of US-Egypt relations, an official from State had asked Kamel about the "unbalanced" criticism of the United States in the Egyptian press.[3] Kamel didn't have a good answer. But a little over a week later he returned to State and showed them an article that had just been published in the *New York Times*. It claimed that the Egyptian government had "purged" twenty-five pro-communist writers from Egyptian daily *al-Gumhuriyyah*—the same newspaper that the official from State had been referring to. Kamel appeared to take responsibility for the purge, saying that he had made "representations" to Nasser "blaming Communists on the newspaper's staff for its characteristically anti-American bias."[4] After the summit, State circulated a report of the incident. It appeared to be proof that Nasser once again was softening his outlook toward the United States.[5]

Nonetheless, while Nasser perhaps was privately indicating that he remained interested in friendly relations with the United States, the image coming out of the summit (especially the threats against Israel's water project) continued to paint him as a demagogue. Thus, the director of the World Bank, George Woods, said during a speech in Tokyo that the bank would no longer lend to countries like Egypt. Nasser had institutionalized foreign properties in the past, said Woods—no doubt a reference to Nasser's infamous nationalization of the Suez Canal in 1956. This upset Nasser, leading him to lash out at the World Bank even though he still needed its help. "It is clear that the director of the International Bank is giving himself the freedom to interfere in the internal affairs of the independent countries," went an editorial in *Al-Ahram*. The article went on to note that Egypt had not requested a loan from the bank, and that Nasser believed the bank should be reformed so that it "may become a genuine machine for development and for international cooperation and not a machine for threatening and illegally interfering in the affairs of the developing countries." From Washington, Nasser was looking more and more like an enigma. If he truly wanted Western capital to jumpstart Egypt's economy, as Kamel had indicated to Bundy, he had an unusual way of showing it—especially by attacking a cornerstone of American-backed international finance.[6]

Komer took it upon himself to puzzle out the reason behind Nasser's distress. He had dinner with Carl Kaysen, the former deputy national security adviser under Bundy, who had returned to the ivory tower at Harvard University in 1963 as a professor of political economy. The two exchanged a "possible brief for Andreas Papandreou in talk w/UAR."[7] Kaysen was a close friend of and informal adviser to Papandreou, who's father, Georgios, had recently become the prime minister of Greece. Andreas was his deputy prime minister and admittedly was an admirer of Nasser. Over the summer, with a hint of Nasserism in his voice, Andreas even had spoken publicly about breaking Greece's "dependence" on the United States.[8]

The brief, presumably discussed over dinner by Komer and Kaysen, painted a bleak picture of Egypt's economy. A portion of it went:

> The data leaves much to be desired, but it is clear that the UAR growth rate is dependent on resources provided through foreign grants and credits in one form or other. The question is whether the UAR can continue to attract the level of resources required to maintain its growth rate. During the past several years, it has utilized its Western long-term borrowing potential to a point perhaps beyond its capacity to repay, and also has exhausted such sources as the IMF. Commercial banking interests have expressed increasing reluctance to extend credits, and balances on clearing accounts are a high level. A foreseeable significant source

of hard currency credits is Kuwait (with its vast oil resources), whose political interests apparently outweigh purely economic considerations.

In short, Nasser needed new capital or else Egypt's economy faced indefinite stagnation.[9]

Komer subsequently began to collect other reports and articles about Egypt's economic outlook. One article in particular, by Seymour Freidin of the *New York Herald Tribune*, claimed that "Nasser is Flat Broke", and that he was in a panic. Referencing Egypt's first loan payment due to the Soviet Union for the Aswan High Dam, Freidin wrote: "Nasser's economic troubleshooters have been scurrying around the bigger banking institutions in the Western world, asking for terms on a big loan to the upcoming liability." According to the director of economic affairs at the US embassy in Cairo, Edwin Moline, Freidin's other claims were inaccurate. Contrary to the journalist's claims, Nasser had carried out the IMF's request in May to reduce Egypt's short-term debts by 14 percent. He had also abided by his agreement with the IMF not to take out any additional medium-term debt. Moreover, Moline dismissed as "patent nonsense" another claim by Freidin that Nasser expected to pay his debts "on expectations alone from Libyan oil in near future."[10]

Moline wrote to State that he was concerned about the dangers of such inconsistent reporting about Nasser. "I have worried for some time at the cumulative effect of various articles unfriendly to the UAR which contribute so much to the poor public image which is constantly mentioned to me as part of the reason it is so difficult to carry on consistently with our aid program here," he wrote. Specifically, Moline had received word that the director of a bank in Philadelphia had printed copies of Freidin's article for a board meeting that had been called to discuss cancelling Egypt's line of credit at the bank. "His four colleagues were unanimously of the opinion that the article was nonsense," wrote Moline, "but I am not sure that other readers will be so perceptive." Indeed, such reporting threatened to increase congressional opposition to Nasser—public outrage about the Egyptian leader meant congressmen would have more incensed constituents to appease than usual.[11]

Komer collected Moline's correspondence alongside the brief he exchanged with Kaysen. He began to piece together exactly what had been driving Nasser's aggressive behavior over the summer. Rodger Davies (director of the Office of Near Eastern Affairs, Bureau of Near Eastern and South Asian Affairs) soon began sending additional diplomatic correspondence to Komer that highlighted a growing backlash against Nasser in US political circles.[12]

For example, there was the report of General Paul Adams's (Commander in Chief, United States Strike Forces aka CINCSTRIKE) visit to the US embassy in London, during which he openly complained about the administration's policy toward Nasser. "What is needed is a bit of toughening in our policy toward him," Adams said. "Instead of giving him more aid, we should first cut our aid in half. And then, if he still doesn't behave, we should cut it altogether." The general was responsible for coordinating military operations in conflicts where the United States was asked to intervene. He was on his way to Tehran to talk to the Shah, who was worried about Nasser. Indeed, Britain, Iran, and the Kurds of Iraq had recently failed at an attempt to overthrow the Nasserist President of Iraq, Abdul Salam Arif.[13] A staff member at the US embassy in

London told Adams that the United States only provided 18 percent of Nasser's wheat. America simply did not have the type of leverage needed to "bring him [Nasser] to heel," as Adams wanted. The staff member also mentioned Badeau, and his well circulated reports about how it would take time to build up a relationship with Nasser. "The General snorted," reported the staff member. He described Ambassador Badeau as caring more for the Arabs than for US interests. "What we need in the UAR," he insisted, "is someone who actively tries to protect our interests in the Middle East." Adams bemoaned State's handling of Nasser. He believed the US military was in danger of losing access to important bases in the Middle East—bases which CINCSTRIKE needed in order to be able to deploy; especially Wheelus. Adams said the staff member was flat out wrong about US aid to Nasser. The United States provided 50 percent of Nasser's wheat, not 18 percent, he insisted. "Many Americans . . . [are] beginning to be fed up with our policy on Nasser," he said. The hapless embassy official later wrote to State, "Since the General's preoccupation with Nasser took up the entire time allotted, no one else could speak. I fear, however, that the General went away unshaken in his conviction that the Department of State is supine in its handling of Nasser." Indeed, the episode was one of many indications that there was a growing backlash against Nasser.[14]

Thus, both Talbot and Komer planned to meet with Kamel ahead of the nonaligned summit in October. "We think it important for the Ambassador to know that we see positive actions which the Conference could take," wrote Rodger Davies to Talbot, in preparation for the important discussion. "We also see a number of pitfalls." Talbot planned to give Kamel a presentation that would explain America's position on a number of Cold War issues; including, among other things, the benefit of "economic development" in nonaligned nations.

A potential flaw in this outreach, however, was that Kaissouni, Nasser's economic adviser, had just launched a campaign to become chairman of the UN's Trade and Development Board. State officials reluctantly felt that his ascension should be blocked given Nasser's abysmal handling of Egypt's economy. As Davies reasoned to Talbot, "You may wish to inform him that we think it only fair that consideration should first be given to a candidate from a developed country."[15]

Kaissouni's campaign was an awkward situation to handle at a time when Talbot and Komer were working to make progress with Nasser. No doubt it had to be handled delicately in order to avoid upsetting Nasser. Talbot's meeting with Kamel, however, got cancelled at the last minute. It was now up to Komer, alone, to send a strong message to Nasser ahead of the nonaligned summit.

Before meeting with Kamel for lunch, Komer prepared a list of issues that "discouraged" him most about US-Egypt relations. It included, inter alia: "Arab-Is. not in icebox any more"; lack of any aid made US-Egypt relations an "exercise in futility," which Komer compared to "closing [the] barn door after [the] horse is gone." Komer also wrote about the upcoming nonaligned summit, "Gt. [great?] tendency to flog dead anti-col. [colonial] horse." These were Komer's private thoughts. And they reveal that he maintained a realistic assessment of Nasser despite his regular campaigning for policies based on optimism. Komer's lunch with Kamel was to be the frank and forthcoming discussion he had hoped McCloy would have with Nasser before the summits.[16]

At lunch the next day, Kamel started off by saying the two countries needed to resume "an upward momentum" in their relations. Woods's speech "had created great suspicion in Cairo." Kamel hoped the Johnson administration "could find some formula for assuaging UAR feeling." To that end, he asked, could the United States "get George Woods to say something nice, for example?"

Kamel also brought up economic aid. It was vital that Johnson approve a new PL 480 deal and the outstanding $20 million loan, he said. Komer replied, "it would be better to make a fresh start and avoid a wrangle over whether conditions for this loan had or had not been met." Kamel countered. "Without such an agreement the US would have absolutely no leverage in Cairo," he said. Kamel framed aid as the key to bringing the United States and Egypt into a "*de facto* alliance." He added, for good measure, that such a relationship could "end Soviet hopes of dominating the ME [Middle East]."

Although Komer agreed with the sentiment behind Kamel's argument, he was not willing to simply roll over in light of the recent difficulties. Nasser was unreliable. And that made it difficult to openly support him. As Komer later wrote: "I heartily agreed with the objective of achieving new forward movement toward US-UAR reconciliation but emphasized the political and economical roadblocks . . . there were many who questioned whether the UAR's development program was sufficiently promising enough to justify substantial external support. Even more important, however, numerous policy issues—Yemen, Jordan, Libyan bases, South Arabia, Cyprus—kept cropping up in the way of any long-term program." Komer brought up the Jordan waters issue, saying he feared that Nasser no longer was capable of containing the Arab-Israeli conflict after it had been unleashed in such a fashion at the two Arab summits. Interestingly, "Kamel fully agreed."

Kamel asked Komer how the two countries could keep their relationship on "an even keel." Komer brought up Johnson's election in November and told him it was important that Nasser "avoid any spats" before then. "These could easily become partisan issues," Komer said, meaning that Johnson would have no choice but to choose saving his political career over Nasser. Komer also brought up the nonaligned summit, telling Kamel that Nasser should "exert a moderating influence" over the summit in order to demonstrate his willingness to cooperate with the United States.

The final topic was Kaissouni's candidacy for the UN committee chair. From Cairo's perspective, Kamel said, the Johnson administration's objection was hostile. "Why did the US unnecessarily offend Kaissouni, who was . . . [a] friend?" Kamel asked. He pleaded for the United States "not [to] ask for trouble" and to avoid making it another issue between the two countries.

Despite the uncomfortable nature of some of the issues discussed, the meeting was promising. It gave Komer the opportunity to air his grievances from the summer and get a warning to Nasser before the start of the nonaligned summit. However, what the United States really needed was positive action from Nasser, not more empty promises via Kamel. Even Komer was beginning to get disheartened about the prospects of getting along with Nasser. "Throughout the luncheon Kamel wove in his standard pitch about his own stake in stronger US-UAR ties, his direct pipeline to Nasser, etc," wrote Komer in a memorandum of their conversation. "I gave him my most sympathetic ear."[17] Indeed, it was becoming a tired tune.

This time, however, Nasser heeded the warning Komer sent through Kamel. Moreover, Nasser did his best to send a friendly message to the administration through McCloy, when the two men finally met on September 28. As McCloy told State during his debriefing, Nasser appeared to be more receptive to arms limitations than before. Nasser also confided to McCloy that, while internal and external pressures kept him from being able to show too much restraint toward Israel, he personally did not see an Arab-Israeli war as a "feasible" option for the Arab states. It was a meaningful gesture from Nasser to demonstrate his willingness to cooperate. And it was exactly what Komer had wanted to see.[18]

Having received some reassurance from Nasser, State raced to get a message to the nonaligned summit before the Soviets sent theirs. It went: "We Americans live in a diversified society. We are a nation of many minority groups—from almost every land. For this reason, we cherish as a guiding principle the right of men and of groups to hold diverse views so long, of course, as the expression of those views does not interfere with the security or welfare of others." It was a message of good faith intended to show that while the administration was still open to working with Nasser, it needed to see further restraint from him at the summit.[19] This was a good start toward warmer relations. But, once again, Nasser sent back a mixed message.

Although Nasser gave a relatively restrained speech at the summit's opening ceremony, it was what happened behind the scenes that was controversial.[20] Specifically, on Nasser's orders, Congolese prime minister Moise Tshombe's plane was refused landing rights in Egypt. Tshombe was forced to spend the night in Athens. Once he finally arrived in Egypt the next day, Tshombe was ostracized by the other heads of state and ultimately denied entry to the summit proceedings. At the summit Nasser said, "a threat to world peace is that a trade in mercenaries is being practiced without honor and without shame." It was a veiled reference to the Congolese government's hiring of South African mercenaries to stamp out a rebellion that had started when the country declared independence from Belgium in 1960. Indeed, Nasser considered Tshombe an enemy. Tshombe was fighting the pro-communist rebels in Congo, whom Nasser supported. And Tshombe was rumored to have taken part in the assassination of the country's first independent leader, Lumumba, whom Nasser considered a close friend. In 1963, Tshombe was exiled after the UN seized the separatist territory under his control. However, in the summer of 1964, he was invited back to Congo to join a new Western leaning coalition government—which was allegedly formed at America's behest. In short, Nasser and the other neutralist leaders viewed Tshombe as a Western-backed stooge in their midst.[21]

In response to Nasser's treatment of Tshombe at the summit, the Congolese government surrounded Egypt's embassy in Leopoldville with a police cordon. Nasser, in turn, detained and threatened to hold Tshombe until the Congolese police dispersed from Egypt's diplomatic compound. The *New York Times* subsequently described Tshombe as Nasser's "hostage." "Despite its seriousness, the situation still had elements of comedy," went one article. "Mr. Nasser, who first strenuously opposed Mr. Tshombe's efforts to reach [Egypt] and then tried to persuade him to leave, was put in the awkward position of now preventing him from leaving." Indeed, Nasser had patched one problem with the United States, only to open the door to another. More importantly, he managed to do so under international scrutiny.[22]

Although a third-party issue once again threatened to become a hot button issue between the United States and Egypt, Lucius Battle, who was now on the ground in Cairo, was in no position to forge a reconciliation with Nasser. While there was no doubt that Battle had been well briefed ahead of his arrival in Cairo, even writing to Komer, "I am very grateful for all your help in briefing me and guiding me during the last days in Washington," the delay over his confirmation and subsequently late arrival kept him from being able to strike up a relationship with Nasser at just the right time. In short, the administration had little recourse to redirect Nasser in Cairo.[23]

Komer, for his part, continued to scan diplomatic correspondence to get a better understanding of Nasser's state of mind. For example, he studied a memorandum of a meeting that had taken place in Cairo shortly after the nonaligned summit. In attendance had been James Spain from State (who was visiting), Donald Bergus (a staff member at the US embassy in Cairo), and Hassan Sabri al-Khouli, who, as it will be recalled, was an adviser to Nasser and often communicated on his behalf. The meeting had been called to discuss US-Egypt relations. Spain and Bergus did their best to convince Khouli that Johnson would warm up to Nasser after the US presidential election. They explained that Johnson merely needed time to review US policy toward Egypt and to formulate his own approach when he was finally free of the restraints of running a political campaign. Khouli accepted the argument. However, he observed that the relationship had been fundamentally altered in the wake of Kennedy's death—which, from his angle, indicated a policy shift. According to a report of their conversation: "In the course of the conversation Hassan Sabri let it be known that thus far, at least, the death of President Kennedy had removed a personal element in the relations between the two countries which had not been replaced. There had, of course, been some correspondence between President Johnson and President Nasser. But where President Kennedy's letters had been frank and friendly, President Johnson's letters had been more in the nature of the usual formal correspondence between Chiefs of State." Khouli even went so far to say that it had been a period of "hell" since Kennedy's assassination. It must have been a surprising comment for Komer to read; after all, he was the one who drafted both Kennedy and Johnson's correspondence with Nasser.[24]

But Khouli was not entirely incorrect. True, Johnson and Nasser exchanged niceties from time to time. But there was never a level of trust between the two men in the way that there had been under Kennedy. In response to Johnson's friendly message to the nonaligned summit, Nasser sent back a "courtesy message" to thank him.[25] He wrote, "Your message to the second conference of the chiefs of state of the nonaligned countries was appreciated and highly valued . . . our sincere greetings and good wishes for the progress and continued prosperity of your country in a world in which peace, security, and friendship will prevail."[26] Likewise, Nasser sent a courtesy message to Johnson after he won the presidential election in November. "I am indeed happy to express sincere congratulations on the grand confidence placed in you by the great American people and delighted by the outcome of the American elections," he wrote. "The people of the United Arab Republic followed these elections with full interest and felt that they had an impact on many issues of international importance with direct influence on all peoples."[27]

Johnson, for his part, also sent generic replies to Nasser, writing, "I deeply appreciate your kind message of congratulations on my election as President of the United States, and extend to you and the people of the United Arab Republic my sincere good wishes."[28] However, this was the extent of their communication in the fall of 1964, when relations were still somewhat uncertain in the wake of two back-to-back administrative transitional periods directly affecting Egypt's pipeline to the United States —the death of Kennedy and the resignation of Badeau. Indeed, the two leaders' messages were perfunctory, and performed more in obligation as heads of state rather than an indication of anything special in their relationship—as opposed to the Kennedy era.

Now that the US presidential election was over, Nasser needed a sign from Johnson. However, this was going to be difficult. Before Johnson won the election, the White House received numerous letters from congressmen who were anxious to cut off all aid to Egypt. In response to one letter, Komer wrote to Bundy, "[Congressman] Ryan's letter about cutting off aid to Egypt is, I assume, one of many we've received before the election for the record. Now that we've won. I've stiffened State's draft reply just a bit to clue Ryan without being argumentative." Indeed, Komer thought it was time for Johnson to get serious about engaging Nasser.[29]

Almost immediately after the election, Komer attempted to jumpstart a discussion about Middle East policy. Specifically, he wanted to conduct a reappraisal of the Kennedy era's generous approach to foreign assistance. His thinking was not unlike an embattled prime minister that gambles on early parliamentary elections in order to make or break their agenda. Indeed, what Komer desired was a test of his political capital in order to determine the feasibility of pushing through friendly approaches to Nasser in an unfriendly environment.

Since Badeau's resignation, Egypt had requested an additional $70 million under the existing PL 480 deal, a $20 million loan for development projects (in addition to the outstanding one for commodities), and a new PL 480 agreement to replace the three-year one that was due to expire on June 30, 1965. Because of the election, no movement had been made to get Johnson to focus on these issues.

On November 17, Komer presented Bundy with a draft of a National Security Action Memorandum (NSAM) on foreign assistance. Komer intended for the NSAM to bring significant attention to the issue, and to pave the way for Johnson to finally formulate his own approach vis-à-vis Nasser. Komer also wanted Johnson to consider federal funding for Salhia. Although it was a more extensive development project than any that had been considered under Kennedy, it no doubt had the potential to usher in a new era in US-Egypt relations. It still was premature to bring the matter before Johnson. So, Komer asked Saunders to produce a study on the project by mid-December in order to understand the costs and politics involved in completing such a large construction project on time.

Komer asked for a reappraisal of foreign assistance not because he changed his mind about the redirection strategy; rather, he wanted to get Johnson on board and fully backing the policy. "Mac: We face a series of tough decisions on aid to UAR in next few months," wrote Komer to Bundy. "Given all the Hill letters, etc about UAR program, I should think LBJ would want to have final say." Komer was still "strongly" in favor of giving aid to Egypt. But he wanted it to be "accompanied by a more active diplomacy aimed at getting more for our money."

Two days later, Bundy replied, "Good idea. [But] redo—make less Presidential." Komer's first draft of the NSAM read like a barking of orders.[30] Komer produced two more drafts before Bundy signed off. "Third time's a charm," Komer wrote. "Sorry to be so slow on uptake." He joked, "On reflection, I'm worried that my 'stock is high at State.' I must not be doing my job." Indeed, Komer was ready, once again, to play the gadfly role.[31]

On November 20, Bundy signed off on Komer's work, officially making it NSAM no. 319. Specifically, it asked State, the Secretary of Agriculture, and AID to produce studies on the benefits and disadvantages of giving aid to Egypt in the fiscal year of 1965–6. "Given the Congressional and other criticism of aid to the UAR," went the memorandum, which had been entirely written by Komer but appeared in Bundy's name, "I think it would be desirable to let the President review our policy on this matter before any new decisions are taken . . . he should be fully apprised of the case for any new aid measures, particularly since they entail potential domestic reactions." The memorandum asked for their studies by mid-December. "So I suggest that you provide him [Johnson] in due course with your recommendations," went the NSAM, "together with an analysis of what we expect to gain from such aid and what leverage it provides us." For good measure, Komer added at the end, "It might also be useful to discuss what other alternatives are open to us."[32]

While Komer's intentions with the NSAM were forward looking, there was no way he could have foreseen that the timing was not right for a reappraisal of the current policy. Indeed, pressures continued to mount on Nasser, with Khrushchev being unexpectedly thrown out of power in Moscow, a Nasserist military regime in neighboring Sudan being similarly ousted, and Nasser himself reportedly dealing with an outpouring of critical public opinion in Egypt that claimed he was too involved in socialist-inspired activism—both at home and abroad. "The general trend of criticism has been that Nasser's foreign policies have been too far to the East, and that his internal policies have carried socialism too far," wrote Thomas Hughes, the head of research at State. "The worsening economic situation in the UAR in fact is attributable in great part to the radial socialization measures instituted by Nasser in 1961; it has been accentuated by the Yemen war and by repercussions of his anti-imperialist campaign against the West." Indeed, the Egyptian economy, which had suffered for years from Nasser's wasteful spending and fiscal neglect, was beginning to bite Nasser back.

In order to address the Egyptian public's concerns, and to briskly brush them away, Nasser delivered a 2 1/2-hour speech to the Egyptian National Assembly on November 12. He highlighted his foreign policy, saying that (unpopular) loans to African countries were made in the spirit of "unselfishness and cooperation." He pointed out that Israel made similar loans, the implication being that Egypt was going to lose influence in Africa if it no longer made them. Nasser also claimed that relations with the United States were better than ever under his leadership. According to Hughes, "He stressed UAR efforts to preserve good relations with the United States, maintaining that there were no direct problems between the UAR and the United States, although there were differences on such matters as Israel, the Congo, and US bases in the area."

Nasser fought back against the claim that he spent too much money on the military budget. He mostly deflected, but he noted that Israel's annual defense spending was much higher for a nation of its size. Nasser also took questions on Yemen, claiming that once-and-for-all he would put an end to the "gossip" about his misuse of military funds—though he did so only behind closed doors.

From afar, in Washington, Hughes speculated that Nasser appeared concerned by the shake-up of the Soviet leadership. Nasser, however, remained adamant that he alone possessed the best vision to carry Egypt forward. He asked the Egyptian people for more time to show what could be achieved under his leadership. "Nasser's words contain no admission that his policies themselves may be in error," observed Hughes. "Nasser made it clear in his speech that his external and internal policies are inextricably interlinked, and he has committed himself too deeply to them to be able to reverse his field."[33]

Having now made it past the two summits a little worse for the wear, US-Egypt relations continued to hobble on. Nasser had indicated that he needed American economic assistance. Nevertheless, his desperation for a gesture of good faith from Johnson soon led him to take a series of missteps that would place US-Egypt relations at their lowest point since Eisenhower. In the process, Komer's campaign to convince Johnson of the merits of a friendly approach to Nasser was sidelined.

9

Communication Breakdown

Coincidentally, it was at the very moment that Nasser was busy defending his policies at home, implying that he would soon be attempting to get closer to the United States, that a new third-party problem suddenly crept up between Egypt and the United States: Congo.

In August 1964, a rebel group suspected to have ties to Nasser overran the US embassy in Leopoldville. They took hostage the staff (at least the ones who did not escape) and several hundred civilians. For the next 110 days, the United States attempted to secure their release. On November 24, negotiations broke down, and the rebels claimed they could no longer guarantee the safety of the hostages. In response, the United States and Belgium (which also had hostages taken) launched a joint rescue operation, which was successful.[1]

Back in Washington, Rodger Davies from State paid a visit to the Egyptian residence to hand Kamel an official statement about the operation. Kamel, in turn, handed Davies a document in Arabic that denied Egypt's involvement in the hostage-taking. Davies replied that while State appreciated Kamel's "assurances," it was more concerned about the fact that on the day of the mission *Al-Ahram* produced an editorial that "could be interpreted as a call for African support for the rebels." The contents of the editorial were later broadcast by Radio Cairo and transmitted over African airwaves. Additionally, Davies said, the United States was "disturbed" by reports of Chinese and Algerian weapons being discovered at an airport in Congo that was owned and operated by Egypt.

If these two incidents were not bad enough, continued Davies, the United States was even more disturbed by the fact that in recent days the Egyptian press (including the same newspaper that Kamel earlier claimed to have "purged") ran a number of hostile articles including, among other things, criticism of US policy in Vietnam, claims that the United States was intentionally starving India, stories of clandestine US plots against the Tanzan Republic, accusations that the US ambassador to Lebanon had interfered in local elections, and allegations of a supposed joint British/American attack on the Egyptian embassy in Khartoum. The last item, in particular, had been depicted by a cartoon showing Uncle Sams and John Bulls attacking the embassy while disguised as Africans. Davies added that an American publication, *Time Magazine*, wanted to run a story about Egyptian officials planting anti-Western stories in their press to fulfill the terms of an agreement it had with Moscow. *Time* possessed proof that the anti-Western propaganda was one of the terms of an aid package that Nasser had signed with Khrushchev. Davies told Kamel that the Johnson administration had intervened at the last minute and successfully convinced *Time* not to run the story. However, in light of the recent events, the administration was reconsidering its objection to its publication.

No doubt this was a veiled threat, by Davies, regarding Egypt's continued eligibility to receive PL 480 aid. Congress would never stand for such behavior from Nasser. Kamel admitted there was indeed a problem. He said he would consult with the Egyptian foreign ministry at once.[2]

Neither of the two men realized the extent to which the unfolding crisis threatened to undo US-Egypt relations. Back in Egypt, Congolese students responded to the American-Belgian rescue operation in an uproar. Specifically, on November 28, which also happened to be the US holiday of Thanksgiving, hundreds of Congolese students formed a large mob on the streets of Cairo. The mob marched to the US embassy compound and burned down the newly built John F. Kennedy Library. Afterwards, they marched to the gates of the US embassy itself. They threw bricks, tore up flowerpots, and chanted at the gates while a line of US marines stood with their arms linked, protecting the embassy behind them. One enterprising member of the mob even threw a heavy pot through the window of Battle's office—which was unoccupied at the time.

With the situation at the US embassy quickly getting out of control, the commander of the marines called Battle at home, where he had been celebrating Thanksgiving with his family—apparently unaware of the mayhem nearby. The marines were not authorized to use their weapons, but they had to restore order, the commander told Battle. More importantly, they needed to protect the sensitive files inside the embassy.

Battle left for the embassy at once. When he arrived, he miraculously walked through the crowd unharmed. Then, he waited at the gates to be let in. Eventually, the mob dispersed. "It was a disastrous situation," Battle later recalled. "In order to get there, I had to pass both the [Egyptian] fire and police department building. In neither case did I see any activity. I passed these buildings and went to the embassy." Battle suspected the Egyptian authorities had not responded because they were complicit.[3]

After the mob dispersed, Battle immediately delivered a "note of protest" to the acting foreign minister, Abu Shadi, who, in turn, acted surprised. The Egyptian authorities had done all they could to stop the protestors, Shadi said. It was not their fault the Congolese students had been so upset. However, the international news agencies were already reporting the spectacle of Battle managing to walk all the way from his home to the embassy compound before the police and fire departments had bothered to show up. The whole world now knew what happened.

In Washington, where it was still the day before Thanksgiving, Jernegan met with a representative from the Egyptian embassy. US-Egypt relations were already the subject of much negative speculation, Jernegan said. How could the administration get the American public to see things any differently now that there had been a direct attack on US property? "Thus, [the] attack on [the] Embassy, while in itself [is] not [an] incident of grave severity," remarked Jernegan, "[it]could have [an] effect out of proportion to [the] actual damage done." In other words, it was sure to invoke congressional opposition to giving Egypt any further PL 480 aid.[4]

Kamel was away in New York for the holidays. However, he immediately called the executive secretary of state, Benjamin Read, and offered his sincerest apologies to the president and secretary of state. Read recommended to Kamel that he follow up the phone call with a request to Cairo to "offer compensation for the damage and publicly express regret." US officials were most upset about the fact that the Egyptian authorities had been notably "remiss" during the incident, and that they remained so in its aftermath.[5]

Komer immediately weighed in on the situation. "I've actively needled State and AID . . . on responding suitably to [the] Cairo library burning," he told Bundy. "All agree we should be tough in demanding compensation and regrets, but fear that going further might cost more than it gained." Komer also told Bundy that in the course of the conversation with Kamel, State had linked the incident to the administration's ability to continue aid in the future. Komer, however, did not want to cut off aid—even if it turned out that Nasser himself had sanctioned the mob. Instead, Komer proposed a slight delay of the previously scheduled aid shipments, writing in reference to one set of cargo that was already at the docks, "we won't hurry this along." However, this was the extent of Komer's interest in punishing Nasser.

Komer was far more concerned about the big picture: the United States had objectives in the Middle East, so it could not afford to be at odds with Nasser. For example, Komer was still hoping to get Nasser to call off the Arab boycott against Chase Manhattan Bank at a December 15 meeting of the Arab League. Komer wrote to Bundy with emphasis, "So instead I've passed word not to be in any hurry to discuss *new* aid to UAR (which will worry them plenty, since they're aching). This is far more sensible, and they can hardly complain about it just now." He added, "Let's remember too that we just one-upped all these guys in the Congo so they're naturally feeling frustrated."[6]

Indeed, a few days later, Congo was the main topic at hand when Rusk met with Egypt's foreign minister, Mahmud Riad, UN representative, Mohamed El-Kony, and Kamel at the November 1964 session of the UN General Assembly. At the beginning of their conversation, Rusk brought up the library incident, saying that "an exchange of notes on this subject would permit . . . [both countries] to remove it from the agenda of bilateral problems." Riad replied that the incident had been "unlucky" and "not predicted." He insisted that Nasser wanted "to keep relations with the United States on very good terms . . . [He] wished to strive constantly to develop better relations and closer friendships."[7]

Nevertheless, when Rusk defended the rescue operation in Congo, saying that the United States had ran out of options to ensure the safety of the hostages, Riad replied it was a shared feeling among the nonaligned countries that the US controlled "the policy decisions of the Congo Government." Therefore, the United States could not be completely surprised about having received such a terrible backlash in Cairo in the aftermath of the rescue operation. Rusk countered it was not the United States that had put Tshombe into power. Nevertheless, the United States could not demand his removal, lest it be seen as an actual demonstration of meddling in Congo's affairs.

No doubt it was a difficult conversation. US-Egypt relations were at their lowest since Eisenhower. Rusk ended the conversation with advice for Nasser. He should discuss issues with Battle on a regular basis, said Rusk. He noted that the ambassador enjoyed the "full confidence" of Johnson and himself.[8] It was a lame attempt to steer US-Egypt relations back on track.

The Johnson administration's restrained response to the library burning, as spearheaded by Komer, appeared to work. Several days after the incident, Nasser formally apologized and offered to pay compensation. Komer mulled over the best response to move relations forward. On December 2, he wrote to Johnson: "We're persuaded that to overtly tie any aid delays to the library burning would cost more in terms of UAR reactions than its worth." He informed Johnson that he wanted to tie up new aid to Nasser rather than delay anything related to the existing agreement. It will "be less risky," Komer argued.[9]

It was important for the United States to remain in communication with Nasser in light of his apology and offer of compensation. Doing so required being tough and friendly at the same time. Nasser had to understand that the United States wouldn't accept similar attacks in the future. But to push him away over the incident was to walk away from relations altogether.

To that end, State began drafting a letter from Johnson to Nasser, in order to officially express the administration's dissatisfaction with the way Egyptian officials had handled the crisis. Komer ended up revising much of the letter. He thought it was important to strike the right tone with Nasser. He wanted to be firm, but respectful; not overly harsh or condescending. Indeed, he thought it would be wise to conjure up the ghost of Kennedy himself in order to give a second chance to the defunct idea that Johnson was the continuation of a better era. As Komer wrote to one of Johnson's most trusted personal advisers, Jack Valenti, it was a "Kennedy-style redo of [the] Nasser letter."[10]

Next, Komer explained his strategy to Johnson. He had to convince the president of the merit of sending a message to Nasser in the wake of the incident. Komer stressed to Johnson that the message would be delivered as a "friendly oral message" in order to avoid public scrutiny. He said he hoped the correspondence would help Nasser make the right decision about Congo, and stressed how important it was to reestablish communication with Nasser if the administration hoped to have any leverage with him in the future. "It is couched as a polite statement of our position," Komer wrote. He added with emphasis, "*It's important to get this word to Nasser before he goes too far on the Congo, and gets locked in a struggle with us, from which we'll both lose.*" Komer also wrote that it would not hurt if only one time the United States flatly rejected a new aid request from Egypt until Nasser ended his involvement in the Congo. "Since Nasser is hoping for [a] continuation of US food aid, and has a request pending right now, this is a good time to hit him," Komer wrote.[11]

Inserting Johnson into the equation was necessary to get Nasser's attention, but it was Battle who had to do the heavy lifting in Cairo. It was time for him to try his hand at the redirection strategy. To that end, White House and State officials coordinated on a list of talking points for Battle to bring up with Nasser. Battle needed to hit a reset button with Nasser in light of the difficulties. As framed by his talking points, he had to convince Nasser that "there seems to you to be an urgent need for a re-examination and revalidation of US/UAR collaboration. We need to restart the political dialogue which characterized the Kennedy/Badeau period. We need to find means of cooperating in other ways than just the US providing aid, and then having its library burned."[12]

This was no ordinary diplomatic meeting. Battle had to invoke both Kennedy and Badeau in order to persuade Nasser that he was on his side.

Though the diplomatic outreach to Nasser in the wake of the library burning consumed Komer's time, reports started to come into him in response to NSAM no. 319. Talbot wrote State's report. It called for continuing all previously scheduled aid shipments to Egypt, as well as signing a new annual aid agreement immediately after the expiration of the current one. Talbot wrote to Rusk to justify his recommendations:

> UAR support for the Congo rebels and the currently pro-Soviet line in the UAR press illustrate a trend toward deterioration of our position in Egypt. American interests are also jeopardized by the UAR's mounting economic problems, which if uncorrected could upset the uneasy *status quo* in the area.
>
> We believe that the best hope of reversing these trends lies in resuming the high-level dialogue with the UARG and consolidating the momentum of US-UAR economic cooperation.[13]

AID's response to the NSAM was similar. It called for continuing to use aid to redirect Nasser; especially in light of the current difficulties between the two countries. With everyone's reports in hand, Komer wrote to Talbot, "We hope to start clearing Monday—provided atmospheric conditions are favorable." Indeed, with anger toward Nasser still fresh in Washington, it was not yet the right time to call for sending generous amounts of aid to Egypt in order to essentially buy off Nasser.[14]

Komer was still against giving any new aid to Nasser for the time being. However, at the same time, he wanted Johnson to get used to the idea that dealing with Nasser was in his best interest. Thus, on December 21, Komer wrote directly to Johnson and encouraged him to invite Nasser to Washington. "Despite all the trouble we're having with him right now," Komer wrote, "this is in fact the best reason for bringing him here." Kennedy had tried to invite Nasser twice. However, each time the "omens weren't right," wrote Komer.

Komer attempted to paint Nasser as a worthy adversary who required a certain level of attention from Johnson. "No matter how much trouble Nasser seems to be causing us, the overriding case for continuing to deal with him is that he could cause us infinitely more if he tried," he wrote. Komer made sure to add that the Soviets were "bidding heavily" for Nasser's "full support."

Despite the bold request for a Nasser visit, Komer was realistic about the signals that Nasser was capable of showing the United States. And he was open with Johnson about the limitations of a relationship with Nasser. "One key to influencing Nasser is to treat him like a first-class citizen," Komer wrote. "Having him here could obligate him to say and do things which would be worth $300 million in aid . . . Of course, this Arab won't change his spots regardless of how well we treat him. Limited cooperation is the best we could expect."

Komer boldly dangled the proposed visit as an opportunity for Johnson to once-and-for-all make a decision about Nasser. He stressed: "If you failed to reach a meeting of minds, we could *then* back away from aid." At the bottom of the memo, he gave Johnson the opportunity to check the box next to a lighthearted, "You're fired" option, or an "I'll think about it" option. For the time being, however, Johnson did not respond to Komer's request.[15]

Before sending the memorandum, Komer had written to Bundy, "Here's how I'd beard the lion in his den. If not persuasive enough, I'll try again." Bundy had signed off on the exercise. However, the two men were being wildly presumptuous with the approach. Unbeknown to Komer and Bundy was the fact that Johnson was upset about Komer's decision to continue any aid to Egypt in the wake of the library burning. Johnson privately told others in the administration that he could not understand why the United States should ever bother to continue dealing with Nasser.[16]

The timing could not have been worse to ask Johnson to reconsider Nasser. On December 18, three days before Komer made the request for a Nasser visit, Egypt mistakenly shot down a private American plane in the desert, just outside of Cairo. The Egyptians' official story was that due to faulty equipment, the plane had not made proper contact with air traffic control. Egyptian authorities had mistakenly thought the plane belonged to Israel due to the direction it had come from. Coincidentally, the plane belonged to John Mecom, a wealthy American oil tycoon, and a close friend of Johnson's. Mecom was not on the plane, but an American pilot and his Swedish passenger died on impact. While US officials believed Egypt's claim about the incident being an accident, it was what happened afterwards that caused a further divide between the two countries during an already troubled period. Two days after the incident, Nasser's deputy supply minister, Ramzy Stino, was reportedly so anxious about Egypt's economic situation that he called on Battle to discuss wheat assistance. Battle, however, was in no mood to talk. He reportedly said to Stino, "This is absolutely an inopportune moment to go into any question of this sort with me."

Back in Washington, Saunders commented to Bundy, "Unfortunately, however, Saturday's plane incident raised Battle's blood pressure to the point he may have fallen into a booby trap . . . the Egyptians may have misread . . . [Battle's reaction] as a falt [sic] turndown."[17] Indeed, a few days later, on a train ride north of Cairo to give his annual speech at Port Said marking the anniversary of the 1956 Suez War, Nasser heard from his vehemently anti-American Prime Minister, Ali Sabri, that Battle's retort had been an "ultimatum" of sorts.[18]

Nasser responded by lashing out at the United States in his speech. He even criticized Battle by name, saying that the ambassador could go "drink from the sea"—an Egyptian euphemism for "go to hell." Nasser proudly proclaimed in his speech that the United States would never again be able to hold aid over his head. "We shall not sell our independence for 30, 40, 50 million pounds," he declared. "If the Americans think that they can give us some aid in order to come and dominate us and dominate our policy tell them 'we are sorry.'"[19]

It is possible that Nasser may have felt emboldened by the presence of the Soviet deputy prime minister at his side during the speech, who had headed a special mission to Cairo just to assure Nasser that the new regime in Moscow planned to honor and possibly increase the amount of aid that had been promised by Khrushchev in April. China, too, was showing interest in Nasser by issuing a $50 million interest free loan. There was no doubt, however, that Nasser was blaming the United States for all of his economic problems. The night before the speech, an unexpected visit to an American intelligence source from Nasser's chief of intelligence, Salah Nasir, confirmed that Nasser felt there had been a clear "deterioration in relations." The source noted that "Nasir's distress over the situation was clearly evident."[20]

Back in Washington, the administration immediately went into crisis mode after receiving news of the Port Said speech. Rusk, having been the first to learn of it right before a previously planned news conference for that same day, made an off-the-cuff remark to the press that "relationships are reciprocal." The question had been posed to him, whether the administration would immediately cut off PL 480 aid to Egypt as a result of Nasser's speech. Rusk said, "if relations are to be good, both sides must make important investments in those relationships." After the conference, he immediately put a gag order on any further comments to the press about the latest crisis. Anything said could be misperceived as inflammatory.[21]

As bad as the Port Said speech was, Rusk shot down the option of recalling Battle from Cairo. He told State officials that it had taken a significant amount of time to get Battle confirmed and settled in Cairo in the first place. Therefore, it made little sense to start the process over again.[22]

Later that day, a group of State officials gathered to discuss the situation. Talbot opened up the discussion by noting the press was more than likely going to misinterpret Rusk's response at the press conference as an indication of a coming confrontation between the administration and Nasser. "[We should] sit on our hands [instead]," he said. He thought it would be unwise to pull Nasser's aid since the Soviets seemed ready to step in at a moment's notice. The group agreed. It was necessary to continue existing aid to Nasser, but not to dole out any new aid—just like Komer wanted. However, another official said, "Take a look at the reverse of the coin, how much would we pay to dislodge the Soviets from an enhanced position in the Near East and Africa." He went on, "For all the vast Soviet investment, so far they have received few dividends. Their fortunes would look up if US-UAR [relations] deteriorate." He proposed giving new aid to Nasser in order to keep the Soviets from taking advantage of the situation. Talbot chimed in. He revealed to the group that "pro-West elements" in Nasser's government had reached out before the Mecom incident and said that Nasser was drifting toward Moscow. The only thing that could stop him, they said, was US aid. Whether these Egyptian officials had come to US officials on their own volition, or had been sent by Nasser, the sentiment remained the same: no matter what he said in public, Nasser seemed to need US support now more than ever. Regardless of the political situation, Egypt's economy was still on the brink of a collapse.[23]

After the meeting, Saunders sat down in his office to play out the ramifications of a rapid downward spiral in US-Egypt relations. "The problem now is to maintain our displeased posture without tampering with the big carrot [i.e., aid]," he wrote to Bundy. "Nasser is reacting à la Aswan [i.e., 1956] as if he expected us to pull the rug completely again."[24] Indeed, it was beginning to feel like Komer's prediction of such a scenario back in April, when Britain had done its best to pressure the administration to discontinue aid, was coming to fruition.

Komer also wrote to Bundy. "I fully realize [the] possible gathering Congressional storm, but I hope you agree that now is the time to play it cool." He pointed out that emotions had gotten a hold of both Battle and Nasser in the situation. He hoped to avoid any further escalation by letting cooler heads prevail.[25]

A few days later, it was New Year's Eve. Talbot and Davies went to Rusk's office late at night to discuss with him, among other things, US-Egypt relations. They too counseled letting cooler heads prevail. Since Nasser's speech, journalists had been approaching US officials for clues on how the administration planned to respond to the recent difficulties. But nothing concrete had yet been decided. Thus, the problem the three men considered was how to move forward with Nasser since his relationship with Battle was so strained. Talbot regretted sending Nasser an oral message after the library burning instead of a written letter. "Since some Arabs, including Nasser, regard an oral message as being sent from a senior to a lesser official, it is problematic whether we get a letter in response to the President's message," he said. But communication was vital to moving forward in the wake of the two incidents. He noted that Nasser could reach out via "long un-used" underground channels to get directly in touch with US officials, should he too feel the relationship had taken too fatal of a stumble. In fact, Talbot was told, Nasser already had.[26]

Indeed, Nasser appeared to privately feel that he had been duped by Sabri, who had more than likely played up the Battle-Stino conversation in order to rattle Nasser's cage before the speech at Port Said. In the days following the speech, dozens of Egyptian officials and private citizens reached out to various American sources to express how regretful Nasser was about his rhetoric.[27]

With this new information in hand, and still sitting in Rusk's office late on New Year's Eve, Talbot, Davies, and Rusk settled on a formula for dealing with the press. Talbot "planned to emphasize that while we could not have close relations with the UAR given some basic differences, our national interests require reasonably good working relations." Rusk wanted him to add "that there are people in the UAR and Arab world who are extremely concerned about relations between the US and UAR." Rusk was concerned about appearing too vulnerable to "UAR pressures," lest Nasser get "an exaggerated idea of his capabilities." He wanted Nasser to understand that he was on very thin ice.

The three men agreed to proceed cautiously in light of Johnson's objection to continuing any aid to Egypt. In the meantime, State was going to have the embassy in Cairo produce a study of Egypt's wheat situation, since a shipment under PL 480 was scheduled to depart in the coming weeks. They decided, however, to leave Egyptian officials in the dark for the time being. It was important not to publicly preempt Johnson's ability to make a decision on whether he wanted to move forward with any aid to Egypt. Nevertheless, they considered informing Johnson of an offer from Nasser to build a new library for the United States in Cairo, which they thought might soften him up to the idea of a reconciliation.[28]

"It would be *an grande geste* [a grand gesture]," wrote Komer to Bundy, earlier that same day. "It costs us nothing and would help calm down press furors." Indeed,

Rusk, Talbot, Davies, Battle, and Komer all thought it would be a good idea. They understood, however, that recent events made it impossible to proceed without Johnson's approval. Komer wrote, "[Rusk] thought President [Johnson] would want to clear this personally."[29]

Bundy gave his consent. Afterwards, Komer immediately sent a memorandum to Johnson entitled, "Handling Nasser in 1965." Foremost, he assured Johnson that Nasser wanted to avoid a break in diplomatic relations. Nasser had been misled about the Battle-Stino conversation by anti-American Egyptian officials, Komer pointed out. "What finally triggered his 23 December outburst was a highly colored report from his anti-US Supply Minister of an 'insulting' interview with our Ambassador [Battle] who allegedly delivered an ultimatum on US aid. His speech was a warning in typical Nasser style that he could and would get along without our food, if we pushed him too hard."

Komer attempted to put some pressure on Johnson, noting that Nasser was regretful in the aftermath of the speech because he knew that he needed America's aid. Of course, "unless we want to break with him," Komer rhetorically asked. "To do so, most of your Middle East experts are convinced, *would cost us more than we could gain*, and make 1965 a mighty troubled year in the Middle East. If we go to war with Nasser, we're less likely to lick him than to make him a hero."

However, there was congressional opposition to consider with any friendly approach to Nasser. "*How can we play Nasser in 1965 in a way that will keep the pot from boiling over, as well as defend your domestic flank?*" asked Komer with emphasis. His response was to: (1) send former Treasury Secretary Robert Anderson to Cairo as a personal envoy of Johnson's (Nasser liked Anderson); (2) explain to the American public that the administration could not "take food from the mouths of common people because of the mistake of their leaders"; and (3) hold off until summer 1965 (when the current PL 480 deal expired) any new aid to Egypt in order to satisfy congressional pressure to get tough on Nasser. Komer argued that such an approach could "forestall new confrontations like Vietnam." He added, "We've had four years of relative peace and stability in the Middle East, partly because of shifted footwork and occasionally swallowing our pride. Unless the domestic heat becomes unbearable, I sincerely urge the same for 1965."[30]

In conclusion, both State and Komer were telling Johnson to continue the existing aid agreement with Nasser, but to hold out any additional aid as a carrot to Nasser that he could eventually obtain with a demonstration of restrained behavior. Of course, such a strategy relied on Congress not standing in the way.

10

Congress Reacts

As fate would have it, the domestic heat soon did become "unbearable," as Komer predicted. In the wake of the Port Said speech, Congress started to interfere with the administration's ability to continue giving any aid to Nasser.

Shortly after New Year's, Kamel requested a meeting with Rusk. State wanted Rusk to say that the administration was moving ahead with the previously scheduled PL 480 shipments of wheat and flour. Komer sent over a gentle reminder to State that it needed to receive clearance from the White House first. "I favor this modest added investment on simple grounds that we're not going to be able to get things out of Nasser unless we're prepared to continue at least existing programs," Komer wrote to Bundy. "However, I'll clue you before any sign-off because I'm sure we as well as Rusk would want an LBJ nod." It was not quite clear yet whether Johnson would approve sending aid under the existing PL 480 agreement in light of his apparent frustration with Nasser in the wake of the Mecom and library burning incidents.[1]

Rusk now was firmly on board for continuing existing aid to Nasser as an immediate lifeline. And he was also prepared to testify to the Senate Foreign Relations Committee on the importance of maintaining the current aid shipments. Johnson, however, was preparing to make a statement to Congress on aid that was intended to launch an aggressive war against world hunger. He was planning to translate some of the sweeping reforms of his popular domestic program, the "Great Society," into a new and ambitious foreign policy initiative that would require him to have flexibility over dispensing aid. The problems with Nasser threatened to derail Johnson's big plans. This added to the uncertainty about the president's position on resuming aid shipments to Cairo.[2]

Komer, for his part, recognized there was an issue with sending aid to Egypt at the same time that Johnson was planning to make his statement to Congress—the inevitable backlash from giving aid to Nasser, in the wake of two back-to-back incidents, was sure to give Congress reason to oppose Johnson's new aid initiative. Rusk, however, had already made up his mind about the shipments. "Perhaps reacting to others who speak as he did only recently, SecState [Rusk] seems rather firmly signed on to continuing existing aid to Nasser, while holding off any new commitments," Komer wrote to Bundy. In other words, Rusk was suddenly taking the lead on the administration's policy toward Egypt.

With Rusk, strangely, in the driver's seat, Komer was temporarily out of the loop. Thus, when a PL 480 "advisory committee" made up of officials from AID and the Bureau of Budget planned to meet with congressmen about Johnson's aid initiative, and one of them indicated that he planned to bring up the issue of aid to Egypt at the congressional meeting, Komer was at a loss on how to advise the group. Instead, he recommended that they talk to Rusk. Komer wrote to Bundy, "Rusk must know a lot more about LBJ's views than I do, and has been carrying [the] job of explaining our UAR policy on [Capitol] Hill. I assume he'll say we're following [a] 'wait and see' policy, 'but please don't bind our hands.' Need we do more?"[3]

Notwithstanding his small attempt at playing the easygoing junior official, Komer could not leave the issue alone. He didn't like not being in the driver's seat of policy. The next day, he wrote again to Bundy. "Mac: The gathering Congressional storm over aid to the UAR seems to be reaching such proportions that our decision may be made for us if we're not careful. The finger-wagging in the Foreign Aid message (unless quietly counterpointed) may well be read on the Hill as *carte blanche*." Quite simply, Komer did not think Rusk was being strategic enough with Congress. Rusk could not steamroll congressional opposition to aid for Nasser and then expect Congress to grant Johnson the flexibility he sought on the following year's foreign aid budget.[4]

Johnson was already preparing for battle against Congress over foreign aid. His annual message to Congress about foreign aid stated that it was a president's job to determine the administering of it. The message ended with, "I call upon the Congress to join with me . . . and to provide the tools to do the job." Johnson didn't need the conflict with Nasser to add any additional trouble for him on Capitol Hill.[5]

"Perhaps Talbot and I are running too scared," Komer wrote to Bundy the day before the statement was to be delivered to Congress, "but when I checked my concern out with him he felt the same way. He's going to work on Rusk, but we both feel that the only effective way to halt the gathering storm is probably for the President himself to let us pass the word quietly that he doesn't want to be boxed in."

Komer noted that the current strategy not to discuss with Egypt any new aid had already made Nasser nervous enough to retreat from his aggressive stance at Port Said. "But if we lose control of our end of this delicate game and are forced to cut off his wheat (especially by public Congressional fiat) he'll react violently," wrote Komer. "I think you know I say this as a realpolitician, not a do-gooder; I just hate to see us fight battles we aren't going to win." Bundy wrote back, "Speak to me."[6]

Nonetheless, Komer was soon proven right: the administration was presented with legislation that threatened to cut off all aid to Egypt. Specifically, on January 26, a congressman from Illinois added an amendment to the 1965 appropriations bill. According to Komer, it stated that "no part of this money could be used to finance Title I sales to UAR for the rest of FY [fiscal year] 1965." The House of Representatives [henceforth House] approved the amendment by a vote of 204 to 177. The new legislation meant that the administration would not even be able to continue the existing PL 480 agreement, let alone consider any future aid agreements with Egypt. In other words, it threatened to undermine the entire basis of US-Egypt relations. Under the proposed legislation, which still needed to be approved in the Senate, there could be no economic incentives for Nasser in return for his moderation. This would effectively mean the end of the redirection strategy.

Talbot immediately paid a visit to Kamel to get a warning to Nasser. Nasser had to refrain from "violently" reacting, Talbot said. He reminded Kamel that the legislation was not yet a *fait accompli* since it still had to be approved by the Senate. Talbot emphasized that the Johnson administration firmly opposed the legislation. They would do everything in their power to stop it, he said.

After learning about the amendment, Komer wrote to Bundy: "Naturally, this comes at a lousy time . . . We can't afford to cut off aid to UAR just when we face an oncoming Jordan Waters and perhaps Congo crisis, but at the same time this is a hard one for the President to get out in front." Indeed, it had finally come down to a situation where Johnson would have to put his political relationships on the line in order to save Nasser.

To make matters worse, Talbot learned that the Senate was going to call for a vote soon, which reduced the amount of time the administration would have to quietly lobby against it. The odds were "2-1" against the administration, Komer told Bundy. He proposed having Rusk approach the senate majority leader, Mike Mansfield, who was a friend of Johnson's, and ask him to delay the vote in order buy time for the administration to launch its lobbying campaign. "This seems important enough for an LBJ call to Mansfield," Komer wrote.[7]

Things were heating up in Washington over Nasser in ways they previously hadn't under Kennedy. But, to make matters worse, in Cairo, Battle began to act in a way that threatened to undermine Komer's attempts to justify a continued relationship with Nasser.

To be sure, it had been nothing but difficulty upon difficulty for Battle as he attempted to transition to his new role as ambassador. Unlike Badeau, Battle did not speak Arabic. He also lacked a basic understanding of Middle Eastern history and culture. "I felt very deficient because of my lack of Middle East experience," Battle later recalled. Indeed, he had been woefully unprepared for the back-to-back crises that had brutally swept up US-Egypt relations into a maelstrom during the opening weeks of his arrival in Cairo.[8]

In addition to Battle's inexperience and the unexpected hardships, State wondered whether there was a problem with intelligence gathering in Cairo. "Through contacts with a few high-level officials (notably Nasser, Sabri, Sharaf, and Haikal) the Embassy has maintained good coverage . . . notably on government policies," went a memo written in the wake of the library burning. However, continued the memo, the embassy was lacking insight into the political dynamics within Nasser's inner circle. State wanted more information on "embryonic opposition movements" against Nasser and on the mood of the Egyptian people themselves. It also wanted a better grasp of military issues like troop movements to and from Yemen, missile production, and clandestine Egyptian operations in foreign countries. It was these gaps in intelligence, in particular, which was holding the administration back from formulating a more effective policy vis-à-vis Nasser, believed officials at State. Indeed, with such gaps it was impossible to know whether Egyptian officials really had been complicit in the library burning.

At the same time, the relationship between the United States and Egypt was so tenuous that State felt it had to move carefully in Cairo. "We consider it particularly important in Egypt that we engage in absolutely no political action or even preparation for some," went one memo. "In a country where our policies are suspect and our assets are so slender and insecure, it is essential to avoid any involvement in domestic affairs."[9]

Indeed, US-Egypt relations were so strained that Egyptian authorities took it upon themselves to check up on every officer in the US embassy in an effort to clamp down on the possibility of there being a member of staff having a dual role as a spy. Nasser had been somewhat suspicious of the embassy staff ever since an incident in 1962, when an Egyptian informant was discovered by the secret police and imprisoned for espionage. The Egyptian police later convinced the informant's mother and wife to visit the embassy on several occasions and demand "back pay," as a way to smoke out whether the informant actually had been in the employment of US intelligence handlers.[10]

"It is recommended that the Embassy proper should avoid chest-nut pulling," wrote State in the aftermath of the library burning. However, with idle time following the incidents came a barrage of policy recommendations from Battle that was at times contradictory, vague, and seemingly fuelled on emotional responses to the events that had played out since his arrival in Cairo. Eventually, Talbot decided to recall Battle for consultations in Washington. State informed Battle that they would quietly bring him home during Johnson's inauguration week in January. In reality, Talbot and Komer themselves planned to have an intervention with Battle, as they had initially done with Badeau in the first months of his service, which subsequently had turned the former ambassador into a more effective ally for their redirection strategy.[11]

"Luke's reporting has taken about a 180 [degree] turn since Xmas," wrote Komer to Bundy, "from tearful pleas not to wreck our UAR policy to stern warning not to be so soft." Komer confided in Bundy that he was losing "confidence" in Battle and the rest of the embassy. Indeed, the embassy had taken the rather unusual step of writing a joint minute with the British embassy. Together, US and British staffers urged Johnson to immediately cut off aid to Nasser. Komer called it "the last straw." He thought it was irresponsible for Battle to openly say and write such things without including an examination of "the costs of a break with Nasser." Indeed, in the midst of a conflict with Congress it was risky to have the ambassador openly echoing the anti-Nasser politicians in Washington.[12]

A meeting was tentatively scheduled so that Johnson also could have a word with Battle. Komer and Talbot wanted to set Battle straight first themselves, then have him meet with the president on record to show that the administration was unified behind Battle. However, the meeting with Johnson had to be cancelled at the last minute because he went to the hospital for stomach pain. Always plagued with unexpected difficulty, from his delayed confirmation to being a target of Egyptian propagandists, Battle was once again deprived of the legitimacy he so badly needed. A key aspect of Battle's trip to Washington had been the presidential meeting. Nevertheless, the embassy in Cairo wrote to State that Nasser, more than likely, was still going to want to meet with Battle upon his return to Cairo. Nasser was aware that Battle was in

Washington. And he would want to know what Johnson had to say about the situation on Capitol Hill.[13]

With Battle's meeting with Johnson getting cancelled, Komer proposed drafting a "carefully phrased" directive that would outline the topics the ambassador was allowed "to draw on" with Nasser. Komer wanted to be vague with Nasser. Indeed, the administration could not say one way or another whether Congress would succeed in shutting down the one element (aid) that had kept US-Egypt relations somewhat alive since Johnson had taken office. But it was important to give Nasser some hope. "If Nasser asks Luke about aid (which I doubt)," Komer wrote to Talbot, evidently disagreeing with the embassy that Nasser would even dare to raise the issue at such a fragile time in US-Egypt relations, "Luke could be authorized to say that the US intends to continue meeting [the] present commitments insofar as circumstances permit, but that the President did not discuss the details of aid policy with him."[14]

Komer's directive instructed Battle to paint Johnson as having his hands tied behind his back. He wanted to give Nasser just enough hope in order to put him on his best behavior. However, Komer also wanted to make it clear to Nasser that he was mostly to blame for the legislation. In other words, Komer once again was attempting to redirect Nasser from Washington:

> When you see Nasser you may draw on the following as appropriate. The President was quite specific on his desire to maintain a friendly relationship with the UAR if the US is given an opportunity to do so. He wanted Nasser to know personally that, just as he understands the importance of not affronting the dignity of other nations, he makes no bones about his feeling that countries like the UAR often seem to have a double standard about respecting the dignity of the US. After all, we didn't burn Nasser's library, nor did we tell him off publicly or privately.
>
> In the President's view, it is crucially important that foreign leaders not underestimate the impact of such developments as hostile speeches . . . In a democracy like the US, the top leadership must take fully into account popular and Congressional reactions to remarks and actions by foreign nations that simply cannot be explained away . . . .
>
> The President is fully aware of the many differences between US and UAR policies, particularly on Israel and the Congo. The more these issues crowd to the forefront, the more difficult it is to maintain a cooperative US/UAR relationship on bilateral issues . . . ..
>
> He feels that the efforts of President Kennedy and himself over the last four years are ample evidence that the US is interested in helping the UAR to grow and prosper. In fact, he thinks the ball is now in Nasser's court. But he wishes Battle to reassure Nasser, that within the limits of flexibility imposed by the current situation, we continue to desire a satisfactory relationship with the UAR on aid and other matters.[15]

Perhaps because Komer was attempting to put so many words into Johnson's mouth, Rusk got involved and took the unusual step of editing the directive himself. He rewrote it to sound much softer. In response, Komer wrote to an ally at AID,

William Gaud, "Bill: For your amusement this is what I proposed we say to Nasser. I dictated this in ten minutes Saturday night and three days later State came up with the mouse you saw. I gave up in disgust."[16] Indeed, nowhere in the final draft did it explicitly mention that Nasser was the one responsible for the current conflict or that he needed to moderate his behavior in order to fix the relationship. The final paragraph of the new version went:

> If Nasser raises the question of future aid, you may say that in your discussions in Washington you found hope that US/UAR relations would improve to permit the continuation of our cooperation. The President thinks that American actions of the last four years show the USG's keen interest in helping the UAR grow and prosper. He is sincere in his hope that we can resolve the differences which have arisen over the Congo and other matter and turn our attention to better understanding of each other's problems and further consolidation of our relationship.[17]

On January 27, Komer wrote to Bundy, "Since Rusk personally fiddled with attached, I'm not going to argue the case." He agreed with an addition by State letting Nasser know that Johnson personally opposed the limitations the House had placed on PL 480 aid to Egypt. "This will give him credit with Nasser even if Congress misbehaves," Komer wrote. Surprisingly, Johnson agreed too. "The President is determined to oppose this limitation," went the directive. However, at Komer's behest, a modest indictment of Nasser was included: "Clearly the actions of the UAR and the statement of its leaders can be major factors in determining the outcome of the Administration's efforts with Congress. The Congo is the most immediate issue now facing us." Nasser would now have some indication of Johnson's disagreement with Congress, which would hopefully help the Egyptian leader understand how crucial his next steps could be for the future of US-Egypt relations. It was at least a partial victory for Komer and his redirection strategy.[18]

Fortunately for all parties—Nasser and the Johnson administration—the administration soon won a major victory on Capitol Hill concerning the amendment to stop all aid to Egypt. On January 27, Rusk went to convince the Senate Foreign Relations Committee that Johnson needed maneuverability in order to be able to effectively deal with Nasser. In response, the Senate passed the amendment on February 4, but with an added proviso that Johnson could approve aid to Egypt under the existing PL 480 deal if he determined it was in the nation's "interest." Later that same day, Johnson gave a special news conference encouraging the House to adopt the same language that had been added into the Senate's version. Several days later, the House followed suit. To be sure, it had been a close call, but the administration won the flexibility it needed to be able to deal with Nasser.[19]

Everything was now in place to get relations between the two countries back on track. On February 1, Battle met with Nasser for one hour. It was the first time that the two of them had met since the Port Said speech. Battle began by saying that Johnson intended to have good relations with Egypt. Nasser too was apparently ready to move forward. As Battle reported, "At this point the President interrupted me and referred to the December 23 speech in a slightly embarrassed manner. He seemed to want to remove the speech from our relationship but without admission of error. He stated that nothing personal was intended . . ." Nasser then brought up aid. He said that he appreciated it, and hoped that it would continue. However, he added his "expressed requirement that the UAR be independent in its actions."

After Battle brought up the Congo situation, which then led him to mention the conflict with Congress over aid, Nasser again brought the conversation back to the Port Said speech. Nasser was truly sorry. He seemed to be relieved to hear that Johnson personally opposed the limitations Congress had sought to put on aid. "Those speeches every year by your Congress and your press," said Nasser, throwing up his hands in the air. "And I read all these articles by the correspondents," he added in reference to an article in the *New York Times* that claimed he was in control of Egypt's media. Earlier in the conversation, Battle had mentioned how the Egyptian press had been hostile toward Johnson and himself. "It is much better now than it was five or six year ago," Nasser said, "but you may not believe it."

Shortly thereafter, the meeting ended on amicable terms. At first impression, it seemed to represent a reset in Battle and Nasser's relationship. "President Nasser stated he hoped I was enjoying Cairo," wrote Battle to State. "I stated I had been fairly busy and laughed. He also laughed and said he hoped things would quiet down for us."[20]

Interestingly, the meeting had been somewhat of a success due to Rusk's avoidance of finger-wagging at Nasser. It was the first time that Komer had been overridden by Rusk on a matter of strategy with Nasser. The two men now agreed on the benefits of having good relations with Nasser. But Rusk, apparently, thought it necessary to tiptoe around Nasser, while Komer preferred to have an honest and open line with him. Constant communication was the main component of Komer's redirection strategy. It had worked under Kennedy and there was no reason it could not work under Johnson, he believed.

11

Komer's Gamble

One of the (many) challenges for US Middle East policy was balancing the needs of multiple allies who did not all get along. Giving weapons to one country could lead to another country making a similar request in order to maintain parity, thus leading to an arms race. This scenario is exactly what happened in 1965, when Jordan asked the Johnson administration for military equipment. Komer planned to deal with the request by offering the same equipment to Israel—Tel Aviv was skittish over the threats emanating from the Arab summits. But threatening to overturn a long-standing US policy not to contribute to the arms race in the Middle East put Komer at loggerheads with Rusk, who began to take even more interest in running Middle East policy.

Earlier that year, the King of Jordan, Hussein bin Talal, had come to the Johnson administration with a problem: the United Arab Command, the joint Arab military force that had been created at the first Arab summit, was requiring all member states to maintain certain arms capabilities. Jordan was being pressured to purchase equipment from the Soviet Union. Hussein, however, was a loyal American ally. He did not want to start doing business with Moscow. This put the administration in a quagmire: it could sell Jordan the equipment and contradict its policy to limit the arms race in the Middle East, or it could consent to Hussein doing a deal with Moscow. The equipment Hussein was asking for were American M-48 tanks and supersonic aircraft, which by no means were "defensive" in nature, and thus would surely lead to Israel augmenting its arms capabilities in response.

State reluctantly recommended to Johnson that he make the sale because it would keep Hussein from turning to Moscow. They saw good relations with Hussein and the other "conservative" monarchies as a "back-up plan" should Nasser ever decide to lash out at the United States. "If we cannot with dignity avoid a confrontation with the UAR, it has the power in the area to attack our special positions and to mobilize most if not all other Arabs into an anti-Israel front, thus effecting polarization since the Soviets would exploit the opportunity to give all-out support to the Arabs against Israel," went one report. It went on to identify that if Nasser had the ability to unite the Arabs and take punitive action against the United States, it would lead to catastrophic problems for America in the Middle East. The potential problems listed in State's report included, "cancellation of our MATs [military air traffic] and commercial airline rights, inspection of vessels transiting the Suez for radioactive hazards, stepped-up pressure against the Wheelus base agreement, removal of UNEF [United Nations Emergency Forces] from Egyptian soil with the consequent threat to the Israeli port of Eilat and of a direct Israeli-UAR military confrontation [which Nasser later did in the run-up to the 1967 War], furthering stirring up of other Arab states against Israel, etc." Once again, the administration found itself in a difficult position over a third-party issue, all because of Nasser.[1]

At an NSC meeting on February 1, which covered both Vietnam and the potential equipment sale to Jordan, the acting secretary of state, George Ball (Rusk was on a temporary leave of absence), laid out the situation for senior foreign policy advisers in the Johnson administration. Everyone then took turns explaining their positions. Some officials were in favor of the sale because they thought Jordan would inevitably get the equipment from the Soviet Union; others were opposed, because they thought the Israelis would demand that the Johnson administration give them a similar deal. After hearing out his advisers, Johnson came to a decision. "There is no problem in providing Jordan with the tanks they request," he said. But he added that they "should be told to buy their supersonic planes in Europe [like Israel had done via West Germany with the tanks]. If they do not wish to do so, then Mr. Talbot [who was leaving for Jordan] should cable us to this effect and await our reply. He should stay in Amman if it appears that the King is about to break off negotiations with us."

Ball pushed back. He pointed out that Hussein had been compelled to form closer relations with Nasser at the first Arab summit because of "attempts on his life"—which, at the time, everyone attributed to Egyptian agents. If Hussein could not get the planes from the United States, Ball said, he more than likely would turn to Moscow in order to maintain his improved relationship with Nasser. Myer Feldman countered that Jordan was a recipient of US aid. If Congress viewed the equipment deal as giving carte blanche to the Arab states to attack Israel, they might pass an amendment to pull Jordan's aid, he said. Instead, he recommended pressuring Nasser "to stop pushing King Hussein so hard."

Komer had another idea. "We should try out the hard-line on Hussein," he said, "not mentioning the supersonic planes in the beginning. Then if he insists, we should fall back and regroup . . . King Hussein is not going to jump the reservation at once. In trying to save Hussein we may kill him." Komer suggested a wait-and-see approach. If the United States rushed into a decision to sell planes to Jordan, then Israel would more than likely come to the administration looking for a similar deal. This could hurt Hussein even more than denying his request, Komer said, because Nasser could then say that Hussein "was a bad Arab" for buying the planes from the United States when he could have bought them from Moscow; especially if buying the planes from the United States led to Israel also acquiring them. "We should take this in two bites and only sell the planes if the Soviets make a firm offer to do so," Komer advised.

The vice president, Hubert Humphrey, agreed with Komer. He reminded the group that an arms sale to Jordan had the ability to sabotage their hard work on Johnson's foreign aid bill. "King Hussein is on the US dole," he said. "If we sell him supersonic planes, we will have all hell to pay. The sale of modern tanks we could possibly get away with but the sale of supersonic would create an impossible situation." Johnson seemed to agree with both Komer and Humphrey. He turned to Talbot and said, "Mr. Talbot, before the MIG's [Soviet planes] arrive in Jordan, please call us." In other words, it was a green light to take the situation in "two bites" as Komer suggested. Talbot would start with the tanks—supersonic planes were off the table for now.[2]

Two days later, however, Johnson began to have cold feet about selling any equipment to Jordan. His sudden reluctance came after a phone call with Ball on February 3, who informed Johnson that the Senate had officially adopted the more conciliatory language of the aid amendment (see Chapter 10). Johnson immediately replied, "not to let Talbot go and make any deal." Talbot was no longer even allowed to offer the tanks. "This is a very explosive thing," Johnson said to Ball. "We can never get anything in the Congress again unless we are careful."[3]

After learning about Johnson's sudden reversal, officials from State and the White House combined their efforts to persuade him to reconsider. Two days later, their efforts were a success and Johnson gave in.[4] Given the uncertainty of the situation, it would have been wise not to unduly rock Johnson's boat. Komer, however, had an idea. And he couldn't resist bringing it to Johnson.

On February 6, Komer wrote to Johnson. He observed that a deal with Hussein was necessary in order to keep "the Soviets and UAR out" of Jordan. However, he also encouraged Johnson to authorize a similar deal for Israel. Maintaining Israel's ability to fight the Arab states was necessary in order to keep the Arab states from feeling like they could attack Tel Aviv at will, Komer argued. A war like that would require the United States "to step in and to stop it." He added, "Since this basic policy reversal on our part (from avoiding [arms] sales to making them) is probably inevitable, there's a case for [also] making it [to Israel] now!"

Komer proposed privately informing Nasser about the two deals, lest news of a possible US arms deal with Israel leak. "I personally favor an approach to Nasser if only to tell him what we plan to do," Komer wrote. "But not before we get Hussein signed on. Then nothing will be lost from trying to convince Nasser not to scream." Komer offered to go to Israel himself to sell the idea of a dual arms deal. At the very least, he thought it was important to send a delegation to Israel to temper their reaction to Hussein's deal. He added that if the delegation to Israel was "authorized to offer arms sales," the plan to sell equipment to Jordan without upsetting Israel "could succeed." Jack Valenti and Bill Moyers, two close advisers to Johnson, got a hold of the proposal. They agreed with Komer, which likely helped convince Johnson to let him go to Israel.[5]

Before leaving for Israel, Komer excitedly walked Bundy (who was in Vietnam) through his thinking. "It gradually dawned on me that we were three-quarters pregnant anyway. If Hussein accepted our package he'd have to tell [the] UAC [United Arab Command] in Cairo; once it then came out that [the] US [is] selling [arms] to Jordan, we'd be trapped." In order to manage Nasser's reaction to the arms sale to Israel, Komer proposed to Bundy that a letter be written from Johnson to Nasser, as well as sending a respected emissary to Egypt like Robert Anderson, who was a good friend of Nasser's. Komer, however, urged waiting to do either of those things until after Hussein agreed to a deal that only included tanks.[6]

This was another one of Komer's multistep plans. He hoped to conduct two arms deals that would simultaneously appease Jordan and Israel, while keeping Nasser from lashing out over the sale to Israel.

On February 7, Talbot met with Hussein for more than two hours at his palace in Aman. Hussein insisted that he needed the supersonic planes too. Talbot reported to Washington: "On non-availability of US supersonic aircraft, King [Hussein] contented himself with [the] quiet assertion that if Western European aircraft could have done the job he would not have troubled [the] USG with [a] request for American aircraft."[7]

After much back-and-forth, however, and days filled with long conversations between the two men, Hussein finally gave in. He tentatively agreed to buy tanks from the United States and to look into buying planes from France. Now all the Johnson administration needed was for Israel to accept the deal and agree to keep silent about it. However, there was a problem: in October, several West German newspapers had leaked details of the secret tank deal with Israel. Now the German chancellor was announcing that his government was going to cancel the sale, even though only 60 out of the expected 150 tanks had been delivered. In mid-February, Israeli officials asked Komer, now in Tel Aviv, whether the Johnson administration would consider directly selling them the remaining 90 tanks.[8]

Once again, it was Nasser stirring up a third-party issue that would impact US-Egypt relations. Evidently, Nasser had found out about the West Germany-Israel tank deal at the end of January. In response, he began to dangle Arab recognition of East Germany as a way to exert power over the West Germans. At a meeting with the West German ambassador, Nasser reportedly said, "If the arms deal with Israel continues we shall reconsider our whole position and shall definitely recognize East Germany." Nasser added that he had invited the East German leader, Walter Ulbricht, to visit Cairo in late February in order to discuss details. West Germany was reportedly in a panic. And Israel was fuming about not receiving all of its tanks.[9] Johnson, for his part, felt bad about the whole situation, saying to Rusk over the phone, "I got him [the Chancellor of West Germany] into a jam with the Jews and I just feel terrible about it."[10]

Having returned to Washington after what he had hoped would be a quick trip to Israel to tell them in person about the arms deal with Jordan, Komer had to go back and negotiate a more complicated arms deal with the Israelis. This time, however, Komer was to be joined in Tel Aviv by Averell Harriman, a veteran diplomat who was sent by Johnson as a high-profile envoy to sweeten the negotiations. Nasser had managed to complicate an already complicated situation. Israeli officials were not happy about Hussein getting tanks, and they certainly were not happy that Nasser always seemed to get his way—which, in their eyes, was confirmed by the US arms deal with Jordan. As Komer wrote to Johnson, "The embattled Israelis regarded our Hill fight to continue aid to Nasser as a capitulation after he thumbed his nose at us, burned our library and shot down our plane." What the Israelis needed was some reassurance from Johnson that he was still their friend too.[11]

Rusk, now back from his leave of absence, was not happy about the whole situation. He unexpectedly took a hard-line approach to the arms negotiations with Israel. Specifically, he saw it as an opportunity to force Israel's hand on a number of issues that had bothered him for quite some time. For one thing, he wanted Israel to agree to start handling all of its disputes with the Arab states over the Jordan River at the UN, rather than resorting to unilateral military action. He was especially worried that US arms would be used by Israel to attack the Arab water diversion projects, which were now being built as a way to deprive Israel of the Jordan waters. Moreover, Rusk wanted Israel to officially accept IAEA safeguards for its nuclear reactor at Dimona—which meant getting Israel's consent to regular inspections. Komer, for his part, was less than pleased with the more difficult negotiations he suddenly found himself in—which was largely due to Rusk. Komer observed to Bundy that the deal Rusk wanted for Israel was looking "lighter" than the one for Jordan.[12] The ambitious attempt to appease both Israel and Jordan had reached an unexpected roadblock.

While the Israeli part of Komer's multistep plan had temporarily stalled, there was still the issue of getting Nasser to keep silent about the potential equipment sale to Israel. State jumped the gun and drafted a letter to Nasser to explain the respective equipment deals with Israel and Jordan. But Komer did not approve of this strategy. He firmly put his foot down, writing "Mr. President, this draft letter to Nasser is not very good. In fact, its brisk tone seems more likely to arouse a violent reaction than the reverse . . . Therefore, suggest you remand it for redrafting." Komer pointed out there was no urgency to send a letter to Nasser before both agreements had been finalized with Israel and Jordan. Komer not so modestly reminded the president that strategy was everything when executing policy. It was good to be open with Nasser, but doing so at the wrong time could sabotage everything.[13]

Indeed, the execution of the plan to keep Nasser calm about the equipment sales was falling apart. While Komer had acted on his original idea to have Robert Anderson meet with Egyptian officials and smooth things over with Nasser, it fell through at the last minute. The meeting was to take place in Beirut, but Nasser apparently felt that the presence of his top officials in Lebanon could not be concealed. Komer wrote to Johnson, "An added reason for letting this one [the letter to Nasser] slide for the moment is that we don't want to get Nasser's wind up until we get King Hussein and the Israelis signed, sealed, and delivered."[14]

Indeed, Komer's concern about timing turned out to be well-founded, as his negotiations in Israel went on for three weeks. When Harriman joined Komer in Tel Aviv at the end of February, rumors began to fly that there was a high-profile mission to discuss putting a NATO base in Israel. Back in Washington, Walt Rostow and Bill Polk began to worry about keeping Nasser in the dark any longer, lest the rumors get out of hand. "Polk has convinced WWR [Walt Whitman Rostow] that time is running out on us quickly that Nasser may pop off any day in a way he'll find it difficult to back away from later," wrote Saunders to Bundy. "He thinks it essential we get back to thinking about an emissary to Cairo."[15]

Nevertheless, it was not until mid-March that Komer finally completed an agreement with Israel. It was called a "Memorandum of Understanding." In return for Israel's promise not to interfere with US equipment sales to Jordan and an agreement not to be the first country to go nuclear in the Middle East, the United States promised to oppose aggression from the Arab states against Israel, sell twenty-four planes (if they could not be purchased from any Western European countries), and sell to Israel on generous credit terms any of the equipment it sold to Jordan. Most importantly, the administration committed to ensuring that Israel received the rest of the tanks from the aborted West German deal.[16]

Reaching the agreement had cost substantial time and energy, and further strained the already tenuous relationship between Komer and Rusk. On March 13, Komer wrote to Johnson, "While I may be prejudiced (and also too tired to see the matter in the round), I think we finally came out all right—and without giving more than we'd have to give sooner or later anyway to our Israeli friends."[17] Komer, however, privately confided in Bundy that perhaps he had been too confident about his ambitious multistep plan to appease Israel, Jordan, and Nasser all at the same time. "You may recall my prediction about six weeks of haggling needed to get [the] Israelis signed on to [the] Jordan arms sale," he wrote. "However, I was wrong in assuring President [Johnson] that adding [the] major concession of [a] willingness [to] make direct sales [to] Israel too[,] at long last[,] would permit [a] quick agreement. Perhaps this was possible if negotiation[s] [had been] confined [to] these two issues."

Indeed, the negotiations had not been confined to only those issues because Rusk had insisted on a more comprehensive arrangement that dealt with several long-standing issues at once. By proposing to sell arms to Israel in the first place, Komer had reversed a long-standing policy not to sell American arms in the Middle East—a policy that Rusk had always strongly supported. If the Johnson administration was going to reverse this long-standing policy, then Rusk believed it was only fair to maximize the number of concessions the United States received from Israel in return.[18]

Now that an agreement had been reached with Israel, and Jordan agreed to sign its deal for the tanks, it was time to brief Nasser. Komer compared the situation to the 1962 sale of Hawk missiles to Israel when Kennedy had sent an emissary to Nasser in order to temper his reaction. "Nasser may still blow up," Komer wrote to Johnson, "but a high level approach to him will at least reduce this risk and at any rate pressure him from claiming that we're acting behind his back."

Komer proposed sending a "friendly but not apologetic" letter from Johnson, and having Battle explain the details of the dual arms sales to Israel and Jordan in person, in order to avoid any written record that could be leaked. "This protects you," Komer wrote to Johnson. Though he added for good measure, "we strongly doubt Nasser would violate your confidence lest he close up a useful channel. He never has before."

Komer carefully described to Johnson his plan for dealing with Nasser: "The letter has been carefully drafted to give Nasser the minimum number of handles for response. Its length is both to make the best case for arms to Israel and to avoid highlighting this too starkly. It gently tells him that sales to Jordan and Israel are exceptions to our continuing policy . . . It also renews our offer to explore mutual arms controls as a better road, and ends up by saying we hope to continue economic cooperation if he'll let us do so." Komer encouraged Johnson to sign the letter immediately. "The letter is on the green *for signature*, so you don't have to approve it twice," he stressed.[19]

Johnson, however, did not approve Komer's letter. He thought it was too long. Instead, he called in Bundy and had him dictate a shorter one, which did not include all of Komer's original points. Noticeably absent was any reference to economic cooperation. Johnson agreed with Komer that Battle should be the primary person dealing with Nasser on the arms issue. The new letter went, "You will, I know, share my view that the best way to deal with difficulties of this kind is to discuss them man to man, with full respect for each other's rights and responsibilities. I have therefore asked Ambassador Battle to seek an appointment with you to bring this personal message and to discuss with you the issues of current importance in the Near East that concern us both." The letter was as vague as possible to ensure the details of the complicated arms sales didn't leak and undercut Johnson's well-known opposition to arms proliferation. Indeed, Johnson made it clear in the letter that he was still committed to arms control: "The problem which needs this kind of discussion is that of the best way of dealing temperately and responsibly with the growing arms race in the Middle East."[20]

Komer begrudgingly went along with Johnson and Bundy's rewrite. However, he still attempted to exert control over State's talking points for Battle. "Here is a much more persuasive version of Battle's talking points," Komer wrote to Bundy, "designed to maximize the incentive to Nasser not to break crockery [fine china]. I left in most of State's wording, simply to avoid undue breaking of crockery at last minute. I anticipate no trouble with State, if we just send this back as a revision [the] White House wanted." This time, however, State also refused to implement all of Komer's points. Komer was losing a degree of control over both policy and strategy.[21]

On March 24, Battle met with Nasser for over an hour. Nasser had just been reelected as the president of Egypt and was in a good mood. He thanked Battle for giving him advance notice of his "movements and intentions" to brief him on the Harriman mission to Israel. "He so strongly implied that if he had not received my message his speech might have been different," Battle reported.

Battle began by handing Nasser the letter from Johnson. Nasser read it two times "with great care." As he set the letter down, and was about to say something, Battle politely interrupted, asking him to wait until Battle explained everything. "I went very slowly," Battle reported, "watching him closely as I proceeded."

After Battle finished explaining the details of the dual arms deals with Israel and Jordan, and spoke also about the previous deal between West Germany and Israel, Nasser said, "This gives me a good opportunity to talk about a number of things." He admitted to Battle that he already knew about Israel's tank deal with West Germany. He alluded to the fact that it had caused the current conflict with West Germany. Nasser, however, insisted that he had invited Ulbricht to visit Cairo on his own. There had been no prodding from Moscow, he said.

Nasser wanted more details about how the United States planned to handle the cancelled deal between West Germany and Israel. "I suppose you are now going to match all the tanks they haven't delivered," he said. "We don't know how many were promised or delivered although our military consider that 80 percent have been received." Battle followed his strict instructions from State to make clear to Nasser that Israel was not getting any special favors on the pricing of the equipment it could purchase—the price would be the same that was offered to all buyers. It was important for Nasser to feel that this was a one-time affair, and that the United States had not made the decision lightly—it was not about choosing one side over the other. Nasser, however, lamented the fact that the United States was contributing to the arms race in the Middle East at all. "You have told me you are going to sell arms to Israel. The pressure from my military will be to equal its arms," he said. "The pressure from my military resulting from the German deliveries, even though the amount is uncertain, had already been forthcoming." Battle replied that now the United States and Egypt needed to work together to reduce the "unfortunate" arms race in the Middle East. Nasser had no comment.

Despite the tense circumstances of the meeting, it went better than expected. According to Battle, "The conversation . . . could not have been more cordial. His tone was friendly, warm, and more in sorrow than in anger (after he learned of our intentions). The only real emotion came with respect to the tank sale by the Germans."[22] Miraculously, Komer's plan had worked: Jordan was able to buy the equipment it needed from the United States, Israel now felt more secure about its relationship with the United States, and Nasser responded well to the Johnson administration being transparent with him. For the first time in a long time, the administration had achieved a major victory. It was beginning to look like the United States was on the verge of reaching the balanced position in the Middle East that Komer had fought so long and hard to achieve.

12

Johnson's Reluctance

With progress vis-à-vis Nasser on the horizon, Komer renewed his efforts to convince Johnson of the merits of giving aid to Egypt. Once again, however, Congress was standing in the way with its dislike of Nasser.

In the middle of the six weeks of arms negotiations with Israel and Jordan, Egyptian officials sought a resumption of PL 480 aid, which had been temporarily placed on hold during the problems with Congress over the library burning. US officials had been too consumed with the Israel-Jordan arms negotiations to properly deal with the request. Battle, however, took the time to write to State that he saw "another Aswan Dam" coming—albeit on a minor scale—if the administration did not resume aid to Egypt.[1]

State replied to Battle to keep the situation frozen (as best he could) until the administration was able to brief Nasser on the arms sale to Israel. In the meantime, Egypt could fulfill its corn requirements by obtaining credit from the federally subsidized Credit Commodities Corporation (CCC)—which was essentially a loan that needed to be repaid in three years, but was still better than the standard market rates and market repayment period of eighteen months. Also, nongovernmental charity agencies were authorized to begin planning for a program that provided free school lunches to 3.4 million Egyptian children, and US embassy officials were authorized to discuss with Egyptian officials preliminary plans for spending US holdings of Egyptian pounds received from PL 480 sales—a portion of which the United States was contractually obligated to spend on development projects. "This at least puts us in a position to say, 'yes', or 'not now,'" wrote Saunders to Bundy on March 10, "[and] to permit current business to continue while reserving our two big political cards—the $37 million and a new agreement." Indeed, $37 million of Title I PL 480 aid from the existing agreement remained untouched. It had been frozen since Nasser's Port Said speech, and Johnson had not yet authorized its release. Johnson was reluctant to clash with Congress again.[2]

In light of Johnson's hesitation to resume PL 480 aid, State pushed for moving forward with CCC sales. They were typically seen as less controversial and did not require approval from Congress. Saunders wrote to Bundy that State saw CCC sales "as a low-key signal to Nasser that we're still in business[,] to keep him from setting us up too readily beside his West German target." Surprisingly, Bundy shot down the idea. He didn't explain his reasons, but perhaps he too was reluctant to reopen the conflict with Congress over aid to Egypt. "They [the Egyptians] can appeal to LBJ if they want," Bundy wrote.[3]

Saunders disagreed with Bundy. He immediately wrote to Komer that Bundy was turning something routine into a higher level political issue. Komer replied that he too disagreed with Bundy's decision. But he was heading to London for a week and did not have time to do anything about it.[4]

The situation stewed for a few more weeks without Komer involved to move things along. In late March, however, after learning of the promising meeting between Battle and Nasser about the Israeli arms deal, Komer jumped back into the fray and attempted to get Bundy on board for CCC sales. He wrote to Bundy that both State and AID were "itching" to go ahead with a $10 million credit for Egypt. "They feel it would be a good follow-up signal to Nasser's mild reaction to Battle's pitch," he wrote. Komer reasoned to Bundy that a sale on "slightly softer than normal commercial terms," did not categorize as "aid" per se. Bundy still refused.[5]

Meanwhile, Egypt's economic situation continued to rapidly decline. On March 29, Battle reported a "private personal meeting" he had with Kaissouni, who paid him a visit to say that Egypt was facing its most serious food shortage to date. Kaissouni confided in Battle that Egypt had only a month's supply of wheat left. Battle replied that PL 480 was out of the question for the time being. However, he took the unauthorized step of mentioning a possible CCC deal. Kaissouni said that Egypt also had a cash flow shortage, so taking out another loan, as required for a CCC sale, would not work. A few days later, however, Kaissouni returned and inquired about the terms of a CCC sale. Since Battle was still unauthorized to make any deals on his own (indeed his authority was still diminished due to his earlier outburst concerning the cold treatment of Nasser in Washington), he said he would immediately make inquiries with State.[6]

Back in Washington, Komer used the telegram to try to convince Bundy about the merit of a CCC sale. He wrote with emphasis, "Luke [Battle] necessarily had to be pretty unforthcoming with key UAR economic minister Kaissouni. This worries me— we want to keep [the] UAR on a short tether, *but not make Nasser think he's lost the US so [that he] might as well bash us over [the] arms to Israel!*" In other words, Komer wanted to be able to give something to Nasser in order to keep him quiet about the Israeli arms sale.[7]

Bundy now better understood Komer's thinking. But it was not him who had held up the CCC sales, it was Johnson. Komer immediately wrote to Johnson: "We'd be chary were it not that Nasser reacted very mildly when we told him about limited US arms sales to Israel. While this may be only the lull before the storm, it would make life a lot easier for us if he kept quiet. Therefore, State and our Ambassador see the CCC offer as a small and low key signal that we're still interested in doing business if he's a good boy." But Johnson remained reluctant to give anything to Nasser. He feared doing so would lead to another dispute with Congress and would affect his ability to gain control over foreign aid. He put a check on the line next to "Disapprove" and wrote "see me."[8]

A few days later, Komer had a short meeting with Johnson and made his best case for helping Nasser. It was a productive meeting: Johnson was somewhat convinced. He gave Komer permission to map out a strategy for resuming aid to Nasser. Komer could study the situation and come up with a convincing argument for making the CCC deal—but that was all, for the time being. "This will do for now," Komer wrote to Bundy, "and I'm organizing a new look at the $37 million Title I commitment [i.e., PL 480]."⁹

With a yellow light from Johnson, Komer chose to move quickly before it turned red again. He had little regard for slow moving bureaucratic procedure. He wanted to push Johnson to endorse the CCC option while he had him somewhat interested. On April 1, Komer drafted a memo to Johnson to convince him of the merits of a CCC sale. He stressed that since the CCC was technically a "financing agent," the administration would have no problem justifying what was merely the facilitation of a "*private dollar sale.*" "*It isn't aid*," Komer stressed. Indeed, the way it worked was a private American supplier sold food to Egypt under a financial guarantee from a private US bank in case Egypt failed to repay.

Komer reasoned that a CCC sale was not even "much of a carrot for Nasser." In 1964, State had offered on two occasions to sell wheat to him on CCC credit. Both times they had been rebuffed since it was not the type of aid Nasser preferred. He only wanted PL 480.

In the draft memo, Komer also reminded Johnson that a simple credit agreement did not require a press release from the Department of Agriculture, which would mitigate the chances of Congress even getting involved in the matter. In other words, there did not have to be a large battle over CCC, which is what Johnson feared most.

State and AID recommended telling a few friendly members of Congress about the deal anyways. That way, if news of it leaked out, it would be possible to argue after the fact that the deal had been processed through proper channels, and not done to skirt congressional opposition over aid to Egypt.

"We are living on pins and needles lest Nasser blow the whistle on US arms sales to Jordan and Israel," Komer argued. "Even a minor gesture like the above could do a lot to keep alive Nasser's hope that he can still do business with the US." In Komer's eyes, the likely consequence of leaving Nasser out to dry, during a serious economic crisis, was that he would go public about Johnson's arms sale to Israel; it was too great a risk. "Once he decides he can't [get aid], we're in for a blow," Komer wrote. "In fact, one problem is that the above gesture is too piddling to accomplish much. The real test will come over the remaining $37 million in Title I PL 480."¹⁰

No doubt, it was a strongly argued memo. But Komer sat on it for six days before sending it to Johnson. First, he wanted to test the waters on Capitol Hill, albeit without raising too many waves for Johnson, since he technically had not approved such an approach. In the meantime, Komer showed the draft memo to Bundy: "Mac: Here's [the] most convincing re-argument on [a] $10 million CCC sale to UAR I can think up." Larry O'Brien, Johnson's adviser on congressional relations, had suggested to Komer that he get in touch with at least six members of Congress. "Should I?" Komer asked Bundy. "It's a lot of sweat for a piddling signal." Bundy replied: "Yes, with O'Brien. What it is *not* of sweat for is the President's own judgement, and the more sweat now, the less later." In other words, if Johnson had more information at his disposal about how Congress would react to a CCC sale, he was more likely to approve it.¹¹

With Bundy's support, Komer set himself to writing a "congressional strategy on the UAR." On April 3, he sent it to Douglas McArthur II, assistant secretary of state for legislative affairs (and nephew of the famous military general), to get the approval of the congressional experts at State. Komer planned a quiet, yet aggressive sell of the CCC deal on Capitol Hill. He wrote up as his main talking point for Congress: "An essential ingredient in the US bag of tricks to deal with the upcoming ME [Middle East] crisis is some room to maneuver with Nasser, particularly some carrots to dangle before him as visible evidence that it is still possible to get some US support if he behaves reasonable." To be sure, Komer was planning to pitch these legislators the same policy and strategy that he had spearheaded under Kennedy: promising aid to Nasser in order to redirect him on issues that were in America's interest.[12]

On April 6, Komer updated Bundy to let him know that he and McArthur were going to "sound out key [congressional] leaders on aid to [the] UAR." Komer worried their efforts would be ineffective without Johnson's support. Indeed, at the time, the House Foreign Affairs Subcommittee on Near Eastern Affairs was entertaining no less than eight "anti-Nasser amendments." In Komer's words, these were "library burning gimmicks." The chairman of the subcommittee, Lawrence Fountain, privately admitted to Komer that he too was feeling pressure to introduce an anti-Nasser amendment—though it would be a more "innocuous" one intended to "fob" off the more aggressive ones.

What Komer needed on Capitol Hill was clout. He wrote to Bundy, "Gaud and Macomber [administrators at AID] say we could win on the Hill if LBJ would only authorize us to say: 'The President wants room to maneuver on this Nasser affair, just as he insisted last January. So please don't force him to fight all over again, and twist arms to defeat another series of nuisance amendments.'" Komer asked Bundy to get more involved. He wanted Bundy to mention Komer's efforts at his weekly Tuesday lunch-meeting with Johnson.

Komer was getting increasingly concerned about leaving Nasser high and dry on his economic problems; especially when he had the ability to sabotage the dual arms agreements with Israel and Jordan. Komer stressed to Bundy, "Mac, believe me when I stress the real depth of my conviction that *we've got to have some room to maneuver with Nasser if we're going to avert a major crisis in the Middle East.*" He added, "I may not know my Congress but I do know my Arabs."

To give Bundy an example of Nasser's ability to sabotage the arms agreements, Komer brought up a recent telegram from the US embassy in Libya. Evidently, when the US ambassador briefed the Libyan prime minister about the arms deals, the latter replied, "if *the other Arabs raised cain about this, even King Idris would be unable to let* ... *[you] stay at Wheelus.*" This was said in spite of the fact that Idris allegedly wanted the United States to remain in Libya. As for "other Arabs," Komer wrote, "read Nasser, whose propaganda machine dominates the Arab world."

Komer described the CCC sale to Bundy in terms of a Kennedy-like move on foreign policy. It was a way to get in front of a potential crisis with Nasser, he argued, rather than being forced into the difficult position of dealing with one later on. "So preventive diplomacy now is cheap at the price," he wrote to Bundy, "*and worth the President's effort.*" Komer added as a personal aside: "You know I'm tough-minded when we have to fight. But I'd rather pay blackmail to avoid it just now, when so many other problems crowd our plate."[13]

No doubt, Komer was getting desperate; he was being treated like a Cassandra. That same day, he wrote a second memo to Bundy: "Mac, I'm pressing the panic button on aid to UAR. I'm not fighting the problem; in fact I'm prepared to go join the battle if only LBJ will let me, and give us a little ammo." With so much pressure from Komer, Bundy gave in: he would ask Johnson to quietly back Komer's approach on Capitol Hill.[14]

The next day, Komer sent Johnson the earlier memo he had drafted on the merits of a CCC sale. After six days of limited congressional lobbying, he was able to add to it that he had already received a "favorable reaction" from at least one congressman. It was apparently enough for Johnson to give Komer the green light to approach Congress in his name. Johnson replied, "Bob, see that MacArthur, O'Brien, Ball and Co. check with all [the] appropriate chairman and leaders before we move. Then give me [the] results at once." It was a step in the right direction.[15]

The next day, Komer wrote to O'Brien to let him know that he had received Johnson's permission to proceed more aggressively on Capitol Hill. Komer wanted to move quickly to make up for lost time. He wrote to O'Brien, "Our sense is that we ought to move fast unless you think we should handle the matter otherwise."[16]

Komer immediately went to Capitol Hill himself, where he received mostly positive responses. On April 9, Komer briefed Johnson on his progress. A few of the congressmen wanted to wait until after the House was done marking up the 1966 aid bill in order to avoid prompting more anti-Nasser congressmen to introduce amendments into the bill that could potentially restrict aid to Egypt. The Senate had already settled on the language of a symbolically restrictive amendment on aid to Egypt. It was similar to the one that had been introduced in January, which gave Johnson the power to use his discretion on foreign aid. However, the House was still undecided. A number of congressmen who were friendly to the administration were continuing to fend off anti-Nasser amendments.

Komer suggested to Johnson that they keep Nasser in a holding pattern for a few weeks longer, until the House was done marking up the bill. The only potential problem, Komer pointed out, was that a decision on the remaining $37 million of PL 480 aid would also have to be delayed. This was an issue because the existing PL 480 agreement was set to expire on June 30 and there was not yet a new agreement to take its place. Presumably, Johnson was fine with waiting (indeed, he was never in a rush when it came to dealing with Nasser). Meanwhile, Komer had continued leeway to continue lobbying on Capitol Hill in order to ensure that congressional support for a CCC sale was ironclad.[17]

On April 14, Komer wrote again to Johnson. This time he was able to report that he had received all of the necessary sign-offs from congressional leaders and the chairmen of the relevant committees. "All are willing to play ball," he wrote. "We and State see urgency in proceeding with this private signal, given the continued leaks about likely US arms sales to Nasser's Arab enemies as well as Israel." He added, "We doubt the UAR will really be interested, so [we] see this as chiefly a means of buying time." Komer added that he and State managed to get a congressman to introduce "relatively painless language" into the aid bill that called for suspending aid "to countries which don't take adequate measures to protect US property." It was essentially the same innocuous amendment that had been passed in the Senate.

Having now possibly steamrolled Johnson's fears about making a CCC sale, Komer decided it was time to push him on authorizing the remaining $37 million in PL 480 aid—which Komer now believed was more important than the CCC sale. Time was running out to get the aid considered, vetted, and approved before the June 30 deadline. Komer wrote to Johnson, "[Nasser] clearly sees the $37 million as the real test of whether he can any longer get any cheap US food, which is his chief incentive not to cause us undue trouble."[18]

Ironically, after all his hard work on Capitol Hill, Komer was no longer focusing on the CCC sale. A CCC sale required the administration to bring in a private bank as a guarantor for the loan, which Komer realized would take too long (if it was at all possible) given the difficult political environment surrounding Nasser. Indeed, one congressman had offered his support for CCC sales only on the condition that it required no contingent liability from the federal government. However, Komer still needed Johnson to approve the CCC sale so that he could buy more time to work out a strategy for the $37 million. "All we must do is tell [the] UAR that any CCC credit sale would be dependent upon availability of private guarantees," he wrote to Bundy. Komer described how such a process would work: "[Department of] Agriculture gives a loan to a US firm (say Cargill) which in turn gives a loan to the foreign buyer after getting a guarantee from a private US bank. Thus, the US firm or US bank would take the rap in case of default." The federal government would merely play the role of financier. Komer proposed contacting Chase Manhattan Bank, which was ironic given Nasser's earlier organization of an Arab boycott against the bank.

Komer stressed to Bundy that Johnson needed to weigh in quickly. "Mac: Here's the report the President asked for on UAR credit sale. Hope you'll make it night reading; the longer we wait the more we're asking for trouble."[19]

However, Johnson continued to hesitate about giving anything to Nasser, whether it be through a middle man, in the case of the CCC sale, or the federal government, in the case of the $37 million. He avoided Komer's memo. "Do we need LBJ's approval before we even say we'll even 'consider' CCC?" an exasperated Komer asked Bundy on April 16, two days after the report had been submitted to the President. He wanted anything, no matter how small, that could give Nasser reason to have faith in Johnson. "If you've been unable to reach LBJ, couldn't we go this far?" Komer asked. Indeed, it was a Friday, and Talbot was scheduled to meet with Nasser on Sunday. Komer desperately wanted Talbot to be able to deliver good news to Nasser.[20]

13

Rusk Takes Over

The reason for Talbot's visit to Cairo was to give a general review of US-Egypt relations—it was a routine annual visit he made to all the Arab capitals. However, it soon became clear that Nasser had higher expectations for the meeting. For him, it was a litmus test for determining whether the Johnson administration planned to resume aid. In the wake of the reconciliation between Nasser and Battle at the end of March, scores of Egyptian officials had inquired with their US counterparts about the administration's intentions toward Nasser. The most common question asked was: Is aid still on the table?[1]

On April 1, a little over two weeks before Talbot's meeting with Nasser in Cairo, Rusk sat down for a meeting with Kamel in Washington at the latter's invitation. Kamel began by saying that the economic situation in Egypt was getting more serious. Nasser needed help from the United States or he would lose control of the country, Kamel said. He added that Nasser was willing to buy food through CCC sales while the administration figured out a way to release the remaining $37 million of PL 480 aid. Rusk replied that the administration was not in a position to give any aid to Egypt while the Congo fiasco still loomed large in the minds of congressmen. He ended the conversation with a stern warning: Nasser needed to demonstrate he was no longer sending weapons to the rebels in Congo. Kamel, however, insisted that it was Nasser who needed a demonstration of good faith since there had been no new aid agreements between the two countries in over two years.[2]

A week later, Komer himself sat down with Kamel for what he called "a long deferred session." The two had not met since their talk before the nonaligned summit in October. Kamel began the meeting repeating the same talking points he had used with Rusk. Komer replied that he needed Nasser to restrain himself if the administration was to be able to get him the aid that he so desperately needed. "I gave him a persistent but soft sell," Komer reported in a memorandum of the conversation. Kamel gave a strong sell. "He emphasized how the UAR had managed to avoid interfering with our essential interests—oil, bases, preventing Soviet penetration, and keeping the Israeli issue in the icebox." This was a similar set of talking points that Kamel often made in Washington. The general gist was that Nasser was liable to lash out against the United States on any of these issues—if he was trifled with.

However, there was one new element to this meeting: according to Kamel, Nasser had "approved a firm invitation" for Komer to visit Cairo. "He urged that I give him a reply as soon as possible," Komer reported. It was an intriguing invitation. It suggested that Nasser understood who was on his side in Washington. Komer had never been out in the open in US-Egypt relations—he was a figure in the shadows. Komer used the unexpected invitation to his advantage by explaining to Kamel his concerns about the direction of US-Egypt relations. There was no reason not to do this, since Komer must have realized after the invitation that he had acquired some capital in Cairo. Komer repeated that Nasser needed to remain calm and patient if he was to be able to help get Nasser the aid that Egypt so badly needed.

Komer "reminded" Kamel that he was "one of those" in the Johnson administration who worked hard to improve US-Egypt relations. However, as he saw it, the relationship needed to be more of a "two way street." Nasser had taken up a number of positions that placed him in direct conflict with American interests—not least, Yemen, Cyprus, Libya, and the Congo—and it was time for him to smarten up. "Those who like myself ... [take] a long view of the mutuality of interest between us ... [are] hard put to it to point to any concrete evidence of Cairo's desire to do business with [America]," said Komer to Kamel. "I ... [am] afraid that suspicions on both sides ... [have] mounted to the point where new signals ... [are] essential."

Nasser needed to clearly demonstrate his intent to be more of a friend to America, reasoned Komer. He brought up recent attacks in the Egyptian press about US operations in Vietnam to illustrate his point. Kamel, however, insisted that Nasser was already doing enough to help America's position in the Middle East. "I will forebear recording the rest of Kamel's remarks, as they were a familiar phonograph record," Komer later wrote. Indeed, Kamel had a habit of reminding his American interlocutors that Nasser was keeping the Arab-Israeli conflict contained and resisting Soviet encroachment in the Middle East. But this was not enough to get Johnson's interest.

Komer was interested in directly speaking to Nasser in order to get him to understand exactly what he needed to do to win over Johnson. In other words, he wanted to accept Kamel's invitation to visit Cairo and take a stab at redirecting Nasser.[3]

Two days after his meeting with Kamel, Komer wrote to Bundy: "While I don't really believe Kamel when he says 'Nasser' has invited me, I've little doubt that Cairo has endorsed the idea of suitable US visitors, and that there might be merit in my going. I'm just about the junior guy who could still talk with Gamal as representing LBJ's thinking." Komer proposed that he follow up Talbot's trip to Cairo with a trip of his own. "In fact," Komer wrote, "Nasser would listen more to me than Phil [Talbot]." Komer also proposed sending Harriman or even Bundy himself. Due to the difficult battle he was anticipating with Congress to get the remaining $37 million released, he thought sending multiple visitors was a "cheap" but important gesture to make. "I'm ready to serve if chosen," he wrote. He then added with a hint of exhaustion: "(after my vacation)."[4]

On April 13, Komer wrote to Bundy again about a possible trip to Cairo. Both Battle and Kamel had rejected a Harriman visit since he was scheduled to visit Israel. The point of a visit was to publicize it as a sign of improving relations between Egypt and the United States, the two of them said, respectively. A trip to Israel and Egypt, as

Harriman was doing, meant possibly sending the wrong signal, worldwide, that Nasser was negotiating an armistice over the Jordan River conflict.

With there already being drama surrounding the possible trip to Cairo, Komer briefly wondered whether anyone from the administration should go. There was no point in bothering to redirect Nasser if there was nothing to give him. "We need to be able, not only to tell Nasser to behave," he wrote to Bundy, "but to offer some prospect of reward if he does." Komer wrote in jest, "I'd hate to postpone [my] spring vacation yet again, lest my bride lose all confidence in us both."

The two men agreed to wait until after Talbot's routine trip to make a decision about a possible follow-up trip by Komer or somebody else from the administration. Indeed, there was one more consideration to make: Rusk suddenly had decided to steer US-Egypt relations toward a resolution of the Congo conflict. But Rusk's approach did not align with Komer's desire not to prod Nasser too much while he waited for a decision on aid. Komer was worried that Nasser might leak the details of the Israeli and Jordanian arms agreements out of spite.[5]

In his April 1 meeting with Kamel, Rusk framed Nasser's involvement in Congo as the main obstacle to improving US-Egypt relations. Specifically, he connected the issue to the war in Vietnam, saying that the administration was wary of Egypt supplying guns to the rebels since it was currently dealing with "blocking arms infiltration into South Vietnam." Kamel claimed that Nasser was no longer involved in Congo. Therefore, it no longer even was an issue on the table. The two of them subsequently argued. Rusk replied that if the question of aid to Egypt came up in Congress before he had had a chance to see a decrease in Egypt's involvement in Congo, then, as secretary of state, he would be unable to authorize any new agreements or even approve resuming the existing PL 480 agreement. According to a memorandum of their conversation, "Secretary [Rusk] said that, while he comprehended Kamel's broad approach to US-UAR relations, Congo was [an] issue that loomed largest in his talks with Congress and this was [the] handiest lever by which to get [the] US-UAR relationship back on track."[6]

Rusk's stern message was received in Cairo. When Talbot and Battle had a preliminary meeting with Kaissouni and former Foreign Minister (now foreign affairs advisor) Mahmoud Fawzi in Cairo, on April 15—ahead of the more important meeting with Nasser—the majority of their five-hour conversation dealt with Congo. Like Rusk, Talbot compared Egypt's involvement in Congo to the guerrilla warfare the United States was experiencing in Vietnam. He said that smaller communist nations across the world were sending their "soldiers and terrorists across frontiers." The United States, Talbot said, was labeling the phenomenon as a third form of aggression—after nuclear and conventional war. According to a memorandum of their conversation, Talbot said that the United States was "troubled when UAR fingers [are] seen in difficult situations elsewhere, as in South Arabia Federation, Persian Gulf, North Africa, Cyprus, etc." This image of Egypt behaving like North Vietnam was lethal to the preservation of US-Egypt relations, Talbot said. This was a serious accusation that Talbot was raising. But Fawzi "thanked" Talbot for his "candor," and expressed relief that Egypt's foreign affairs "was the extent of our [US-Egypt] problems." Talbot and Battle were somewhat dumbfounded by Fawzi's "mild response." They wondered what Nasser had planned and whether he would take a more hard-line approach when he saw Talbot.[7]

But Talbot and Battle's concern did not deter Rusk. Back in Washington, he continued to stress the importance of settling Congo once and for all. To that end, State sent Talbot a script for his talk with Nasser, which had been heavily revised by Rusk himself. It went, "'Satisfactory climate' [between the US and Egypt] cannot be defined in terms of specific issues. It will [be] obtain[ed] when [the] sum total of UARG positions on major issues between us[,] reflects [a] conscious Egyptian effort to adapt to USG requirements. However, improvement in regard to Congo must be part of [the] picture."[8]

After reading the directive, Komer wrote to Bundy, "Unfortunately, both [Rusk and Ball] continue to make some UAR pullback on the Congo the test of our future relations." According to Komer, most State officials disagreed with Rusk's approach. Instead, they tended to agree with Komer that it was more important to focus on resuming aid to Nasser in order to buy his continued silence about the arms sale to Israel. Komer worried that Rusk was making US aid to Egypt contingent on a meaningless concession from Nasser (i.e., Congo). Komer did not like the new direction in which Rusk was taking his redirection strategy. "I regard this as serious business," he wrote to Bundy with a hint of annoyance about the whole situation. "Why give Nasser a chance to get off the hook by doing something less important than what we really want?" Komer pointed out that the American press was now reporting that the United States was "winning" in Congo. Therefore, it was unlikely that Congress would any longer object to aid over Congo—quite simply, there was nothing to object. There were more serious issues to redirect Nasser on—such as the Jordan River, Yemen, and inter-Arab relations. Although Komer strongly believed that Rusk was going down the wrong path with Nasser, he agreed to capitulate to Rusk's steering of policy and not "fight the problem."[9] After all, Rusk outranked Komer.

On April 18, Talbot and Battle sat down with Nasser for a two-and-a-half-hour meeting that was mostly about Congo. They believed Nasser had been briefed about the earlier conversation with Kaissouni and Fawzi, as he was noticeably well prepared for the meeting. Talbot reported that Nasser "had done his homework sufficiently well so almost all points I had raised were skillfully woven into his comments and responses to my questions." Nasser understood that this conversation was a test of sorts on whether he would cooperate with the Johnson administration.

It had been thirteen months since Talbot last met Nasser to discuss arms control. Much had changed: Badeau's resignation, Johnson's election victory, and the intermittent conflicts that had so far plagued US-Egypt relations in 1965. From Nasser's point of view, the meeting represented an important opportunity to get the relationship back on track. He began by saying that he had been following a "fairly stiff line" vis-à-vis the United States as a measure of protection against the economic pressures the Johnson administration had been placing on him. However, he flatly stated that he no longer was providing arms to rebel groups in Congo. Referring to Talbot's last visit to Cairo (which had been to discuss arms control), Nasser said that he would accept IAEA safeguards on any nuclear reactor that was ultimately built in Egypt.

Nasser then read down a list of recent problems between the United States and Egypt, noting all of the ways in which he would no longer contribute to them—including: (1) Arab diversionary projects on the Jordan River, which he said would not exceed the original water allocations designated under an American-led plan to fairly allocate the water between the riparian states—including Israel (the Arabs had officially rejected the plan, so this was a major concession from Nasser); and (2), the Cyprus conflict, which he claimed to have lost interest in. Nasser also reiterated his intention to remain quiet about the US arms agreements with Israel and Jordan.

Talbot was impressed with Nasser's concessions. Indeed, the Egyptian leader had delivered on the Congo issue quicker than expected, and also had rather remarkably reversed his position on a wider variety of issues. However, as Komer had feared, Talbot had nothing to offer Nasser in return, thus leaving the Egyptian leader empty-handed. The only thing Talbot could say, rather lamely, was that the administration would now "consider" a CCC sale of wheat and corn. And the only comment he could make about the $37 million of remaining aid was that he hoped there would be a "prompt decision" about it. Talbot did not even have authority to assure Nasser that the administration would consider entering talks for a new PL 480 agreement to replace the existing one when it expired on June 30.

Despite the awkwardness of his inability to offer anything of value to Nasser, Talbot hailed the conversation as a turning point in US-Egypt relations. He wrote to Rusk and urged him to issue an immediate authorization of the CCC sales—known as a purchase authority. "I have now had many hours of talk with UARG officials," Talbot wrote. "It is apparent to Ambassador [Battle] and me that Nasser's decision to tell us no arms [are] being sent to Congolese rebels represents [a] firm UARG policy decision to attempt to meet [the] conditions we have laid down for completion [of the] existing PL 480 agreements." Talbot added that it was time to consider discussing a new PL 480 agreement. "That, rather than further dialogue on the existing agreement, seems to me [to be] the proper occasion for further examination of the many and real problems remaining between [the] US and the UAR."[10]

After hearing about Talbot's meeting with Nasser, Komer reluctantly praised Rusk's approach. "It shows the merits of playing hard to get on aid now and then," he wrote to Bundy, "so long as one doesn't overdo it (Congress may yet undermine this promising trend)." With Nasser laying down his arms in Congo, Rusk was ready to move forward with the remaining $37 million of PL 480 aid. Ball agreed to take the news to Capitol Hill himself in order to push for an immediate release of funds. Komer, however, was nervous that the two of them were moving too fast and without any regard for strategy. Nasser had explicitly asked that it remain private he had reversed his position on Congo, as well as his acquiescence to America's arms arrangement with Israel. With markups on the 1966 aid bill ongoing, Komer thought it was prudent to quietly move forward with the CCC sales for the time being, lest any ambitious congressman decide to make a public statement of victory and leak news of Nasser's capitulations.[11]

The next day, Komer wrote to Bundy about travelling to Egypt. "Only remaining question is *my possible descent on Nasser.*" He proposed holding off on a decision for a few weeks in order to leave room after Talbot's trip. However, there was still much to reassure Nasser about. The $37 million was still an issue. Johnson was unwilling to release it after he learned that the House was still considering barring any aid to Egypt in the 1966 aid bill. Since Rusk had forced the Congo issue, above all else, Komer thought it was important to reassure Nasser about the $37 million and be upfront with him about the delay. Communication was the cornerstone of his approach to Nasser.

It was clear that getting the $37 million was going to be a difficult battle. "Your own gloom shakes me," Komer wrote to Bundy. "It is crucially important someone like myself (known to Nasser as LBJ's man) break the news on LBJ's behalf that the $37 million is just not possible till the aid bill is passed." Komer agreed with Talbot that the timing was right to "dangle" a new one-year PL 480 agreement "in order to keep Nasser quiet." Indeed, Nasser now had made three major concessions: silence on the Israeli arms deal, distancing himself from the rebels in Congo, and committing himself to IAEA controls. And the Johnson administration awkwardly had nothing to offer him in return.[12]

14

The $37 Million

Now that Nasser had made a number of concessions, Komer thought it was important to get Johnson to release the remaining $37 million of PL 480 aid. To that end, Komer continued to push for preventative diplomacy measures in order to keep Nasser from lashing out at the United States and exposing the arms arrangement with Israel. However, Komer and Rusk continued to clash over the best approach to take with Nasser. To Komer's dismay, Rusk's approach was becoming more dominant.

On April 20, Komer wrote to Bundy, encouraging him to bring up Nasser at the next Tuesday lunch-meeting with Johnson. "We must get a clear sign-off on tactics towards the UAR!" he wrote. He added with emphasis, "As I read it, we seem to be winning a battle with Nasser, *if only we know how to negotiate the truce.*" Komer pointed out that Nasser needed aid badly enough that he was apparently willing to back down from long-standing positions. Specifically, Komer applauded Nasser's continued silence on the Jordan waters issue and the arms agreement with Israel. He noted, however, that Nasser's pulling back from the Congo was more of an "inevitable" recognition that the rebels were losing. And Nasser's commitment to IAEA safeguards was nothing novel. "*Nonetheless,*" Komer wrote with emphasis, "*if LBJ wants to avoid a Middle East crisis over the Jordan Waters, he can only do so with the tacit collaboration of Gamal Abdel Nasser.*" In other words, Johnson needed to get over his reluctance to give aid to Nasser. He had to stand up to Congress.

Komer wanted to do three things to move the ball forward with Nasser: (1) proceed with a CCC sale "as a quick response," even though he did not think Nasser actually wanted it; (2) ensure that the House passed the 1966 aid bill with nothing stronger than the restrictive amendment that had been passed in the Senate; and (3) release the remaining $37 million of PL 480 aid after the 1966 aid bill was done being marked up—it was important not to ruffle any feathers before the funding for Johnson's other programs was fully finalized. Komer believed the $37 million was the only "carrot" that could win Nasser's trust. He wanted Johnson to understand that. "To Nasser, this will be the real test of whether we're willing to do business," he wrote to Bundy. "If we don't go through with the $37 million, we can kiss our victory goodbye."

In spite of his drive to steer Johnson toward Nasser, Komer understood that Johnson was becomingly increasingly preoccupied with the Vietnam War. Indeed, Johnson had just committed two more Marine battalions and 20,000 more soldiers to the war and, apparently, he was nervous that he had overextended the armed forces. Komer wanted Bundy to play on Johnson's fears about overextension. Specifically, he wanted Bundy to argue at his weekly lunch with Johnson that keeping the Middle East "quiet" was relatively simple to accomplish with "a few tools of the trade," and that it was important to do so in order to head off another hot spot from forming when the administration already had too much on its plate. "I too would rather sacrifice Nasser than the aid bill," Komer wrote. "But I'm confident that if we can only show the President this problem, he will vote our way."[1] Komer was desperate to get Johnson to pay attention to Nasser.

On April 24, Komer again pressed Bundy about the trip to Cairo. It was important to let Nasser know that his concessions had not been for nothing. Komer very much wanted to do it himself. "*Faute de mieux ['want of a better alternative']*, I'd still see merit in telling Gamal that LBJ definitely wants to do business, but that [the] Congressional problem is mighty real (I could speak from experience now)," Komer wrote. He added with emphasis, "*In short, Gamal should hang on a little while longer.*"

Komer's efforts to get Johnson more engaged on Nasser fell flat. At the Tuesday lunch meeting with Bundy, Johnson said he was reluctant to even authorize hints to Egyptian officials that he would eventually release the $37 million of PL 480 aid, lest word leak out and sabotage the 1966 aid bill. Komer's solution was to tell Nasser that Johnson would immediately move toward a new one-year PL 480 agreement once the 1966 aid bill was approved; however, in the meantime, Nasser had to continue patiently waiting for the $37 million from the 1962 agreement with Kennedy. Komer wrote to Bundy, "If LBJ won't go this far now, it would still be a good line in mid-June [just before the 1962 agreement expired]." He added for humor, "assuming we weren't at war by then." No doubt it was a joke, but Komer really was worried about Nasser acting out to disrupt Johnson's continued silence.

Indeed, Komer worried so much about Johnson's stalling and Rusk's new hard-line approach, that he argued to Bundy the two men were causing unnecessary strife with Nasser, which could lead to immediate problems for the United States in the Middle East. "All in all, there are still so many issues on which Nasser could cause us real ME trouble this year," he wrote to Bundy, "that I see wisdom in buying him off to the extent US opinion will permit—or stringing him along as much as possible to the extent it won't." Komer added, "My dropping in on Cairo would be useful enough to this end that I suggest we try it out pronto on LBJ and then Rusk or Ball." From Komer's vantage point, it was better to get Johnson on board for the trip, then present a fait accompli to Rusk. Without a presidential stamp, Rusk would shoot the trip down given his dislike of Komer.[2]

At least Komer had Talbot to argue his case at State; or so he believed. When Komer broached his possible trip to Cairo with his usually erstwhile companion, Talbot shot him down. Instead, Talbot proposed inviting Fawzi to Washington because Nasser reportedly wanted him to deliver a letter to Johnson. Talbot pointed out that the United States always sent visitors to Nasser, but neither Kennedy nor Johnson had ever invited a high-level Egyptian to visit. According to Nasser's confidante, Heikal, in a conversation with Battle a few days after Talbot had left Cairo, Nasser was upset that his idea to send Fawzi had not been immediately received with more enthusiasm in Washington. It was unfortunate, Heikal pointed out, that the suggestion had been received "very low key . . . as [an] after-thought." Johnson's silence was becoming deafening for Nasser.[3]

Before departing for a two-week vacation to Italy, Komer again pressed Bundy for authorization to visit Cairo. He was even willing to come home early from vacation for it. Komer proposed, at the very least, telling Kamel that Johnson was "willing" to let Komer go if Nasser was "still interested." "Yes," Bundy surprisingly responded. Perhaps he was broken down from Komer's badgering or just shared Komer's concern about leaving Nasser in the dark after the latter's concessions to Talbot. Regardless, Komer was right to want to reassure Nasser: it soon became apparent that the Egyptian leader was losing faith that Johnson would ever come through with the aid that Egypt so badly needed.[4]

On May 1, Nasser gave his annual May Day speech, during which he devoted more time to domestic affairs than usual. Nasser declared that Egyptians needed to work harder. There were no natural resources, like petroleum, to make the country inherently rich. What caught the attention of officials in Washington, however, was a minor reference to the arms agreement with Israel. Nasser said:

Israel, and imperialism everywhere behind it, is arming and threatening us. Germany has supplied Israel with arms free of charge. Britain is arming Israel and so is France. Nowadays something new has come into the picture. Two years ago America decided to arm Israel with rockets for air defense. Now she has decided to arm Israel with military weapons. What does this mean? It means that Israel and those behind her represent a perpetual danger to us.

It was a quick, but dangerous reference to the US-Israel arms agreement; especially dangerous if the press asked follow-up questions.

Nasser also referred to the imminent expiration of the PL 480 deal he had signed with Kennedy three years prior. He implied that the United States was going to cut off Egypt altogether. Nasser said:

In 1956, after the aggression, we were faced with economic pressure. We were taking American aid and it stopped. We did not perish. We worked and doubled our national income. In 1957, 1958, 1959 there was no aid. We had been getting wheat before 1956 under agreements with America and payment was made in Egyptian pounds. This aid was cut off after the aggression but we went ahead and worked hard and developed our country . . . After 1960, America started again to give us wheat for Egyptian pounds which were lent back to us . . . We concluded a three year agreement which will expire next month. Until now America has not taken any steps to renew the agreement. We have asked for its renewal. But the indications so far are that there will be no renewal.

Nasser was being honest. However, there was the possibility that his honesty could lead to a backlash against the United States from the other Arab countries, who would do so in order to show solidarity with the powerful Arab leader.

Nasser concluded his speech by saying that Egyptians were prepared to "eat half a loaf" of bread in order to survive. "What I am saying is that we are facing a stage of economic pressure similar to the one we faced in 1956," he said. "I say there is not one single Egyptian who is prepared to yield his self-respect." While the rhetoric was not inflammatory, the underlying message was provocative: it indicated that Egypt and the United States would soon be at odds if there was no aid.

Battle immediately wrote to State. It was clear that Nasser had purposefully chosen to inform the Egyptian people about the US arms agreement with Israel. Nevertheless, Battle dismissed the announcement as "low key and in [the] context [of] arms supplies from [the] West in general." While Battle drew parallels between the May Day speech and Nasser's earlier speech at Port Said in December, he noted that this time Nasser had delivered his message in a "calm and dignified manner." Indeed, Nasser had, at least, acknowledged that America's aid was essential for Egypt's prosperity. Battle surmised that the speech was intended to exert pressure on the United States to sign a new PL 480 deal rather than an emotional outburst like the one at Port Said. It was a surprising display of statesmanship from the Egyptian leader, the ambassador claimed.[5]

What happened next, however, was even more surprising. And it seemingly proved Battle's assessment of the situation correct. On May 3, the Egyptian Ministry of Supply sent the US embassy in Cairo an official request for a CCC sale of corn. Nobody from the Johnson administration had actually expected Nasser to ask for a CCC sale. However, the letter accompanying the request mentioned that in light of "various conversations," Egypt was ready to move forward with a CCC sale. Battle assumed it was a reference to Talbot's opening the door to such a sale in his talk with Nasser. Battle wrote: "In my view [the] request is not only [an] effort [to] cover corn requirements [for the] remainder [of] this year[,] but is also an even more important first test [of] our intentions in [the] aftermath [of the] Nasser-Talbot talks and [the] UAR decision re Congo. I cannot overstate how critical I consider it in current circumstances that our reply be prompt and affirmative." The US-Egypt relationship had come to a vital crossroads; which path Nasser would take, a friendly or a hostile one, depended on how the Johnson administration handled aid.[6]

Inconveniently, Komer was still on vacation in Italy. Therefore, on May 4, Saunders took the lead in Komer's absence and forwarded both of Battle's telegrams to Bundy ahead of the weekly Tuesday lunch-meeting with Johnson. By now, the administration was considering sending US marines to Santo Domingo (i.e., the Dominican Republic), where a coup had deposed the American-installed leader. "If Dominican and Vietnamese issues don't crowd everything else off the plate, Rusk may bring up the question of *CCC corn credit for the UAR*," Saunders wrote to Bundy. "Whether you get to this at lunch or not, we'll have to try it again soon. If it doesn't come up, Talbot will probably be after you." Indeed, State was pushing for an immediate decision on the aid issue.[7] It was beginning to look like Nasser would receive a favorable outcome in Washington. Mostly, he had his newfound conciliatory tone to thank for that—US officials were seizing it to push for more aid.

However, as fate would have it, that same day, US intelligence services received information that Egypt made two flights to Sudan on a route their planes typically took when delivering arms to the rebels in Congo. Rusk was livid. He once again held up the CCC deal because of the Congo. Rusk also completely shot down the idea of Komer visiting Cairo. Saunders wrote to Bundy, "I gather Rusk told you he didn't think RWK [Robert Komer] should talk to Nasser unless he could say something about the undelivered $37 million in food." Significantly, Rusk had missed the point of Komer's proposed trip: Komer wanted to reach out to Nasser precisely because the administration had nothing yet to offer him in terms of aid. It was preventative diplomacy that Komer was pushing for and Rusk was missing the point.[8]

If relations between Egypt and the United States were a two-way street, as US officials often characterized them to their Egyptian counterparts, then communication was vital in order to reassure Nasser that his concessions to Talbot had been received in Washington and would be rewarded in due time. This is what Komer wanted, but his redirection strategy conflicted with Rusk's more hard-line approach. In essence, it was an issue of Rusk being inconsistent. His frequent pivoting between being too hard or soft on Nasser conflicted with the consistency that was required for a successful redirection strategy.

Time was ticking: Nasser soon got impatient about the delay on his CCC request and struck a deal with China, instead, for corn. In the meantime, he didn't give up on seeking aid from the United States. He wrote a letter to Johnson that Fawzi hand-delivered to Battle on May 15. In it, Nasser reiterated the concessions he had given to Talbot. This time, however, they were in writing. Nasser signed off with a warm message for Johnson: "Please accept, dear President, kindest respects and very best wishes." No doubt, Nasser was still hoping to get a response from Johnson about CCC, the $37 million of remaining PL 480, and a new PL 480 agreement to replace the expiring one; however, he was getting more and more impatient with Johnson's silence.[9]

Komer understood Nasser's impatience. After returning from his vacation, he immediately wrote to Bundy, describing Nasser's letter as "highly forthcoming" and "encouraging." "Reading between the lines," Komer wrote, "this guy is really asking for a truce." Komer identified four aspects of the letter that he found particularly groundbreaking: (1) Nasser was asking for "good relations with US"; (2) he claimed that he was not looking for a war against Israel; (3) he claimed he did not want an arms race in the Middle East; and (4) he promised to focus on internal development. "Which is [the] very line we've been peddling to him for five years," Komer wrote. Indeed, Nasser was admitting that he needed America's help to get Egypt's economy back on its feet, and therefore he was willing to make concessions. More importantly, he was willing to listen to the United States, this time around, in order to stabilize his economy for the long run.

"Here is further convincing evidence that Gamal wants a rapprochement," Komer wrote to Bundy. He added that it was an "opening for a frank oral reply on behalf of LBJ, delivered by one of his junior hatchet men [i.e., Komer]." Bundy merely responded, "Staff meeting Tues."[10] Evidently, Komer did not yet know the extent to which Rusk was putting his foot down on extending any olive branches to Nasser.

But Komer continued to feel strongly about reaching out to Nasser. Nasser required reassurance that his concessions to Talbot, now in writing to Johnson, had not been in vain. Nonetheless, discussions about Komer's proposed trip to Cairo suddenly fell by the wayside as Nasser grew increasingly impatient with Johnson and lashed out. The window of time for Komer's preventative diplomacy approach was gone. The administration was left scrambling to react to events rather than being in a position to prevent them.

On May 16, *Al-Ahram* published an article that unexpectedly rehashed the conflict over American overseas bases by attacking Libya's King Idris and his continued support of America's access to Wheelus Air Base. It went: "The popular masses in Libya are demanding the liquidation of the Wheelus imperialist base and the withdrawal of the foreign troops from the country. These bases and troops threaten the security of the whole region and the freedom of its peoples, and they have been used before to threaten the national liberation movement and to hamper its development and progress." At the same time, Egyptian radio launched an unexpected propaganda campaign against Jordan (another key American ally), for not doing enough to contribute to the Palestinian liberation cause. While the two propaganda instances were isolated, they were no doubt a worrisome sign.[11]

On May 21, State wrote to Battle, "We are accustomed to UARG's taking one line with us and another with the Arabs, but lately we have sensed [a] greater degree of ambivalence than usual. We can understand [the] compulsion [the] Egyptian regime must feel to present itself to [the Egyptian] public in [the] best possible light, to placate [the] Soviet Union, to throw up an anti-American smoke screen to camouflage [the] fact of its pulling back on the Congo, and even to prod [the] USG a bit." State also was willing to concede that Nasser was probably resorting to anti-American propaganda in order to prepare for any domestic blowback he was expecting if he did not receive American aid. Nonetheless, his possible return to demagoguery threatened to derail any chances of him receiving that aid. Therefore, the situation was concerning. Indeed, concerning enough that it got Rusk to change his mind about the best approach to Nasser.[12]

On May 31, Rusk was ready to ask Johnson to release the remaining $37 million of PL 480 aid in order to stem what appeared to be the opening of a new conflict between the two countries. Rusk also took the unusual step of personally checking in with congressional leaders from both political parties in order to ensure they would not cause problems over the release. Komer was relieved. He wrote a memorandum for Johnson, which he attached to Rusk's recommendation. "This bribe is probably essential to avoid a major ruckus in the Middle East," he wrote. "Nasser has made clear that he sees our suspension of shipments since December as an act of economic pressure." Komer remarked that the "pressures . . . to date" had worked to get Nasser out of Congo. However, he warned that should the administration delay aid any longer, Nasser was likely to lash out at the United States. He added with emphasis: "Past experience amply shows that in such a case (e.g. the Aswan Dam) his response is to show that he too has teeth. *The sad fact of the matter is that Nasser can hurt us more than we can hurt him.*" This was the crux of the matter for Komer: he still deeply believed that failure to engage Nasser meant disaster for the United States in the Middle East.

Komer mentioned oil, overseas bases, and the Arab-Israeli dispute as potential hot button issues that Nasser could immediately exploit to hurt the United States. "Last but not least," Komer wrote, "if we cut Nasser off he has nowhere to go but Moscow, which can force him to cause trouble as the price of its support." In Komer's eyes, Johnson was running the risk of undermining the entire enterprise of Kennedy's careful diplomacy in the Middle East.

Komer felt he had to get Johnson to respond quickly with some sort of concession in order to keep the situation somewhat contained. He reminded Johnson that the $37 million of PL 480 would only provide enough food to last for a few months. The real battle, Komer wrote, would be coming up with an entirely new aid agreement for Nasser. Only at that point, Komer stressed, should Nasser be made to understand that a continuation of aid was contingent on his "continued good behavior." In other words, Nasser required carrots for the time being, not sticks. It was a strong sell by Komer. This time, however, he had the added benefit of having Rusk's support.[13]

Ironically, while Komer and Rusk were no longer working against each other, Bundy happened to disagree with both of them. He told Johnson not to release the $37 million. It was one of the rare times he ever decided against Komer. Bundy, for his part, was nervous about Congress. He wrote to Johnson: "The Secretary and Bob Komer are both ready to go ahead on this and I am sure they are right from every point of view but that of Congressional reaction." The Senate was not due to authorize the 1966 aid bill for another ten days. Bundy recommended telling Nasser "informally" that the administration would hold off on the $37 million for another couple of weeks. "He keeps his mouth shut on this sort of thing because it is in his interest to do so," Bundy wrote. No doubt Bundy was getting impatient after years of careful balancing efforts with Nasser.

Bundy advised Johnson not to make a decision right away—he was going to schedule a discussion for the following week's Tuesday lunch-meeting. "So this particular paper is for information and not for decision," he wrote. Johnson replied by circling the words "telling Nasser informally that we expect to be able to go ahead in the next couple of weeks," and writing, "We tell Nasser—we hope to go $17 [million] in 2 or 3 wks & perhaps can get Congress to go along shortly thereafter but ask him to bear with us with [the] other 20 [million]." To be sure, this was a compromise by Johnson to keep Nasser from lashing out. Crucially, however, it was also a signal from Johnson that he was considering getting tougher on Nasser by giving him money in smaller increments rather than in lump sums like Kennedy. This was the opposite of Kennedy's policy—giving Nasser large sums of money up front in hopes that he would use it wisely and not act against America's interests—and it was the first instance in which Johnson put his own spin on US-Egypt relations.[14]

On June 2, State instructed Battle to "privately" inform Nasser about Johnson's decision to split the $37 million of PL 480 into smaller increments. "We leave to you [the] paraphrasing of [the] message in such [a] way that Nasser will get the point that we desire [to] get on with improving relations[,] but that timing of [the] purchase authorizations is necessarily linked to progress of [the] foreign aid bill," wrote State. "He should of course also be reminded that untoward developments in [the] area could obviously limit Executive Branch capability to deal with Congressional critics of some aspects of [the] aid program."[15] Komer had revised the telegram. He also issued strict instructions that its distribution "be most closely held." Komer may have had his doubts about Johnson's approach, but he was a loyal aide to the president.[16]

Rusk, however, was a wildcard. At the same time that the telegram was being sent to Battle, word got to Komer that Rusk planned to tell congressional leadership about the deal anyways. Rusk had privately given his word to the congressional leadership that he would inform them of any decisions Johnson made regarding PL 480 aid to Egypt. And the congressional advisers at State reminded Rusk that he had an obligation to keep his word to Congress. According to Komer, "none of [them at State] . . . unfortunately knew the score, i.e. that the whole purpose of LBJ's private word to Nasser was to *avoid* publicity on PL 480 till the [1966] aid bill was through." Talbot had missed the meeting at State when Rusk decided to inform Congress about the split PL 480 payment. And Komer did not find out about the meeting until it was too late. "So I warned all concerned to be discreet, and gently questioned the Secretary's decision," Komer informed Bundy. "I only hope the cat isn't out of the bag. It would be hell if some Congressman called LBJ and mentioned he'd been told that LBJ was going forward with the UAR deal."[17]

Rusk continued to act on his own despite concern from the White House over his approach. For the next week-and-a-half, Rusk and Douglas McArthur went to Capitol Hill to brief members of Congress about the deal. Ultimately, congressional leadership from both political parties approved Johnson's decision to go ahead with the $37 million in increments. They claimed to understand that Johnson needed "flexibility and leverage" to deal with Nasser. Rusk had almost sabotaged the $37 million of PL 480. Nonetheless, he managed to emerge from his initial misstep with a victory. Johnson now had congressional backing for the release. But this did not alter Johnson's continued hesitancy about Nasser in general.[18]

On June 15, Komer wrote to Johnson, asking for *"final approval on the $37 million [of] food for the UAR."* The Department of Agriculture had informed Komer that without Johnson's approval they could not begin processing the release. The paperwork had to be signed immediately in order to meet the June 30 expiration of the 1962 PL 480 agreement. "The matter is now urgent," Komer wrote. "The half-promise we gave Nasser kept him quiet but he's on edge to see if we come through." Komer assured Johnson there would be no publicity on the matter. Johnson still hesitated, however, and let the memo sit on his desk.[19]

Later that same day, Johnson asked Rusk over the phone, "Should we let them have that $37 million?" "I think we ought to, Mr. President," Rusk replied. He encouraged Johnson to move forward with the split payment. He added, "I think we've had some real dividends from the pressures we've put into this and I think we ought not to make ourselves responsible for the street riots and things like that they may well have there." Presumably, Rusk was implying that denying Nasser the aid any longer could lead to protests in Egypt over mass hunger. Johnson, however, didn't respond. He moved on to discussing Vietnam.[20]

The next day, Rusk wrote to Johnson, recommending that he immediately approve a "resumption of Public Law 480 Title I sales to the UAR." But Johnson still hesitated. It was clear that he really didn't want to deal with Nasser. Perhaps he never believed his idea to split the $37 million would be so well-received within his administration and on Capitol Hill. Komer wrote again to Johnson the next day. "This is a messy problem, and will generate some flak however we move. But the Secretary of State makes a powerful case for giving Nasser just enough rope to limit the risk of a difficult confrontation in the Near East." Komer added, "I can only add my sober judgement as your Middle East hand that he's dead right." This time, Bundy agreed with Rusk and Komer. He wrote at the bottom of the memo for Johnson: "I am absolutely sure we should do this—because if we don't the explosion will be our fault. We can haggle like hell in the next phase."[21]

But Johnson continued to hesitate. Later that day, Komer wrote to Bundy: "Mac: I don't panic easily but I'm getting mighty nervous about our Nasser enterprise. Latest reading from Cairo is that we're close to the point of no return unless we proffer our long dangling thin carrot." Specifically, Komer worried that the press might find out about Egypt selling rice to Cuba and the Soviet Union. This was a violation of a clause in PL 480 aid, which stipulated that recipients of American aid could not sell products to the two communist countries. Kamel told US officials that Nasser would not do it again. And he added that it could be discussed further after the $37 million was released. To be sure, this was only a minor issue. So Komer began to wonder whether Johnson had other reasons for sitting on a decision for so long.[22]

The next day, Komer wrote again to Bundy. He expressed his concern that Johnson was purposely delaying aid to Egypt—as well as to India and Pakistan, two other neutralist countries that badly needed immediate help. Komer wondered whether he and Bundy had done a sufficient job explaining to Johnson the risks of his continued delay.

It was clear to Komer that Johnson had no patience for troublesome leaders like Nasser. But the president's inability to see the long-term benefit of redirecting Nasser meant that he was on the verge of losing any upper hand the United States still had in the relationship. "I realize that President [Johnson] is also seeking to educate the town by playing hard to get, and have been enthusiastically cooperating to this end," Komer wrote. "But I also sense that the President hasn't much confidence in the advice of his personal staff (or in me at least) when we tell him that the time has come to dangle a carrot instead of use a stick." He reminded Bundy that no new loans had been given to Egypt in eighteen months—the length of time that Johnson had been in office—and that the expiration of the 1962 PL 480 agreement was fast approaching.

From Komer's vantage point, it was becoming less about the time restraints and more about the fact that Johnson was just too hard on Nasser. Johnson had an unrealistic view that he could "break" Nasser, Komer wrote. Nasser "knows and calls it economic pressure." Komer added that it only took Nasser to make "a speech or do something else to retaliate" to turn the entire US-Egypt relationship on its head. If Johnson waited any longer, Komer reasoned, it would only take one wrong move from Nasser to make it impossible to give him anything at all. "If we did [go through with aid at that point], it would look as though we were caving to pressure," Komer wrote. Nasser had to be given aid *before* he lashed out, not after.

Komer feared that Johnson's stalling threatened to create a serious crisis for the administration that it could ill afford. "Another aspect of the problem bothers me," Komer wrote. "We've got plenty of trouble just now in Vietnam and Santo Domingo without asking for too much in South Asia and the Near East as well. So I see the prescription as being a judicious mixture of preventive medicine and active diplomacy." Komer had worked for years to head off potential crises with Nasser. He understood that Nasser's desperation for aid in this instance made him all the more likely to lash out at the United States.

Komer had been one of the key architects behind the strategy to use aid as a political lever on Nasser. And he, most of all, had stayed close to the lever for most of the Kennedy and Johnson years in order to keep Nasser on a tight leash. But now he was saying that it was time to let go; before Johnson pushed Nasser too far. It was not an easy decision for Komer either—paying off Nasser didn't make him feel good. But he felt it was the right call. And he was not willing to back down until Johnson made it. "It would be easy to stop agitating and bend with the wind," Komer wrote to Bundy with the air of the dramatic. "But it's not in my makeup."[23]

Fortunately, three days later, Johnson finally gave in. Komer was relieved. Talbot immediately went to tell Kamel the good news. Kamel also was relieved. He asked Talbot to "convey to President Johnson officially the thanks of his Government for his 'wise and courageous' decision." The next day, Johnson put a check mark next to the approve box on Komer's memo from the week before. After six months of nonstop tension in the wake of the Port Said speech—when all aid to Egypt had been placed on hold—US-Egypt relations were finally ready to move forward.[24]

Getting Johnson to the mark had been difficult. And it would have been prudent for Komer not to push Johnson too far. However, with one small victory achieved, Komer attempted to move on to the next one. Specifically, he decided it was important for the $37 million to be dispersed in one lump sum rather than in two separate installments as Johnson wanted. He asked Bundy to lend his support. "I like the two idea," Komer wrote, "but there just won't be time." Johnson still had to sign a "Presidential Determination" justifying his decision to give aid to Egypt, as required by the amendment to the Foreign Assistance Act that was passed in February. Johnson had until June 30 (nine days) to sign the paperwork and make it official, lest he wanted to get into a dispute with Congress over extending the deadline.[25]

Komer saw this as a potential roadblock that could undo his hard work getting Johnson to the mark. He wrote to Johnson, in regard to breaking up the $37 million into installments, that "two bites would just prolong any arguments." He pushed Johnson, who apparently was still wary about the deal, to sign the "Presidential Determination" immediately. Komer assured Johnson that it would "not be published." Komer was not taking any chances on bureaucratic procedure. He wrote to Bundy: "Budget would be very unhappy if *LBJ* didn't sign [the] UAR determination. Also, Rusk hesitates to move till LBJ signs." He added in exasperation, "Ye Gods."[26]

On June 22, Johnson finally signed all of the necessary paperwork to give Nasser the $37 million of PL 480. State planned to make a quiet announcement the following day, though they planned to keep Johnson out of it as much as possible. "Batten down the hatches for a minor blow," wrote Komer in anticipation of some minor blowback. He suggested inviting over Jewish senators and congressmen to State in order to help "cover any flap."[27]

When the announcement about the $37 million was finally made on June 23 there were only minor complaints, most of which came from a few congressmen who had been kept in the dark about the matter. Thus, Komer (with Rusk's assistance) had pulled off an important victory in US-Egypt relations. Indeed, the release of the $37 million had been a saving grace. Unknown by the administration, Nasser had managed to secure a deal with the Soviet Union for 300,000 tons of wheat, which he planned to announce with large fanfare on July 1—the day after the expiration of the 1962 PL 480 agreement. Evidently, after everything, Nasser had lost faith in Johnson. Rusk's hijacking of policy—forcing Nasser's hands on Congo, standing in the way of the CCC sales, and preventing Komer from visiting Cairo—had almost undone US-Egypt relations. All Nasser had required was more communication, which is exactly what Komer had been asking to provide him.[28]

15

Another Long Summer

Even though Johnson came through in the end with the $37 million, Nasser was angry that he had been left in the lurch until the last minute. In the summer of 1965, Nasser sought to understand where he stood with Johnson. In the meantime, Komer waited patiently for the right time to ask Johnson about signing a new PL 480 agreement.

The Soviets just barely missed an opportunity to claim the sole credit for bailing out Nasser. And because the Americans preempted Nasser's big announcement planned for July 1, the claim could not be made that Soviet pressure had forced the United States to release the $37 million. It was an accidental, but clear, victory for the Johnson administration. Komer wrote to Bundy, after learning about the Soviets' deal with Nasser, "From [a] foreign policy viewpoint we just made it." The $37 million provided 50 days' worth of food for Egypt. In conjunction with Egypt's projected crop yields, the food supply was expected to last until January 1966. "Our *clearest gain* is relief from pressure for a new [PL 480] agreement," stressed Saunders to Bundy on June 25. However, given the unexpected competition from Moscow's aid, the Johnson administration could not afford to sit back.[1]

Indeed, the Soviet deal sounded better in term of the wheat provided (300,000 tons), but the American deal looked better on paper. It provided 175,000 tons of wheat, 170,000 tons of flour, and $17 million worth of miscellaneous food items like vegetable oil, milk, and tobacco. The Egyptian press, however, was describing the Soviet deal as the better one. Saunders admitted to Bundy that "the Cairo article gives the Soviets a nice propaganda play." Johnson had come through in the end with the $37 million, but he was not getting the credit in the Arab world that Komer had expected. To make matters worse, because State had requested minimal press coverage of the $37 million in order to avoid "flak," the American press was instead highlighting the surprisingly generous amount of wheat provided by Moscow.[2]

No doubt looking to capitalize on the favorable press reports it was receiving, the Soviets decided to make an early delivery of their wheat, which was received in Alexandria on June 27. An accompanying message declared that the Soviet Union intended to support Egypt's "struggle . . . [by] all means." It was a reminder that Moscow had been a friend in 1956 (by providing funding for Aswan Dam), when Nasser needed one most.[3]

Nasser, for his part, received the Soviets' message loud and clear: Moscow expected him to show his appreciation. Shortly after the arrival of Soviet wheat, the Egyptian press began to criticize American aid, while lavishly praising the Soviets. For example, an article in *Al-Ahram* declared: "Foreign aid is no more monopolized by the US. There are other nations now competing in this field with the US even within the Western bloc. The loser in the long run will be the US government." Later that day, a broadcast on Radio Cairo declared: "We do not get wheat from the US as charity or aid, as its trumpets make out; we buy it at the full price, which includes profit." The next day, an article in an Egyptian weekly, *Akhbar al-Yom,* declared: "The Americans might be able to reach the moon, to swim in space and somersault in the air, but they—through the US Congress's course of action—will not reach the hearts of masses in developing, struggling and heroic nations . . . such as the UAR."

By comparison, the Soviets' wheat was celebrated with favorable front page coverage. One publication, for example, declared that the Soviet Union "fully appreciates the policy of nonalignment adopted by the UAR."[4]

Back in Washington, officials were confused by the propaganda. Even a routine intelligence briefing for Johnson made note of it. Bundy sent the briefing over to Komer, asking, "Is it this bad?" Komer replied, "Yes, it is this bad." However, he assured Bundy that it was probably no more than Nasser's fleeting frustration at having been made to wait so long for the $37 million. Komer surmised that Nasser was also upset because of the cancellation of his big announcement planned for July 1. Komer urged letting cooler heads prevail in Washington despite Nasser's seeming lack of appreciation for American aid. He wrote, "I still see our resumption as a very smart move to forestall a full-scale confrontation. Sticks and stones . . . you know."[5]

Bundy was not convinced by Komer's argument; he was upset about Nasser's attitude. After all, Bundy had gone out on a limb with Komer and Rusk to get Johnson on board for the $37 million. It didn't make sense how Nasser was behaving, and it made it difficult to figure out how to proceed with him.

To see for himself what was going on in Cairo, Bundy asked to see a copy of the memorandum from the meeting when Talbot informed Kamel of Johnson's decision to release the $37 million. It showed that Kamel had expressed nothing but gratitude upon hearing about the resumption of aid. Another memorandum Bundy read showed that Kaissouni had reacted with "tremendous pleasure" when Battle informed him of the good news about the $37 million. To make matters more confusing for Bundy, a high-level Egyptian official told Battle that Nasser was extremely happy about the $37 million. The Egyptian official added that Nasser had only taken the Soviets' wheat because he believed Johnson no longer was interested in giving aid to Egypt. These reports contradicted the propaganda emanating from Cairo.

Battle, Komer, and a group of NSC staffers were all in agreement that the administration had to overlook Nasser's "outbursts" and maintain "dignified detachment." They wrote this assessment in a memo to Bundy. A far more important matter to consider than Nasser's propaganda about Soviet wheat, the group wrote, was what to do about a new PL 480 agreement now that the old one had expired. Indeed, Komer wanted a plan for how to move forward on that front. The administration could not continue to react to crises with Nasser. It needed to be able to redirect him in order to avoid those crises from even occurring.[6]

At the beginning of July, Komer asked the CIA to see an advanced copy of an intelligence report entitled, "Soviet wheat for the UAR." He wanted to understand how to proceed with a new PL 480 agreement that could counteract the Soviets pulling Nasser even further into their orbit. The report showed Komer that, in mid-June, when Nasser realized that Egypt's wheat supply would run out in August, he made deals to buy wheat from Mexico and Argentina in addition to the arrangement with the Soviets. Komer highlighted a portion of the report which concluded that Nasser was unlikely to buy wheat from these two countries again, as they had made it available to him "only under fairly stringent terms." What this revealed to Komer was that Nasser was merely looking for the most generous benefactor; it didn't matter who was first.[7]

This gave Komer an idea, which he wrote up for Johnson: In order to lure Nasser back, Komer wanted to give him the impression that Johnson was immediately extending additional aid on extremely generous terms. Komer, however, wanted to give Nasser this impression without actually giving him anything. That way, the administration could keep Nasser's interest until Johnson was ready to conclude a new PL 480 agreement in the fall—which would presumably occur after the 1966 aid bill made it through Congress.

Komer, however, was reluctant to approach Johnson with his idea. There were rumors circulating that he had misled Johnson about the urgency of releasing the $37 million. Komer was being painted as a Cassandra. Komer wrote to Bundy before sending the memo to Johnson. "Attached [is] worth a weekend try. The President is apparently operating on a fair amount of bum info gleamed from the press and raw intelligence. Shall we step up our memo writing to him?" he facetiously asked. Despite the controversy surrounding Komer, Bundy approved the memo and sent it to Johnson.[8]

It began with a modest defense of releasing the $37 million when they did: "We moved just in time to spoil partly a big Soviet propaganda coup." Komer informed Johnson that in order to receive the wheat, Nasser had to convince the Soviets to divert some of their own incoming shipments of wheat from Canada and Australia. Indeed, the Soviet Union had its own problems balancing the supply of wheat, just like Egypt. The Soviets were not capable of maintaining a large wheat program for Egypt like the United States. Nasser had acted "in desperation" when he contacted Moscow for wheat. Komer reminded Johnson that the $37 million was more than just about feeding Egypt. It was also about gaining leverage over Nasser in order to redirect him on issues that affected America's interests in the Middle East. Thus, Komer wrote:

> There's a rumor that you feel we led you astray on the UAR by painting a grim picture of its inability to get food. I don't believe this, because we put the case on straight *political* grounds of preventing a real bust-up between the US and UAR. Our chief hope was to forestall total dependence on the Soviets for wheat as well as arms. We're still in this ballgame if we choose.

Komer shared his idea with Johnson about enticing Nasser with a fictitious offer of generous aid. He explained that there was $30 million worth of unanswered CCC requests from Egypt. He recommended that Johnson sign purchase authorizations for all of them. The caveat, Komer wrote, was that Egypt would not actually qualify with private American banks for the CCC loans due to its low foreign currency reserves and poor credit. The only institution that could theoretically support the CCC sales was the Export-Import Bank (EXIM), and Komer proposed secretly barring the institution from insuring any new CCC sales to Egypt. Komer stressed, *"we can have our cake and eat it too. Is this OK?"* he asked. Johnson wrote back, "See me –L." Bundy wrote with emphasis underneath Johnson's message: "Bob, I think *you* should do this."[9] Indeed, it was still unclear how Johnson felt about things involving Nasser—only Komer had the necessary enthusiasm to convince the president.

Komer was well-equipped for the challenge. After a short meeting with Johnson on July 7, he was given permission to proceed with his scheme. Komer wrote for the record with emphasis: *"However he did so on my representation that in fact very little if anything would move this route because the UAR's very tight foreign exchange position and heavy commitments for other grain purchases made it extremely unlikely that it could get US bank credit for such sales."* Komer, once again, had put himself on the line in order to save his redirection strategy. It was risky making offers to Nasser and simultaneously sabotaging those offers.

To put his plan into motion, Komer contacted the Department of Agriculture and AID to let them know that under no circumstances could Egypt be given any leniency on repayments of old CCC sales. It was important not to relieve Nasser's current balance of payments, lest the banks decide to give him a second chance. Komer also insisted that all new applications of CCC credit for Egypt had to be "cleared with the White House first." Komer contacted the head of the EXIM bank, Harold Linder, and explained that the bank was not allowed, under any circumstance, to insure any new CCC sales to Egypt. It was not a problem, replied Linder, who told Komer he had "no intention anyway" of helping Nasser.

Thus, a sudden release of CCC credit to Egypt was approved by Johnson under a false premise; nobody actually expected Egypt to qualify with any of the banks. Komer was ready to sit back for the rest of the summer and wait for Johnson to greenlight discussions for a new PL 480 agreement. Once again, however, Rusk intervened.[10]

It is unclear why, but on July 15, Rusk met with Kamel and opened the door for a new PL 480 agreement. The meeting had been called at Kamel's behest in order to convey Nasser's appreciation for the $37 million. Kamel was doing his best to make up for the pro-Soviet propaganda in Cairo. He praised Johnson's decision to release the $37 million, saying that it had led to the "normalization of US-UAR relations."

Kamel said the struggle over the $37 million had demonstrated that the two countries still had much work to do to find common ground. It was not helpful for either country if they continued to focus on their political differences. According to a memorandum of the conversation, Kamel said that "events obstructing US-UAR relations were not organic." The implication was that both sides had to commit to improving relations and not continue coming up with ways to harm the other side. Nasser was ready to do this, Kamel said. Despite the Soviet propaganda, the situation between Egypt and the United States was not as bad as it seemed, Kamel claimed. Specifically, he underscored that the Arab-Israeli "problem" was still in the "ice box," and that Nasser had stopped sending arms to Congo. "Patience, restraint, good will and diplomacy clearly brought beneficial results," he said. He added that Nasser was not turning to communism despite accepting wheat from the Soviets.

These were all positive signs during a time of uncertainty. Kamel, however, cautioned that if the Johnson administration did not offer a new PL 480 agreement in the near future, then Nasser would have no choice but to seek relief from Moscow again. Nasser authorized him to formally request a new agreement. To that end, Kamel asked Rusk for four things: (1) starting talks for a new PL 480 agreement immediately; (2) securing assistance from the International Bank for Reconstruction and Development (more commonly known as the "World Bank") to improve Egypt's economic situation; (3) encouraging American companies to invest in Egypt; and (4) mutual containment of the Arab-Israeli "problem" by keeping it in the "ice box."

Kamel was essentially asking to take politics out of US-Egypt relations for the time being. In response to a question from Rusk about the Soviet propaganda, Kamel said it was unhelpful to focus on the "trivia" of newspaper clippings. He asked Rusk to bring Egypt's dire economic needs before "President [Johnson], to the Congress and other key US Government officials" as soon as possible. He warned that if the United States did not help soon, then Nasser would have no choice but to turn to Moscow.

Rusk replied that although it was desirable from America's perspective to improve bilateral relations with Egypt, it was still not clear what interests the two countries exactly had in common. Nasser needed to understand that America's political system worked differently than Egypt's. "As professional diplomats we . . . [can] agree that passing irritants should be overlooked," Rusk said. "The President, however, as manager of . . . [the American] political system . . . [cannot] not do so." He explained to Kamel that Johnson was beholden to the American people. He governed the country at their pleasure. Unless it became more clear that it was in the country's interest to deal with Egypt, Johnson was essentially powerless to push through a new PL 480 agreement.

Kamel replied that Nasser was willing to work with the United States. As evidence he brought up a television interview with CBS in which Nasser had said nice things about Johnson. Kamel asked Rusk to take time to consider what Nasser had said. According to a report, Kamel reasoned: "It was not necessary to sign an agreement now, but important to initiate talks promptly. President Nasser would appreciate knowing exactly what the situation was. This was a very serious matter to the UAR." Rusk agreed to meet again in a few weeks' time.[11]

After hearing about the meeting, Komer immediately wrote to Bundy. He was upset that, once again, Rusk had so little regard for strategy. Johnson was not yet ready to consider a new PL 480 agreement. Komer understood that. He told Talbot to let Rusk take the lead with Kamel. Rusk could take the heat from Johnson. "Why should we India and UAR lovers have to do all the dirty work?" he facetiously asked Bundy. "Since it was Rusk himself who opened this new round with Kamel (I would have waited), let him bell the cat (and us suggest the compromise)." Komer believed a more appropriate time for starting PL 480 talks was in late August, just before Nasser was scheduled to visit Moscow. It was important to get Nasser hooked on a good deal before the Soviets offered him anything. Until then, Komer wrote, "there's merit in keeping Nasser guessing for a while about our future intentions."

As for what a new PL 480 agreement would look like, Komer proposed a "*one-year austere deal*" for $80–$100 million, which was considerably lower than the $123 million Nasser had received in 1965. "This would both keep Nasser on the hook and remind him we're playing him on a short line," Komer told Bundy. He also proposed signing the agreement when Congress was out of session for summer recess. That way, reasoned Komer, the administration could avoid a "flat Hill ban" on aid to Egypt in 1966.[12] Komer, however, was in the dark on the fact that Nasser was about to take a series of steps that would throw off any hopes for a quiet summer.

The problems began on July 22, when Battle was unexpectedly summoned by Fawzi from a lunch he had been having with a group of Western ambassadors. The reason for the interruption was that the US embassy's political attaché, Bruce Odell, had been caught handing over a list of questions to an Egyptian journalist, Mustapha Amin, who sometimes had access to Nasser. The Egyptian authorities were accusing the two men of spying. Battle strongly denied the charge. He stressed that the arrest should not be allowed to damage relations between the two countries. Fawzi agreed with Battle that the incident should not damage diplomatic relations. In fact, Fawzi appeared to be deeply upset about the incident. According to Battle, Fawzi conducted himself "more in sorrow than in anger." Fawzi promised that Nasser would not publicize the arrest, nor would Egyptian newspapers make any mention of it.[13] It was a promising sign that the situation would be contained.

The next day, however, Nasser appeared to be emotional and upset when he gave his annual speech to mark the anniversary of the 1952 revolution that brought him to power. Although he did not outright refer to Odell's arrest, he was critical of US foreign policy in general. He accused the United States of attempting to use aid to control him. He also made a vague reference to US "arms agreements" in the Middle East. Nasser, however, was not referring to the secret arms arrangement between the United States and Israel. Rather his comment was about Yemen. Specifically, Nasser claimed that the royalists were using American weapons. The implication was that the United States was siding with Faisal in Yemen. Nasser angrily declared that Saudi Arabia's aggression in Yemen had to be dealt with once and for all. He said he intended to attack Saudi military bases if they did not immediately stop the weapons flowing into Yemen.[14]

Back in Washington, Komer was worried. "*We may have to fasten our seat belts on the UAR,*" he stressed to Bundy the day after the speech. "Aside from blowing (and twisting) all our arms control efforts, Nasser rightly convicts us of political pressure." He added, "Playing this game has its costs; for example, our $37 million may have come too late, since Gamal had already burned his bridges." Komer thought the best strategy for dealing with Nasser's latest diatribe was to "stay loose and see." Nasser appeared to be mounting a pressure campaign for a new PL 480 agreement, Komer reasoned, which was worrisome since Johnson already was seen as a "hard case" in the third world in light of the invasion of the Dominican Republic. On the other hand, Komer theorized the speech could merely be a warning to back down on Yemen, where Faisal was once again asking the United States to get involved. "I'm a good soldier and will gladly attack as well as retreat," Komer wrote, "but we ought to keep asking ourselves how many troubles we want on our plate just now."[15]

Four days later, Rusk met with Kamel to tell him that the administration was not yet ready to move forward with talks for a new PL 480 agreement. Instead, he said, the two countries needed to conduct their relations "low key" and "get them off front pages and into diplomatic channels." It was an attempt to diffuse things. But Kamel replied that it was important to give Nasser a small gesture before he visited Moscow. He asked whether the administration could at least promise to discuss a new agreement? Rusk pointed out that Nasser's speech calling US aid "pressures" had not helped the situation; particularly since Congress still had strong "reservations" about Nasser. The 1966 aid bill was still waiting for final approval in the House, Rusk said. Now was not the time for Nasser to stir up trouble.

Kamel replied with a stern warning: Nasser would turn to Moscow, he said. According to a memorandum of their conversation, "Kamel said he thought Nasser's motive in citing US pressure was to underline [a] vital Egyptian interest in wheat. [The] [c]rux is[,] if [the] US does not supply food others will. Egypt has maintained [a] non-aligned policy thus far, but failure [to] obtain US wheat would expose it to Communist domination." Kamel compared the situation to Eisenhower's decision to withdraw funding for Aswan Dam in 1956. The reference—a symbolic threat to hurt American interests in the Middle East as Nasser did once before to Britain and France—failed to move Rusk. He replied that Nasser should not overestimate Johnson's power over Congress. The only way to move forward, Rusk said, was to "keep matters quiet." Doing so would hopefully allow the two countries to work out a new PL 480 agreement in the near future.

The conversation should have stopped there. But Kamel was persistent. Nasser did not understand the president's inability to override "domestic pressures." He added that Nasser was beginning to suspect Johnson was using aid as a means to "embarrass and overthrow him." Should Nasser "become convinced [of the] validity [of] his suspicions, he would react violently and irrationally regardless of [the] consequences," Kamel said. There was no symbolism about 1955 this time. Kamel plainly made a threat.[16]

In spite of Nasser's rhetoric and Kamel's threats, Johnson still wanted to wait to discuss a new PL 480 agreement. Komer understood Johnson's reluctance. However, in the meantime, Komer wanted to make a small gesture in order to keep Nasser calm. In mid-August, Komer wrote a memo to Bundy under the facetious title of "Cats and Dogs." He informed Bundy that he had just approved a minor CCC sale to Egypt; it was for tobacco. "I've said yes, since tobacco sure ain't food and these sales bring in dollars," Komer wrote to Bundy, in justification of his decision. He was aware of his promise to Johnson not to let any of the CCC requests go through. But Komer assured Bundy that the EXIM Bank had been kept out of the deal. No doubt it was a minor flex of Komer's power in Washington, but he hoped it would go a long way in Cairo.[17]

As the summer of 1965 marched on, difficulties between the Johnson administration and Nasser continued to pile up. Surprisingly, Yemen once again became an issue when Egyptian planes crossed into Saudi Arabia and flew over select military bases. Since it appeared Nasser was making good on his threat to bomb the bases, Faisal sent word through his defense minister that he wanted Johnson to send a squadron of planes—just as Kennedy had done with Operation Hard Surface in 1963—as well as a destroyer. "The story is repeating itself," wrote Komer to Johnson. Komer noted that should Nasser "launch a full-scale attack on Saudi Arabia," the United States would have to reconsider all of its policies. Under that scenario, neutrality couldn't be maintained. But Komer stressed to Johnson that "we want to keep the pressure on both [the] Saudis and Egyptians to talk out a Yemen settlement themselves." Nobody in the administration wanted to get dragged into Yemen again; yet something had to be done. Komer proposed approving a plan from State and the DOD to send a "500 man rifle team" to Saudi Arabia for two weeks. "This isn't as risky or as expensive as an air squadron," he wrote to Johnson, "but I think State and DOD ought to get your express approval before starting down this Yemen road again." Johnson agreed with him. He wrote back, "See me. L." Bundy later translated it for Komer as, "for action as indicated."[18]

In the midst of the Yemen conflict suddenly heating up, Kamel asked to meet with Rodger Davies (director of Near Eastern Affairs) no less than two times in August. Each time, Kamel pressed for a new PL 480 agreement despite Rusk's earlier rejection. Kamel said that Nasser was growing impatient with the United States. He brought up Nasser's upcoming trip to Moscow and warned that the Egyptian leader was getting closer to the Soviets.

Kamel also said that Nasser was becoming agitated about Yemen. Indeed, there were now more Egyptian troops there than ever. Egyptian military officials were blaming their operational impasse on America's support for Saudi Arabia. They claimed to have found American weapons near the locations of several battles. Egyptian officials had already approached their American counterparts in Yemen and Cairo, asking whether the United States would refrain from intervening if Nasser attacked Saudi bases. According to a report of one such conversation: "The Saudis were hiding behind US skirts and were supporting Royalists in belief [the] US [was] committed to protect them if [the] Egyptians responded in force."

Kamel claimed to Davies that Nasser wanted to negotiate a truce with Faisal as soon as possible. However, Faisal's confidence in American support was keeping him from the negotiating table.

All of these issues—Yemen, PL 480, and even pressure from Moscow—were taking a toll on Nasser. Kamel stressed to Davies that a new PL 480 aid agreement would help to alleviate some of that pressure. The ambassador painted the situation as an imminent spiral into conflict between the United States and Egypt if the Johnson administration did not communicate to Nasser about the prospects of American aid.[19]

On August 18, Kamel's warning was seemingly amplified in a telegram from Battle. He said that America's "staunchest friends" in Cairo were pressing him to find out when Johnson was going to authorize talks for a new PL 480 agreement. Battle was concerned. He observed that while a new agreement would "not guarantee a new honeymoon in US-UAR relations," without an agreement the US embassy in Cairo would soon be reduced to "roughly that of [the] British at present, i.e., little useful contact with UAR authorities and little or no influence on such matters as UAR policies on Palestine, the Arabian Peninsula or Libya." Indeed, Britain had been sidelined in

Middle Eastern affairs since the 1950s, when it had a falling out with Nasser over the Suez Canal. This was driving Battle's present concern: the United States could soon find itself replaced in the Middle East—by the Soviets.

Battle asked to return to the United States in the fall for consultations; specifically, for "reassessing and redefining US policy towards [the] UAR." The next day, State gave him a greenlight to come home in mid-September. Stated added, for Battle's own benefit, that only after the 1966 aid bill had been finalized would Johnson possibly consider approving talks for a new PL 480 agreement. In other words, Nasser had to be patient.[20]

Nasser did not want to wait. Instead, he took steps to demonstrate his desire for a new aid agreement immediately—not least, by engineering a surprising truce with Faisal. On August 24, after three days of talks between Faisal and Nasser, the two leaders signed a document called the Jidda Agreement. In short, the agreement included the following steps for a peaceful resolution of Yemen's civil war, now in its third year: (1) a "popular plebiscite" for the Yemeni people to determine their own system of government, which was to be held "not later than 23rd November 1966"; (2) a transitional period to make preparations for the plebiscite; (3) the establishment of an "interim congress" made up of fifty members "representing all national forces and decision-making elements of the Yemeni people"; (4) a "joint neutral committee" made up of representatives from Egypt and Saudi Arabia to oversee the interim congress; (5) "The Kingdom of Saudi Arabia shall immediately cease all operations involving the supply of military assistance in any form or the use of Saudi territory for action against Yemen"; (6) "The United Arab Republic shall withdraw its military forces from Yemen within ten months starting on 23rd November 1965"; (7) "Armed clashes in Yemen shall be halted forthwith" and a "joint peace committee" established to observe a ceasefire; (8) the establishment of a joint Egyptian-Saudi military force "to crush any deviation from this agreement or any action to obstruct it or any troubles standing in the way of its successful implementation"; and (9) "Direct contact shall be established between President Gamal Abdel-Nasser and His Majesty King Feisal to avoid any difficulties hampering the implementation of this agreement." There were also two secret side deals which stipulated that: (1) Saudi Arabia and Egypt would each pick half of the fifty members (i.e., 25 each) of the interim congress; and (2) none of the former Imam's family could serve in the congress.

The Jidda Agreement was nothing short of a miracle: Nasser was reversing his long-held reluctance to give Faisal any say over Yemen's future.[21]

Even more surprising, from Washington's view, is that it was later learned Nasser arranged the talks and signed the agreement, in part, to appease the United States. According to a report of a conversation with Zakaria Muhieddin, a staunchly pro-America deputy prime minister in Egypt: "Nasser had given orders to concentrate on domestic problems and withdrawal from Yemen [was] one aspect [of] this. [The] UAR was doing exactly what [the] USG had been asking it to do, and although primarily for [its] own reasons, and not because [it was] begging for US aid, [Nasser] hoped that [the] withdrawal would have [a] beneficial effect on [the] US attitude toward aid for [the] UAR."[22]

Having contained the Yemen conflict for the time being, Nasser wasted no time turning to Washington. The day after the Jidda Agreement was signed, Kamel lobbied for a new PL 480 agreement. So eager was Kamel that, at a party for Middle East ambassadors on Johnson's presidential yacht, the Sequoia, he tracked down Johnson to talk about PL 480. Then he cornered Bundy to convince him to sit down for a formal meeting.

The next day, with Komer at his side, Bundy found himself sitting down with Kamel for the first time since their heated meeting almost a year earlier. It was awkward: Nasser had unexpectedly delivered on Yemen, but Johnson was still waiting for the 1966 foreign aid bill to get passed. All Bundy could tell Kamel was that Johnson and Rusk planned to make a "careful review" of US-Egypt relations. He acknowledged the helpful steps Nasser had taken on Yemen. But there was nothing else Bundy could offer. No doubt aware that Nasser's expectations for the meeting were high, particularly in light of his diplomatic breakthrough on Yemen, Bundy kept his statements to Kamel as noncommittal as possible, noting that the United States "wanted good relations with key countries like the UAR."[23]

"In return," Komer later wrote for the record, "he [Bundy] got an abbreviated version of the now famous Kamel speech." Indeed, Kamel once again claimed that Egypt and the United States were at a "crossroads." Nasser immediately needed aid in order not to lose his "stabilizing influence in the Middle East." As for what exactly Kamel meant by this, in Komer's paraphrased words: "Despite regrettable incidents, no basic US interests in the Middle East had been harmed; the Israeli problem was in the ice box, etc." Kamel added that Nasser had been "humiliated" by the long period without aid after the Port Said speech. Now Nasser was even beginning to believe that the CIA was out to get him—which was more than likely a reference to the Odell incident. Bundy immediately dismissed the last point: the CIA was not out to get Nasser. Nevertheless, this part of the conversation was disturbing enough that Komer sent a copy of it to Richard Helms, the incoming director of the CIA. Komer warned State that the memorandum "should receive only limited distribution."[24]

Kamel's efforts in Washington were getting nowhere. Nasser, however, continued to do his best to demonstrate to the Johnson administration that he was ready to talk about PL 480. Thus, when Nasser visited Moscow, he even refrained from making any criticism about the United States.

Of course, Nasser did not receive the warm welcome from the Soviets he had expected, which may have been a significant contributing factor to his sudden friendliness toward the United States. In fact, Nasser received very little from Moscow. Brezhnev told him that the visit was more about getting to "know you better as a human being" and to "establish personal friendships." The Soviets also pressured Nasser to get closer to their ally—his foe—Syria.[25]

But Nasser continued to hold his tongue on the United States well after the Moscow trip, and even at the third Arab summit in September, which was held in Morocco this time rather than in Egypt. As Komer pointed out to Johnson:

We reserve judgment on how Nasser came out until more of the clandestine reports are in, but so far it looks as if he made no effort to dominate [at the summit] and was relatively restrained. He stuck to the position that no military action against Israel is possible in the near future. So we continue to get a picture of a somewhat subdued Nasser, although he may have adopted a wait-and-see attitude toward us until he finds out how we answer his food requests. We have indications too, that government censors have been weeding anti-US noises out of the Cairo press recently.

Johnson initialed "L" to show that he read the memo, but he still did not indicate any sign of being ready to consider a new PL 480 agreement.[26]

Due to the many positive signals coming out of Cairo, Komer, for his part, thought it was past time to consider entering talks over a new PL 480 agreement. On September 21, he wrote to Bundy, "Battle . . . ought to see LBJ for at least five minutes on-the-record to enhance Luke's credibility in parleying with Nasser." He added, "Better yet would be to use this as an occasion for a half hour analysis of 'where now with Nasser.'" Komer asked, "Once [the 1966 foreign] aid bill is passed, would LBJ consider giving us a little ammo at least?"[27]

The next day, Komer wrote directly to Johnson. He encouraged him to take the meeting with Battle, writing, "It needs to be known that Battle saw you." Komer also informed Johnson that he and Rusk planned to "make the case" for a new PL 480 agreement after the foreign aid bill made it through Congress. "But this can be done in writing later," he added.[28]

Komer was getting ready for another major campaign in Washington on Nasser's behalf. But it would be his last time doing so before leaving for Vietnam.

16

Komer's Final Campaign

Over the rest of the summer, Komer more or less resigned himself to heading off minor crises emanating out of Congress. One such crisis led him to meet with a group of congressmen who were on the verge of making anti-Nasser speeches on Capitol Hill. Komer convinced them not to. The congressmen were upset over news reports that Nasser had sold for a profit "almost half" of the corn he had received from the United States under PL 480. While it was true some of the corn had been sold, the United States had no recourse for monitoring how Nasser actually used the food once it arrived in Egypt. As Saunders wrote to Komer, "AID says that, once they purchase the stuff, we normally consider it beyond our control." Nonetheless, to silence his critics, Nasser gave away corn to the Egyptian people at an equivalent amount to the stocks he had sold; this was subsequently verified through an audit by the US embassy. The problem had been kept low key and dealt with immediately on both sides.

However, when a routine letter to a congressman, who inquired about the incident, was sent by Johnson's congressional adviser, Larry O'Brien, who wrote, "Please be assured that your comments will be carefully considered," the response was mistakenly hailed by a reporter from the Israeli publication, *Haaretz*, as a sign that the White House and State were not in sync on policy. Indeed, State had already released a statement saying that it was "indifferent" to the corn controversy. O'Brien's letter, though it was brief, gave the impression that Johnson was upset with Nasser. The corn incident was stirring up trouble in Washington—in multiple ways—and it was out of proportion with the severity of Nasser's mistake.

In a separate incident involving Nasser, which Komer involved himself in, a congressman mistakenly believed he had valid intelligence that Nasser was building up his arms capabilities to a greater degree than the administration realized. The ambitious congressman wanted to publicly call for the cancellation of all aid to Egypt. Komer subsequently met with the congressman and informed him that his intelligence was invalid. Indeed, the congressman had been misled by a pair of Israeli lobbyists.

In a separate incident, again involving Nasser, a congressman used the House floor to publicly criticize Johnson for being friendly to Nasser. The congressman said that Congress needed to cancel aid to Egypt because Johnson was propping up Nasser with US dollars. Komer met with the congressman to set the record straight.

After a long and exhausting summer of dealing with these types of issues, Komer was once again ready to assume the driver's seat of policy. Specifically, he made it his mission to convince Johnson to authorize a new PL 480 agreement.[1]

In late September, two days after the foreign aid bill finally made it through Congress, Komer asked Johnson to take a hard look at an earlier proposal from Rusk concerning PL 480. He noted that all he and Rusk wanted was authorization to talk to Egyptian officials about a new agreement. However, as Komer himself pointed out to Johnson, "even to start talking does imply we'd go ahead."

According to Komer, the future of US-Egypt relations depended on a new PL 480 agreement. Nasser had taken a number of steps to show that he was ready to have a constructive relationship. Now Johnson had to reciprocate. Komer, however, acknowledged that the new PL 480 agreement had to be different than the previous, three-year one that had been signed under Kennedy. Nasser needed to understand that he could no longer challenge the United States and still receive its aid. "All agree we should be much less generous than in the past and keep Nasser on a short rein," Komer wrote to Johnson. "But State and our Ambassador argue cogently that some food is useful insurance to keep this key Arab country from taking a strongly anti-US course and becoming too dependent on the USSR and Red China." Komer added, "They're right on straight foreign policy grounds—moreover, we've now faced Nasser down and shown we're not to be trifled with. But if we flatly cut him off (and he halfway believes we have), he'll have no incentive to think twice about shafting us." In other words, Johnson had already demonstrated to Nasser that he was not as forthcoming with aid as Kennedy. It was clear to Nasser, at that point, that Johnson would not suffer in silence any missteps by the Egyptian leader. However, what Komer was trying to explain to Johnson was that if he personally did not like Nasser, he still had to give him at least some aid in order to avoid serious problems for the United States in the Middle East.

Of course, Komer was willing to admit that the American public's dislike for Nasser was a serious matter to consider. Komer understood that Johnson was hesitant to do anything to harm his approval ratings—particularly in light of the growing anti-war movement over Vietnam. To that end, he informed Johnson that Nasser's recent steps to end the conflicts in Yemen and Congo had bought him some goodwill in Washington. Indeed, when Battle was home for consultations and went to visit old friends on Capitol Hill, he was given the impression that "anti-Nasserism" was in decline.

Thus, Komer pushed Johnson to approve the talks for a new PL 480 agreement, stressing that it was the right time to consider entering negotiations with Nasser. Komer suggested initiating the talks immediately and offering only a six-month agreement, worth $50 million, to get the ball rolling. "Anything beyond this he'd have to take in Title IV dollar sales (which are good business for us)," Komer wrote to Johnson. "Then we'd be giving much less than in the last three-year $400 million plus Title I agreement, and Nasser would know he was on his good behavior." A Title IV agreement, versus Title I, meant that a portion would be made repayable to the US government in dollars—rather than in Egyptian pounds. It was similar to CCC sales, except that the terms were more lenient, and the federal government was the sole financier instead of a third-party bank.

Evidently, Johnson was willing to hear Komer out. He checked off an option on the memo that said, "Let's have [the] talk Rusk wants first." However, Johnson crossed out "Rusk wants first," indicating that he wanted to talk only to Komer.[2] It was a small sign that Komer had earned back the president's trust.

To be sure, Komer had his work cut out for him: Johnson had been avoiding the aid to Egypt issue for the better part of the summer. For over three months he ignored repeated requests from Rusk, Komer, and Bundy to approve a routine Title III program for Egypt—which simply allowed American charities to provide good works, like free lunch for schoolchildren. The program was running out of funding. On September 13, Komer wrote to Johnson in desperation after seeing so many of the Title III requests denied. "In the UAR, the case for going ahead is essentially not to burn all our bridges to Nasser, who seems to feel that we're doing so," Komer wrote. "While he's currently on the defensive, he's a dangerous animal when cornered . . . Resuming Title III won't buy us much but it's a highly useful indicator that we still hope to better relations." Komer added, "We've always billed Title III as non-political, so letting it drift now would be a sharp signal to Nasser that we're pulling away. [Ambassador] Battle reports straws in the wind that Nasser is beginning to worry more about his domestic problems and less about meddling abroad. Time alone will prove this, but there's merit in our keeping the door slightly ajar in case he does."

At that point, Komer was desperate to make any type of friendly gesture toward Nasser. In early October, when Johnson reluctantly approved spending $11.4 million on Title III programs, Komer pushed State to run a press release, which was subsequently featured on the front pages of several major Egyptian newspapers. "Occasionally, we do get State to produce a little publicity return," Komer told Bundy. "In general, the President's policy of playing hard to get is paying a return in making it news when we do come through." Komer wanted it to be clear to Nasser, as well as to the Egyptian people themselves, that Johnson was "giving them something." His efforts appeared to pay off. Shortly thereafter, Nasser endeavored to show Johnson that he was ready to get serious about fixing Egypt's economy. There was no mistaking that Nasser wanted a new PL 480 agreement.[3]

As if to further prove his good faith toward the United States, at the beginning of October 1965, Nasser got rid of his longtime anti-American prime minister, Ali Sabri, and appointed Zakaria Muhieddin, who was known for being pro-American. One of Muhieddin's first acts was to send Kaissouni to Washington. On October 7, Kaissouni and Kamel met with Walt Rostow at State. Rostow was a highly regarded economist, having written an influential book called, *The Stages of Economic Growth*. Meeting Rostow was a message to Johnson that Nasser no longer would be half-hearted about economic reform. The Egyptian officials told Rostow that Nasser was ready to work with the West. Kaissouni said that many Egyptians were fed up with the cost of the war in Yemen. Indeed, US officials estimated that Yemen was the heaviest strain on Egypt's economy.

Winding down expenditures on Yemen was a good first step. But Egypt still needed to garner foreign capital and undergo internal reforms. Since Nasser had lashed out at international financial institutions, like the World Bank, on multiple occasions, this would be a challenge. Kaissouni told Rostow that he recently had met with George

Woods (the president of the World Bank), and had convinced Woods to look into establishing an international consortium for development—which, as it will be recalled, is what Kamel had proposed to Bundy in the fall of 1964.

Rostow bluntly asked Kaissouni: "Is your government really prepared for the sustained stability in relations with the West which that kind of assistance demands, if it is to be successful?" Kaissouni replied, without hesitation, "it is." As the two Egyptians were headed out the door, Kamel turned to Rostow and said, "[do] not let Minister Kaissouni down before his colleagues in Cairo." He mentioned the importance Nasser was putting on a meeting between Kaissouni and Rusk that was scheduled for October 12.[4]

Rusk received the warning. On October 11, he visited Johnson, who was at a hospital in Bethesda Maryland, recovering from gall bladder surgery. Rusk broached the possibility of a new PL 480 agreement. Like Komer, Rusk stressed that it could be a "short-term PL 480 agreement." He then pushed Johnson for an answer so that he could give Kaissouni good news the next day. But Johnson denied the request. He wrote back to Rusk later that day:

> Dean,
>
> At 5:10 p.m. this afternoon, ten minutes after you left, I reviewed your memorandum on US aid to the UAR.
>
> This has not given me time that I need to decide the matter. I need further information about the rice sales, and, frankly, if a decision must be made today, I would have to disapprove the recommendation.
>
> I am sure that if these PL-480 shipments are resumed to Nasser, many other governments who have insulted us in like manner, will immediately demand new agreements also.
>
> Get me more material, and we will talk about it after I get out of the hospital.
>
> Sincerely,
>
> /S/[5]

Johnson was still reluctant to give Nasser anything. In part, he was simply intolerant of Nasser's politics. But adding to his general hesitation to work with Nasser, this time, was the fact that Nasser, once again, had sold agricultural products in a way that violated the bylaws of PL 480. Specifically, Nasser had been caught selling rice to several communist countries—including Cuba. Johnson did not like the fact that Nasser was profiting from trade with America's enemies.

Once again, Rusk had rushed into action with little regard for strategy. After seeing Johnson's memo to Rusk, Bundy wrote to Komer: "(1) We guessed right; (2) Get the rice picture straight." Rusk had erred by approaching Johnson without a solution to the rice story, which was being covered negatively in the American press. As a result, Bundy and Komer took it upon themselves to change Johnson's mind.[6]

At his meeting with Kaissouni the next day, Rusk had nothing to offer. He had little choice but to say that the matter was before Johnson, and that Johnson was waiting to take a comprehensive look at PL 480 until after he got out of the hospital. Kaissouni reluctantly agreed to wait. Indeed, it appeared a reasonable request with Johnson being sick. But Rusk had not been entirely forthcoming with Kaissouni, which was a more significant problem for diplomatic relations in the long run.

There was no escaping the fact that despite Nasser's positive steps in 1965, Johnson just could not bring himself to work with Nasser. Moreover, as Rusk privately wrote to Battle after the meeting with Kaissouni: "FYI. [The] [p]rincipal problem here is not the political issues with Egypt, which have improved in important ways, but certain policy questions regarding PL 480 as a whole which President [Johnson] wishes to be clearer. For example, the policy of sending large quantities of PL 480 food on extraordinary generous terms to countries who are themselves food exporters or to countries who use their own foreign exchange to buy food in other markets needs clarification." It was no longer enough that Nasser had taken steps to rehabilitate his image in Washington. Johnson was just too upset to learn that Nasser had exported 40 percent of his rice to communist countries when the United States was taking care of the remainder of Egypt's food requirements.[7] Once again, Johnson had to be brought to the mark.

Komer asked his junior partner, Saunders, to look into the rice situation. Komer himself was too busy. Bundy had just asked him to be his Deputy National Security Adviser. But Saunders rose to the challenge and came up with a creative solution in the spirit of Komer: he devised a plan to have Nasser sell his rice to the United States. The administration needed to find 300,000 tons of rice for South Vietnam. And the Department of Agriculture was having trouble finding it due to a worldwide rice shortage. Nasser had rice to sell, and the United States had mouths to feed in Southeast Asia.

On October 22, Saunders wrote to a colleague, James Spain, who was the head of research and intelligence on the Middle East and South Asia at State. Saunders asked Spain for input on his plan. "Jim: This is just my first effort to sort this problem out for myself," Saunders wrote. "After you've reflected on it, perhaps you could give me a call." Saunders added, "Strictly *entre-nous* [between ourselves]." Perhaps Komer's mistrust of the standard Washington bureaucracy, which tended to block creative plans like Saunders's, had rubbed off on Saunders; or, maybe Saunders shared Komer's sentiments about dealing with Nasser, while also understanding the risks of openly appearing to favor Nasser. Either way, Saunders was being strategic—and acting like Komer. Spain expressed his approval of the plan. So Saunders then sent the proposal to Komer himself.[8]

Saunders understood that it was dangerous to give Nasser the impression that the United States was desperate for rice, so his idea was to make the new PL 480 agreement contingent on Nasser agreeing to sell it. Instead of the United States appearing desperate for rice, Saunders was hoping to use Nasser's desperation for aid to America's benefit. Under Saunders's plan, if Nasser agreed to sell the United States 50,000–70,000 tons of rice, he could then get a Title I agreement with the option to buy additional food under a reasonable Title IV agreement. If Nasser refused to sell the rice to America, then he would be told that he had to buy all of his food under Title IV. That way, there was a built-in incentive for Nasser to sell his rice to the United States.[9]

Komer liked Saunders's idea. On October 25, Komer wrote to Bill Macomber, an assistant administrator at AID: "I gather that whatever other rice availabilities may be, we could almost certainly use at least 50,000 tons of UAR rice in 1965." He suggested that State and AID move "promptly" on Saunders's plan "if at all on for PL 480 for the UAR." Johnson still needed to indicate his readiness for a new PL 480 agreement. But Komer wanted a plan in place in case Johnson suddenly chose to authorize negotiations. To that end, he took the liberty of drafting up a telegram to the US embassy in Cairo to explain the complicated rice scheme.[10]

As Saunders and Komer were working on the rice angle to convince Johnson about the merits of a new PL 480 agreement, Kamel was stressing to State that time was running out to get a new agreement in front of Nasser. Egyptian newspapers were running a mock countdown—according to which, the United States had three weeks to start the negotiations.

Once again, Rusk acted on his own. On October 27, he went to Johnson's ranch in Texas and handed the president two proposals for a new PL 480 agreement. The two options were: (1) a combination of Title I (worth $70 million) and Title IV (worth $70 million) under a one-year agreement (but requiring a review at six months); or (2), only Title IV for $98 million. Rusk preferred the first option. Komer, however, thought both options were "more generous" than needed. Evidently, Rusk had overpromised Kaissouni in their meeting and was feeling pressure to deliver.

Komer understood that Johnson would never suddenly become interested in giving aid to Nasser just for the sake of continuing Kennedy's policy. Rather, Komer needed to provide Johnson with a good reason to do business with Nasser. Thus, he put forth the rice scheme. "I *favor* on foreign policy grounds *asking Nasser for non-dollar rice*," Komer wrote to Bundy on October 27. "It limits his foreign exchange for buying Soviet arms, reminds him we expect a return for our largesse, and even gives him an excuse to claim he's not just taking a dole." Komer strongly encouraged conditioning the new PL 480 agreement on Nasser selling his rice. Bundy sent word to Johnson's ranch.[11]

To Komer's surprise, Johnson liked the idea. He tentatively approved putting together a "food arrangement with Egypt." Rusk begrudgingly went along. Later that day, William Gaud from AID sent Komer a comprehensive report on Egypt's latest rice crops, writing, "Bob: You may be able to use this information on Egyptian rice in your latest wild scheme. I understand our colleagues in State are now beginning to see the beauty of your plan."[12]

A few days later, State, AID and the Department of Agriculture came up with a joint proposal that incorporated the rice scheme. It was a one-year agreement, worth $100 million, that was divided 75/25 between Titles I and IV sales. It required no down payment and the repayment period was fifteen years, with a modest 2.5 percent interest rate. Additionally, Nasser would be required to sell 100,000 tons of rice. A final stipulation was added to the agreement, and it was brimming with historical symbolism given Nasser's previous denigration of British and French influence in the region when he nationalized the Suez Canal: Nasser had to allow the United States to pay its Suez Canal tolls using Egyptian pounds received as payment for Title I sales. Nasser would receive no US dollars from US ships navigating the canal.[13]

Komer strongly advised Johnson to approve the new agreement: "Rusk's new package seems to meet the criteria you gave him at the ranch. In fact, it is tough enough that Nasser may insist on arguing about it, even though our Embassy says he's by now almost desperate enough to grasp at any straw." Komer emphasized that the proposed deal was far less generous than what Kennedy gave in 1962. Kennedy's three-year PL 480 agreement had allowed for $130–$150 million in Title I sales per year. Nasser also had wanted a multiyear agreement from the Johnson administration; but he was only getting one year. Komer advised Johnson that making the proposed deal any tougher meant risking the rice needed for South Vietnam. He stressed that the proposed agreement was "politically defensible" given that its terms were stricter than previous PL 480 agreements. Johnson, however, hesitated. The memo sat untouched on his desk for days.[14]

As a result, Komer began to worry that a one-year agreement was still too generous in Johnson's eyes. Thus, Komer wrote to Bundy that he should recommend making the deal tougher in order to get Johnson interested: "I assume this memo has been sent to the Ranch. If no answer yet, urge you to tickle. If LBJ still won't buy, I suggest cutting the duration from one year to six months and halving all the sums involved." Komer wanted to get any deal in front of Nasser—no matter how small. It was the only way to move forward with the Egyptian leader, he believed.

After a few more days of waiting, Johnson finally replied to Komer's original memo: "I want to talk to Rusk and Bundy about this Thursday." Three days later, Johnson met with them both and approved entering talks for a six-month agreement worth $54.75 million. Crucially, Komer had managed to read Johnson correctly. More importantly, his active monitoring of the situation had been pivotal in avoiding a lengthy delay.[15]

With Johnson's approval in hand, the next step was taking care of the domestic politics involved in a new PL 480 agreement with Egypt. Nasser was still a controversial figure in Washington, after all.

No doubt Komer was relieved to have Johnson finally on board for a new diplomatic outreach to Nasser—he immediately took care of all the bureaucratic paperwork himself. But Komer's pace concerned State. They wanted to proceed more slowly. They also wanted to get Johnson's approval of the negotiations on record, lest word get out that there were ongoing talks with Egypt about a new PL 480 agreement. It was important that the talks were conducted quietly in order to avoid unnecessary political fallout. At the same time, the talks had to be seen as legitimate. If word of them did leak out, the administration would not want them to be construed as a secret from the American public. But Komer did not want to give Johnson any reason to reconsider his decision to move forward on aid for Egypt. It had taken many months to convince Johnson to even consider talking about a new deal with Egyptian officials. Thus, Komer wrote to State, "Since the President had already made the policy decision, we did not feel it necessary to burden him with a determination now on an exercise which might yet be abortive."[16]

However, word soon did start to leak that the administration was pursuing a new aid deal with Nasser. Administration officials believed it was coming from Israel, which did not want to see Nasser emerge from his economic crisis with help from Johnson. On November 9, the Israeli ambassador told Rostow over lunch that the administration was making a big mistake by offering Nasser a new PL 480 agreement. He argued that "external frustration and internal pressure" were just beginning to get

Nasser to moderate his behavior; any amount of aid from the United States would essentially "bail him out." After the meeting, news travelled fast of the tentative PL 480 agreement, indicating that the Israeli ambassador had put a pressure campaign into play. Later that same day, Senator Stuart Symington (D. Missouri) asked State officials to meet in his office over "reports" that the administration was "considering a new PL 480 program for the UAR." He stressed that Johnson had to balance any new aid to Nasser by allowing Israel to buy "supersonic" planes directly from the United States. After a brief chat with Komer over the phone, however, Symington promised not to go public with news of the negotiations. Nonetheless, shortly thereafter, a number of other pro-Israel lawmakers began writing letters to Johnson to voice their collective concerns. Komer attempted to manage the group by writing a letter in Bundy's name.[17]

Komer wrote: "The President cannot help but feel that the type of statements you propose would only complicate his task and unfairly expose him on matters where our full case cannot be made public." No doubt, as Komer earlier had learned on Capitol Hill, presidential authority was powerful. But, this time, Komer overstepped by presuming to speak for Johnson. Bundy wrote back to Komer, with emphasis: "Bob: For god sake! *Don't ever* use President the way you do in [the] last paragraph without having checked with him!!"[18] Komer replied, "You caught me on the hip, though rightly so. I was worried over Symington not listening unless [the] reply seemed Presidential. If LBJ OKed the UAR deal, I assumed he would hardly cavil at our using his name to defend it. But I should have said so—and [I] am red-faced." Clearly, Komer wanted Johnson to stand behind the talks with Egypt; so he tried alternative ways to make this happen.[19]

On November 24, Komer wrote to Johnson's two closest advisers, Jake Jacobsen and Bill Moyers, asking them to press Johnson for permission to make "a low key oral release" about the talks. "We'll get flak in any case," Komer wrote, "but Bundy and I agree there's advantage in putting out [the] story ourselves rather than just letting it leak." The plan worked: two days later, Johnson consented to an oral release.[20]

With Johnson's backing now made public, Komer began to write to senators and congressmen in defense of the proposed PL 480 agreement. He also went up to Capitol Hill, once again, to explain in person the pressing reasons (in Komer's view) for a new agreement with Nasser. Nonetheless, this time, Komer was more careful to check in with Bundy, writing, "Mac: Just glance before I send. I'm new at writing Senators."[21]

Despite his concerns, Komer's meetings on Capitol Hill went better than expected. After meeting with Symington, Komer observed that the senator appeared appreciative that the administration was dealing with the matter with a "degree of candor." [22] Other lawmakers liked the fresh strategy of giving Nasser smaller aid packages in six-month increments. One senator said to Douglas MacArthur he was "glad to learn that we had abandoned the idea of a one year program for if we had negotiated a one year program he would have been obliged to oppose it with all his strength and he felt the end result would have been the passage by Congress of legislation which would absolutely prohibit any shipments to the UAR next year. The Senator said that he thought the program we had in mind was 'realistic.'" In other words, Komer definitely had made the right call with the six-months term for the tentative deal.[23]

As Komer made progress getting lawmakers in Washington on board behind a new PL 480 deal with Egypt, negotiations moved forward in Cairo. The process began with State giving Battle permission to inform Kaissouni about the proposed deal. In light of the stringent terms Johnson was offering Nasser, Kaissouni was seen as the Egyptian official most likely to be receptive. So he was the first one approached. "Kaissouni [is] not only in [a] position [to] better understand [the] implications [of a] new agreement [for Egypt's economic outlook,] but [is] less likely [to] react emotionally about possible 'strings' or penalties," reasoned State.

There was significant concern that Nasser would have an off-the-cuff response to the six-months term of the new PL 480 agreement. Therefore, Battle was instructed to meet with Nasser separately: not to talk about PL 480, but US-Egypt relations in general. Both State and Komer believed it was necessary to understand where Nasser stood with the United States before proceeding. That way, they could best determine how the two countries could move forward along areas of "cooperation."[24]

On November 24, Battle went to see Nasser. By that point, the Egyptian leader was aware of the proposed deal and, surprisingly, had nothing negative to say about the terms. Instead, Nasser expressed nothing but gratitude for Johnson's authorization of the talks. "We have nothing to gain from bad relations [with] your country," he said, "and we will do everything possible to improve them."

Even when the conversation moved to Yemen—normally a sensitive issue between the two countries—Nasser remained upbeat. "Do you know we have had over 70,000 troops there?" he asked Battle. It was an astonishing admission from Nasser of how heavily extended, militarily, he had been. Battle replied that he had not been aware of that figure. Evidently, Nasser was looking to increase his capital with the Johnson administration. Nasser told Battle that his military commanders had been preparing to go to war against Saudi Arabia, and that it had taken considerable effort to hold off their "pressure" and come to an understanding with Faisal in Jidda. Nasser asked Battle to ensure that the administration kept in touch with Faisal, and "do all possible [to] keep anything from going wrong."

The two men, Battle and Nasser, had not had a substantial discussion for several months. It was an opportunity to see where the United States and Nasser stood respectively on issues that had affected their relations for most of 1965. The meeting turned emotional when the arms deal with Israel came up. Nasser said, "If you sell planes to Israel, we will buy planes. If you sell tanks to Israel, we will buy tanks." Despite this warning, Nasser was relatively restrained. As Battle later wrote, the meeting had been "embarrassingly friendly." Indeed, Nasser once again apologized for his speech at Port Said. In this way, he appeared determined to stay out of trouble in order to get the new PL 480 agreement finalized. "Obviously he wishes desperately [to] get back in good graces with us," Battle reported to State, "and will[,] I believe[,] try in his own way to do his part."[25]

These were all positive signs—Komer's successful lobbying in Washington and Nasser's warm reception of Battle in Cairo. It was important to keep the momentum going. To that end, at Komer's urging, Johnson approved an outstanding request by Egypt to release $2.5 million for ongoing technical assistance programs—which allowed for sending United States experts to Egypt, and for sending Egyptian personnel to the United States to receive training and "exposure to American ideas and ideals." "We have held up this minor matter till the UAR food program was launched," wrote Komer to Johnson. "This is the only on-going dollar aid program we have left in the UAR. State makes the case that it maintains useful person-to-person contact and that termination now would jar our slowly improving relations with the UAR." No doubt, it was a minor gesture to sweeten the mood of the PL 480 talks in Cairo.[26]

Nonetheless, the talks proved difficult, despite the sudden warming between Washington and Cairo. Until the very end, Nasser's negotiators were adamant that the rice scheme would not work because the 1965 crop yields had been lower than expected. Moreover, the Egyptians stressed that the cornerstone of Muheidden's economic reforms, which the United States had encouraged, involved expanding Egypt's foreign currency holdings through its rice exports. Egypt badly needed the funds from these sales, said the Egyptians. On strict instruction from Washington, the American negotiators remained firm on the rice issue. On December 21, Nasser's negotiators finally relented. Battle wrote to State, "UAR, finally realizing that [the] whole agreement might fail on this point, reluctantly and under protest[,] accepted." On December 27, after all the terms of the agreement were finalized, the Egyptian negotiators pressed for signing it before New Year's Eve, which left only three days to get Johnson's approval and signature for the required "Presidential Determination." (This was due to the amendment to the foreign aid bill that required the president to determine that giving aid to Egypt was in the nation's interest.) In other words, Johnson did not have any time for second thoughts.[27]

On December 28, Komer wrote to Johnson: "Since we've already taken our Congressional flack as a result of the decision to go ahead and since the UAR has met our stiff terms, to hold any longer would tend to defeat the purpose of the exercise." Komer added: "It also makes sense to go ahead before Congress comes back." Komer observed that Nasser had been "relatively quiet." Komer was holding his breath, lest Nasser's silence be interrupted by a sudden diatribe against the United States or some other Western country. He advised Johnson to sign the new agreement without any delay. The next day, Johnson approved the deal, thus symbolically ending a tumultuous and uncertain year in US-Egypt relations. The relationship was finally ready to move forward.[28]

17

Sadat's Visit

With PL 480 back in the picture, it seemed like US-Egypt relations were finally back on track. However, it soon became apparent through a visit to the United States by Anwar Sadat—the head of Egypt's parliament—that the Egyptians were getting frustrated because they did not think the United States was giving the relationship enough attention. Moreover, Nasser was secretly upset about the six-months term of the new PL 480 agreement.

Back in June 1965, when Johnson's officials were in the middle of dealing with Congress to release the $37 million, Nasser's officials had floated the idea of a high-level visit by the head of the national assembly, Anwar Sadat. Komer tried to get Johnson to approve. "For obvious reasons we have rarely had any top UAR officials here," he wrote, "while the Soviets go out of their way to invite Nasser and his people to Moscow." Johnson replied, "Lunch if you suggest. L." However, Kamel later informed Talbot that Nasser felt the timing was not yet right for such a visit. According to a memorandum of their conversation, Kamel said: "The Sadat visit would be best put off until the beginning of the next session of Congress. He thought repair work on US-UAR relations would have to continue for the next six months and that any possible disruption to a quiet handling of the situation during this period should be avoided."[1]

On December 14, in the middle of the PL 480 negotiations, Sadat himself asked if he could visit in February. One Egyptian official said to Battle that Sadat hoped the new aid deal would be concluded by then, so that the visit could be framed as "a new beginning" between the two countries. Moreover, Sadat hoped that he could be greeted at the airport by Rusk—which would send a message to the rest of the world that Egyptian officials were no longer received at arm's length in America.[2]

State wanted it to be clear to Sadat, and by extension Nasser, that any trip would be purely symbolic, and not an opportunity to deal with substantive issues. "We anticipate no QUOTE positive results END QUOTE [from the] visit except laying groundwork [for an] improved understanding in visitors of US institutions, a few high officials, people, and way of life," State wrote to Battle. "We hope [the] familiarity gained [from Sadat's visit] may serve as [a] basis [for] better understanding [of] things American and thus serve as [a] basis [for] better future relations [between the two countries]."[3]

On January 20, three weeks after the signing of the new PL 480 agreement, Rusk encouraged Johnson to approve the visit. Komer also wrote to Johnson: "Sadat ain't

Nasser, but he's the highest ranking Egyptian ever to visit officially." He reminded Johnson of his prior approval of the visit in June, and asked the president to approve it again on the grounds that Israel's foreign minister, Abba Eban, was also asking for a meeting around that same time. "The Egyptians constantly are received in Moscow, so it makes sense to let them see that the door is open here too," Komer wrote. The next day, Johnson wrote back, "I'll see both of them. L."[4]

With Johnson's approval secured, State gave Battle permission to tell Sadat. They instructed Battle to describe the trip as a cultural event, rather than an opportunity for substantive talks: "FYI. We believe US-UAR relations [are] best served by [a] visit emphasizing [a] red carpet rather than substance[,] and hope [to] avoid encounters that could unleash hostile public criticism [both in Egypt and the US] that [are] never far from [the] surface."[5]

Battle wrote back to State that the US embassy staff were "gratified" that Johnson would even be able to meet with Sadat. However, he warned that Sadat's assistants were beginning to question whether the planned diplomatic protocols of the trip would be appropriate for an official of Sadat's stature. Sadat was adamant about Rusk meeting him at the airport. After State dodged the question, Battle wrote a "personal" telegram to Rusk, encouraging him to welcome Sadat as he would expect Vice President Hubert Humphrey to be welcomed in Cairo. "This is essentially [a] petty matter in our eyes but it [is] obviously looming large in UAR view," Battle wrote. "Sadat [is the] first senior UAR official to visit us and [the] Egyptians [are] concerned that he receive [an] adequate red carpet." Egyptian officials would not drop the issue.[6]

Therefore, State felt it necessary to dampen the Egyptians' expectations. Kamel was summoned to State, where he was told that Sadat's trip was being funded under a routine grant that paid for foreign officials to visit the United States and "familiarize" themselves with the country and "its people." In other words, from Washington's standpoint, Sadat's visit was no different than the routine visits of other foreign officials—Sadat was not considered a high-level visitor. Battle reluctantly agreed to echo the message in Cairo. However, he warned State that Sadat was a member of the original clique that had brought Nasser into power in 1952. Sadat had the ear of Nasser. And Battle stressed that Sadat would want to "bring home [a] bacon of some sort." There was no doubt that the Egyptians viewed it as a historic visit. Fawzi let Battle know that Sadat would be flanked by several high officials during his trip. Battle believed they were coming in order to "advise" Sadat for "substantial discussions" with US officials.[7] The Egyptians simply weren't getting the message.

On February 23, Sadat came to the White House flanked by Kamel and Ahmad Hassan al-Feqi, an undersecretary in the Egyptian foreign ministry. Johnson started off the meeting by noting that relations between the two countries had somewhat improved. However, he noted that the main problem between the two countries boiled down to a public relations issue. Johnson said he understood that Nasser had his own "problems." However, he asked that Egyptian officials put themselves "in his shoes." He compared himself to a goldfish in a bowl; the entire country was watching his every move, he said. "That . . . [is] the character of American democracy." Johnson told Sadat that he could not force Congress to allow him to give aid to Egypt at any point in time. Instead, he had to be strategic, and show Congress that US-Egypt relations were steadily improving. Johnson then got personal with Sadat. He told him that he was often an object of intense public scrutiny. Political opponents tried to bate him in order to get him to react in a way that could bring him down. But he would not give "them that pleasure." The implication was that neither could Nasser. Johnson said, "When your government has something to say to us, you just tell Ambassador Kamel to put on his hat and come down here. Let's not talk about it in public."[8]

The meeting ended on a positive note. Johnson asked that the conversation remain private. Sadat could tell the gathered press outside that they had discussed "mutual problems," but he wanted to start keeping US-Egypt relations "out of the public forum." Indeed, an hour before the meeting, Komer had sent an urgent message to Johnson. The day before, Nasser's annual speech to mark the anniversary of the revolution that brought him into power had been unexpectedly emotional. Komer instructed Johnson to keep Sadat calm in front of the press. "We don't want him popping off in the West Lobby," Komer warned.[9]

Nasser's speech seemed to indicate that another period of difficulty with the United States was coming in the near future. Israel had nuclear capabilities because of the United States, Nasser said. And Faisal was reneging on the Jidda Agreement. "Should we surrender to Faisal or should we sit ten years in Yemen?" Nasser asked a raucous crowd. "I say, we shall sit for twenty!" Johnson refused to discuss either of the two issues, Israel's nuclear program or Yemen, with Sadat. He stuck to the earlier line that it was not supposed to be a substantive meeting but rather a symbolic one. The thrust of Johnson's message to Sadat, indeed the only point of substance, was that US-Egypt relations needed to be kept out of the public sphere.[10]

Two days later, Rusk reiterated the same message to Sadat. He said that Johnson "believed deeply" that "leaders" who wanted to improve relations "should not engage in polemics." Sadat smiled and said he understood.[11] What else could he say while being a guest in America?

On March 2, Kamel wrote to Komer to thank the administration for receiving Sadat. "I am sure that this important meeting will contribute immensely in cementing and promoting the good relations which exist between our two countries." Kamel added, "May I ask you, my dear Mr. Komer, to be kind enough to convey to the President our thanks and deepest appreciation as well as our hope for his continued success in the leadership of his great country and his tireless efforts for world cooperation and peace." By now, Kamel understood just how important Komer was to the preservation of US-Egypt relations. Komer wrote back: "I am only sorry that I could not myself take the opportunity to meet Mr. El Sadat during his Washington stay." He added, "However, you may regard my door too as always open."[12]

Komer, however, was not yet aware that he would soon be leaving the White House. Indeed, he would not have anything to do with Nasser for the remainder of the Johnson administration. The last ardent supporter of strong US-Egypt relations was about to exit the stage.

Komer's departure from the Middle East portfolio could not come at a worse time. There was no doubt that Nasser was upset about the new "short leash" of American aid under Johnson. In the absence of a redirection strategy to reassure Nasser about his concerns, and without Komer in the picture to act as a gadfly in Washington, communication between the two countries would hit their lowest point since Eisenhower.

Part Three

After Komer
(March 1966–May 1967)

18

Johnson's Men

In March 1966, there was no mistaking that Kennedy's men were now firmly Johnson's men. Komer's replacements had a different approach to policy-making. For one thing, none of them filled the role of being a gadfly, which was problematic since Komer often took matters into his own hands to create diplomatic outreaches to Nasser.

The six-month PL 480 agreement with Egypt went into effect on January 20, 1966. It was the last PL 480 aid that Nasser would ever receive. Following Sadat's visit to the United States, Nasser failed to keep up the spirit of the agreement by refusing to temper his anti-American rhetoric. As US officials watched him make speech after speech decrying "US imperialism" in Vietnam and in the Middle East, a series of changes to NSC personnel and a restructuring of its operations resulted in a different approach to dealing with Nasser.[1] Gone were the days of Komer arguing for continuing aid and convincing others to follow suit.

As seen in Parts 1 and 2 of this book, Komer had been a relentless figure behind the scenes. He was willing to deal with members of Congress to get aid through the legislature, he micromanaged his counterparts at State in order to control their movements, and he somewhat understood how to appeal to Johnson in order to gain his approval. Also, Komer was indispensable to Bundy, and therefore was given a large degree of autonomy (for a mid-level staffer) to drive the administration's policy on Egypt. Komer had played a pivotal role in getting Johnson to extend aid to Nasser on several different occasions during the difficult year of 1965. If Komer had an abnormally large impact on diplomatic relations with Egypt for an NSC staffer, then the opposite was equally true after his departure: his absence spelled trouble for US-Egypt relations.

In the spring of 1966, shortly after Sadat's visit, Johnson's foreign policy team underwent major changes. It began with Bundy suddenly leaving the administration for a new position as director of the Ford Foundation—a nonprofit organization. At the beginning of March, Komer was made the interim national security adviser. Before his departure, Bundy wrote to Johnson that Komer was the ideal candidate to replace him on a permanent basis.[2] Nonetheless, Komer was to be just a placeholder. Instead of maintaining the status quo by sticking with Bundy's designated successor, Johnson decided to restructure the NSC, thereby dispersing Bundy's duties between several different positions. (It will be recalled that Bundy had an unusually significant amount of influence for a National Security Adviser.) At the end of Komer's trial month, March

31, Johnson made the surprising decision to bring Walt Rostow into the White House from State. He, not Komer, was to be the new national security adviser.[3]

Along with the NSC staff shuffling came a change in philosophy. The regional committees within the NSC became an academic enterprise rather than an outlet for presidential action.[4] While Komer had understood that his cohort in Middle East policy-making had been granted special permission by Bundy to skirt the bureaucratic process and "speak for" their superiors—telling an interviewer, at one point that, "the Middle East was being a sideshow with sort of decentralized decision-making"[5]—he also later acknowledged that the situation drastically changed after his departure.[6]

Rostow had an entirely different approach than Bundy—which, ironically, had led to the two men clashing when Rostow initially served as Bundy's deputy national security adviser at the beginning of the Kennedy administration. As Johnson's new national security adviser, Rostow returned the NSC to its role as a "paper-mill," which was a clear reversal of the Kennedy era approach to foreign policy. But this had always been Rostow's approach, which is why initially he had clashed with Kennedy's emphasis on action rather than deliberation. As Bundy later recalled, "I've always thought that one of the reasons . . . President [Kennedy] put Walt Rostow in the Department of State was so he wouldn't have to read quite so many papers which he didn't have to decide on." Johnson apparently felt differently. He now expected analysis from the NSC rather than recommendations for immediate action.[7]

When Rostow held his first NSC staff meeting, Johnson made a quick appearance to tell the staffers that he wanted information and ideas from them that could not be found in newspapers. "Your President wants ten ideas a week from each of you," he said. "Cut it to nine, but one will give me satisfaction. Dream your dreams and let me have them."[8] Crucially, this now meant that Johnson was somewhat removed from the NSC. Although he occasionally read their reports—which Rostow would selectively pick and choose for him—policy decisions were mostly made at the Tuesday lunch-meetings in the company of a few senior officials. And these lunches were often entirely dominated by the Vietnam War; especially now that Johnson asked for weekly briefings on its progress.[9]

Rostow's appointment also led to a fundamental shift in how the administration perceived Nasser. Above all else, Rostow was an economics scholar. In 1960 he produced a well-received book about the evolution of democracies, *The Stages of Economic Growth: A Non-Communist Manifesto*. In it, he argued that nuclear weapons were a paradox for powerful countries like the United States. Although nuclear states had awesome power at their fingertips, the threat of mutually assured destruction between the nuclear states meant that such power could never be reasonably used. Therefore, there existed two realms of foreign policy within a nuclear state, Rostow wrote. The first was the stalemate between countries with nuclear weapons. The second was the "main business of the world," consisting of "diplomacy, economic policy, and conventional weapons of a low order." Thus, "the major powers from day to day operate under great restraint with respect to powers whose military potential in no way approximates their own." The leaders of smaller, nonnuclear states, such as Nasser, had "found ways of exploiting this paradox."[10] While in Rostow's worldview, aid was a tool that could be used for helping developing countries (like Egypt) that were on the verge of obtaining a self-sustaining economy, by 1966 Nasser had proven himself to be wasteful on ideological causes, like the war in Yemen, and inflicted harm upon American interests. This made him less deserving of America's help. Ironically, Rostow had initially shared Komer's enthusiasm for redirecting Nasser through aid. However, he later came to see Nasser as "such a mixed-up character"; a "sucker" even.[11]

No doubt, from Johnson's perspective at the time, Rostow was an ideal candidate for bringing fresh solutions to the quagmire in Vietnam; especially for getting the noncommunist part of the country, South Vietnam, onto its feet. However, what Johnson may have believed was good for his Vietnam policy, actually brought significant harm to his Middle East policy. The only person capable of bending Johnson's ear and making the case for working with Nasser had been Komer. However, instead of having Komer return to his previous role as the NSC's top Middle East adviser, Johnson shifted him out of Middle East policy altogether. Johnson wanted to apply Komer's persistence, especially his qualities as a gadfly, toward ending the Vietnam War.

At that point, Johnson was beginning to focus on nation-building in Vietnam. And he wanted Komer to be in charge on the ground.[12] Komer's new position was announced via a National Security Action Memoranda. "In my view it is essential to designate a specific focal point for the direction, coordination and supervision in Washington of US non-military programs for peaceful construction relating to Vietnam," Johnson declared. "I have accordingly designated Mr. Robert W. Komer as Special Assistant to me for carrying out this responsibility."[13]

Shortly after the NSAM was made public, Kamel wrote to Komer, congratulating him on his new position. Komer wrote back, "You may be sure that even though I am moving on to new responsibilities, I will continue to watch with great interest the enterprise which has concerned both of us so keenly over the past five years." No doubt, these were thoughtful parting words; indicative of the spirit in which Komer had committed himself to revitalizing US-Egypt relations under Kennedy and later Johnson. However, despite his promise to stay involved, Komer would never return to Middle Eastern affairs during the Johnson administration—much to the dismay of Egyptian officials.[14]

Officially, William Howard Wriggins replaced Komer as the senior NSC adviser on Near East/South Asian affairs. However, it was Wriggins's deputy, Harold Saunders, who became the de facto Middle East staffer at the White House. As it will be recalled, Saunders had already been in the NSC for four years as Komer's junior partner.[15]

Wriggins was an expert on South Asia. Therefore, he let Saunders take the lead on Middle Eastern affairs.[16] Indeed, Wriggins's official title as senior Middle East adviser had more to do with the odd "shot-gun marriage" of Near East and South Asia affairs within the NSC, which is how one staffer characterized the bureaucratic restructuring of Johnson's foreign policy staff.[17]

Saunders was very different than Komer. For one thing, he was seen by his peers as a Middle East wonk. Also, he was not as much of an optimist when it came to Nasser. His reports were realistic about the low prospect of warm relations between the United States and Egypt while Nasser remained in power.

As will be seen in Part 3 of this book, Saunders accurately predicted the coming break in US-Egypt relations that would occur in May 1967. Saunders, however, lacked Komer's raw political skills and understanding of Washington, which made him incapable of playing the gadfly role that Komer had so masterfully deployed over the years to keep US-Egypt relations afloat. Only after the Arab-Israeli war in June 1967, when US-Egypt relations were officially severed at Nasser's behest, did Saunders come to hold any sway over Johnson.[18]

Alongside changes at the NSC, there were also structural changes at State. Specifically, a "Country Directorate" system was established, which meant that each country was assigned a Country Director and their assistant.[19] For Egypt, in 1966, the role of Country Director fell to Donald Bergus and his assistant, George Bennsky—a holdover from the NEA bureau's economic desk. Bennsky would later describe 1966 as a particularly difficult year for dealing with Egypt from Washington: "the Egyptians, themselves, would keep doing things that would cause Washington politicos to be upset with them. And even when they weren't doing things they had reached that reputation where they were suspected of doing them."[20]

In 1966, Rusk began to put off dealing with Nasser. Talbot, having become the US ambassador to Greece, was no longer around to continue Komer's redirection strategy at State.

Without Kennedy, Badeau, and now Talbot, and most importantly, without another Komer in the White House to act as a gadfly, important decisions about Egypt were left on State's backburner for too long in 1966. As a result, America's relations with Egypt rapidly deteriorated in the year leading up to the 1967 War. Komer later remarked that his most important job in Washington had been to de-escalate tensions between the United States and Nasser. "Remember, I was not a great cold warrior," he said. "How to do business with Nasser was an attempt to defuse the Middle East dragon. So most of my exercises were low posture exercises."[21]

Without Komer at the helm, or a strong ambassador in Cairo, there was no one left to defuse the problems that would subsequently arise between the United States and Nasser. Tragedy was right around the corner.

19

A New Policy

The beginning of the end for US-Egypt relations came on June 18, 1966, when Rostow noted in a memo to Johnson that Nasser's "economy is in worse shape than ever—[foreign cash] reserves are all but exhausted." The six-month PL 480 agreement was set to expire in twelve days, on June 30. Back in March, Nasser had asked for a new one-year PL 480 agreement worth $150 million. His request, however, went unanswered in the middle of all the personnel changes and Johnson's growing preoccupation with Vietnam. By the time Rostow wrote to Johnson about Egypt's economic woes, it was past time to give Nasser a response to his request. Nasser needed American aid immediately in order to avoid Egypt's impending economic disaster. All of Johnson's advisers, however, were telling him not to renew aid to Egypt.[1]

The underlying issue was a realization that Nasser was becoming more and more hostile toward the United States, despite the many years of trying to moderate him through aid. Saunders, the new Komer, was tentatively part of a group that called for leaving Nasser high and dry on aid for a time. He wrote in a memo: "As far as I can see, we have just about reached the end of our rope. We really can't argue any more that we are buying influence with Nasser via PL 480. To justify sending more food, we need more to show for our aid. So the problem is how to get something and still give enough to keep this door open."[2]

Saunders was wrestling with the futility of continuing to help a hostile leader when there was so little benefit visible to the naked eye. Therefore, he wondered whether the timing was right for a new strategy. He wrote to Wriggins, "our chief political problem in the UAR is that Nasser is a revolutionary—not the sort of rational calculator of priorities . . . whom we can work with." To be sure, this was a 180-degree turn from what Komer had written to Bundy shortly before the first Arab summit in 1964. Komer had believed that Nasser was the type of leader who would ultimately listen to the United States. Saunders was not so sure anymore.[3]

To be sure, this shift in Saunders's thinking was part of the larger ideological transformation in Johnson's administration. Nasser, for his part, never really changed. Since the 1950s, he consistently had alternated between warm and cool periods vis-à-vis the West. But although Johnson's officials would continue to wrestle over the aid issue up until the outbreak of the 1967 War, several factors combined that ushered the end of American aid to Nasser as it was: the departure of Bundy and Komer, Johnson and Rusk's growing preoccupation with the war in Vietnam, and a smaller wheat crop in the American Midwest. To make matters worse, a global drought brought famine to India in 1966, requiring the United States to give away a large portion of its agricultural surplus. This left the administration in short supply to meet its aid commitments to other countries.[4]

The latter development, more than anything, led Johnson to place a greater emphasis on sending aid to countries that really needed it. And a massive PL 480 deal for India, in the wake of the famine, showed Johnson that aid could only turn adversaries into friends if the former were actually receptive to change. Even Komer, who never seemed to lose faith in Nasser's ability to change, characterized Johnson's White House meeting with India's president, Indira Gandhi, as a "fitting . . . valedictory as your Mid-East hand" and as the most important US foreign policy meeting "since Kennedy met Khrushchev in Vienna."[5]

In return for an aid program that combined IMF loans with American aid, Johnson convinced Gandhi to implement liberalizing economic reforms in India. Komer hailed the program as the "real McCoy," and told Johnson that he had helped "500 million people in the largest country in the Free World." The program became considered by many in the administration a new standard for how the United States should conduct economic assistance to all developing nations. Rusk subsequently instructed all embassies and legations to share with their host governments news of India and America's new partnership. Johnson asked to see the replies. He had reason to be proud: he was told that his outreach to India had put the country on a direct path to economic independence.[6]

By choosing Walt Rostow to be his new national security adviser, Johnson no doubt found the perfect partner to join him in engineering similar large-scale economic assistance programs for other countries that would be responsive to America's help. Thus, when Saunders wrote to Wriggins, in May 1966, about reappraising US-Egypt relations, he was thinking along the lines of Johnson's new approach to economic assistance and considering how to apply it to the situation with Nasser. The approach used on India, however, was not applicable to Nasser's circumstances. Saunders understood that Nasser was probably incapable of making the same sweeping changes Gandhi had. After all, the United States had already "tried [and failed] for five years to 'turn Nasser inward'—to help him begin weighing his development priorities against his foreign revolutionary aims."[7]

Saunders was not alone in thinking that it was time for the United States to reevaluate its economic outreach to Nasser. Indeed, as Rostow noted in his memo to Johnson about Egypt's economic problems, numerous officials at State and in the White House were "just fed up" with Nasser.[8] These officials, however, did not advocate for a complete break in aid to Egypt. Rather, most of them believed it was necessary to temporarily withhold aid in order to get Nasser to moderate his rhetoric. This position was halfway between Komer's emphasis on consistent aid to keep Nasser engaged at all times and Johnson's seeming antipathy toward Nasser. These officials were still interested in working with Nasser, but just not to the same extent as before.

The problem was this: besides Moscow, Egypt had nowhere else to turn for economic assistance. Private investment was simply not an option. When Boeing was considering selling planes to Egypt on credit from the Export-Import Bank, Bennsky observed, "we hope always that private ties can help," and instructed Harold Linder, president and chairman of the Export-Import Bank, accordingly. Linder, however, was "skeptical" that Egypt could afford to take on new debt. William Wolle from State agreed. According to him, Egypt's currency reserves were "under $10 million; short term credit heavily overdrawn and UAR credit rating at rock bottom. Cotton crop is threatened by [a] leaf worm and [the] anti-feudalism campaign will cause a new nose-dive in industrial and agricultural efficiency via a new round of sequestration [i.e., forcing businesses to declare bankruptcy]." Nasser was still not taking the correct steps to fix Egypt's economy. Private investment was likely a waste of money.[9]

Rusk, for his part, did not want Johnson to give Nasser a new PL 480 agreement because of Nasser's anti-American rhetoric—which, strangely enough, had increased exponentially since he received the six-month PL 480 agreement. But, considering Egypt's serious economic problems, Rusk did not envision a complete break in aid to Egypt. Instead, he advised Johnson to approve a $50 million CCC sale, which would have better credit terms than a commercial market sale. At the same time, Rusk thought it was important to maintain Title III programs, which provided social initiatives like lunches for Egyptian schoolchildren. Rostow supported Rusk's recommendations. He wrote to Johnson, "Nasser badly needs this food—and on heavily concessional terms if he can get them." The thinking behind the proposal was that Nasser would reconsider his hostile rhetoric and reckless economic policies if he felt the sting of no PL 480 aid for a little while. Johnson agreed with this approach and approved both of Rusks's recommendations.[10]

On June 20, Battle was instructed to notify Kaissouni that the administration would consider resuming PL 480 aid to Egypt at a later date. Egypt's request for a new one-year agreement would not be approved due the "present overall state of US relations with [the] UAR." Nonetheless, Egypt could still get wheat from the United States through a CCC sale, which was capable of holding the country over until September or October 1966. If relations between the two countries improved by then, Nasser could reapply for a new PL 480 agreement. State wrote to Battle, "we do not want give [a] negative response and sincerely hope [that the] overall climate [of] US–UAR relations will improve enough in [the] future to make [a] favorable response possible."[11]

It was a calculated policy that was intended to provide some assistance to Egypt while still incentivizing Nasser to reform. Although Nasser wanted to immediately obtain aid—specifically wheat—through the more favorable terms of a PL 480 agreement, he was receiving lower interest rates through the CCC than he would from commercial market vendors.[12] Saunders observed that while it was a "'no' on PL 480 for the time being . . . all other lines [are] open to Nasser."[13] Nasser was not being cut off; but the administration was putting away its carrots for the time being and picking up sticks.

It soon became clear, however, that Nasser was extremely troubled by the vague rejection. He only wanted PL 480 aid, not CCC sales. Battle had received no pushback when he delivered the news in Cairo. Nasser, however, made sure his disappointment was felt directly in Washington. He promptly sent Kamel, who had been on leave in Cairo, to express his concerns.

Kamel embarked on a series of meetings to persuade US officials to resume PL 480 aid. In the first meeting, which took place at State on June 24, he highlighted Nasser's steps to attract Western business to Egypt. (One of Kamel's examples was that Nasser had lifted restraints on American oil companies prospecting for oil on the Sinai Peninsula.) Kamel said that Nasser was willing to wait until after America's congressional elections in November to request another PL 480 agreement—but only if the administration informally committed itself to a one-year agreement in the meantime. Kamel warned that Nasser would turn to Moscow in the absence of any informal commitment from the United States. The Soviet Premier, Alexei Kosygin, had visited Cairo in May and had left Nasser on the verge of accepting Soviet wheat, Kamel said. He advised that the administration quickly put together an aid package for Nasser in order to prevent that from happening. No doubt, it was a hard sell, but Kamel ultimately was rebuffed by his American interlocutors. If Nasser wanted to send a positive message to Johnson, Kamel was told, then Nasser should focus on winding down the war in Yemen.[14] Indeed, Nasser effectively had torn up the Jidda Agreement when Britain announced that it would be leaving Southern Arabia in 1968. Nasser suddenly renewed his interest in Yemen and moved Egyptian troops to the border areas in order to be ready to move in after the British left the area. The United States was not happy that Nasser was backtracking from what had looked like a promising peace agreement with Faisal.[15]

Kamel was not deterred by the negative response he received at State. And he continued to play up the threat of the Soviets increasing their position in the Middle East as if he truly believed it would play on the Americans' Cold War fears and convince them to reconsider a new PL 480 agreement. The next official Kamel tried to convince was Rusk. Egypt could stop the left-wing Arab states from coming under Moscow's control, Kamel said. But first, it "was important that Egypt not feel it was being cornered" by the United States. Like his previous effort, this threat failed too. Rusk said to Kamel, it was his own opinion that Nasser's political agenda was the root of all problems between the United States and Egypt. He pointed out that Nasser had been making speeches about the Vietnam War. The administration wanted him to tone down this anti-American rhetoric. The United States could "live with silence but not abuse," Kamel was told.[16]

Two weeks later, at a follow-up meeting with Kamel, Rusk remained firm. All aid issues would be on hold until after the congressional elections in November, he said. Rusk added that it was a window of opportunity for Nasser to walk back his anti-American speeches. Kamel disagreed. He replied that Nasser would receive the news with anxiety.[17]

Nasser apparently did not appreciate the extent to which he had damaged, once again, his image in Washington by making anti-American speeches and tearing up the Jidda Agreement. On July 14, the US Speaker of the House "reneged" on a private agreement he had with the Johnson administration not to introduce any new anti-Egypt amendments. That morning he put up for debate a new amendment to the 1966 appropriations bill that would require Johnson to justify any form of assistance to Egypt—not just PL 480. Another proposed amendment would require Johnson to personally contact the Speaker within a month of making any such determination.

Wriggins wrote to Rostow that the "alternative legislation seemed much worse, i.e. a compete prohibition of any assistance, leaving the President no authority at all."[18]

Nonetheless, the legislation under consideration posed a serious political threat to Johnson: he no longer could approve any form of assistance to Egypt unless he was willing to do so publicly and go on the record to defend it. Without Nasser's cooperation and restraint, Johnson would soon have no maneuverability to give Nasser anything. Nasser somewhat heeded the message. On July 23, he gave his annual speech to mark the 1952 revolution that brought him into power. He told his captivated audience that Egypt would not be getting any more aid from the United States; now they would have to use the nation's dwindling hard currency reserves to buy food for starving Egyptians. It was policy disagreements with the United States that led to the suspension of PL 480, Nasser said, nothing more. However, he made sure to blame Congress rather than the Johnson administration.

Back in Washington, officials interpreted the speech as Nasser's way of accepting the offer of CCC sales. American newspapers, however, characterized the speech as the latest in a long line of anti-American rhetoric.[19] Rostow attempted to convince Johnson that Nasser had reacted as well as could be expected considering his disappointment over PL 480. "His tone was more-in-sorrow-than-in-anger," Rostow wrote, "and he took some pains to explain the terms of past food deals to prepare his people for cutting back on other imports to buy food."[20]

Saunders agreed with Rostow. In fact, he sent Komer, who had already started working on the Vietnam portfolio, a copy of Rostow's memo to Johnson. Saunders prefaced it with the words, "Bon appetite." Included was an update for his old boss: "Kamel's line is to push his favorite theme that the UAR is ready to do business with us. He is just back from Cairo and argues they really mean it this time. As you can see from the attached, I feel Nasser's speech Friday was acquiescence in our decision only to sell wheat on CCC credit for the time being. I did not read it as a major anti-US blast the way the *Washington Post* did. I am sure he would like to get back into the PL 480 business but meanwhile [he] has to explain to his people why he'll have to divert currency from other imports."[21] Reaching out to Komer was sensible. There was much for Saunders to be uncertain about given the potential for a downward spiral in US-Egypt relations.

But Saunders was right: Nasser was interested in CCC credit. Shortly after his speech, Nasser sent a team of negotiators to the United States to talk with banks about providing coverage for the full $50 million that had been offered to him. This is what Rostow and Rusk had wanted to happen when they encouraged Johnson to hold off on PL 480.

A small crisis emerged, however, when the secretary of agriculture, Orville Freeman, voiced his opposition to the CCC sales more than a month after they had been authorized by Johnson. Evidently, Freeman was worried that the foreign aid bill for 1967, which Johnson cared deeply about given his success with India, would be revised because Congress would not approve of the CCC sales and, therefore, it would seek retribution on Johnson for authorizing them. Freeman wrote to Rusk that Egypt's credit was too close to the brink of collapse to approve $50 million worth of CCC credit. Saunders believed that Freeman was probably correct about Egypt's credit crunch.[22] However, the administration was already aware of Egypt's credit situation, and had decided to extend the credit anyways in order to keep diplomatic relations afloat.[23] Freeman was gently rebuffed; but not before he had a chance to offend a few Egyptian officials: specifically, an associate of Kamel's, who later reported to State that he had been "treated like a dog" by "two low-level CCC employees." US-Egypt relations were repeatedly encountering rough seas on the way to stabilization.[24]

At the beginning of August, Kamel asked for a meeting with Johnson—both Rusk and Rostow thought it was a good idea. Rostow wrote to Johnson that a meeting with Kamel would probably help "keep the lines of communication open" between the two countries. Nasser clearly still desired good relations with the West, Rostow wrote, and hopefully relations between the United States and Egypt would eventually improve enough for Johnson to authorize a new PL 480 agreement. However, in the meantime, Rostow added, the meeting would probably be the last substantive communication between the two countries until after the US midterm elections. Therefore, because of the meeting's significance, he thought it would be wise to get a "solid brief" from State and get Johnson properly prepared.

The meeting with Kamel was no doubt the most significant diplomatic outreach to Nasser since Komer had left the NSC five months earlier. And there was optimism among officials at State and the White House that Kamel's request for the meeting was in the spirit of Johnson's message to Sadat back in February. "When your government has something to say to us, you just tell Ambassador Kamel to put on his hat and come on down here," Johnson had said. "Let's not talk about it in public."[25]

Saunders agreed with Rostow that Johnson needed to be properly prepared for the meeting in order to make it "an important substantive talk."[26] To that end, he set himself to the task of producing a background paper for Johnson about the major issues that had affected relations between the two countries since spring 1966. Saunders wanted Johnson to seriously consider the long-term implications of helping Nasser. If the United States recommitted itself to feeding Egypt, he wrote, then it would have a large economic burden to shoulder if Egypt's economy continued to decline. "Economic ineffectiveness remains a major roadblock," Saunders lamented, "a big self-help push would be needed [from Nasser] before we could give any more aid." Saunders, however, reasoned that good relations with Nasser were still important for protecting America's interests in the Middle East.[27]

Kamel also prepared extensively for the meeting. "Ambassador Kamel invited me to lunch yesterday chiefly to lay the groundwork for his prospective meeting with the President," wrote Saunders for the record, a few days before the meeting. Kamel framed his meeting with Johnson as the first high level discussion between the two countries since Sadat's visit in February.

The lunch-meeting between Saunders and Kamel was highly informative. Kamel had called it to convey to Saunders what Nasser wanted to say to Johnson through Kamel, as well as what Nasser hoped to hear from Johnson in response. Kamel said that Nasser was ready to offer a number of concessions, which Kamel laid out for Saunders as: "(1) Nasser wants good personal relations with the President. (2) The UAR would accept nuclear safeguards if we could persuade Israel to do the same. (3) The UAR will continue to keep the Israeli issue 'in the icebox.' (4) He wants to get out of Yemen and hopes we will support Kuwaiti mediation." In return, Kamel said, Nasser wanted Johnson to appreciate these concessions, and to convey his appreciation in an informal letter to Nasser after the meeting. It was very important for Nasser to see a sign from Johnson that PL 480 aid would be extended to Egypt soon, he said. Nasser saw PL 480 as a "political symbol" that represented the state of US-Egypt relations. According to Saunders's report, Kamel said: "To end this aid would amount to telling Nasser, as he would see it, that we are out to upset him."

Saunders told Kamel that he would make sure Johnson was aware of the extra significance Nasser was placing on the meeting. He then added into the conversation his own assessment of the problems between the United States and Egypt. Saunders said that Nasser's anti-American rhetoric showed he did not trust the United States, therefore making it difficult—if not impossible—to have better relations with him. Nasser's refusal to repay the IMF for previous loans made him appear unserious about economic reform. Furthermore, Nasser did not heed the advice of his own economic advisers, which gave observers the impression that "politics are likely to derail sensible economic programs at any moment" in Egypt. Johnson was looking more and more into funding projects in India and Pakistan rather than Egypt, Saunders said, because those countries had made "economic development . . . [a] top political priority."[28]

Based on Saunders's conversation with Kamel, Rostow provided talking points for Johnson that more or less gave Nasser the response he seemed to be expecting. However, Rostow advised Johnson it was important that he not commit to signing a new PL 480 agreement. Nasser needed to implement meaningful economic reforms if he wanted to show that he was ready for the more serious type of development projects that Johnson and Rostow were envisioning under their new economic assistance policy. The point of the meeting was "to keep a line open," Rostow emphasized. In the meantime, he hoped that Nasser would agree to get another standby loan from the IMF.[29]

State's talking points for Johnson intentionally omitted any mention of PL 480 because they thought it was too controversial of an issue for Johnson even to bring up with Kamel. This concerned Saunders, however. He reasoned to Rostow that although Johnson had already communicated his intention not to completely close the door on PL 480, Kamel needed to hear that from Johnson himself in order to really believe it. If there was no mention of PL 480, wrote Saunders, it would leave room for suspicion and second-guessing in Cairo. Nasser would convince himself that the new policy was, "No more aid."[30]

The expectations in Cairo for Kamel and Johnson's meeting were high. Since, for the time being, the administration was not offering any carrots to Nasser, it was important that the diplomatic overtones were conducted in a way that could keep Nasser from feeling like he was being abandoned. The emphasis was on aesthetics rather than substance.

The meeting occurred on August 12. Crucially, it didn't come anywhere close to meeting the high expectations that Nasser had placed on it. Indeed, Kamel left the oval office feeling empty-handed, as Saunders had feared. The meeting lasted only twenty minutes. Johnson arrived over two hours late because his schedule had been overbooked. Moreover, he was "in a hurry" to get to his ranch in Texas. Kamel, however, was "very long winded" for his part, which did not make Johnson particularly receptive.[31]

In his presentation to Johnson, Kamel again emphasized that American aid was necessary to keep Nasser from turning to Moscow. Nasser had sent "signals" to the United States to demonstrate his good intentions, Kamel said, but had received no response. Johnson agreed that relations could be normalized. However, instead of following Saunders's advice to indicate that PL 480 was not entirely off the table, Johnson was elusive. He said that he could not give Kamel a definitive answer at that particular point in time. In this way, Johnson failed to assuage Nasser's main concern: the Egyptian leader wanted to hear that PL 480 was more likely to be offered than not. Before Johnson departed, Kamel tried once again to convince him of the importance of PL 480 and the expectation in Cairo for a new agreement.[32] Johnson, however, rushed out of the meeting, eager to get through his next few appointments and then on the plane to Texas. Later that day, almost immediately after boarding Air Force One, he took a two-hour nap. Exhausted and overscheduled, Johnson's meeting with Kamel was unsatisfactory for the expectations that had been placed on it.[33]

In the aftermath of the disappointing meeting, Saunders started to get more concerned about US-Egypt relations. Specifically, he was afraid that Nasser would turn to the Soviets as Kamel was threatening. A few days after the meeting, he wrote to Rostow: "We have had several indications over the past few months that the UAR may indeed be approaching closer to the 'crossroads' that Kamel talked about. Even if one discounts his cries of doom, one cannot completely dismiss other analysts." Saunders wanted to bring to Rostow's attention one incident in particular: Egyptian diplomats in Moscow had approached their American counterparts in order to sound out the administration's position on PL 480. "They painted a gloomy picture of UAR slippage under Soviet control as the only alternative," Saunders wrote. The setting of the warning, the heart of the Soviet republics, was almost like a dare to the United States: give us aid or else.

Officials at State shared Saunders's concern. Thus, they proposed immediately untangling aid from the "political arena." Despite Saunders's earlier reluctance to continue down the same well-worn path with Nasser that had been traversed since Kennedy (i.e., Komer's redirection strategy), he agreed with State that it was important to find a way to once again extend PL 480 to Egypt. To that end, he offered the following policy line to Rostow that the administration could begin trying out on Egyptian officials: "Because of our own limited food and money supplies, our aid must go increasingly to those governments that can get results." The emphasis would be placed on getting Nasser to actually turn his economy around. Instead of continuing to perseverate over Nasser's politics, Saunders argued, the administration could work on getting him to deal with global financial institutions—like the IMF. Saunders added:

We have never defined the conditions of our aid in quite this way. However, it may be increasingly important in a country like the UAR to begin talking about the real reason why we have trouble doing business there. To be sure, we would like to see Nasser get out of Yemen. We would like to see him leave South Arabia alone. We hope he will keep Israel in the "ice box." But even if he did all of these political things—and he won't—there would still be one big obstacle [Egypt's economy] to our joining in his development effort.[34]

Rostow liked the idea. Thus, Saunders's exact line was used by Robert Anderson on a visit to Cairo in early September. Although the former treasury secretary was in Egypt for private reasons, Rusk himself briefed Anderson in order to have him serve as an informal emissary. Anderson met with Kaissouni and Zakaria Muheidden, Nasser's pro-American prime minister, respectively. He made it clear to both officials that the Johnson administration expected material changes from Nasser, not just more empty promises. The Egyptian government had to refrain from politics and focus on internal development. Kaissouni and Muheidden agreed that Egypt badly needed America's help to fix its economy. No doubt, this was a step in the right direction. David G. Nes, the chargé d'affaires at the US embassy in Cairo, reported to Washington that "the visit has been useful and that repetition of [the] line we have been taking here and in . . . [Washington] by well-known Americans outside . . . [government] is all too good."

Indeed, Anderson's message was well received in Cairo. Before he returned to the United States, Kaissouni reached out for additional advice. Kaissouni said he was scheduled to meet with IMF officials to discuss upcoming payments for loans that Egypt was not able to make. Anderson told Kaissouni to inform the banking organizations ahead of time that Egypt was unable to make the payments. That way, Anderson said, the IMF would take Kaissouni more seriously and not wait with resentment for Egypt to default. It was prudent advice and, most importantly, a step toward a new kind of dialogue between the two countries: fixing Egypt's economic problems once-and-for-all.[35]

Nonetheless, while Anderson's meetings with the two most pro Western officials in Cairo (Kaissouni and Muheidden) had gone well, his later meeting with Nasser did not. Among other things, Nasser was pessimistic about dealing with the IMF. They were being too hard in their talks with Kaissouni, he said. Nasser was also upset about PL 480. At one point, he asked Anderson whether Johnson wanted food riots in the streets of Egypt. Nasser strongly hinted that he would turn to the Soviets if he needed aid badly enough. And he strongly implied that they would help him if he asked. Egypt "must keep balance between [the] East and West," he said. "If we lean too far in the direction of the East, we get complaints from you and if we go the other way, the Russians complain. The Russians gave us the High Dam [Aswan] and even supplied skilled workers when we did not have them. They sent wheat shipments when you stopped. These are things we cannot forget."

In spite of Nasser's obvious frustration about PL 480, the meeting with Anderson yielded a few positive results. For one thing, Nasser said he was willing to meet Johnson on political issues, including keeping Israel in the "ice-box," publicly accepting nuclear safeguards, and devoting all "available resources" to the Salhia development project that Anderson was spearheading. Anderson, for his part, was adamant with Nasser about economic reform, saying that the "key" to solving all of Egypt's problems was reaching an immediate agreement with the IMF for a new loan.[36]

Back in Washington, however, Saunders was feeling pessimistic after reading about Anderson's meeting with Nasser. He wrote to Wriggins, "Three things strike me about the attached: (1) Nasser's total lack of candor; (2) Nasser's apparent lack of perception about what is missing in our current relationship; (3) My conclusion that Anderson's meeting with Nasser was not a discussion but a case of two men each talking past each other." Saunders did not believe that Nasser was actually getting the message about economic reform.[37] The administration was in danger of heading down the same beaten path with him that it had travelled on so many times before. Saunders was no longer convinced that Kennedy's policies were viable for dealing with the Egyptian leader.

Nevertheless, the redirection strategy, spearheaded by Komer under Kennedy, was the only tool the administration had for steering Nasser out of trouble. Therefore, in light of signs that relations between the two countries were heading toward even choppier waters, the administration considered reopening the personal lines of communication with Nasser à la Kennedy. Nasser's daughter was getting married and planned to honeymoon in the United States. Wriggins suggested a "father-to-father message" to "cultivate a personal relationship" with Nasser. Johnson approved. And the letter was sent.[38]

A week later, Rusk recommended to Johnson that he receive Nasser's daughter and son-in-law at the White House. Rostow agreed with the idea. He suggested that Johnson meet with the two of them for a few minutes in the Rose Garden. Afterwards, they could take a tour of the White House. Rostow liked the idea because it was "a unique opportunity for personal diplomacy." Although the meeting would not be publicized, since the families of foreign leaders were never extended such attention, Nasser no doubt would be honored by the gesture. Rostow stressed the importance of showing Nasser that there were no personal disagreements between him and Johnson; particularly given the absence of PL 480. Nasser too often was treated like a "leper" by US officials, Rostow added. Extending an invitation to his daughter and son-in-law would go a long way toward rectifying that. Johnson approved.[39]

A few days before the visit, Rostow prepared Johnson. He explained that Nasser's daughter and son-in-law had been married the previous October, but they had begun living together only in spring 1966. This was because Islamic custom dated marriage from the signing of the wedding contract, not when couples began living together. It is unclear why Rostow wished to inform Johnson of the conditions of their marriage, other than perhaps he wished to save Johnson the potential embarrassment of making any offensive comments to Nasser's daughter—something Johnson was prone to doing. The same memo was sent to Mrs. Johnson, who had volunteered to take the couple on a tour of the White House.[40]

The visit went well. A month later, Nasser sent a warm thank you letter to Johnson that resembled the friendlier dialogue of the Kennedy era:

I have heard a great deal from Mona [Nasser's daughter] regarding her experience. She is still extremely enthusiastic about everything she saw, heard, and felt during the time she spent with you all. In particular, she speaks with warmth of the cordiality and kindness extended to her by Your Excellency and Mrs. Johnson. For all that she is most grateful.

As I write you these lines to express my deep thanks, my wife joins me by sending heartfelt greetings to your wife, as mother to a mother.

Please accept, Dear President, my very best wishes for happiness to yourself and your family.[41]

Battle informed the administration that Nasser had handwritten the original draft of the letter himself before having it translated into English. It was an indication of the level of care the Egyptian leader had placed on the visit. Saunders wanted to make sure Johnson actually read the letter because "there is no harm in the President's realizing that Nasser is capable of human emotion, even though as a politician he sometimes looks to us like the devil."[42] Rostow agreed and wondered whether the visit had temporarily saved US-Egypt relations.[43] Kennedy's brand of personal diplomacy once again seemed like the best approach to take with Nasser.

Meanwhile, Nasser began sending signals that he was getting more serious about economic reform. He awarded Kaissouni with a position as deputy prime minister and named an economics wonk, Nazih Deif, as the new minister of finance. Deif, who was viewed by the US embassy in Cairo as "the keenest economist in the Egyptian government," was in charge now of talking to the IMF. Nasser seemed to be following Anderson's advice to secure a new IMF loan.

In early October, Deif came to Washington for an annual meeting held by the IMF. State urged having Rostow meet with him to discuss economic reform. Saunders agreed, writing to Rostow, "We want to be sure Nasser gets the message that we view his pending agreement with the IMF as a watershed." Indeed, Deif was the type of pragmatist who Saunders believed was capable of leading Nasser toward more sensible economic planning. A lot was riding on officials like Deif convincing Nasser to sign a new agreement with the IMF in order to demonstrate his commitment to fixing Egypt's economy. "The decision whether to accept the IMF package is now up to Nasser alone," wrote Saunders to Rostow. "His agreement to go along with the IMF would be essential symbolic recognition that he can't go on running an economy from the seat of his political pants. Unless he sets a more rational course, we're going to have a tougher and tougher time selling even PL 480. I don't see the IMF agreement as a panacea, but without it I think five years of hopeful experimentation (which began in your office in 1961) are about to breathe their last."[44]

Rostow agreed. On September 29, he and Saunders met with Deif and Kamel for an hour. Evidently, Deif was a keen student of Rostow's theories of economics. Deif, however, said that while it was important to come to terms with the IMF, he believed their focus on devaluating the Egyptian pound was misguided. "Devaluation would not only cause unnecessary political burdens; it doesn't fit the UAR's problems," he passionately argued. "The UAR could export as much as it could produce of products like cotton, rice, and petroleum and will not soon be able to export manufactured items—not because of the exchange rate but because it lacks the quality control which might make UAR products marketable at competitive prices abroad." Rostow replied that everything Deif said "makes economic sense." But, he added, "The problems the

UAR faces are familiar in countries at this stage of development." Rostow then urged Deif to accept the IMF's conditions for the sake of "establishing the UAR's future credit worthiness." He reasoned that "the UAR government's current serious efforts to come to terms with these problems might be the break we [have] all been hoping for." Egypt had the ability to accomplish great things, Rostow said. Its "real future . . . [lies] in becoming a model of development in the Middle East." Coming from Rostow, those words must have been seen by the two Egyptians as a sign that the administration would once again offer economic assistance.

Before the conversation ended, Rostow asked if there was anything else that needed to be discussed. Kamel "then stepped in." He said that he had "instructions" from Nasser to ask Rostow for two things: (1) an immediate sign from Johnson that he would "consider a new PL 480 agreement" after the midterm elections in November; and (2) he wanted the administration to "use its good offices with the IMF to precipitate an agreement." Rostow replied that, as a matter of principle, the administration did not interfere with the IMF. Kamel replied, "there [are] . . . ways to talk to the IMF." Rostow was firm: the administration could not intervene with the IMF. Despite the awkwardness of Kamel's request, according to a memorandum of the conversation, "The meeting ended in the extremely warm atmosphere in which it had been carried on. Though no promises had been made, the party left with the feeling they had had a friendly hearing in the White House."[45]

To be sure, there had been a series of positive developments in US-Egypt relations despite the absence of PL 480 to keep Nasser from lashing out: Anderson's well-received trip to Cairo, Johnson's warm reception of Nasser's daughter and son-in-law, and Rostow's informative meeting with Deif. Nonetheless, Nasser soon sabotaged these positive developments by slipping back into anti-American propaganda.

Indeed, Nasser claimed to be confused by what he perceived as hot and cold signals from the Johnson administration; particularly since his daughter told him that Johnson had approached her at the White House and said that he hoped he and her father could be "friends." According to one of Nasser's trusted confidantes, "Nasser, who was a reserved man, could not understand this behaviour at all. He wondered what it all meant."[46]

Therefore, instead of heeding the multiple warnings to remain patient on PL 480 and to demonstrate his commitment to economic reform, Nasser once again turned to propaganda. Specifically, he joined Moscow in claiming that the United States was behind a failed coup attempt in Syria. On October 1, *Al-Ahram* claimed that the failed coup had been promoted and organized by the CIA, which had been revealed by one of the conspirators who fled to Cairo in order to confess.[47] The story coincided with an interview by Sallal (of Yemen), who claimed to have removed a number of his cabinet ministers for "collaborating with agents of the United States and Saudi Arabia."[48]

Thereafter, anti-American rumors continued to fly. On October 4, Cairo's Domestic Radio Service picked up a story from the Lebanese press, claiming that Jordanian officials had conspired with their CIA contacts to initiate the Syrian coup. America and Israel were described by the broadcast as the "essential tools" of the plot.[49] At the same time, Moscow's *Pravda* also referred to the plot. It stated that a Syrian coup had been "encouraged by imperialist powers headed by the United States."[50]

With the additional support from Moscow, Egypt then stepped up its attacks. On October 6, the radio show, Voice of Palestine, broadcasted the details of the coup. Specifically, it was attributed to the "CIA's extreme concern over the development of events in Syria and the current nationalist trend of the Damascus government."[51] One report even claimed that the US ambassador in Jordan had sent a "coded radio message . . . concerning the readiness of American soldiers to land in Israel to support the Jordanian plot to invade Syria."[52]

With no knowledge of an alleged CIA plot to destabilize Syria, State was puzzled by the propaganda emanating from Egypt. In a phone call with Rusk, Egypt's foreign minister, Mahmoud Riad, attempted to downplay the affair. He claimed that the rumor had actually been started by Jordan. Thus, Riad assured Rusk, Nasser did not intend to pursue the matter any further. Nonetheless, Riad attempted to use State's concern to his benefit by pressuring Rusk for a decision on PL 480. He claimed that the rumor had been unavoidable due to the fact that the United States had close relations with Israel, Saudi Arabia, and Jordan. Relations such as these made the United States an easy target for Arab suspicion, Riad said. These countries were opposed to Nasser's vision of revolutionary progress in the Middle East—the type of progress that could help the region stand tall above the fracas of the East-West, Cold War competition. The entire affair appeared to be no less than a pressure tactic to get the administration to immediately extend a new PL 480 agreement.[53]

Nasser soon began to turn the screws even harder. Specifically, he made a surprising claim to a visiting American lawyer, James Birdsall, that he had proof, which he was willing to show, that the CIA was plotting to kill him and then impose a Western-oriented government in Egypt. Unwilling to call Nasser's bluff, Birdsall refused to examine any evidence as a private citizen. Rusk, however, wanted to know more. He advised Battle to visit Nasser and to look at the evidence himself.[54] When Battle finally met with Nasser on December 10, the Egyptian leader was unwilling to provide the evidence, nor did he wish to discuss it any further.[55]

Ironically, it was in the midst of this renewed turbulence between the two countries that Egyptian officials began to think about Komer, and once again extended an invitation for him to visit Cairo. It also happened to be the beginning of the month (November) that the administration had promised to reconsider PL 480. Komer had always been in favor of letting cooler heads prevail. Thus, perhaps Egyptian officials hoped he would once again bend Johnson's ear enough to get a new PL 480 agreement. Saunders wrote to Komer: "I am doing my duty to Rodger Davies and Ambassador Kamel in passing this message. UAR Foreign Minister Riyad has asked Kamel to tell you that if you ever can return from Vietnam via Cairo, you will be most welcome." Saunders added, "As I recall, you had an invitation on your previous incarnation which you never picked up." Komer, however, was too preoccupied with Vietnam to take up the offer.[56]

As 1966 marched into 1967, a year in which there would be a third Arab-Israeli war, US-Egypt relations were sinking lower and lower. Indeed, it was only a month later that Saunders would write to Rostow with a hint of sorrow, "The Kennedy experiment is over."[57] Komer's years of hard work were being undone. The problems would only get worse after November, as communication between the two countries continued to decline. Once again, a major problem was Rusk. He was too busy dealing with Vietnam to consider strategy toward Nasser. Indeed, as he said to Kamel in the summer of 1966, "We've got a war in Asia, we've got no time for this Arab thing!"[58]

20

Nasser's Last Stand

After congressional midterm elections in November 1966, Nasser made strong attempts to get Johnson to make good on his promise to consider a new PL 480 agreement. As secretary of state, it was Rusk's role to put any PL 480 proposal in front of the president. Rusk, however, avoided it—he was too busy with the Vietnam War. But without Komer in the picture, there was nobody in the administration capable of bending Johnson's ear in the absence of any action from Rusk.

Around the same time that Nasser made the startling claim of a CIA plot against him, he once again directed Kamel to restart PL 480 negotiations. It was November 1966, congressional elections were over, and the administration had promised to reconsider aid; but there was still no movement from the administration toward an agreement. Thus, Kamel began to paint the issue as a serious crisis in US-Egypt relations. On November 23, he made an outburst in front of Rusk, unexpectedly crying out over lunch that Americans should not "starve Egyptians."[1] Four days later, he urgently called the deputy executive secretary at State, John P. Walsh, and explained his concern. Kamel warned that the situation was getting dire: US-Egypt relations were deteriorating. Nasser was getting closer to turning to Moscow for help, Kamel said.[2]

On December 1, Saunders and Wriggins wrote to Rostow to complain that Rusk urgently needed to approve a new PL 480 agreement or at least spend some time considering it. They warned, "we badly need to get him to focus on the UAR." The two officials also proposed having Rusk visit Nasser on the way to a previously scheduled trip to Paris. Nasser needed a positive sign from the administration, they wrote:

> The main problem in our UAR relations is lack of confidence. Nasser believes we're out to get him, and the fact that our high level travellers bypass him just confirms his belief. The Egyptians still consider that postponement (for pressing US reasons) of the Secretary's scheduled visit last spring was a calculated slight, but the invitation has been repeated.

The two officials pushed for resuming PL 480 aid for Egypt on the basis that "Nasser could behave much worse and do much greater damage to our interests." Saunders, now more concerned about the state of affairs than before, envisioned "some new base for our relationship, though less ambitious than our 1962 effort."[3] Wriggins wrote to

Rostow separately and pleaded with him to talk to Rusk on the plane about PL 480. "The attached memo outlines our thoughts," he wrote, "and describes . . . decisions we should not let drift until the Secretary returns." Rusk, however, declined the invitation to visit Egypt. He also refused to make a decision about PL 480.[4]

Saunders and Wriggins' campaign was subsequently taken up by an interdepartmental group of White House and State officials. The group agreed that it was important for the preservation of American interests in the Middle East that Rusk put some form of a PL 480 proposal on Johnson's desk. Specifically, they advised the immediate sale of $50–$70 million worth of foodstuff to Egypt under another short-term PL 480 agreement.[5]

Meanwhile, in what appeared to be an attempt to pressure the administration to make a decision about PL 480, Nasser started a rumor that he once again was getting wheat from the Soviet Union. In a conversation with the Canadian ambassador on December 11, he said that he no longer cared about PL 480; it had been important only because it had been a factor in Egypt's long-term economic planning. "In any event," Nasser said, Egypt had "been able to meet part of . . . [its] food needs by [an] arrangement with [the] Russians as . . . [was] done in [a] smaller way last year." In response to the ambassador's question on whether the amount of wheat would be greater than the 300,000 tons received in June of 1965, "Nasser said the amount was supposed to be a secret."

Battle surmised that Nasser had chosen to tell the Canadian ambassador because he knew that the two of them (Battle and the ambassador) were close friends. Battle, however, also believed that Nasser was telling the truth about the Soviet wheat. "I see no reason for Nasser misleading us at this point regarding [the] amount of what he can obtain with Russian cooperation," he wrote to State. Battle subsequently panicked, believing that Nasser had firmly turned to Moscow as Kamel had warned he would do all along. Thus, he soon began to second-guess the policymakers back in Washington with a barrage of urgent telegrams.[6]

Nasser, for his part, continued to apply pressure on the United States. When Rusk got back from his trip in late December, and still had not made a decision about PL 480, Kamel asked for an emergency meeting with the Secretary. According to a memorandum of their conversation, "'He said that he was speaking under instructions." Kamel insisted that Nasser wanted peace in Yemen, did not wish to provoke the British in South Arabia, and had no interest in "exciting the Arab-Israel problem." Most importantly, he wanted strong relations with the United States. According to a memorandum of their conversation, "Kamel had maintained continuous contact on these points with the US Government over the past months. Nothing had happened. He feared the consequences if this state of affairs continued." Kamel added for effect: "Egypt has wheat supplies for only one and one-half months. The Egyptians . . . [will] know why they . . . [are] starving."

Kamel claimed that he had a plan to establish peace in the Middle East and asked the administration to send aid to Egypt "within hours" if it wanted the plan to come to fruition. The plan was: (1) work to repair the relations between Nasser and Faisal; and (2) a major initiative to "freeze" the Arab-Israeli conflict, which was heating up again over a controversial Israeli military raid into the Jordanian village of Samu in late November. (Israel's military raid was to destroy the homes of terrorists. For several months, these terrorists had increased their operations through pinprick attacks inside Israeli territory.) Syria had been clamoring for war ever since and Nasser was under pressure to respond. Rusk asked if the "plan" Kamel was proposing had been included in his instructions from Nasser. It had not. But Kamel said he could definitely "sell it to Cairo."

Rusk said that he would bring Kamel's plan before Johnson. To that end, he asked that the two of them meet again the following week to give him some time. Before concluding the meeting, Rusk inquired about the rumor of Soviet wheat, asking whether it was true. Kamel evaded the question.[7] No doubt, Rusk was trying to read Kamel and determine whether the threat of Nasser turning to Moscow was really just a bluff.

Before Rusk met with Kamel again, Battle wrote directly to Rusk and criticized him for dragging his feet on PL 480. He wrote, "I am deeply disturbed at [the] drift and deterioration [of the] US position stemming in large part from [a] strong Egyptian belief [that] we are long overdue in giving them [an] answer to their request of last March for additional food." Battle had seen the interdepartmental group's recommendation for an immediate PL 480 agreement. He wrote, "I strongly concur and urge your approval and that of the President of the recommendation contained therein." He desperately urged Rusk to give Kamel some sort of indication that the administration intended to sign a new PL 480 agreement.[8]

In spite of Battle's strong concerns from Cairo, when Rusk met with Kamel on January 12, he said that he was still was not ready to give Kamel an answer about PL 480 because he "had not had a chance to discuss the matter with the President." Kamel replied that he was sorry he had to keep asking the administration for a decision. However, "for six months he had been giving tranquilizers to Cairo. His little pharmacy was now exhausted." Kamel added that Nasser carefully followed his meetings with US officials and was asking for regular reports. "Egypt must have wheat," Kamel said. "Failure to get it would cause the greatest repercussions on all our [i.e., America's] relations and interests in the Near East and even on US relations with the Soviet Union." PL 480 was even more important than Aswan had been in the 1950s, Kamel said, once again referring to the lowest point in the history of US-Egypt relations—a moment, no less, that had led to war in the Middle East in the absence of US aid. In response to the historical reference, Rusk asked if he could "pose a personal question" to Kamel: How could Rusk convince Johnson to resume aid to Egypt if all he had to bring before him was a "threat" that "something bad would happen?"

Indeed, Rusk was on to something. US officials had always secretly laughed off Kamel's threats. Maybe it was time to be honest with the ambassador that his threats failed to move the administration any closer to a decision.

Kamel did not provide a direct response to Rusk's question. But he did his best to explain just how dire the economic situation was in Egypt. He described Nasser's desperation over Egypt's dwindling food resources. He explained to Rusk that there would be a famine in Egypt if Nasser did not procure wheat. Thus, Kamel was not making empty threats: without American aid, Nasser would have no other choice but to turn to Moscow. If the administration followed his advice, he said, then the Middle East would be closed to the Soviets and Egypt could achieve full economic independence within three years. However, if the United States abandoned Egypt, Kamel said, Nasser could potentially open up new hot spots in the Middle East that would directly affect the United States. "Who knows who brought us to Yemen," he said, "and who knows who will bring us into other situations if you leave us?" The implication was that without PL 480 as a moderating force, Nasser would set his sights on Southern Arabia once the British left in 1968. By leveling with Rusk just how concerned Nasser was about the food shortage, Kamel had started off his argument on good footing. But Rusk did not appreciate the new threat about Nasser stirring up even more conflict in the region if the United States did not feed Egypt.[9]

A few days later, Kamel met with Rostow, who heavily admonished the Egyptian ambassador for threatening Rusk. According to the memorandum of what Rostow said: "It was time he [Kamel] stopped describing Cairo's acceptance of Soviet wheat as a threat to the United States and started thinking of it as a threat to the UAR." Kamel heeded the warning. A few days later, he met with Saunders. He said he was very sorry for giving the impression that he was making threats. However, it was inevitable that Nasser would seek help from Moscow if necessary. A "sick man needs moral support from more than one quarter," Kamel said. Kamel was getting more and more frustrated. "He retained his composure throughout," Saunders observed, "but was more emphatic than I have ever seen him."[10]

Nasser's desperation and the administration's indifference were splitting any foundation left in US-Egypt relations. Thus, some US officials took it upon themselves to spur Rusk into action.

On January 26, William J. Handley, the acting assistant secretary of state for Near Eastern and South Asian affairs, wrote to Rusk. He reminded the Secretary of Kamel's argument that a failure to resume aid would be "to the detriment of Western and moderate interests" in the Middle East. To that end, he encouraged Rusk to immediately sign off on a PL 480 proposal to send to Johnson. Handley wrote: "Ambassador Kamel continues to press for a decision on his government's PL-480 request. He is again attempting to put off Cairo by telling them that you have been too busy testifying on the Hill to finish up the consultations necessary to get a decision this week on this important and delicate matter. While he agrees that setting a time limit is not helpful, he says his government is growing ever more insistent for an answer. Thus he has reported to Cairo that he hopes to get the decision from you this week." In other words, Kamel had set a deadline for Rusk.

Handley presented Rusk with the terms of a potential deal that had been designed by the same interdepartmental group of State and White House officials that had pushed for resuming aid to Egypt. There were two options favored by the group (both of which involved a new six month PL 480 agreement): (1) an immediate agreement consisting of wheat (which, as it will be recalled, Egypt needed most of all) and other commodities; or (2) a "carrot and stick" approach, consisting of a large amount of commodities other than wheat (however, the "prospect of future wheat assistance" would be "held out to the UAR"). The second option was certainly less desirable for

Nasser because he would need to demonstrate restraint toward the United States in order to eventually receive the wheat; however, the sale of other foodstuff would alleviate Egypt's food shortage in the meantime.

The interdepartmental group favored either of the two options, as the "reactions of Egypt, the most powerful Arab country, can be detrimental to our interests," wrote Handley. In other words, getting anything to Nasser at this point was deemed essential for preserving US interests in the Middle East. Officials from AID, however, offered a dissenting point of view. They were in favor of selling only 250,000 tons of wheat to Egypt under a deal worth $16 million. They were willing to extend the amount to $25 million if other commodities were included. The intention behind AID's proposal was to match the amount of the Soviet Union's alleged wheat offer—though, it was later discovered there was, in fact, no Soviet offer to Cairo.[11]

Despite having the outline of a PL 480 deal now sitting directly on his desk and having numerous officials from different agencies and departments prodding him, Rusk continued not to make any movement on the PL 480 issue. He was holding everything up. But without Komer there to go around the Secretary, there was little hope of getting an aid package together to reassure Nasser.

As a result of Rusk's foot-dragging, Donald Bergus, the country director for Egypt at State, left for Cairo at the end of January 1967 in order to sound out Egyptian officials. Reporting on his talks, he sent a telegram to Washington noting that the failure to reach a new PL 480 agreement had already tarnished America's image in the Middle East. The situation was so dire, in fact, that it would require grand gestures to make up for it. In other words, in spite of the fact that State officials (other than Rusk) desperately wanted to make it clear to Nasser that an aid package was in the pipeline, it was already too late: Nasser was washing his hand of the United States. Indeed, as Battle wrote to State:

> Bergus and [Richard] Parker left with [the] impression [that the] UARG [is] becoming increasingly convinced that [a] broad US–UAR confrontation is unavoidable. There is little basis for believing that Egyptians any longer flinch at such a possibility. In Egypt, as elsewhere in this part of [the] world, there is [a] strong streak of fatalism.[12]

Wriggins wrote to Rostow to complain about Rusk dragging his feet: "We are coming to the point of bad manners, as well as exhausting our credibility. No doubt Secretary Rusk has been under tremendous pressure to deal with Vietnam . . . But there must be some way of inducing him to focus on this problem."[13] Rostow had to take matters into his own hands in order to avoid a conflagration in the Middle East.

On February 14, Rostow laid everything on the table for Johnson. Informing Johnson of the many meetings that Kamel had with Rusk and other officials in Washington, Rostow arranged for Johnson to make a final decision on PL 480 at the Tuesday lunch-meeting scheduled for later that day. Rostow wrote: "Our purpose at lunch is to get a sense of your priorities." He included for Johnson his own assessment that it was a difficult decision to make. "We're all reluctant to picture the consequences of a break with Nasser," he wrote. "Arguing that line rubs us all the wrong way because no one likes the idea of paying off a bully."

Rostow personally favored resuming aid to Egypt because he was impressed by Nasser's new economic advisers. Therefore, he did his best to convince Johnson that Nasser was "the most powerful figure in the Middle East" and that Egypt was poised for cutting-edge research "to demonstrate what can be done in agricultural production and population control." Rostow also underscored Nasser's ability to lash out at America's interests in the Middle East; especially his ability to undermine Israel's security. Finally, Rostow brought to light for Johnson the shared concerns of United States and Egyptian officials that the two countries were "rapidly sliding into a showdown."[14]

There is little doubt that the Johnson administration dragged its feet too long on giving an answer to Egypt about PL 480, but there exists no record of the Tuesday lunch-meeting to indicate which direction Johnson considered going next. A memo about a side conversation between Rostow and Robert Anderson, however, indicates that Rusk had "anxiety that an Egyptian concessional grain deal could blow the aid bill in the Congress." Anderson hoped that Johnson would be willing to authorize an interim deal for Egypt to "buy a little time" with Nasser. "Hunger," Anderson said, "is a real possibility which could blow Nasser's reaction into violence which would tear apart the Middle East." But there is no record to indicate whether Johnson heeded Anderson's advice or was even made aware of it.[15]

With no decision in sight, Nasser did lash out at the United States a week later in his annual February 22 speech, which was far more hostile than the speech he had given a little over a year earlier at Port Said. Instead of continuing to wait for the administration to make up its mind while the Egyptian economy got worse on a daily basis, Nasser said that Egypt no longer wanted American aid. He subsequently delivered a sermon that denounced the machinations of "American imperialism." According to a British observer:

> Unlike previous speeches in the last year this one dealt almost wholly with foreign affairs. Economic difficulties, which he has in previous speeches displayed pre- occupation and concern, were relegated to a brief section as something already dealt with. The speech was demagogic, colloquial and confident.

Specifically, Nasser painted the Americans as aggressors in the Middle East. He claimed they were attempting to exert their influence over him through economic assistance—just like the imperial powers of Europe had attempted to bend the will of Egypt's monarchy before Nasser came to power.[16] Nasser said:

> The Americans get angry if they are attacked and want to silence us. They threatened us but we were not intimidated by their threats. We went along our path and America stopped all aid to us including, principally, her supply of £E60 million worth of wheat. If we kept silent in return for this wheat, the Americans would take us by the scruff of our necks and never let us go.[17]

Nasser identified America as the modern equivalent of an imperial power, claiming that it was out for domination over the entire Middle East, and thus making it clear that he viewed himself as the last line of defense against America's imperial machinations. Nasser said:

> We could not submit to economic pressure or threats, because by refusing to submit we should be defending the Arab revolution, the Arab struggle, Arab sovereignty and Arab nationalism . . . Let me tell you that we are a hundred percent independent country and we are ready to sacrifice £E 60 million. I knew that we should be in difficulties . . . But I was sure that every inhabitant of this country, if he had to choose between submitting to the Americans and receiving no aid, would say: "We won't have the aid."[18]

As aptly noted by a British observer, "the predominant thought in Nasser's mind when he made this speech was to make sure his people laid the blame for their privations at the door of the United States."[19] Likewise, another British observer viewed Nasser's speech as an indication "that the UAR wants to step up her hostility to the 'traditionalists' Arab governments and to the Western world." He also noted that Nasser was "assuming that they would get no further American aid."[20]

Indeed, the reality of Egypt's economy and the finality of American aid appeared to be driving Nasser into conflict with the United States. Further deflecting from the dismal performance of Egypt's economy, Nasser highlighted all of the positive work that he had done in order to prepare the Arab world for an invasion of Israel; and, in the process, effectively again broke his promise not to take the Arab-Israeli issue out of the "icebox." Nasser said:

> In December 1963 I called for unified Arab action. On behalf of Palestine, and for the convening of the Summit Conference . . . If you remember, in 1963 I said that while certain Arab countries talked about Israel and the recovery of Palestine, in their secret councils they admitted that they were incapable of defending their existence on their own. We therefore had to meet at an Arab Summit Conference to discuss means of ensuring the defence of the whole Arab homeland, and then work for the restoration of Palestine to its people.[21]

Nasser announced that it was now time for a "new stage" in the Arab struggle against Israel. "We are only at the beginning and there are still many obstacles ahead," he said, "but this [Arab unity] is the only true formula and it is essential for the confrontation of imperialism and Israel."[22]

Nasser claimed that he was the tail that wagged the dog of Palestinian liberation. He juxtaposed this image with "America's constant attempts to liquidate the Palestine problem and the Palestinian people." Just like in 1956, when Nasser had nationalized the Suez Canal in a grand gesture of Egyptian triumph over the West, he seemed intent on preparing Egypt for a similarly ambitious move. In short, this was the great calamity that Komer had warned about years before if the United States completely cut off Nasser—Aswan was getting a sequel.[23]

In the absence of American aid, Nasser oversaw a massive restructuring of Egypt's economy that began to make his leadership look more and more like a socialist dictatorship. First, a Supreme Control Committee was established with the purpose "to keep a watch on the counter-revolution everywhere."[24] The committee's mandate was to make public sector companies more efficient. Draconian measures were implemented, including: massive layoffs, decreased salaries, mandatory reviews for board chairmen over the age of 65, and a complete overhaul in production management that required business leaders to conduct themselves as "political leaders" with the power to get rid of workers who were found to have "deviated" and thus negatively impacted the company's production quota.

At the same time as the restructuring of the public sector companies, the Arab Socialist Union (ASU), Egypt's only political party, was also restructured to increase its influence over the state.[25] According to Nasser's appointed head of the ASU, the former anti-American prime minister, Ali Sabri, the guiding philosophy for the party's activities was based entirely on the "revolutionary thought of the leader of the revolution"; the understanding being that Nasser was in charge of the ASU and that any indication of governmental checks and balances was illusionary.[26] According to Sabri, the ASU had contacts with every echelon of Egyptian society and was tasked with planning and implementing policies before measures were even brought before the parliamentary body of the National Assembly. The assembly was important in its own right, claimed Sabri, yet it was inevitably destined to a lesser role in comparison to the omnipotent ASU.[27]

These heavy-handed policies from Nasser did little to fix Egypt's ailing economy. Moreover, the Egyptian public was becoming critical of the public sector companies. And the chairmen of the boards, in return, were critical of Nasser's new policies.[28] In short, it was not the type of economic reform that US officials had envisioned for Egypt. Instead, it gave the impression that Nasser was getting ready to get closer to Moscow by implementing reforms along communist lines.

Nasser appeared to be done waiting for Johnson to come through with aid. Indeed, the day after Nasser's hostile speech, Battle reported from Cairo that Nasser was planning to sack Kamel and replace him with someone less friendly.[29] Ironically, Battle had just found out that he too was being replaced as ambassador. He was going to take up Talbot's old position back at State. Once again, the administration did not have an immediate replacement for the ambassadorship.[30] US-Egypt relations were rapidly crumbling under Johnson's watch. In the following weeks, leading up to the outbreak of the 1967 War, Nasser continued to lash out even more.

21

Cold Shoulders

When Battle made his farewell calls with Egyptian officials at the end of February 1967, he was given a clear indication that diplomatic relations between the two countries were already soured beyond repair. Sadat, for example, made reference to the low point in relations under the direction of Eisenhower's secretary of state, John Foster Dulles: "US policy in [the] Middle East and particularly toward [the] UAR [is] even worse than that of John Foster Dulles. Dulles . . . said flatly [that the] UAR [is] broke and [the] US . . . [has] no intention of providing aid." The Johnson administration, however, "dangled hope of aid and never gave [an] answer." This is the reason why Nasser had lashed out at the United States in his speech, Sadat said.[1]

The most critical warning sign came from Nasser himself, on March 4, when Battle paid a final and "emotional" visit. The meeting was routine at first. However, Nasser began to lecture Battle after the diplomat brought up the possibility of the United States once again arbitrating an agreement between Saudi Arabia and Egypt to end the civil war in Yemen. Battle wrote to State:

> Nasser then launched into [a] thirty minute tirade of [the] most emotional character yet displayed in my meetings with him. He said [the] UAR [is a] proud, independent country with its own dignity. He had decided in thinking over my call to him to be very frank and he hoped I would not take offence at anything he said, but he must deal lucidly and frankly with issues. [The] UAR would not respond [to] US pressure. It did not want American wheat. During [the] time we had provided wheat he had gone to bed each night disturbed that [the] UAR [was] dependent on [the] US for food and [he] had resented each item in [the] American or world press reminding [the] UAR that five out of each eight loaves of its bread were provided by [the] US. [The] UAR would not accept interference by other countries.

Battle told State that he was concerned about Nasser's state of mind. "Nasser was more emotional than I have ever seen him," he wrote, "and at moments developed [a] glaze over [his] eyes typical of that we have seen when he makes speeches."[2]

Battle asked Nasser why he was so suspicious of the United States. "He admitted I was right when I said he was suspicious. It grew out of his background and he still found himself nervous about writing down telephone numbers, for example, which he always committed to memory. He also hesitated about writing letters and [was] reluctant [to] commit himself to paper, even in reply [to] correspondence [from] other presidents (presumably US) which [were] sometimes delayed due to his suspicious nature." Nasser appeared to be bordering on the delusional: he was adamant with Battle that the CIA was plotting to topple him.[3] Significantly, Nasser's suspicion was shared by every other high-level official Battle met with that week.[4]

Nasser remained defiant for the remainder of the conversation with Battle, launching diatribe upon diatribe against the Johnson administration. Ultimately, he ended the conversation with a threat. "If any country attempted [to] hurt [the] UAR," he said, "[the] UAR would respond and no doubt could do damage [to the] US and other countries."[5] This farewell visit was remarkably different than the friendlier one between Nasser and Badeau three years earlier.

What came next was even more startling. The farewell visit with Battle, in which Nasser formally rescinded his request for PL 480 aid, became a launching pad for a propaganda campaign against the United States. Shortly afterwards, Egyptian daily, *Al-Ahram*, released a series of eight articles that critically examined the history of US policy toward Egypt. Using the metaphor of a "spider's cobweb" to describe American involvement in Arab affairs, it was noted that "the cobweb's threads were cut off" when Nasser rejected American aid in his farewell meeting with Battle.[6]

On March 17, *Al-Ahram* displayed the alleged text of what Nasser had said to Battle:

[W]hile appreciating and thanking you for all the facilities accorded to us in the wheat question, we want nothing now. In Feb 1966, we requested you to supply us with wheat. Since then we have neither renewed the request nor reminded you of it . . . We have been very patient with all the pressure you have applied to us because of the wheat, but our patience has run out. Please know that the value of this country and of its struggle lies basically in its capacity in all conditions to withstand all sorts of pressure–economic, military, or psychological.[7]

Two days after Battle's final meeting with Nasser, Johnson received from Rostow a forwarded telegram written by Saunders, who was "quietly touring" Egypt on Rostow's instructions. Saunders reasoned that it was time to give in and offer a new PL 480 agreement to Nasser. It was in America's best interest, he wrote, to deal with what is "clearly [the] chief power in [the] Middle East." Anything to the contrary, he argued, would cause Egyptian officials to believe that the United States was attempting to undercut Nasser. According to Saunders:

My main reason for arguing this case is that our biggest problem in Cairo today is that no amount of logic [is] sufficient [to] persuade [the] Egyptians that everything we do in [the] Near East [is] not directed at them. It [is] amazing what shreds of evidence they have woven together to prove this to themselves. These [are] not just debating points. Every official I talked to from [the] Foreign Minister on down obviously sincerely believes this. [The] [m]ain thread [of] this fabric of illogic seems be [a] philosophy [that] those not helping them must be against them.[8]

Officials at State agreed with Saunders's assessment. Bergus lamented about the state of affairs in a telegram to Battle: "At issue is the question as to whether the US can in fact accept the proposition that some at least of the Near East states are fully sovereign, are jealous of their sovereignty and are legitimately entitled to that jealousy." Specifically, Bergus was commenting about the rumored CIA operations in Egypt.[9]

Bleak predictions about the future of US-Egypt relations continued apace. At lunch with Rodger Davies on March 6, Kamel said that he "had just received highly secret indications from Cairo that matters would probably become much worse unless . . . [the US] acted at once." Continuing on, Kamel said that "malevolent forces around Nasser had not only persuaded him that future US-UAR relations were black but had practically convinced Nasser that he had nothing to lose and possibly much to gain by proceeding [to] create [a] crisis in US-UAR relations."[10]

Indeed, a little over two months later, Nasser would effectively declare war against Israel—thus forcing the United States, once-and-for-all, to choose a side in the Arab-Israel conflict. Striving for neutralism in the Middle East was no longer an option for the Johnson administration. Battle wrote to State that he regretted having to leave Cairo during one of the lowest points in the history of US-Egypt relations. Indeed, in one fell swoop, Nasser permanently took the Arab-Israel dispute out of the icebox. US-Egypt relations would never be the same for the remainder of his life.[11]

22

US-Egypt Relations Unbound

In the two months that followed Battle's farewell call with Nasser, there was a slew of anti-American propaganda that seemed to equate the United States and Israel as one common enemy. On March 18, the Arab League approved a resolution that condemned "the hostile attitude adopted by the United States to the Palestine problem." Moreover, in a dig against US-Israel relations, the council asserted that the "United States has no right to interfere in the affairs of the Palestinian people."[1] In the month of April, *Al-Ahram's* series of articles continued to criticize US foreign policy, while Egypt's "Foreign Relations Committee" met for a joint session on Israeli aggression and problems in US-Egypt relations.[2]

Nasser also continued to lay groundwork for the "new stage" of Arab unity against Israel that he had spoken of in February. After Israel downed six Syrian jets in an air battle on April 7, he sent his prime minister to Syria to discuss the terms of a joint defense agreement that originally had been signed in October but had not yet been officially activated. A joint communiqué declared: "The statements of the American and Zionist authorities have disclosed that the arming of Arab reaction [e.g., Jordan and Saudi Arabia] is directed principally against the revolution of the Arab masses . . . Israel's latest move against the Syrian regime is no more than a manifestation of the overall imperial and reactionary plans." The statement intended to link America, Israel, and Nasser's Arab rivals as one in the same, in order to paint the image of a nefarious Western-backed plot to control the region.

Then, in a twist of fate, two Americans from AID were arrested in Yemen on April 25 for allegedly shooting bazooka rounds into an ammunitions dump.[3] In reality, the two workers were part of a crew that was building new roads in Yemen. However, they happened to be near an area where Egypt was training fighters for an army that would eventually go into Southern Arabia after Britain left. The incident was symbolic given that AID was the federal department that administered PL 480 aid. Although Rostow believed that the incident was a coincidence, he informed Johnson that Egyptian officials in Yemen took advantage of the situation in order to pilfer CIA documents from the US embassy safe.[4]

Soon afterwards, Nasser followed up the incident with renewed criticism aimed toward the United States and Israel. On May 2, he gave what British observers described as an "important historic speech." Notably, he continued his earlier boast about rejecting American economic pressure. This time, however, he called for collective Arab resistance against American imperialism, noting that, personally, he was "not prepared to sell even a grain of sand of this country's soil against 100 million dollars."[5] Likewise, President Sallal of Yemen joined Nasser in noting that the detained AID workers were hired "to implement CIA plans" to impose American dominance in the region.[6]

Nasser's speech also played on Egypt's historical disagreements with Britain, which Nasser now associated with the United States. At the end of the speech, he reiterated his call for a war against Israel, noting that it was the first step toward eradicating foreign influence in the Middle East. He said:

> It is an unremitting struggle, and we stand with the revolutionary forces against imperialism in every Arab country, against imperialism everywhere, for imperialism will not stop working against us. They won't stop plotting, for we are the real resistance to them; we represent our nation's power to endure, our nation's will to live, our nation's aspirations to freedom and to be rid of imperialism and its allies, the first of which is Zionist racialism in Israel.[7]

The jump from rhetoric to war footing did not occur until May 14, when Egyptian troops suddenly marched through the streets of Cairo and headed into the Sinai Peninsula—the stretch of mostly empty land that bridged Egypt and Israel.

The official justification for Egypt's war footing was Israeli threats to attack Syria. But within the extensive news commentary and various political speeches in favor of military action there was a consistent anti-American sentiment. In most instances it took the form of describing Israel as an American satellite. "The people will have no mercy on imperialist installations [i.e., Israel]," went one broadcast. "The United States will not be able to escape punishment."[8]

At first, Nasser remained silent about the turn of events and allowed the Egyptian press to spread his propaganda. The tactic notably worked on May 21, when Saudi Arabia did a sudden about-face and publicly praised Nasser:

> Perhaps now you realize full well and appreciate that if the United Arab Republic says something, it carries it out; if it promises something, it fulfills that promise; and if it is put to the test by serious events or if it is forced by liars to reveal its might, we find it the most intrepid and the strongest among the states and among mankind. It is brave and trustworthy in facing Zionism and imperialism and a shield to all Arabism and Islam, under the leadership of the pioneer of Arab nationalism, brother President Jamal Abd-an Nasir.[9]

Finally, on May 22, Nasser made his first public appearance since the initial mobilization. When announcing a blockade on Israeli shipping through the Straits of Tiran, Israel's only south-bound point of access, he proudly concluded the announcement with an affirmation of Egyptian strength. "We are not scared by imperialist, Zionist, or reactionary campaigns," he said. "We are independent, and we know the taste of freedom. We have built a strong national army and achieved our objectives. We are building our country."[10] The rhetoric was noticeably yet another rejection of American aid. Nasser was saying that he was a proud and independent leader.

At the same time, *Radio Cairo* had a noticeable spike in anti-American commentary. According to one program, "The United States should also know that there is something else stronger than US might and muscles . . . it is the willpower of the Arabs and their decisive and firm refusal to concede any of their territory or rights."[11] Another popular program openly declared war against the United States:

> We challenge you Israel. No, in fact we do not address the challenge to you, Israel, because you are unworthy of the challenge. But we challenge you America . . . We challenge you to come near, with Israel, to our gulf—The Gulf of Aqaba [in the Tiran Straits]. Our soldiers are there with the most powerful war material known in the Middle East. Behind them stand millions of Arabs, including fidai workers carrying in their hands explosives to blow up every American presence throughout the American homeland.[12]

Likewise, another radio show envisioned a showdown with American forces: "The United States is seeking excuses for an armed intervention against the Arab nation to support Israel. The United States, the number one enemy of popular liberty, is showing very great eagerness and is moving toward active intervention."[13] One newspaper even blamed the United States for instigating the conflict: "The United States [cannot] erase the fact that it has collaborated with Israel in an attempt to create tension or war between Israel and Syria."[14]

The verbal attacks against the United States in the Egyptian press continued unabated, leading *Al-Ahram* to observe that "the confrontation is gradually becoming a confrontation between the Arab nation and the US Government more than between the Arab nation and Israel."[15] At the same time, Nasser continued to garner mass Arab support. On May 26, he said, "Israel today is the United States," effectively declaring that a direct attack on Israel was like a symbolic attack on the United States.[16]

In the midst of this crisis, Johnson sent two private emissaries to Cairo, one of whom was Charles Yost, who, as it will be recalled, had been one of the candidates to be Badeau's replacement. When Yost met with Foreign Minister Riad, he was told that Egypt had badly needed aid. "US policy to the UAR," said Riad, "has seemed in Cairo to be ambiguous and undependable." Riad also said that all Egyptian officials were positive that the CIA had been attempting to topple Nasser. The regime had "documents and tape recordings" to prove the allegation.[17]

To be sure, Nasser was preparing for war against Israel. But the underlying message was that there was going to be payback for his mistreatment at the hands of the Johnson administration.

The historical evidence strongly suggests that Nasser's threat of an all-out Arab war against Israel was partly intended to provoke some sort of response from the United States; perhaps, even, to get the United States to cave in on PL 480. Another emissary Johnson sent to Egypt in the run-up to war was Robert Anderson, who got Nasser to agree either to send Muheidden to the United States or to receive Vice President Humphrey in Cairo in the near future. The hypothetical visits would have been the closest contact between the two countries since Battle's departure, and the highest-level visits since the Eisenhower administration.

For two months the United States did not have an ambassador in Cairo. Eventually, State chose Richard Nolte, who was an expert on the Middle East and fluent in Arabic. He was, perhaps, the closest to a Badeau that the administration could find on short notice. Unfortunately, Nolte was due to present his credentials to Nasser on June 5—the day that Israel would end up launching a surprise attack against Egypt, thus officially beginning the 1967 War. Several days later, US-Egypt relations were officially severed at Nasser's request.[18]

One historian has observed that it was a fait accompli for the other Arab states to join Nasser once he had initiated the sabre-rattling against Israel: "Once war began, other Arab governments lost control of their policies and were sucked in behind the UAR as hapless allies in a war to which their own rivalries had led them."[19] Indeed, even Faisal declared on American television that "all the Arab countries are just as ready to aid Egypt or any other country that is the object of aggression by Israel."[20] In this way, the 1967 War appears to be the major crisis that Komer had often warned about, and for so many years had worked hard to avoid. Nasser was forcing the United States to choose between the Arabs and Israel.

As for Nasser's ultimate intentions toward Israel, it is only possible to speculate about how far he was willing to go. Nonetheless, before the fighting began on June 5, he tried to get word to Johnson, through unofficial channels, that he was not looking for war. He claimed, instead, once again, to be looking for any sign of support from the United States:

> This is the message from Nasser: "Now is the time when all Arab people are waiting to see an act of friendship on the part of the USA. His urgent request is that the US undertake no direct military action in the form of landings, shifting of naval fleet, or otherwise. Nasser assured Siddiqui that the UAR had no intention of fighting. What they are doing is returning to the 1956 frontier. He assured Siddiqui that this matter would soon be terminated without any fighting. He informed Siddiqui that his current actions were intended only to prove to the Arab world that Saudi Arabia and Jordan are false friends. And the Arabs should follow Nasser who is their friend. He also wishes to prove that President Johnson is impartial as between the Arabs and Israel and that he will not take any sides in the present war of nerves. If President Johnson can grant Nasser's request, he can be assured that Nasser will place his entire services at Johnson's disposal."[21]

There was no US strategy for war in 1967—the Johnson administration was caught flat-footed. Instead, the United States sought to avert war by finding an alternative resolution, which culminated in a dogged pursuit to organize an international armada that ultimately was not widely supported nor effective in any capacity to challenge Nasser's blockade against Israeli shipping.

The entire policy of redirecting Nasser had run contrary to the Egyptian leader's political ideology, which called for nonalignment with either superpower in the Cold War[22] and for an active Egyptian role in the political and social spheres of the Middle East and Africa.[23] These were the very same principles which had carried Nasser into power by promising to bring progress to Egypt. Ironically, they would also bring defeat to Egypt in the 1967 War by driving Nasser to take drastic action against Israel, thereby alienating himself even further from the United States.

Most histories have overlooked the collapse of US-Egypt relations as a contributing factor in the origins of the 1967 War. However, the absence of this important geopolitical aspect in the existing literature is an omission of a critical context behind Nasser's unexpected steps in May 1967. Indeed, even Nasser himself claimed that his steps were partially aimed against "the West which created Israel and has despised and ignored us Arabs since 1948 and even before 1948," and which "has shown no consideration whatsoever for us, our feelings, our aspirations in life or our rights."[24] America's food aid was no doubt a political tool to exert influence abroad. However, it was ultimately Nasser's choice to walk away from such American support in 1966 by refusing to tone down his political agenda. Ultimately, it was the combination of these competing sentiments, alongside a volatile regional context, that eventually put the Egyptian leader and the superpower on a collision course over Israel in May 1967.

Conclusion: Applied History

In 2016, two Harvard scholars, Niall Ferguson and Graham Allison, wrote an article for the *Atlantic* called "Why the US President Needs a Council of Historians." Their thesis was that historical knowledge is dangerously absent in US foreign policy-making and that this history deficit sometimes leaves officials drawing blanks about the approaches taken by previous administrations and about the general history and culture of the nations they are dealing with. The two scholars were breathing life into an earlier work by Ernest May and Richard Neustadt, also Harvard scholars, called *Thinking in Time* (not to mention an earlier effort by May called, *"Lessons" of the Past*). Another work in this school of "applied history" is an essay by William H. McNeill, titled, "Why Study History," in which the world history scholar describes history as humanity's "collective memory." According to McNeill, amnesia is just as devastating to a nation's collective memory—affecting its self-understanding and ability to deal with outside nations—as it is to an individual who wakes up with no sense of identity.[1] Taken together, these works demonstrate the important role of history for conducting contemporary policy.

What can be learned from US relations with Egypt during the Kennedy and Johnson administrations that can be applied by later administrations? *The opportunities and limits of personal diplomacy.* Kennedy and his advisers may have been too optimistic about being able to fundamentally change a leader like Nasser, but their redirection strategy did give them influence with him. Johnson, however, didn't appreciate that this influence probably helped keep a partial lid on the Arab-Israeli conflict. Indeed, it made Nasser think about what he might lose if he took drastic action against Israel.

While the continuation of personal diplomacy may not have tempered Nasser's ultimate decision to challenge Israel in 1967, it would have made that decision more complex. Moreover, Johnson potentially could have used his influence either to mitigate or eliminate Nasser's steps.

Ultimately, Nasser bears total responsibility for his decision-making. But by eliminating personal diplomacy, Johnson sacrificed any chance of influencing his choices.

What of Komer and the redirection strategy he spearheaded? This tragedy was told in three parts, which coincided with three distinctive transitional phases in the Johnson administration's policy toward Egypt prior to the 1967 War: The immediate aftermath of Kennedy's assassination, the prolonged period attending Badeau's resignation, and the short interlude after Komer's transition to the Vietnam War. Each of these phases reflected a change in the administration's strategy vis-à-vis Nasser. And success with Nasser in each phase, albeit sometimes fleeting, was often directly related to Komer's behind-the-scenes role (or lack thereof in the case of the final phase).

After Kennedy's assassination in November 1963, Komer did his utmost to ensure that Johnson saw the value of his predecessor's approach to Nasser. However, the personal relationship between Kennedy and Nasser, formed under Komer's guiding hand, vanished with Kennedy's last breath, because Johnson did not present, as Nasser keenly recognized, the same potential for friendly relations that had existed during the Kennedy era.

As Richard Parker, the political attaché at the US embassy in Cairo, later recalled about Johnson's first communication with Nasser: "The letter duly came, and all of us in the embassy thought it was a good letter. It was delivered, and we got word back that Nasser thought the letter was cold. Now the fact is that the letter was drafted by the same people who drafted the earlier ones [e.g., Komer]. But it wasn't the letter, it was the image that stood behind the letter, that had changed, and this affected Nasser's attitude."[2]

With Kennedy no longer in the White House, Badeau—the only visibly remaining link that Nasser had to Kennedy—became more important than ever as the Johnson administration's direct line of communication to the Egyptian president. And with Komer constantly present to steer or support Badeau from Washington, the situation somewhat worked. For example, Badeau was able to talk Nasser down from the foreign bases issue in spring 1964. He also got Nasser to tentatively accept a new arms reduction initiative in the Middle East during his farewell call in June 1964. However, when Badeau left shortly thereafter, there was no one available to immediately take his place, notwithstanding Komer's warning about the dangers of leaving the ambassadorship vacant. There was still a redirection strategy in play, but there was no one in Cairo to apply it.

During the second transitional phase, Congress played a more significant role than before by restricting the administration's ability to give aid to Egypt—the cornerstone of the bilateral relationship since Kennedy signed the multiyear PL 480 agreement in 1962. After Badeau's departure, the administration temporarily drifted away from Nasser because communication between the two countries was virtually nonexistent during Lucius Battle's lengthy confirmation process. By the time Battle arrived in Cairo in September 1964, it was already too late: the administration was missing a representative on the ground who was capable of dealing with Nasser raising problems over US operations in the Congo.

There were also a series of critical miscommunications between the two states. In December 1964, for example, Nasser was misinformed by anti-American officials in his government that Washington was withdrawing aid when it in fact was not. At the White House, Komer was working hard to show Johnson that it was still in his best interest to deal with Nasser despite strained relations. However, in light of the administration's difficult battle with Congress in early 1965 for greater flexibility to continue giving economic assistance to Egypt, Johnson was reluctant to put himself out on the limb for Nasser. Johnson's hesitation led to the redirection strategy's unraveling.

With much difficulty, Komer was eventually able to get Johnson to reopen the relationship with Nasser by restarting PL 480 shipments in June 1965—after they had temporarily been on hold during the extended battle with Congress. Komer also played a key role in getting Johnson to agree to a new PL 480 agreement at the end of 1965 to replace the expired one originally signed under Kennedy.

Nasser, however, rejected the smaller amount of aid that Johnson gave him at the beginning of 1966. Nor did he deem a six-month agreement sufficient, insisting instead on a longer deal like the multiyear one he had obtained under Kennedy. Yet, in the wake of a series of speeches by Nasser about Washington's Vietnam policy, the Johnson administration was reluctant to consider his request for a more substantial aid package. This was the third transitional period in the administration's approach to Nasser. Without Komer in the White House, nobody was left with enough influence that could bypass Rusk to put together a new aid agreement for Nasser. Moreover, by that point, the administration was beginning to change its general philosophy on foreign aid—which essentially meant that Nasser no longer was seen as a worthy recipient of American aid. At that time, the redirection strategy was no longer in play.

When Nasser lashed out against the administration in February 1967, Johnson's officials began to panic and advised Rusk and Johnson to give in to Nasser's demands for aid given the serious threat he posed to America's interests in the Middle East. As far as the available record shows, Johnson and Rusk did not get around to making a final decision in time.[3] Arguably, the absence of Komer as a gadfly in Johnson's Middle East policy left a critical void. Therefore, Komer's departure for Vietnam was an unforeseen axis point of history, around which a chain of events in US-Egypt relations contributed to the environment in which Nasser took his fateful steps against Israel in May 1967.

Crucially, while it was complex regional dynamics that shaped Nasser's actions in May 1967, his steps against Israel appear to have been partially aimed at the United States. Indeed, as Richard Parker observed on the twenty-fifth anniversary of the 1967 War:

> We were pretty frazzled out there. And we did not think that we were getting the sort of support from the Department of State, from the White House, from the government, that we needed in our relations with Egypt. This was an important factor. If you read Nasser's May Day speech of 1967, a third of it is devoted to an attack on the United States, and when this crisis erupted, it was clear to those of us in Cairo that the United States was as much an object of the crisis as anyone else. Nasser was going to destroy our interests.

To be sure, by that point, the Johnson administration was too consumed with the war in Vietnam to be able to take the careful approach with Nasser that Komer had consistently lobbied for. As a major crisis unfolded in the Middle East during the month of May 1967, the United States was an observer of events, reacting to things rather than being in a position or mindset to prevent them. Indeed, this is what Komer himself had to say on the twenty-fifth anniversary of the 1967 War: "Let me tell you that by May 1967 we had 500,000 men in Vietnam, a half million . . . So in the eye of the president, who spent twenty times as much time on Vietnam as he did on the

Arab-Israeli fracas, even at its height, there was no possibility of the United States adopting a military rule or intervening militarily or providing a great deal of support. We were fighting a war already."[4]

At a final meeting between Johnson and Kamel on May 22, before the visibly shaken ambassador made his departure from the United States, there was an air of fatality. It seemed like there was very little Johnson could do to fix the situation apart from having other countries ask Egypt to "handle itself cautiously, write to Nasser, [or] find some way at least to get back to supplying food via CCC credit." Kamel declared that his mission had been a failure. Johnson, for his part, was still reluctant to reach out to Nasser. According to Saunders: "He does not want to appear to be pleading with Nasser at this point."[5]

Nevertheless, Johnson may have come to regret his approach to Nasser in the wake of Komer's departure. This can be seen in his decision to temporarily bring Bundy back into the administration as head of a special White House committee to handle the 1967 War. As Bundy later recalled: "I joined the war after it had begun . . . [Johnson] said, we need somebody. Walt's got a war. I want somebody else to handle the second war, so you stick around."[6] But this was a reaction to a crisis without regard for strategy or policy—the exact scenario that Komer had feared when he devised the redirection strategy under Kennedy.

Alexander Wendt's theory about the changing identity of states is demonstrated in how Johnson's America became less confident in its diplomatic outreach and more consumed by the quagmire in Vietnam to the detriment of its other foreign relations. Nasser's Egypt also went through a transformation in identity. The self-confidence of Nasser's exploits in Yemen at the beginning of this book were replaced with financial ruin—as a result of his interventions in Yemen—and constant suspicion of American covert action that could potentially take advantage of that ruin to bring him out of power.

Komer went to great lengths to hold the two sides together in spite of the fact that he had less approval from Johnson than he had from Kennedy. This was an atypical role for someone in Komer's position. After Komer's time, the Middle East became a more crucial component of American grand strategy; one that gradually replaced the focus on Moscow after the Cold War came to a close in 1991. Since then, individuals have certainly left their mark on US Middle East policy in profound (if not destructive) ways; but none have maintained positive relations in the way that Komer did. US presidents and their advisers never quite seemed to learn the key lesson of the story of US-Egypt relations in the 1960s, which is the power of diplomacy to head off crises rather than waiting to react to them. As a result, the United States has consistently found itself impacted by a region it has little understanding of and no hope of ever controlling.

To a certain extent, the events depicted in this book demonstrate an axiom by Henry Kissinger that American foreign policy is often no more than a "series of moves that have produced a certain result."[7] Do busy policymakers have time to formulate strategies and put them into play? Not when crises, like the 1967 War, begin. Those types of events move too quickly to give policymakers enough time for thorough deliberations. And yet, as pointed out by British historian Christopher Bayly, crises always lurk beneath the surface of bureaucratic daily routines.[8] Therefore, the onus is on policymakers to come up with comprehensive strategies before those crises reach their "critical" stage. Indeed, Komer, a self-professed "gadfly," clearly had a large impact for an adviser with a mid-level position. The lesson in this story is that individuals and their decisions matter.

Notes

Prologue: The Swerve

1 Jay Walz, "Four Test Rockets Launched by Cairo," *New York Times*, July 22, 1962.
2 Memorandum, Brubeck to Bundy, July 28, 1962, *Foreign Relations of the United States Series (FRUS) 1961–1963*, Vol. XVIII, doc. 10.
3 Memorandum, Brubeck to Bundy, August 3, 1962, *FRUS 1961–1963*, Vol. XVIII, doc. 12.
4 Message, Bundy to Kennedy, August 19, 1962, *FRUS 1961–1963*, Vol. XVIII, doc. 23.
5 Letter, Kennedy to Nasser, August 16, 1962, *FRUS 1961–1963*, Vol. XVIII, doc. 22.
6 Nomi Prins, *All the President's Bankers: The Hidden Alliances that Drive American Power* (New York: Nation Books, 2014).

Preface: The Argument and Themes of the Book

1 Matthew F. Jacobs, *Imagining the Middle East: The Building of an American Foreign Policy, 1918–1967* (Chapel Hill: University of North Carolina Press, 2011), pp. 227–8.
2 Alexander Wendt, *Social Theory of International Politics* (Cambridge: Cambridge University Press, 1999), p. 194.
3 Kori Schake, *Safe Passage: The Transition from British to American Hegemony* (Cambridge: Harvard University Press, 2017), p. 28.
4 See John Lewis Gaddis, *Strategies of Containment: A Critical Appraisal of American National Security Policy during the Cold War* (Oxford: Oxford University Press, 2005 revised and expanded edition).
5 See Isaiah Berlin, *The Hedgehog and the Fox: An Essay on Tolstoy's View of History* (New York: Simon and Schuster, 1953).
6 See John Lewis Gaddis, *On Grand Strategy* (New York: Penguin Press, 2018).
7 See, for example, Said K. Aburish, *Nasser: The Last Arab* (New York: Thomas Dunn Books, 2004).
8 Ibid.
9 C. A. Bayly, *The Birth of the Modern World: 1780–1914* (Oxford: Blackwell, 2004), p. 207.
10 See Gamal Abdel Nasser, *Philosophy of the Revolution* (Cairo: Mondiale Press, date unknown), pp. 66–72.
11 Ibid., p. 24.
12 Nasser, "The Egyptian Revolution," *Foreign Affairs* 33, no. 2 (January 1955): 204–5.
13 Ibid., p. 205.
14 Ibid., p. 206.
15 Ibid., p. 207.
16 Robert B. Strassler, ed. *The Landmark Herodotus: The Histories* (New York: Anchor Books, 2007), p. 118.

17 See, Miles Copeland, *The Game of Nations: The Amorality of Power Politics* (New York: Simon and Shuster, 1969), chapters 3 and 4. Copeland describes in great detail how the CIA looked for a leader capable of winning support in Egypt and exerting influence over the Middle East. He believed that Nasser relied on a doctrine of Arab nationalism because it was popular at the time and therefore would also denounce the West as a way to get to the hearts and minds of the Arab people. Copeland's assessment is supported by a CIA report which notes that, "Most Arabs are profoundly influenced by the anti-imperialist and neutralist doctrines of nationalist movements." See, also, CIA National Intelligence Estimate 36–54, "Probable Developments in the Arab States," September 7, 1954, pp. 7–8.

18 Heikal, *Sphinx and Commissar: The Rise and Fall of Soviet Influence in the Arab World* (London: Collins, 1978), p. 20.

19 There is a large body of literature about Nasser manipulating both America and the Soviet Union into seeing him as an asset. See, for example, Malcolm H. Kerr, *Egypt Under Nasser* (New York: Foreign Policy Association, 1963), p. 29; Amos Perlmutter, *Egypt: The Praetorian State* (New Brunswick: Transaction Books, 1974), p. 177; James P. Jankowski, *Nasser's Egypt, Arab Nationalism, and the United Arab Republic* (Boulder and London: Lynne Rienner, 2002), p. 50.

1 Introduction: Kennedy's Men

1 Text of John F. Kennedy, 1960 Democratic National Convention Speech, July 15, 1960, John F. Kennedy Presidential Library (hereafter JFKL).

2 See David Halberstam, *The Best and the Brightest* (New York: Modern Library, 1972).

3 Edmund S. Ions, *The Politics of John F. Kennedy* (London: Routledge, 1967), p. 44.

4 Richard N. Goodwin, "President Lyndon Johnson: The War Within," *New York Times*, August 21, 1988; For the assessment of Kennedy, see Richard Hofstadter, *Anti-Intellectualism in American Life* (New York: Vintage Books, 1962), p. 228.

5 Robert A. Caro, *Means of Ascent* (New York: Vintage Books, 1990), p. 5.

6 Frank Leith Jones, *Blowtorch: Robert Komer, Vietnam, and American Cold War Strategy* (Annapolis: Naval Institute Press, 2013), pp. 65–6.

7 Tim Weiner, "Robert Komer, 78, Figure in Vietnam, Dies," *New York Times*, April 12, 2000.

8 Komer Fifth Oral History (hereafter OH), December 22, 1969, JFKL, p. 54.

9 Jernegan First OH, March 12, 1969, JFKL, p. 30.

10 Ibid., p. 31.

11 Komer Fifth OH, December 22, 1969, JFKL, p. 13.

12 Ibid., p. 12.

13 Bundy First OH, March 1964, JFKL, p. 68.

14 Andrew Preston, *The War Council: McGeorge Bundy, the NSC, and Vietnam* (Cambridge: Harvard University Press, 2010), p. 7.

15 Ibid., pp. 46–7.

16 Komer Fifth OH, December 22, 1969, JFKL, pp. 4–5.

17 Ibid., p. 9.

18 Ibid., p. 4.

19 Badeau OH, February 25, 1969, JFKL, p. 1.

20 Bowles First OH, February 2, 1965, JFKL, p. 21.

21 Komer Second OH, July 16, 1964, JFKL, p. 20.

22 Badeau OH, February 25, 1969, JFKL, p. 4.

23 Komer Fifth OH, December 22, 1969, JFKL, p. 44.

24 See Komer Fourth OH, October 31, 1964, JFKL, p. 22.

25 Komer Fifth OH, December 22, 1969, JFKL, p. 22.

26 Ibid., p. 49.

27 Ibid., p. 1.

28 Ibid., p. 50.

29 David Fromkin, "Lyndon Johnson and Foreign Policy: What the New Documents Show," *Foreign Affairs* (January/February 1995). As Johnson said to a friend about Vietnam: "I think that I've got to say that I didn't get you in here, but we're in here by treaty and our national honor's at stake. And if this treaty is no good, none of 'em are any good. Therefore we're here. And being there, we've got to conduct ourselves like men." Odd Arne Westad, *The Cold War: A World History* (New York: Basic Books, 2017), p. 319.

30 Jones, *Blowtorch*, p. 11.

31 Bundy First OH, March 1964, JFKL, p. 71.

32 Komer First OH, June 18, 1964, JFKL, p. 3.

33 See Michael Doran, *Ike's Gamble: America's Rise to Dominance in the Middle East* (New York: Free Press, 2016).

34 Komer First OH, June 18, 1964, JFKL, p. 4.

35 See William J. Burns, *Economic Aid and American Policy toward Egypt, 1955–1981* (Albany: State University of New York Press, 1985).

36 Komer First OH, June 18, 1964, JFKL, p. 4.

37 See Bundy OH, January 30, 1969, Lyndon Baines Johnson Presidential Library (hereafter LBJL), pp. 23–4.

2 Komer's War

1 For more information about the United States and the war in Yemen see a book written by the former US ambassador to Saudi Arabia: Parker T. Hart, *Saudi Arabia and the United States: Birth of a Security Partnership* (Bloomington: Indiana University Press, 1998).

2 See Jesse Ferris, *Nasser's Gamble: How Intervention in Yemen Caused the Six-Day War and the Decline of Egyptian Power* (Princeton: Princeton University Press, 2013).

3 See Roby C. Barrett, *The Greater Middle East and the Cold War: US Foreign Policy under Eisenhower and Kennedy* (London: I.B. Tauris, 2007), pp. 296–7.

4 Memorandum, Komer to Kennedy, March 11, 1963, *FRUS 1961–1963*, Vol. XVIII, doc. 188.

5 Komer Fifth OH, December 22, 1969, JFKL, p. 43.

6 Badeau OH, February 25, 1969, JFKL, p. 15.

7 David Coleman, *The Fourteenth Day: JFK and the Aftermath of the Cuban Missile Crisis* (New York: W.W. Norton, 2012), pp. 11–13; Godfrey Hodgson, "Obituaries: Dean Rusk," *Independent*, December 21, 1994.

8 Komer Second OH, July 16, 1964, JFKL, p. 13.

9 Memorandum, Komer to Kennedy, October 7, 1963, *FRUS 1961–1963*, Vol. XVIII, doc. 334.

10 Memorandum, Komer to Bundy, October 19, 1963, *FRUS 1961–1963*, Vol. XVIII, doc. 344.

11 Telegram, State to Jidda, October 19, 1963, *FRUS 1961–1963*, Vol. XVIII, doc. 346.

12 Telegram, State to Cairo, October 19, 1963, *FRUS 1961–1963*, Vol. XVIII, doc. 347.

13 Telegram, Cairo to State, October 21, 1963, *FRUS 1961–1963*, Vol. XVIII, doc. 348.

14 Telegram, State to Jidda, October 28, 1963, *FRUS 1961–1963*, Vol. XVIII, doc. 350.

15 Memorandum, Komer to Bundy, October 30, 1963, *FRUS 1961–1963*, Vol. XVIII, doc. 351.

16 Letter, Talbot to Bundy, November 6, 1963, *FRUS 1961–1963*, Vol. XVIII, doc. 354.

17 Telegram, State to Cairo, November 20, 1963, *FRUS 1961–1963*, Vol. XVIII, doc. 366.

18 See, for example, Warren Bass, *Support Any Friend: Kennedy's Middle East and the Making of the US-Israel Alliance* (Oxford: Oxford University Press, 2003).

19 Memorandum, Talbot to Rusk, November 23, 1963, *FRUS 1961–1963*, Vol. XVIII, doc. 371.

20 Telegram, State to Cairo, November 20, 1963, *FRUS 1961–1963*, Vol. XVIII, doc. 366. See fn. 4.

21 See, for example, Memorandum, Solbert to Taylor, "Near East Arms Policy," December 2, 1963, *FRUS 1961–1963*, Vol. XVIII, doc. 375. Solbert recommended a "counter draft to State's paper" on arms policy. "We believe that the situation in the Near East has changed sufficiently since our original policy was enunciated to warrant review of US arms policy in the area and the State paper thereon."

22 Telegram 2297, State to Cairo, November 24, 1963, LBJL, National Security Files, Country Files, UAR, Box 158, Vol. 1 (hereafter NSF/UAR/158/1).

23 Telegram, Jidda to State, November 30, 1963, *FRUS 1961–1963*, Vol. XVIII, doc. 372.

24 Telegram, State to Jidda, December 1, 1963, *FRUS 1961–1963*, Vol. XVIII, doc. 373.

25 Memorandum for the Record, "Meeting with the President," December 2, 1963, *FRUS 1961–1963*, Vol. XVIII, doc. 374.

26 Memorandum, Komer to Bundy, December 3, 1963, LBJL, National Security Files, Name Files, Komer Memos, Box 6, Vol. 1.

27 Memorandum, Komer to Bundy, December 3, 1963, LBJL, National Security Files, Name Files, Komer Memos, Box 6, Vol. 1. This memo was a follow-up to the one cited in note 26.

28 Telegram 00731, State to Cairo, December 3, 1963, LBJL, NSF/UAR/158/1.

29 See Burns, *Economic Aid and American Policy toward Egypt*, p. 145.

30 Letter, Talbot to Badeau, December 4, 1963, *FRUS 1961–1963*, Vol. XVIII, doc. 379.

31 Telegram 1267, Cairo to State, December 5, 1963, LBJL, NSF/UAR/158/1.

32 Memorandum of Conversation, "Discussion of Near East Developments and OPEC," December 6, 1963, *FRUS 1961–1963*, Vol. XVIII, doc. 381.

33 Cover Letter, Bundy to Johnson, December 11, 1963, LBJL, National Security Files, Aide Files, Bundy.

34 Memorandum, Joint Chiefs of Staff to McNamara, "Withdrawal of Hard Surface Forces from Saudi Arabia," December 24, 1963, *FRUS 1961–1963*, Vol. XVIII, doc. 393.

35 Telegram, State to UN, December 18, 1963, *FRUS 1961–1963*, Vol. XVIII, doc. 388.

36 Telegram 11411, Cairo to State, December 17, 1963, LBJL, NSF/UAR/158/1.

37 Telegram, State to Jidda, December 19, 1963, *FRUS 1961–1963*, Vol. XVIII, doc. 389.

38 Telegram, State to Cairo, December 23, 1963, *FRUS 1961–1963*, Vol. XVIII, doc. 391.

39 Telegram 11855, State to Cairo, December 23, 1963, LBJL, NSF/UAR/158/1.

40 Information Report, CIA, December 12, 1963, LBJL, NSF/UAR/158/1.

41 Telegram 1441, Cairo to State, December 30, 1963, LBJL, NSF/UAR/158/1.

42 Telegram 1423, Cairo to State, December 26, 1963, LBJL, NSF/UAR/158/1.

43 Telegram 1490, Cairo to State (Part I), January 7, 1964, LBJL, NSF/UAR/158/1.

44 Telegram 1490, Cairo to State 1490 (Part II), January 7, 1964, LBJL, NSF/UAR/158/1.

45 Telegram 1490, Cairo to State (Part III), January 7, 1964, LBJL, NSF/UAR/158/1.

46 Memorandum, Komer to Johnson, January 31, 1964, *FRUS 1964–1968*, Vol. XXI, doc. 321.

3 Nasser's New Frontier

1 Letter, Johnson to Eshkol, January 2, 1964, *FRUS, 1964–1968*, Vol. XVIII, doc. 1.

2 Telegram 1493, Cairo to State, January 7, 1964, LBJL, NSF/UAR/158/1.

3 Telegram 1445, Cairo to State, December 31, 1963, LBJL, NSF/UAR/158/1.

4 Telegram 2984, London to State, December 31, 1963, LBJL, NSF/UAR/158/1.

5 Telegram 3021, London to State, January 2, 1964, LBJL, NSF/UAR/158/1.

6 Telegram 1451, Cairo to State, December 31, 1963, LBJL, NSF/UAR/158/1.

7 Circular Telegram 1178, State to Cairo, January 3, 1964, LBJL, NSF/UAR/158/1.

8 Peking NCNA International Service in English, January 13, 1964, Foreign Broadcast Information Service Daily Report (FBIS), January 14, 1964, B1.

9 Editor Note, FBIS, January 14, 1964, B1.

10 Ibid., B2.

11 Address by President Nasir, Cairo Domestic Service in Arabic, January 13, 1964, FBIS, January 14, 1964, B2.

12 Radio Cairo, January 13, 1964, FBIS, January 14, 1964, B2.

13 Radio Cairo, July 1, 1964, FBIS, July 2, 1964, B2.

14 See Anwar el-Sadat, *In Search of Identity: An Autobiography* (New York: Harper & Row, 1978), p. 192.

15 Efraim Karsh, *Islamic Imperialism: A History* (New Haven: Yale University Press, 2006), p. 157.

16 Address by President Nasir, Cairo Domestic Service in Arabic, January 13, 1964, FBIS, January 14, 1964, B2.

17 Cairo Domestic Service in Arabic, January 13, 1964, FBIS, January 14, 1964, B5.

18 Cairo Domestic Service in Arabic, January 15, 1964, FBIS, January 16, 1964, B3.

19 Damascus Domestic Service in Arabic, January 16, 1964, FBIS, January 16, 1964, D1.

20 Baghdad Domestic Service in Arabic, January 15, 1964, FBIS, January 16, 1964, B2.

21 Cairo Domestic Service in Arabic, January 17, 1964, FBIS, January 20, 1964, B1.

22 CIA Intelligence Information Cable 95010, January 9, 1964, LBJL, NSF/UAR/158/1.

23 Cairo Domestic Service in Arabic, January 19, 1964, FBIS, January 20, 1964, B1.

24 Jerusalem Domestic Service in Arabic, January 19, 1964, FBIS, January 20, 1964, H1.

25 Cairo in Hebrew to Israel, January 17, 1964, FBIS, January 20, 1964, B3.

26 Burns, *Economic Aid and American Policy toward Egypt*, p. 252, n. 50. Burns mistakenly identifies Keating as a Democrat.

27 Thomas G. Paterson, "The Historian as Detective: Senator Kenneth Keating, the Missiles in Cuba, and His Mysterious Sources," *Diplomatic History 11*, no. 1 (January 1987): 67–70.

28 Saunders to Komer, September 10, 1963, LBJL, National Security Files, Files of Robert W. Komer, Box 52 (hereafter NSF/Komer/52).

29 Komer to Bundy, September 10, 1963, LBJL, NSF/Komer/52.

30 Saunders to Komer, September 10, 1963, LBJL, NSF/Komer/52.

31 Komer to Bundy, December 3, 1963, LBJL, NSF/Komer/52.

32 Rex Mortimer, *Indonesian Communism under Sukarno: Ideology and Politics, 1959-1965* (Ithaca: Cornell University Press, 1974), p. 268.

33 Memorandum, Komer for Talbot, December 18, 1963, LBJL, NSF/Komer/51.

34 Komer to Bundy, December 2, 1963, LBJL, NSF/Komer/51.

35 Komer to Bundy, January 7, 1964, LBJL, NSF/Komer/51.

36 See Saunders to Komer, September 10, 1963, LBJL, NSF/Komer/52

37 Saunders to Komer, December 10, 1963, LBJL, NSF/Komer/52.

38 Memorandum, Komer to Bundy, December 30, 1963, LBJL, NSF/UAR/158/1.

39 Letter, Badeau to the President, January 3, 1964, LBJL, NSF/UAR/158/1.

40 Memorandum for the President, "Ambassador Badeau's Analysis of US Policy Toward the UAR," January 14, 1964, LBJL, NSF/UAR/158/1.

41 Memo, Komer to Moyers, January 14, 1964, LBJL, NSF/UAR/158/1. Badeau was coming back to the United States for a teaching job at Columbia University.

42 Handwritten Note, Moyers to Bromley Smith, undated, LBJL, NSF/UAR/158/1.

43 Telegram 1643, Cairo to State (Section I), January 23, 1964, LBJL, NSF/UAR/158/1.

44 Telegram 1643, Cairo to State (Part II), January 23, 1964, LBJL, NSF/UAR/158/1.

45 Telegram 1723, Cairo to State, January 30, 1964, LBJL, NSF/UAR/158/1.

46 Moshe Gat, *Britain and the Conflict in the Middle East, 1964-1967: The Coming of the Six-Day War* (London: Praeger, 2003), p. 68.

47 Telegram 1723, Cairo to State, January 30, 1964, LBJL, NSF/UAR/158/1.

48 Text of Remarks in New York City at the Dinner of the Weizmann Institute of Science, February 6, 1964, Public Papers of the Presidents of the United States: Lyndon B. Johnson, 1963–1964, doc. 175.

49 CIA Intelligence Information Cable 18717, "Nasir's Reaction to President Johnson's Speech at the Weizman Institute," February 13, 1964, LBJL, NSF/UAR/158/1.

50 Telegram 1801, Cairo to State, February 11, 1964, LBJL, NSF/UAR/158/1. The telegram was Limdis, "For Talbot NEA from Ambassador."

51 Komer to Talbot, February 18, 1964, LBJL, NSF/Komer/51.

52 Komer Draft, Letter from Johnson to Nasser, Attachment from Komer to Talbot, February 18, 1964, LBJL, NSF/Komer/51.

53 Draft Letter to Nasser, February 19, 1964, LBJL, NSF/Komer/51.

54 Memorandum, Komer for Johnson, February 18, 1964, LBJL, NSF/Komer/51.

4 Weapons and Bases

1 Owen L. Sirrs, *Nasser and the Missile Age in the Middle East* (London: Routledge, 2006), pp. 227–30.

2 Avner Cohen, *Israel and the Bomb* (New York: Columbia University Press, 1998), pp. 132–3, 156.

3 See Memorandum, Komer for Johnson, February 18, 1964, LBJL, NSF/Komer/51.

4 Komer's notes for a memorandum to the President, but then sent to Bundy, "The UAR/Israeli Missile Problem," February 13, 1964, LBJL, NSF/Komer/53.

5 Memorandum, Komer for Jack Jernegan, March 12, 1964, LBJL, NSF/Komer/53. Marked "CANE."

6 Memorandum, Komer to Talbot, February 21, 1964, LBJL, NSF/Komer/51. Marked "CANE."

7 Komer to Bundy, February 24, 1964, LBJL, NSF/Komer/51.

8 Ibid.

9 Memorandum, Komer for Johnson, February 26, 1964, LBJL, NSF/Komer/51.

10 Komer to Bundy, February 26, 1964, LBJL, NSF/Komer/51. Marked "CANE."

11 Memorandum, Komer for Johnson, February 26, 1964, LBJL, NSF/Komer/51.

12 Copy of Letter, Johnson to Nasser, February 27, 1964, LBJL, NSF/Komer/51. A handwritten note says the letter was sent to the US Embassy in Cairo, reftel 3968.

13 Telegram, State to Cairo, February 29, 1964, *FRUS 1964–1968*, Vol. XVIII, doc. 22.

14 Telegram 4009, State to Cairo (for Talbot), February 29, 1964, LBJL, NSF/UAR/158/1.

15 Telegram 4013, State to Cairo (for Talbot), February 29, 1964, LBJL, NSF/UAR/158/1.

16 Telegram 1995, Cairo (from Talbot) to State (Section I), March 4, 1964, LBJL, NSF/ UAR/158/1.

17 Telegram 1995, Cairo (from Talbot) to State (Section II), March 4, 1964, LBJL, NSF/ UAR/158/1.

18 Telegram 1995, Cairo (from Talbot) to State (Section III), March 4, 1964, LBJL, NSF/ UAR/158/1.

19 Telegram, Cairo to State, March 4, 1964, *FRUS 1964–1968*, Vol. XVIII, doc. 24.

20 CIA Intelligence Information Cable 33036, "Nasir's Comments on His Meeting with Assistant Secretary Talbot," March 5, 1964, LBJL, NSF/UAR/158/1.

21 CIA Intelligence Information Cable 37807, "Nasir's Pressure on Libya for Removal of Foreign Bases," March 12, 1964, LBJL, NSF/UAR/158/1.

22 Telegram 4292, State to Cairo, March 17, 1964, LBJL, NSF/UAR/158/1.

23 Telegram, Cairo to State, March 18, 1964, LBJL, NSF/UAR/158/1.

24 Ibid. Bundy handwrote the remark on a copy of the telegram.

25 Telegram 4292, State to Cairo, March 17, 1964, LBJL, NSF/UAR/158/1. Bundy handwrote his comments on a copy of the telegram and addressed it to Komer.

26 Telegram 4713, London to State, "For the Secretary (Rusk) from Talbot," March 25, 1964, LBJL, NSF/UAR/158/1.

27 Telegram 2234, Cairo to State, March 28, 1964, LBJL, NSF/UAR/158/1.

28 Memorandum for the Record, April 2, 1964, *FRUS 1964–1968*, Vol. XVIII, doc. 35.

29 Telegram 2316, Cairo to State (Section I), April 5, 1964, LBJL, NSF/UAR/158/1.

30 Telegram 2316, Cairo to State (Section II), April 5, 1964, LBJL, NSF/UAR/158/1.

31 Telegram 2316, Cairo to State (Section III), April 5, 1964, LBJL, NSF/UAR/158/1.

32 Saunders to Komer, April 8 1964, LBJL, NSF/Komer/52.

5 Enter Britain

1 Letter, Komer to Badeau (via classified diplomatic pouch to the embassy in Cairo), April 17, 1964, LBJL, NSF/Komer/51.

2 Komer to Dungan, April 1, 1964, LBJL, NSF/Komer/51.

3 Komer to Bundy, April 7, 1964, LBJL, NSF/Komer/51.

4 Komer to Bundy, April 7, 1964, LBJL, NSF/Komer/51.

5 Ibid. Handwritten response from Bundy.

6 Memo, Dungan to Bundy and Komer, April 8, 1964, LBJL, NSF/Komer/51.

7 Komer to Dungan (carbon copy to Bundy), April 9, 1964, LBJL, NSF/Komer/51.

8 Airgram, Cairo to State, "US-UAR Relations: I. Areas of Maneuver," April 11, 1964, LBJL, NSF/UAR/158/1.

9 Telegram 2358, Cairo to State (Section I), April 10, 1964, LBJL, NSF/UAR/158/1.

10 Telegram 2358, Cairo to State (Section II), April 10, 1964, LBJL, NSF/UAR/158/1.

11 Action Memorandum, Talbot to Rusk, "United States Policy toward UAR," April 20, 1964, *FRUS 1964–1968*, Vol. XVIII, doc. 45.

12 Spencer Mawby, *British Policy in Aden and the Protectorates, 1955–1967: Last Outpost of a Middle East Empire* (London: Routledge, 2006), pp. 113–14.

13 CIA Intelligence Information Cable 62297, "UAR Guidance Minister Hatim's Comment about Pamphlet on American Intelligence," April 16, 1964, LBJL, NSF/UAR/158/1.

14 Letter, Komer to Badeau (via classified diplomatic pouch to the embassy in Cairo), April 17, 1964, LBJL, NSF/Komer/51.

15 Memorandum, Komer for Johnson, March 14, 1964, LBJL, NSF/Komer/51.

16 TMT to Komer, April 17, 1964, LBJL, NSF/Komer/51.

17 Memorandum, Komer for Johnson, April 17, 1964, LBJL, NSF/Komer/51.

18 Komer to Bundy, April 21, 1964, LBJL, NSF/Komer/51.

19 Komer to Bundy, April 21, 1964, LBJL, NSF/Komer/51.

20 Memorandum of Conversation, "Countering UAR Pressure against the British Position in Aden," April 27, 1964, *FRUS 1964–1968*, Vol. XXI, doc. 55.

21 Telegram 2440, Cairo to State, "For Crockett and Talbot," April 18, 1964, LBJL, NSF/UAR/158/1.

22 Telegram 2572, Cairo to State, May 2, 1964, LBJL, NSF/UAR/158/1.

23 Telegram 2580, Cairo to State, May 2, 1964, LBJL, NSF/UAR/158/1.

24 Telegram 2583, Cairo to State, May 2, 1964, LBJL, NSF/UAR/158/1.

25 Telegram 2585, Cairo to State (Section I), May 3, 1964, LBJL, NSF/UAR/158/1.

26 Telegram 2583, Cairo to State, May 2, 1964, LBJL, NSF/UAR/158/1.

27 Telegram 2585, Cairo to State (Section II), May 3, 1964, LBJL, NSF/UAR/158/1.

28 Telegram 2586, Cairo to State (Section I), May 4, 1964, LBJL, NSF/UAR/158/1.

29 Telegram 2586, Cairo to State (Section II), May 4, 1964, LBJL, NSF/UAR/158/1.

30 See, for example, Badeau OH, February 25, 1969, JFKL.

31 Telegram 2586, Cairo to State (Section II), May 4, 1964, LBJL, NSF/UAR/158/1.

32 State Circular Telegram 2064, May 5, 1964, LBJL, NSF/UAR/158/1.

33 Saunders to Bundy, May 4, 1964, LBJL, NSF/Komer/51.

34 Saunders to Bundy, May 5, 1964, LBJL, NSF/Komer/51.

35 Saunders to Bundy, May 6, 1964, LBJL, NSF/Komer/52.

36 Handwritten Note, Bundy to Saunders, undated, LBJL, NSF/Komer/52. The note was filed with the document cited in n. 35.

37 See, for example, Sean J. Savage, *JFK, LBJ, and the Democratic Party* (Albany: State University of New York Press, 2004).

38 Memo by Komer, "Press Conference," May 6, 1964, LBJL, NSF/Komer/51.

39 Edwin Dale Jr., "US Allies Irked on Loan to U.A.R.," *New York Times*, May 28, 1964.

40 Saunders to Komer, May 27, 1964, LBJL, NSF/Komer/52.

41 Komer to Bundy, May 28, 1964, LBJL, NSF/Komer/52.

6 Badeau's Final Mission

1 Memorandum for the Record, "Standing Group Meeting on Israeli Requests for US Tanks," April 30, 1964, *FRUS 1964–1968*, Vol. XVIII, doc. 49.

2 Telegram 5168, State to Cairo, May 6, 1964, LBJL, NSF/UAR/158/1.
3 Telegram 2632, Cairo to State, May 8, 1964, LBJL, NSF/UAR/158/1.
4 Telegram 2629, Cairo to State, "From Ambassador for Jernegan," May 8, 1964, LBJL, NSF/UAR/158/1.
5 Telegram 5289, State to Cairo, "For Ambassador from Talbot," May 13, 1964, LBJL, NSF/UAR/158/1.
6 Memorandum, United States Information Agency to Komer, "Arab Reaction to Badeau's Resignation," May 22, 1964, LBJL, NSF/UAR/158/1.
7 Telegram 3588, Moscow to State, May 25, 1964, LBJL, NSF/UAR/158/1.
8 Komer to Bundy, May 26, 1964, LBJL, NSF/UAR/158/1.
9 Memorandum, Johnson to Feldman, "President's Instructions for Feldman-Sloan Mission," May 15, 1964, *FRUS 1964–1968*, Vol. XVIII, doc. 55.
10 Memorandum for Record, "Israeli Tank Discussion with the President," May 16, 1964, *FRUS 1964–1968*, Vol. XVIII, doc. 57.
11 Telegram 5303, State to Cairo, May 14, 1964, LBJL, NSF/UAR/158/1.
12 Telegram 2709, Cairo to State, May 15, 1964, LBJL, NSF/UAR/158/1.
13 Memorandum, Komer for Johnson, May 19, 1964, LBJL, NSF/Komer/51.
14 Komer to Bundy, May 19, 1964, LBJL, NSF/Komer/51.
15 Letter, Johnson to Nasser, May 20, 1964, LBJL, NSF/Komer/51.
16 Memorandum, Komer for Johnson, May 19, 1964, LBJL, NSF/Komer/51.
17 Telegram 5566, State to Cairo, May 28, 1964, LBJL, NSF/UAR/158/1.
18 Telegram 5567, State to Cairo, May 28, 1964, LBJL, NSF/UAR/158/1.
19 Telegram 5592, State to Cairo, May 30, 1964, LBJL, NSF/UAR/158/1.
20 Telegram, Cairo to State, June 8, 1964, *FRUS 1964–1968*, Vol. XVIII, doc. 71.
21 Telephone Conversation, Johnson and Rusk, April 9, 1964, Tape no. WH6404.05, Citation no. 2941, University of Virginia, Miller Center, Secret White House Tapes.

7 Starting Over with/in Cairo

1 Telegram 5444, State to Cairo, May 22, 1964, LBJL, NSF/UAR/158/1; Flash 5449, State to Cairo, May 22, 1964, LBJL, NSF/UAR/158/1; Telegram 2813, Flash, Cairo to State, May 23, 1964, LBJL, NSF/UAR/158/1.
2 Battle OH, July 10, 1991. The Association for Diplomatic Studies and Training, p. 22.
3 Ibid., pp. 22–3.
4 Telegram 2347, Cairo to State (Sections I & II), April 10, 1964, LBJL, NSF/UAR/158/1.
5 Memorandum, Read to Bundy, "Extra-Long Staple Cotton," June 3, 1964, *FRUS 1964–1968*, Vol. IX (Commodities), doc. 221; Komer to Bundy, June 10, 1964, LBJL, NSF/Komer/52.
6 Memorandum, Komer for Johnson, June 3, 1964, LBJL, National Security Files, Country Files, Israel, Box 138, Vol. 2.
7 Memorandum, Talbot to Rusk, "The Palestine Problem, 1964–1965," June 15, 1964, *FRUS 1964–1968*, Vol. XVIII, doc. 73.
8 Memo, Komer and Bundy to Johnson, June 17, 1964, LBJL, NSF/Komer/51.
9 Memo, Saunders to Komer, June 19, 1964, LBJL, NSF/Komer/51.
10 Memorandum, Komer for Johnson, June 29, 1964, LBJL, NSF/Komer/51.

11 Memorandum of Conversation, "US-UAR Relations," June 29, 1964, *FRUS 1964–1968*, Vol. XVIII, doc. 74.

12 Data chart, "US Aid to UAR and Iran," June 5, 1964, LBJL, NSF/Komer/51; Burns, *Economic Aid and American Policy toward Egypt*, p. 160.

13 Letter, Bundy to Mr. Canaday, June 9, 1964, LBJL, NSF/Komer/51.

14 Saunders to Bundy, July 1, 1964, LBJL, NSF/Komer/52.

15 Saunders to Komer, July 17, 1964, LBJL, NSF/Komer/52.

16 Saunders to Komer, July 27, 1964, LBJL, NSF/Komer/51; Uma K. Srivastava, "Impact of P.L. 480 aid on India's money supply and external deb-service obligations: A look ahead (Card Report 44)," The Center for Agricultural and Economic Development (Iowa State University, 1972), p. 3, fn. 7.

17 Memorandum for Talbot, July 28, 1964, LBJL, NSF/Komer/51.

18 Text of Lyndon B. Johnson, Report on the Gulf of Tonkin Incident, August 4, 1964, University of Virginia, Miller Center, Presidential Speeches.

19 Halberstam, *The Best and the Brightest*, p. 478.

20 Ibid., p. 46.

21 Memorandum, Komer to Bundy, July 28, 1964, *FRUS 1964–1968*, Vol. XVIII, doc. 80. Komer wrote to Bundy: "FYI, Nasser is sending a letter to LBJ; our hunch is it may refer to arms limitations. At any rate, it will give us a peg for a lot of things I've been waiting to say to Gamal about Libya, Cyprus, Yemen, Jordan, etc."

22 Memorandum, Komer for Johnson, August 3, 1964, LBJL, NSF/Komer/51.

23 Komer to Bundy, August 3, 1964, LBJL, NSF/Komer/51.

24 Memorandum, Komer for Johnson, August 10, 1964, LBJL, NSF/Komer/51.

25 Komer to Bundy, August 10, 1964, LBJL, NSF/Komer/51.

26 Memorandum for Record, "President's Meeting with UAR Ambassador Kamel August 10, 1964," August 11, 1964, LBJL, NSF/Komer/51.

27 Memorandum of Conversation, "Meeting with UAR Ambassador, August 10, 1964," August 12, 1964, LBJL, NSF/Komer/51.

28 Memorandum, Komer for Johnson, August 11, 1964, LBJL, NSF/Komer/51.

29 Letter, Johnson to Nasser, undated, LBJL, NSF/Komer/51. The letter is attached to Komer's memo to Bundy cited in n. 30.

30 Komer to Bundy, August 11, 1964, LBJL, NSF/Komer/51.

31 Memorandum, Komer for Johnson, August 12, 1965, LBJL, NSF/Komer/51.

32 Memorandum, Komer to Talbot, August 13, 1964, LBJL, NSF/Komer/51.

33 Telegram, State to Cairo, August 24, 1964, *FRUS 1964–1968*, Vol. XVIII, doc. 94. Johnson approved of McCloy's arms mission and even met with him on August 14. See Memorandum, Rusk to Johnson, August 12, 1964, *FRUS 1964*–1968, Vol. XVIII, doc. 89, fn. 1. It was Nasser who rescheduled. As reported by McCloy: "it had been inconvenient for him to meet me at that time and that he was glad that I had been able to adjust myself to his convenience." See Memorandum of Conversation, September 28, 1964, *FRUS 1964–1968*, Vol. XVIII, doc. 96.

34 Memorandum, Komer for Johnson, August 24, 1964, LBJL, NSF/Komer/51.

35 1964 Democratic Party Platform, August 24, 1964, The American Presidency Project, University of California, Santa Barbara.

36 Memorandum for the President, August 26, 1964, LBJL, NSF/Komer/51.

37 Memorandum, Komer for Johnson, August 25, 1964, LBJL, NSF/Komer/51.

38 Komer to Bundy, August 28, 1964, LBJL, NSF/Komer/51.

39 Battle OH, LBJL.

8 Two Summits

1 Moshe Gat, *Britain and the Conflict in the Middle East*, p. 78.
2 Cairo Domestic Service in Arabic, September 11,1964, FBIS, September 14, 1964, B3.
3 Memorandum of Conversation, Curtis Jones and Kamel, "Anti-American Press in Cairo," August 24, 1964, LBJL, NSF/Komer/51.
4 Memorandum of Conversation, Curtis Jones and Kamel, "Anti-American Press in Cairo," September 4, 1964, LBJL, NSF/Komer/51.
5 Read to Bundy, September 15, 1964, LBJL, NSF/Komer/51.
6 Cairo Domestic Service in Arabic, September 14, 1964, FBIS, September 14, 1964, B4.
7 Letter, Carl Kaysen to Komer (Harvard University letterhead), September 15, 1964, LBJL, NSF/Komer/51.
8 See Evanathis Hatzivassilou, *Greece and the Cold War: Front Line State, 1952-1967* (London: Routledge, 2006), pp. 156-7.
9 Brief, "General Comments on the Economy of the UAR," undated, stamped with a date of September 17, 1964 (presumably the date it entered Komer's office), LBJL, NSF/Komer/51. The brief was attached to Kaysen's letter (see n. 7), with Kaysen writing, "I return herewith."
10 Memorandum, "Comments on the Article 'Nasser is Flat Broke,'" September 17, 1964, LBJL, NSF/Komer/51.
11 Moline to James H. Bahti, September 17, 1964, LBJL, NSF/Komer/51.
12 Handwritten Note, Davies to Komer, October 12, 1964, LBJL, NSF/Komer/51.
13 Bryan R. Gibson, *Sold Out? US Foreign Policy, Iraq, the Kurds, and the Cold War* (New York: Palgrave MacMillan, 2015), pp. 86-7.
14 Informal Letter, London to Davies, October 5, 1964, LBJL, NSF/Komer/51.
15 Davies to Talbot, "Your Meeting with Ambassador Kamel," September 22, 1964, LBJL, NSF/Komer/51.
16 Komer, "Note for Lunch w/Kamel," September 23, 1964, LBJL, NSF/Komer/51.
17 Memorandum for the Record, September 23, 1964, LBJL, NSF/Komer/51.
18 Memorandum of Conversation, "McCloy's Impressions of His Meeting with President Nasser on September 28," October 6, 1964, *FRUS 1964–1968*, Vol. XVIII, doc. 98.
19 Telegram 1871, State to Cairo, October 2,1964, LBJL, NSF/Komer/51.
20 Cairo Domestic Service in Arabic, October 5, 1964, FBIS, October 6, 1964, B1–B5.
21 "Nasser Action Reported," *New York Times*, October 6, 1964.
22 Hedrick Smith, "Nasser Is Holding Tshombe Hostage For Cairo's Aides," *New York Times*, October 8, 1964.
23 Letter, Battle to Komer, September 18, 1964, LBJL, NSF/Komer/51.
24 Memorandum of Conversation, "US-UAR Relations," October 17, 1964, LBJL, NSF/Komer/51.
25 Memorandum, Read to Bundy, "Telegram from President Nasser to President Johnson," November 5, 1964, LBJL, NSF/Komer/51.
26 Letter, Nasser to Johnson, October 22, 1964, LBJL, NSF/Komer/51.
27 Telegram 2671, State to Cairo, November 9, 1964, LBJL, NSF/Komer/51.
28 Commercial Cable 04364, November 9, 1964, LBJL, NSF/Komer/51.
29 Letter, Congressman James Roosevelt to Johnson, September 24, 1964, LBJL, NSF/Komer/51; Letter, Congressman Leonard Farbstein to Feldman, October 22, 1964, LBJL, NSF/Komer/51; Letter, Congressman William F. Ryan to Johnson, "PL 480 Aid to UAR," October 19, 1964, LBJL, NSF/Komer/51; Response, Bundy to Congressman

Ryan, November 5, 1964, LBJL, NSF/Komer/51; Komer to Bundy, November 5, 1964, LBJL, NSF/Komer/52.

30 Komer to Bundy, November 17, 1964, LBJL, NSF/Komer/52.

31 Komer to Bundy, November 20, 1964, LBJL, NSF/Komer/52.

32 National Security Action Memorandum No. 319, "US Aid to the UAR," November 20, 1964, LBJL, NSF/Komer/52.

33 Research Memorandum, Hughes to Rusk, "Nasser Defends His Policies Against Rising Public Criticism," November 23, 1964, LBJL, NSF/Komer/51.

9 Communication Breakdown

1 Michael Hoyt Interview, "Captive in the Congo," The Association for Diplomatic Studies and Training.

2 Memorandum of Conversation, "The Congo," Parts I and II, November 24, 1964, NSF/Komer/51; Read to Bundy, December 10, 1964, LBJL, NSF/Komer/51.

3 Battle OH, July 10, 1991, The Association for Diplomatic Studies and Training, pp. 24–7.

4 Telegram, State to Cairo, November 27, 1964, *FRUS 1964–1968*, Vol. XVIII, doc. 110.

5 Read to Bundy, S/S 16626, Attachment "Message from UAR Ambassador Kamel," November 27, 1964, LBJL, NSF/Komer/51.

6 Komer to Bundy, November 27, 1964, LBJL, NSF/Komer/52. Bundy responded, "good sense," and asked Komer to let Johnson know about his plan to continue with only existing aid rather than a full stop.

7 Memorandum of Conversation, "Mob Attack on US Embassy in Cairo," November 30, 1964, LBJL, NSF/Komer/51.

8 Memorandum of Conversation, "The Congo," November 30, 1964, LBJL, NSF/Komer/51.

9 Memorandum, Komer for Johnson, December 2, 1964, LBJL, NSF/Komer/52.

10 Komer to Valenti, December 9, 1964, LBJL, NSF/Komer/51.

11 Memorandum, Komer for Johnson, December 12, 1964, LBJL, NSF/Komer/51.

12 "Supplementary Talking Points," Dictated to Davies's Office by JAK, December 18, 1964, LBJL, NSF/Komer/51.

13 Talbot to Rusk, "US Relations with the UAR – Action Memorandum," December 17, 1964, LBJL, NSF/Komer/51. See, also, Memorandum, Rusk for Johnson, undated, LBJL, NSF/Komer/51; "The Protection of American Interests in the Near East," undated, LBJL, NSF/Komer/51; "US-UAR Balance Sheet," undated, LBJL, NSF/Komer/51.

14 "Country Assistance Strategy Statement, United Arab Republic" by AID, December 1, 1964, LBJL, NSF/Komer/51; Talbot to Komer, December 19, 1964, LBJL, NSF/Komer/51; Komer to Talbot, December 19, 1964, LBJL, NSF/Komer/51.

15 Memorandum for the President, December 21, 1964, LBJL, NSF/Komer/51.

16 Komer to Bundy, December 21, 1964, LBJL, NSF/Komer/51; Memorandum of Conversation (Rusk, Talbot, Davies), "US-UAR Relations, Jordan Arms Request, NE Chiefs of Mission Conference," December 31, 1964, LBJL, NSF/Komer/51.

17 Saunders to Bundy, December 24, 1964, LBJL, NSF/Komer/51.

18 Komer to Bundy, December 30, 1964, LBJL, NSF/Komer/51.

19 "Nasser Rejects Aid Terms," *Chicago Tribune*, December 24, 1964.

20 Hughes to Rusk, "Nasser's Speech and Its Implications for US Policy," December 24, 1964, LBJL, NSF/Komer/51; Battle to State, Tab B, December 27, 1965, LBJL, NSF/Komer/51.
21 Department of State Bulletin, Vol. 52, No. 1333, January 11, 1965, p. 39.
22 Saunders to Bundy, December 24, 1964, LBJL, NSF/Komer/51.
23 Memorandum of Conversation, "US-UAR Relations," December 23, 1964, *FRUS 1964–1968*, Vol. XVIII, doc. 115.
24 Saunders to Bundy, December 24, 1964, LBJL, NSF/Komer/51.
25 Komer to Bundy, December 30, 1964, LBJL, NSF/Komer/51.
26 Memorandum of Conversation, "US-UAR Relations, Jordan Arms Request, NE Chiefs of Mission Conference," December 31, 1964, LBJL, NSF/Komer/51.
27 Jernegan to Rusk, "UAR Feelers Seeking Improved Relations," December 28, 1964, LBJL, NSF/Komer/51; Memorandum of Conversation, "Informal UAR Approach for Improvement of Relations," December 29, 1964, LBJL, NSF/Komer/51.
28 Memorandum of Conversation, "US-UAR Relations, Jordan Arms Request, NE Chiefs of Mission Conference," December 31, 1964, LBJL, NSF/Komer/51.
29 Komer to Bundy, December 31, 1964, LBJL, NSF/Komer/51.
30 Memorandum, Komer for Johnson, December 31, 1964, LBJL, NSF/Komer/51.

10 Congress Reacts

1 Komer to Bundy, January 4, 1965, LBJL, NSF/Komer/52.
2 Kristin L. Ahlberg, *Transplanting the Great Society: Lyndon Johnson and Food for Peace* (Columbia: University of Missouri Press, 2008), pp. 60–75.
3 Komer to Bundy, January 12, 1965, LBJL, NSF/Komer/52.
4 Komer to Bundy, January 13, 1964, LBJL, NSF/Komer/52.
5 Text of Special Message to the Congress on Foreign Aid, January 14, 1965, The American Presidency Project, University of California, Santa Barbara.
6 Komer to Bundy, January 13, 1964, LBJL, NSF/Komer/52.
7 Komer to Bundy, January 26, 1965, LBJL, NSF/Komer/52.
8 Battle OH, July 10, 1991, The Association for Diplomatic Studies and Training, p. 28.
9 Spain to Davies, "The Acquisition of Intelligence in the UAR," November 30, 1964, LBJL, NSF/Komer/51.
10 Letter, George J. Ratham (Regional Security Officer, US Embassy in Cairo) to William Boswell (Director, Office of Security, State), March 14, 1962, LBJL, NSF/Komer/51.
11 Spain to Davies, "The Acquisition of Intelligence in the UAR," November 30, 1964, LBJL, NSF/Komer/51.
12 Komer to Bundy, January 9, 1965, LBJL, NSF/Komer/51.
13 Memorandum, Rusk to Johnson, January 22, 1965, *FRUS 1964–1968*, Vol. XVIII, doc. 125.
14 Komer to Talbot, January 23, 1965, LBJL, NSF/Komer/51.
15 Komer Draft Cable, January 23, 1965, LBJL, NSF/Komer/51.
16 Komer to Gaud, January 26, 1965, LBJL, NSF/Komer/51.
17 Telegram, State to Cairo, January 28, 1965, *FRUS 1964–1968*, Vol. XVIII, doc. 128.
18 Komer to Bundy, January 27, 1965, LBJL, NSF/Komer/51; Telegram, State to Cairo, January 28, 1965, *FRUS 1964–1968*, Vol. XVIII, doc. 128. The directness of the Congo issue was Komer's idea. Johnson indicated his approval of the approach in a phone call

with Komer's secretary, Alice (as indicated in Komer's handwriting on the January 27 memo to Bundy).

19 Editorial Note, *FRUS 1964–1968*, Vol. XVIII, doc. 127.
20 Telegram, Cairo to State, February 1, 1965, *FRUS 1964–1968*, Vol. XVIII, doc. 132.

11 Komer's Gamble

1 Memorandum, Rusk to Johnson, "Jordan Arms Request-Impact on Near East Policy," February 1, 1965, *FRUS 1964–1968*, Vol. XVIII, doc. 129.
2 Summary Notes of the 544th Meeting of the National Security Council, "Vietnam— Arms Sales to Jordan," February 1, 1965, *FRUS 1964–1968*, Vol. XVIII, doc. 130.
3 Editorial Note, *FRUS 1964–1968*, Vol. XVIII, doc. 133.
4 Telephone Conversation, Rusk and Ball, February 5, 1965, *FRUS 1964–1968*, Vol. XVIII, doc. 135.
5 Memorandum, Komer to Johnson, February 6, 1965, *FRUS 1964–1968*, Vol. XVIII, doc. 138.
6 Memorandum, Komer to Bundy, February 7, 1965, *FRUS 1964–1968*, Vol. XVIII, doc. 140.
7 Telegram, Aman to State, February 7, 1965, *FRUS 1964–1968*, Vol. XVIII, doc. 141.
8 Briefing Memorandum by Talbot, February 13, 1965, *FRUS 1964–1968*, Vol. XVIII, doc. 149.
9 Gareth M. Winrow, *The Foreign Policy of the GDR in Africa* (Cambridge: Cambridge University Press, 2009), p. 68.
10 Telephone Conversation, Johnson and Rusk, March 5, 1965, Tape no. WH6503.02, Citation no. 7023, University of Virginia, Miller Center, Secret White House Tapes.
11 Memorandum, Komer to Johnson, February 16, 1965, *FRUS 1964–1968*, Vol. XVIII, doc. 152.
12 Memorandum, Rusk to Johnson, "Near East Arms," February 19, 1965, *FRUS 1964–1968*, Vol. XVIII, doc. 155.
13 Komer to Johnson, February 19, 1965, LBJL, NSF/Komer/51.
14 Memorandum, Komer for Johnson, February 20, 1965, LBJL, NSF/Komer/51.
15 Saunders to Bundy, March 2, 1965, LBJL, NSF/Komer/51.
16 Telegram, State to Aman, March 10, 1965, *FRUS 1964–1968*, Vol. XVIII, doc. 186.
17 Memorandum, Komer to Johnson, March 13, 1965, *FRUS 1964–1968*, Vol. XVIII, doc. 190.
18 Message, Komer to Bundy, March 6, 1965, *FRUS 1964–1968*, Vol. XVIII, doc. 180; See Abraham Ben-Zvi, *Lyndon B. Johnson and the Politics of Arms Sales to Israel: In the Shadow of the Hawk* (London: Frank Cass, 2004), p. 70.
19 Memorandum, Komer for Johnson, March 17, 1965, LBJL, NSF/Komer/51.
20 Letter, Johnson to Nasser, March 18, 1965, *FRUS 1964–1968*, Vol. XVIII, doc. 192; Memorandum, Komer to S/S (Executive Secretariat, Department of State), March 18, 1965, LBJL, NSF/Komer/51.
21 Komer to Bundy, March 18, 1965, LBJL, NSF/Komer/51; See Telegram, State to Cairo, March 18, 1965, *FRUS 1964–1968*, Vol. XVIII, doc. 193. The sent version is noticeably different than the version Komer had written.
22 Telegram, Cairo to State, March 25, 1965, *FRUS 1964–1968*, Vol. XVIII, doc. 197.

12 Johnson's Reluctance

1 Saunders to Bundy, March 10, 1965, LBJL, NSF/Komer/52.
2 Ibid; Saunders to Komer, January 27, 1965, LBJL, NSF/Komer/52.
3 Saunders to Bundy, March 11, 1965, LBJL, NSF/Komer/52; Bundy to Saunders, March 13, 1965, LBJL, NSF/Komer/52.
4 Saunders to Komer, undated, LBJL, NSF/Komer/52.
5 Saunders to Komer, March 25, 1965, LBJL, NSF/Komer/52; Komer to Bundy, March 25, 1965, LBJL, NSF/Komer/52.
6 Telegram 3409 from the Embassy in Cairo to State, March 29, 1965, LBJL, NSF/Komer/52.
7 Komer to Bundy, March 29, 1965, LBJL, NSF/Komer/52.
8 Memorandum, Komer for Johnson, March 29, 1965, LBJL, NSF/Komer/52.
9 Komer to Bundy, March 29, 1965, LBJL, NSF/Komer/52.
10 Draft Memorandum, Komer for Johnson, April 1, 1965, LBJL, NSF/Komer/52.
11 Komer to Bundy, April 1, 1965, LBJL, NSF/Komer/52.
12 Komer to Doug McArthur, April 3, 1965, LBJL, NSF/Komer/51.
13 Komer to Bundy, April 6, 1965, LBJL, NSF/Komer/52.
14 Komer to Bundy, April 6, 1965, LBJL, NSF/Komer/52.
15 Memorandum, Komer for Johnson, April 7, 1965, LBJL, NSF/Komer/52.
16 Memo for Larry O'Brien, April 8, 1965, LBJL, NSF/Komer/52.
17 Memorandum, Komer for Johnson, April 9, 1965, LBJL, NSF/Komer/52.
18 Memorandum, Komer for Johnson, April 14, 1965, LBJL, NSF/Komer/52.
19 Komer to Bundy, April 14, 1965, LBJL, NSF/Komer/52.
20 Komer to Bundy, April 16, 1965, LBJL, NSF/Komer/52.

13 Rusk Takes Over

1 As framed by State in its instructions to Talbot: "This meeting is important to both US and UAR . . . Egyptians are looking for a signal that US declarations of desire to resume aid are sincere . . . [With] Egyptians in grim mood, we wish to accord them such a signal." Telegram, State to Cairo, April 17, 1965, *FRUS 1964–1968*, Vol. XVIII, doc. 207.
2 Telegram, State to Cairo, April 2, 1965, *FRUS 1964–1968*, Vol. XVIII, doc. 200.
3 Memorandum for the Record, April 7, 1965, LBJL, NSF/Komer/51.
4 Komer to Bundy, April 9, 1965, LBJL, NSF/Komer/51.
5 Komer to Bundy, April 13, 1965, LBJL, NSF/Komer/51.
6 Telegram, State to Cairo, April 2, 1965, *FRUS 1964–1968*, Vol. XVIII, doc. 200.
7 Telegram, Cairo to State, April 15, 1965, *FRUS 1964–1968*, Vol. XVIII, doc. 205.
8 Telegram, State to Cairo, "Suggested Scenario for Talbot's Meeting with Nasser,"' April 17, 1965, *FRUS 1964–1968*, Vol. XVIII, doc. 207.
9 Komer to Bundy, April 16, 1965, LBJL, NSF/Komer/51.
10 Telegram from Cairo, April 18, 1965, *FRUS 1964–1968*, Vol. XVIII, doc. 208.
11 Komer to Bundy, April 19, 1965, LBJL, NSF/Komer/51.
12 Komer to Bundy, April 20, 1965, LBJL, NSF/Komer/51.

14 The $37 Million

1   Komer to Bundy, "Tuesday Lunch Item," April 20, 1965, LBJL, NSF/Komer/52.
2   Komer to Bundy, April 24, 1965, LBJL, NSF/Komer/51.
3   Telegram 431, Cairo to Beirut, "For Talbot," April 21, 1965, LBJL, NSF/Komer.
4   Komer to Bundy, April 27, 1965, LBJL, NSF/Komer/51.
5   Telegram 3827, Cairo to State, May 3, 1965, LBJL, NSF/Komer/52.
6   Telegram 3831, Cairo to State, May 3, 1965, LBJL, NSF/Komer/52.
7   Saunders to Bundy, May 4, 1965, LBJL, NSF/Komer/52.
8   Saunders to Bundy, May 5, 1965, LBJL, NSF/Komer/51; Saunders to Bundy, May 12, 1965, LBJL, NSF/Komer/51.
9   John Waterbury, *The Egypt of Nasser and Sadat* (Princeton: Princeton University Press, 1983), p. 95; Telegram, Cairo to State, May 15, 1965, *FRUS 1964–1968*, Vol. XVIII, doc. 215.
10 Komer to Bundy, May 15, 1965, LBJL, NSF/Komer/51.
11 Cairo Domestic Service in Arabic, May 16, 1965, FBIS, May 18, 1965, B1
12 Telegram, State to Cairo, May 21, 1965, *FRUS 1964–1968*, Vol. XVIII, doc. 217.
13 Memorandum, Komer for Johnson, May 31, 1965, LBJL, NSF/Komer/52.
14 Memorandum, Bundy to Johnson, "$37 Million PL 480 Wheat for Egypt," May 31, 1965, *FRUS 1964–1968*, Vol. XVIII, doc. 221.
15 Telegram 7401, State to Cairo, June 2, 1965, LBJL, NSF/UAR/159/4.
16 Memo, Komer to S/S, June 2, 1965, LBJL, NSF/Komer/52.
17 Komer to Bundy, June 2, 1965, LBJL, NSF/Komer/52.
18 Memorandum, "Reaction of Congressional Leadership Regarding the Remaining $37 Million of our Three Year Foreign Aid Commitment to the UAR," June 18, 1965, LBJL, NSF/Komer/52; McArthur to Talbot, "Senate Aid Bill," June 7, 1965, LBJL, NSF/Komer/52; McArthur to Ball, "PL-480 and the United Arab Republic: Information Memorandum," June 9, 1965, LBJL, NSF/Komer/52.
19 Memorandum, Komer for Johnson, June 15, 1965, LBJL, NSF/Komer/52.
20 Telephone Conversation, Johnson and Rusk, June 15, 1965, Tape no. WH6506.04, Citation no. 8137, University of Virginia, Miller Center, Secret White House Tapes.
21 Memorandum, Rusk for Johnson, "Resumption of Public Law 480 Title I Shipments to the United Arab Republic," June 16, 1965, LBJL, NSF/Komer/52; Memorandum for the President, June 17, 1965, LBJL, NSF/Komer/52.
22 Komer to Bundy, June 17, 1965, LBJL, NSF/Komer/52.
23 Komer to Bundy, June 18, 1965, LBJL, NSF/Komer/52.
24 Memorandum of Conversation (Kamel, Talbot, and Sterner), "Presidential Decision to Complete PL-480 Deliveries, UAR Position on Algerian Coup, Postponement of Sadat Visit," June 21, 1965, LBJL, NSF/Komer/52; Memorandum, Komer to Johnson, June 17, 1965, *FRUS 1964–1968*, Vol. XVIII, doc. 225; Memorandum, Komer for Johnson, June 15, 1965, LBJL, NSF/Komer/52.
25 Komer to Bundy, June 21, 1965, LBJL, NSF/Komer/52; Attachment, "Determination that Sale of Surplus Agricultural Commodities to the United Arab Republic Is in the National Interest," with Memorandum, Rusk for Johnson, "Resumption of Public Law 480 Title I Shipments to the United Arab Republic," June 16, 1965, LBJL, NSF/Komer/52; Saunders to Komer, June 21, 1965, LBJL, NSF/Komer/52.
26 Memorandum, Komer for Johnson, June 21, 1965, LBJL, NSF/Komer/52; Komer to Bundy, June 21, 1965, LBJL, NSF/Komer/52.

27 "Answers to Hypothetical Questions on President's Decision to Complete PL-480 Deliveries to UAR," June 22, 1965, LBJL, NSF/Komer/52; Komer to Bundy, June 22, 1965, LBJL, NSF/Komer/52; Komer to Bundy, June 22, 1965, LBJL, NSF/Komer/52; Komer to Bundy, June 22, 1965, LBJL, NSF/Komer/52. Komer wrote to Bundy at least three separate times on June 22.

28 Telegram 4511, Cairo to State, June 22, 1965, LBJL, NSF/UAR/159/4; Komer to Bundy, June 23, 1965, LBJL, NSF/Komer/52.

15 Another Long Summer

1 Komer to Bundy, June 23, 1965, LBJL, NSF/Komer/52; Cairo Domestic Service in Arabic, June 27, 1965, FBIS, June 28, 1965, LBJL, NSF/Komer/52; Saunders to Bundy, June 25, 1965, LBJL, NSF/Komer/52.

2 Saunders to Bundy, June 25, 1965, LBJL, NSF/Komer/52; Note for UAR Economic Files, June 25, 1965, LBJL, NSF/Komer/52.

3 Research Memorandum (RNA-32), Hughes to Rusk, "UAR Makes Wheat Deals with USSR and Argentina," June 28, 1965, LBJL, NSF/Komer/52; Intelligence Note 168, Hughes to Rusk, "Moscow Speeds Wheat to the UAR," June 29, 1965, LBJL, NSF/Komer/52.

4 USIA Daily Reaction Report 123, "Resumption of US Aid Results in UAR Media Attack, Soviet Wheat Aid is Lavishly Praised," June 28, 1965, LBJL, NSF/Komer/52.

5 Bundy to Komer, July 2, 1965, LBJL, NSF/Komer/52; Komer to Bundy, July 6, 1965, LBJL, NSF/Komer/52.

6 Memorandum, USIA for Johnson, June 29, 1965, LBJL, NSF/Komer/52; Memorandum, Read to Bundy, "UAR Reaction to Resumption of US PL-480 Sales," July 2, 1965, LBJL, NSF/Komer/52.

7 Memorandum, CIA to Komer, "Soviet Wheat for the UAR," July 2, 1965, LBJL, NSF/Komer/52.

8 Komer to Bundy, July 2, 1965, LBJL, NSF/Komer/52.

9 Memorandum, Komer for Johnson, July 2, 1965, LBJL, NSF/Komer/52.

10 Memorandum for the Record, July 8, 1965, LBJL, NSF/Komer/52.

11 Memorandum of Conversation, "US-UAR Relations and Request for New PL 480 Agreement," July 15, 1965, LBJL, NSF/Komer/52.

12 Komer to Bundy, July 19, 1965, LBJL, NSF/Komer/52.

13 Tim Weiner, *Legacy of Ashes: The History of the CIA* (New York: Anchor Books, 2007), pp. 326–7; Telegram, Cairo to State, July 22, 1965, *FRUS 1964–1968, XVIII*, doc. 228.

14 Robert Rakove, *Kennedy, Johnson, and the Nonaligned World* (New York: Cambridge University Press, 2013), p. 98; Telegram 632, State to Cairo, July 27, 1965, LBJL, NSF/Komer/53.

15 Komer to Bundy, July 23, 1965, LBJL, NSF/Komer/51.

16 Telegram, State to Cairo, July 26, 1965, *FRUS 1964–1968*, Vol. XVIII, doc. 229.

17 Komer to Bundy, August 11, 1965, LBJL, NSF/Komer/52; Raymond A. Ioanes (Department of Agriculture Administrator) to Komer, August 11, 1965, LBJL, NSF/Komer/52. Another reason to make the sale was because tobacco was one of the most "burdensome surpluses in CCC inventories," according to the Department of Agriculture.

18   Telegram 48, State to Jidda, August 2, 1965, LBJL, NSF/Komer/53; Telegram 973, State
     to Cairo, August 12, 1965, LBJL, NSF/Komer/53; Memorandum, Komer for Johnson,
     August 13, 1965, LBJL, NSF/Komer/51.
19   Memorandum of Conversation, August 3 and 10, 1965, "Luncheon Discussions
     on UAR-US Relations," *FRUS 1964–1968*, Vol. XVIII, doc. 232; Memorandum of
     Conversation, Isam Hanafi and Clifford J. Quinlan at the Embassy in Taiz, "Captured
     American Arms, American Position in Event of UAR Attack on Saudi Arabian Bases,
     UAR and Saudi Arabian Negotiations and a Future Yemen Government," August 1,
     1965, LBJL, NSF/Komer/53; Telegram 374, Cairo to State, August 3, 1965, LBJL, NSF/
     Komer/53; Telegram 390, Cairo to State, August 4, 1965, LBJL, NSF/Komer/53.
20   Telegram, Cairo to State, August 18, 1965, *FRUS 1964–1968*, Vol. XVIII, doc. 233.
21   Telegram "UNN," Cairo to State, August 24, 1965, LBJL, NSF/Komer/53.
22   Telegram 585, Cairo to State, August 26, 1965, LBJL, NSF/Komer/53.
23   Memorandum for Record, August 26, 1965, LBJL, NSF/Komer/51.
24   Ibid; Memorandum for S/S, August 26, 1965, LBJL, NSF/Komer/51.
25   Walter Laqueur, *The Struggle for the Middle East: The Soviet Union and the Middle
     East, 1958–1968* (London: Routledge, 1969), pp. 72–3; Stephen M. Walt, *The Origins
     of Alliances* (Ithaca: Cornell University Press, 1987), p. 91.
26   Memorandum, Komer to Johnson, "Week's Developments in the Near East,"
     September 23, 1965, *FRUS 1964–1968*, Vol. XXI, doc. 9.
27   Komer to Bundy, September 21, 1965, LBJL, NSF/Komer/51.
28   Memorandum, Komer for Johnson, September 22, 1965, LBJL, NSF/Komer/51.

16   Komer's Final Campaign

 1   Saunders to Talbot, July 22, 1965, LBJL, NSF/Komer/52; Letter, Congressman
     Seymour Halpern to Johnson, July 22, 1965, LBJL, NSF/Komer/52; O'Brien to
     Bundy, July 24, 1965, LBJL, NSF/Komer/52; Letter, Larry F. O'Brien to Congressman
     Seymour Halpern, July 24, 1965, LBJL, NSF/Komer/52; Bundy to Komer, July 28,
     LBJL, NSF/Komer/52; Saunders to Komer, July 30, 1965, LBJL, NSF/Komer/52; "State
     Department, White House Disagree on Reaction to Egyptian Press Attacks," *Hebrew
     Daily Press Review*, August 1, 1965, LBJL, NSF/Komer/52; Dictated over phone by
     Rodger Davies, "Sale of Title II Corn by the UAR," August 16, 1965, LBJL, NSF/
     Komer/52; Read to Bundy, with Attachment, "Suggested Response to Congressman
     Halpern's Letter Concerning GAO Report on Title II Grant of Corn to UAR,"
     August 19, 1965, LBJL, NSF/Komer/52; Letter, Komer to Congressman Halpern,
     August 20, 1965, LBJL, NSF/Komer/52; Saunders to Komer, August 12, 1965, LBJL,
     NSF/Komer/51; Saunders, "Answer to Congressman Roosevelt," August 12, 1965,
     LBJL, NSF/Komer/51; Saunders to Komer, August 13, 1965, LBJL, NSF/Komer/51;
     Memorandum for Record by Komer, August 16, 1965, LBJL, NSF/Komer/51; Komer
     to Jake Jacobsen (with an attachment that begins, "Why do we resume aid to a
     country which cusses us out?"), July 21, 1965, LBJL, NSF/Komer/52.
 2   Memorandum, Komer for Johnson, September 24, 1965, LBJL, NSF/Komer/51.
 3   Memorandum, Rusk for Johnson, "Title III PL 480 Programs for the UAR, India and
     Pakistan," August 20, 1965, LBJL, NSF/Komer/52; Memorandum, Bundy for Johnson,
     September 10, 1965, LBJL, NSF/Komer/52; Memorandum, Komer for Johnson,
     September 13, 1965, LBJL, NSF/Komer/52; Saunders to Komer, October 12, 1965,

LBJL, NSF/Komer/52; Saunders to Komer, October 15, 1965, LBJL, NSF/Komer/52; Komer to Bundy, October 26, 1965, LBJL, NSF/Komer/52.

4 Memorandum of Conversation, October 7, 1965, LBJL, NSF/Komer/52.

5 Memorandum, Johnson to Rusk, October 11, 1965, LBJL, NSF/Komer/52.

6 Bundy to Komer, October 12, 1965, LBJL, NSF/Komer/52.

7 Telegram, State to Cairo, "Eyes only for Ambassador from the Secretary, October 13, 1965, *FRUS 1964–1968*, Vol. XVIII, doc. 244.

8 Saunders to Bundy, October 12, 1965, LBJL, NSF/Komer/52; Saunders to Bundy, October 16, 1965, LBJL, NSF/Komer/52; Memorandum, Chester L. Cooper to Bundy, "The Rice Picture," October 16, 1965, LBJL, NSF/Komer/52; Saunders to Spain, October 22, 1965, LBJL, NSF/Komer/52.

9 Saunders to Komer, October 23, 1965, LBJL, NSF/Komer/52.

10 Memorandum, Komer to Bill Macomber, October 25, 1965, LBJL, NSF/Komer/52; Draft Telegram to Cairo, October 28, 1965, LBJL, NSF/Komer/52.

11 Hare to Rusk, "UAR PL-480 Request," October 20, 1965, LBJL, NSF/Komer/52; Memorandum, Rusk to Johnson, "US Aid to the UAR," October 11, 1965, *FRUS 1964–1968*, Vol. XVIII, doc. 243; Komer to Bundy, October 27, 1965, LBJL, NSF/Komer/52.

12 Memorandum of Conversation with Johnson by Rusk, October 27, 1965, LBJL, NSF/Komer/52; Gaud to Komer, October 27, 1965, LBJL, NSF/Komer/52; Memorandum from Ellis to Waters, "UAR Rice Situation," October 21, 1965, LBJL, NSF/Komer/52.

13 Saunders to Komer, November 2, 1965, LBJL, NSF/Komer/52; Saunders to Bundy, November 2, 1965, LBJL, NSF/Komer/52.

14 Memorandum, Komer (and Bundy) to Johnson, "Food for the UAR," November 8, 1965, LBJL, NSF/Komer/52; Memorandum for the President from Rusk, "PL 480 Program for the UAR," November 8, 1965, LBJL, NSF/Komer/52.

15 Komer to Bundy, November 10, 1965, LBJL, NSF/Komer/52.

16 Komer to Bundy, November 17, 1965, LBJL, NSF/Komer/52; Memorandum for Executive Secretary Department of State, November 19, 1965, LBJL, NSF/Komer/52.

17 Memorandum for the Record (Symington, Hare, MacArthur), "PL 480 for the UAR," November 9, 1965, LBJL, NSF/Komer/52; Memorandum for the Record by Komer (Symington phone call), November 9, 1965, LBJL, NSF/Komer/51; Letter, Senator Abraham Ribicoff to Johnson, November 15, 1965, LBJL, NSF/Komer/52; Letter, Senator Hugh Scott to Johnson, November 15, 1965, LBJL, NSF/Komer/52; Letter, Bundy to Senator Symington, November 22, 1965, LBJL, NSF/Komer/52.

18 Draft Letter, Bundy to Symington, November 22, 1965, LBJL, NSF/Komer/52; Bundy to Komer, November 22, 1965, LBJL, NSF/Komer/52.

19 Komer to Bundy, November 22, 1965, LBJL, NSF/Komer/52.

20 Memorandum for Mr. Jake Jacobsen (also pass to Mr. Moyers), "PL 480 Negotiations with UAR," November 24, 1965, LBJL, NSF/Komer/52. According to a note in Komer's handwriting: "11/26: President approved per Alice [Komer's secretary]."

21 Komer to Douglas MacArthur, November 23, 1965, LBJL, NSF/Komer/52; Memorandum for Lee White, November 26, 1965, LBJL, NSF/Komer/52; Letter, Komer to Senator Abraham Ribicoff, November 29, 1965, LBJL, NSF/Komer/52; Letter, Komer to Senator Hugh Scott, November 29, 1965, LBJL, NSF/Komer/52; Komer to Bundy, November 29, 1965, LBJL, NSF/Komer/52.

22 Memorandum for Record (Symington and Komer Talk), November 24, 1965, LBJL, NSF/Komer/52.

23 Memorandum of Conversation, MacArthur and Senator Hickenlooper, "PL 480 For the UAR," November 16, 1965, LBJL, NSF/Komer/52.

24 Telegram, State to Cairo, November 17, 1965, *FRUS 1964–1968*, Vol. XVIII, doc. 252.

25 Telegram, Cairo to State, November 24, 1965, *FRUS 1964–1968*, Vol. XVIII, doc. 253.

26 Memorandum, Ball for Johnson, "Determination that Certain Assistance to the United Arab Republic Is Essential to the National Interest," November 24, 1965, LBJL, NSF/Komer/52; Memorandum, Komer for Johnson, December 16, 1965, LBJL, NSF/Komer/52; Saunders to Jim Clark, December 21, 1965, LBJL, NSF/Komer/52; Saunders to Bromley Smith, December 23, 1965, LBJL, NSF/Komer/52; Memorandum, Bromley Smith for Benjamin Read, December 27, 1965, LBJL, NSF/Komer/52.

27 Telegram 18391, Cairo to State, December 23, 1965, LBJL, NSF/Komer/52.

28 Memorandum, Komer to Johnson (in Texas), December 28, 1965, *FRUS 1964–1968*, Vol. XVIII, doc. 258; Saunders to Komer, December 28, 1965, LBJL, NSF/Komer/52; Memorandum for the Secretary of State, "Determination that Sale of Surplus Agricultural Commodities to the United Arab Republic Is Essential to the National Interest (No. 66-10)," December 29, 1965, LBJL, NSF/Komer/52.

17 Sadat's Visit

1 Memorandum, Komer for Johnson, June 15, 1965, LBJL, NSF/Komer/51; Telegram 4458, Cairo to State, June 19, 1965, LBJL, NSF/Komer/51; Telegram 7828, State to Cairo, June 23, 1965, LBJL, NSF/Komer/51; Memorandum of Conversation (Kamel, Talbot, and Sterner), "Presidential Decision to Complete PL-480 Deliveries, UAR Position on Algerian Coup, Postponement of Sadat Visit," June 21, 1965, LBJL, NSF/Komer/52.

2 Telegram 1461, Cairo to State, December 14, 1965, LBJL, NSF/Komer/51.

3 Telegram 3939, State to Cairo, January 15, 1966, LBJL, NSF/Komer/51.

4 Memorandum, Rusk for Johnson, "United Arab Republic Parliamentary Delegation," January 20, 1966, LBJL, NSF/Komer/51; Memorandum, Komer for Johnson, January 21, 1966, LBJL, NSF/Komer/51.

5 Telegram 4096, State to Cairo, January 24, 1966, LBJL, NSF/Komer/51.

6 Telegram 2263, Cairo to State, February 3, 1966, LBJL, NSF/Komer/51; Telegram 4388, State to Cairo, February 5, 1966, LBJL, NSF/Komer/51; Telegram 2012, Cairo to State, "Personal for Secretary from Ambassador," February 9, 1966, LBJL, NSF/Komer/51.

7 Telegram 4487, State to Cairo, February 10, 1966, LBJL, NSF/Komer/51; Telegram 4620, State to Cairo, February 16, 1966, LBJL, NSF/Komer/51; Telegram 2095, Cairo to State, February 16, 1966, LBJL, NSF/Komer/51.

8 Memorandum of Conversation, "US-UAR Relations, Yemen," February 23, 1966, LBJL, NSF/Komer/51.

9 Ibid; Memorandum, Komer for Johnson, February 23, 1966, LBJL, NSF/Komer/51.

10 "Text of Address by President Gamal Abdel Nasser: At the Great Popular Rally Held by the Arab Socialist Union in Celebration of the Anniversary of Unity Day," February 22, 1966, Cairo, Internet Archive.

11 Telegram, State to Cairo, February 28, 1966, *FRUS 1964–1968*, Vol. XVIII, doc. 277.

12 Letter, Kamel to Komer, March 2, 1966, LBJL, NSF/Komer/51; Letter, Komer to Kamel, March 4, 1966, LBJL, NSF/Komer/51. According to Komer in his letter to Kamel, he could not meet Sadat "owing to the press of business connected with McGeorge Bundy's departure" from the Johnson administration.

18 Johnson's Men

1 For examples of Nasser's rhetoric, see Douglas Little, *American Orientalism: The United States and the Middle East since 1945* (Chapel Hill: University of North Carolina Press, 2009), p. 186. Nasser also allowed the Vietcong to open an office in Cairo in April 1966.

2 Memo, Bundy to Johnson, February 19, 1966, LBJL, Bundy Memos to the President.

3 Editorial Note, *FRUS 1964–1968*, Vol. XXXIII, doc. 164.

4 See Memorandum, Rostow and Smith to Johnson, May 25, 1966, *FRUS 1964–1968*, Vol. XXXIII, doc. 170.

5 Komer Fifth OH, December 22, 1969, JFKL, p. 21.

6 Ibid., p. 14.

7 Bundy First OH, March 1964, JFKL, p. 3.

8 Editorial Note, *FRUS 1964–1968*, Vol. XXXIII, doc. 171.

9 Memorandum, Smith to Johnson, March 31, 1966, *FRUS 1964–1968*, Vol. XXXIII, doc. 165.

10 Walt Rostow, *The Stages of Economic Growth: A Non-Communist Manifesto* (Cambridge: Cambridge University Press, 1960), pp. 125–6.

11 Avner Cohen Interview of Walt Rostow, 1993, Wilson Center, Nuclear Proliferation International History Project. Under Kennedy, Rostow had promoted the prospects of working with Nasser toward the development of Egypt. See Warren Bass, *Support Any Friend*, p. 87.

12 Robert Komer, "Organization and Management of the 'New Model' Pacification Program—1966-1969," Rand Corporation, May 7, 1970. According to one observer, while Kennedy had dismissed Rostow's extreme call for bombing North Vietnam, Johnson took an interest in the embattled adviser's idea and even "appointed a committee" to consider "what some of the implications might be." "It was at this juncture [February 1964] that Johnson began to take Rostow seriously." See David Milne, *America's Rasputin: Walt Rostow and the Vietnam War* (New York: Hill and Wang, 2008), p. 135.

13 NSAM 343, March 28, 1966, LBJL, National Security Files, National Security Action Memorandums, Box 7.

14 Letter, Komer to Kamel, April 12, 1966, LBJL, NSF/Komer/51.

15 See Memorandum, Saunders to Rostow, April 8, 1966, *FRUS, 1964–1968*, Vol. XXXIII, doc. 167.

16 See Wriggins OH, The Association for Diplomatic Studies and Training, March 8, 1995. According to Wriggins, he had been interested in the Middle East, but his real expertise was on South Asia: "So then, when Walt asked me to go over, I took the NEA slot. But there was a splendid man who was already there, Hal Saunders, working on Arab-Israel problems. Saunders became one of my heroes. I mean, he was a marvellous person; who worked so long and patiently on Arab-Israeli relations. He was allegedly my deputy, which was kind of absurd. He knew so much more about the Middle East than I did, so I more or less left that to him. So, I really focused mainly on South Asia."

17 Memorandum, Hamilton to Rostow, May 3, 1967, *FRUS, 1964–1968*, Vol. XXXIII, doc. 176.

18 Wriggins OH, The Association for Diplomatic Studies and Training, March 8, 1995. According to Bundy, Johnson put a premium on administrative action. Of course, this

was at odds with his restructuring of the NSC, which made such action less likely. See Bundy Third OH, March 19, 1969, LBJL, p. 29.

19 See William I. Bacchus, *Foreign Policy and the Bureaucratic Process: The State Department's Country Director System* (Princeton: Princeton University Press, 1974), pp. 7–8.

20 Bennsky OH, The Association for Diplomatic Studies and Training, January 19, 1993, p. 24.

21 Komer Fifth OH, December 22, 1969, JFKL, p. 43.

19 A New Policy

1 Memorandum, Rostow to Johnson, June 18, 1966, *FRUS 1964–1968*, Vol. XVIII, doc. 302.

2 Saunders Memo for the File, May 24, 1966, LBJL, National Security Files, Files of Harold H. Saunders, Box 32 (hereafter NSF/Saunders/32).

3 Saunders to Wriggins, May 20, 1966, LBJL, NSF/Saunders/32.

4 See "The State of Food and Agricultural Assistance 1966," Report by the Food and Agriculture Organization of the United Nations (Rome 1966), p. 1.

5 Memorandum, Komer to Johnson, March 27, 1966, *FRUS 1964–1968*, Vol. XXV, doc. 306.

6 Memorandum, Komer to Johnson, March 29, 1966, *FRUS 1964–1968*, Vol. XXV, doc. 310.

7 Saunders to Wriggins, May 20, 1966, LBJL, NSF/Saunders/32.

8 Memorandum, Rostow to Johnson, June 18, 1966, *FRUS 1964–1968*, Vol. XVIII, doc. 302. See fn. 3.

9 Memorandum, Wriggins for Rostow, "Boeing's hope to sell three Boeing-320s to UAR," July 7, 1966, LBJL, NSF/Saunders/32.

10 Memorandum, Rostow to Johnson, June 18, 1966, *FRUS 1964–1968*, Vol. XVIII, doc. 302.

11 Telegram, State to Cairo, June 20, 1966, *FRUS 1964–1968*, Vol. XVIII, doc. 303.

12 See Memorandum, Rostow to Johnson, June 18, 1966, *FRUS 1964–1968*, Vol. XVIII, doc. 302. The downside was that Nasser could not repay the loans in Egyptian currency. Also, a portion of the funds would not be reinvested in Egypt.

13 Saunders to Bromley Smith, July 9, 1966, LBJL, NSF/Saunders/32.

14 Telegram, State to Cairo, June 27, 1966, *FRUS 1964–1968*, Vol. XVIII, doc. 306. See fn. 3.

15 Nadav Safran, *Saudi Arabia: The Ceaseless Quest For Security* (Ithaca: Cornell University Press, 1988), p. 121.

16 Memorandum of Conversation, July 13, 1966, *FRUS 1964–1968*, Vol. XVIII, doc. 308.

17 Telegram, State to Cairo, July 28, 1966, *FRUS 1964–1968*, Vol. XVIII, doc. 311.

18 Wriggins to Rostow, "Future aid to UAR," July 14, 1966, LBJL, NSF/Saunders/32.

19 See, for example, Hedrick Smith, "Nasser Says US Delays Food Aid Because of Policy Conflicts," *New York Times*, July 23, 1966.

20 Memorandum, Rostow for Johnson, July 23, 1966, LBJL, NSF/Saunders/32.

21 Saunders to Komer, July 25, 1966, LBJL, NSF/Saunders/32.

22 Saunders to Rostow, August 1, 1966, LBJL, NSF/Saunders/32.

23 See Memorandum, Wriggins for Rostow, July 7, 1966, LBJL, NSF/Saunders/32.

24 Memorandum of Conversation, Kamel and Davies, "US-UAR Relations" (Part II), LBJL, NSF/Saunders/32.

25 Memorandum, Rostow for Johnson, "UAR Ambassador's Request to See You," August 3, 1966, LBJL, NSF/Saunders/32.

26 Saunders to Rostow, August 3, 1966, LBJL, NSF/Saunders/32.

27 Possible Main Points for Background Paper, August 3, 1966, LBJL, NSF/Saunders/32.

28 Memorandum for the Record by Saunders, August 10, 1966, LBJL, NSF/Saunders/32.

29 Memorandum, Rostow for Johnson, "Talking Points for Your Meeting with UAR Ambassador Kamel," August 12, 1966, LBJL, NSF/Saunders/32.

30 Saunders to Rostow, August 12, 1966, LBJL, NSF/Saunders/32.

31 President's Daily Diary, August 12, 1966, LBJL; Memorandum for the Record by Wriggins, August 12, 1966, LBJL, NSF/Saunders/32.

32 Memorandum of Conversation, August 12, 1966, *FRUS 1964–1968*, Vol. XVIII, doc. 315.

33 Memorandum for the Record by Wriggins, August 12, 1966, LBJL, NSF/Saunders/32.

34 Memorandum, Saunders for Rostow, August 15, 1966, LBJL, NSF/Saunders/32.

35 Telegram, Cairo to State, September 7, 1966, *FRUS 1964–1968*, Vol. XVIII, doc. 320.

36 Telegram 1296, Cairo to State, August 10, 1966, LBJL, NSF/Saunders/32.

37 Saunders to Wriggins, September 20, 1966, LBJL, NSF/Saunders/32.

38 Memorandum, Wriggins for Johnson, "Letter to Nasser on Daughter's US Honeymoon," August 22, 1966, LBJL, NSF/Saunders/32. See, also, Attachment, "Suggested Reply to Nasser," undated, LBJL, NSF/Saunders/32. According to a handwritten note, the letter was, "Revised 8/23/66 by BKS [Bromley Smith]."

39 Memorandum, Rostow for Johnson, "Receiving President Nasser's Newly Wed Daughter," September 6, 1966, LBJL, NSF/Saunders/32.

40 Memorandum for the President, "Receiving Nasser's Daughter and Son-in-Law," September 12, 1966, LBJL, NSF/Saunders/32. See, also, Saunders to Rostow, September 12, 1966, LBJL, NSF/Saunders/32.

41 Memorandum, Rostow for Johnson, "Letter From Nasser," October 13, 1966, LBJL, NSF/Saunders/32.

42 Saunders to Rostow, October 13, 1966, LBJL, NSF/Saunders/32.

43 Memorandum for the President, "Letter From Nasser," October 13, 1966, LBJL, NSF/Saunders/32.

44 Memorandum, Saunders for Rostow, "Seeing the New Egyptian Treasury Minister," September 22, 1966, LBJL, NSF/Saunders/32.

45 Memorandum of Conversation, September 29, 1966, LBJL, NSF/Saunders/32.

46 Mohamad Heikal, *Nasser: The Cairo Documents: The Private Papers of Nasser* (London: New English Library, 1972), p. 212.

47 "US Anti-Syria Plot Reported by Cairo," *New York Times*, October 2, 1966.

48 Hedrick Smith, "Yemeni Accuses Ex-Ministers," *New York Times*, October 1, 1966.

49 Cairo Domestic Service, October 4,1966, FBIS, October 6, 1966, B2.

50 Hedrick Smith, "Plotting Charged by Arabs," *New York Times*, October 4, 1966.

51 Voice of Palestine, October 6, 1966, FBIS, October 7, 1966, B2.

52 Cairo Domestic Service, October 6, 1966, FBIS, October 7, 1966, B3.

53 Telegram, Rusk to State, October 7, 1966, *FRUS 1964–1968*, Vol. XVIII, doc. 325. See fn. 3.

54 Telegram, State to Cairo, November 21, 1966, *FRUS 1964–1968*, Vol. XVIII, doc. 341.

55 Ibid. See fn. 3. See also Telegram 3230, Cairo to State, December 8, 1966, LBJL, NSF/UAR/160/5.

56 Memorandum, Saunders to Komer, November 1, 1966, LBJL, NSF/Saunders/32.

57 Memorandum, Saunders and Wriggins for Rostow, "UAR Decision Up in the Air," December 1, 1966, LBJL, NSF/Saunders/32.

58 Burns, *Economic Aid and American Policy toward Egypt*, p. 169.

20 Nasser's Last Stand

1 Telegram from State to the Embassy in Egypt, November 25, 1966, *FRUS 1964–1968*, Vol. XVIII, doc. 348.

2 Memorandum for the Record, November 28, 1966, 1966, *FRUS 1964–1968*, Vol. XVIII, doc. 350.

3 Memorandum, Wriggins and Saunders for Rostow, "UAR Decisions Up in the Air," December 1, 1966, LBJL, NSF/Saunders/32.

4 Wriggins to Rostow, December 2, 1966, LBJL, NSF/Saunders/32.

5 Memorandum for the Record by Saunders, December 19, 1966, LBJL, NSF/Saunders/32.

6 Telegram 3340, Cairo to State, December 14, 1966, LBJL, NSF/UAR/160/5. See Telegram 3356, Cairo to State, December 15, 1966, LBJL, NSF/UAR/160/5; Telegram 3392, Cairo to State, December 17, 1966, LBJL, NSF/UAR/160/5; Telegram 3414, Cairo to State, December 19, 1966, LBJL, NSF/UAR/160/5; Telegram 3498, Cairo to State, December 23, 1966, LBJL, NSF/UAR/160/5; Telegram 3540, Cairo to State, December 27, 1966, LBJL, NSF/UAR/160/5; Telegram 3600, Cairo to State, December 31, 1966, LBJL, NSF/UAR/160/5.

7 Memorandum of Conversation, "US-UAR Relations and Near East Stability," December 29, 1966, LBJL, NSF/Saunders/32.

8 Telegram 3753, Cairo to State, "For the Secretary," January 9, 1967, LBJL, NSF/UAR/160/5.

9 Memorandum of Conversation, "US-UAR Relations – Food," January 12, 1967, *FRUS 1964–1968*, Vol. XVIII, doc. 378.

10 Memorandum of Conversation, "Lunch with Ambassador Kamel," January 17, 1966, LBJL, NSF/Saunders/32. Saunders made sure that Rostow saw the memorandum: See Saunders to Bromley Smith, January 17, 1966, LBJL, NSF/Saunders/32

11 Action Memorandum, Handley to Rusk, "PL-480 Assistance for the UAR," January 26, 1967, *FRUS 1964–1968*, Vol. XVIII, doc. 384.

12 Telegram, Cairo to State, February 1, 1967, *FRUS 1964–1968*, Vol. XVIII, doc. 386.

13 Wriggins to Rostow, "State's Continuing Inability to Grasp the UAR Nettle," February 9, 1967, LBJL, NSF/Saunders/32.

14 Memorandum, Rostow for Johnson, "Lunch Discussion of UAR," February 14, 1967, LBJL, NSF/Saunders/32.

15 Memorandum, Rostow for Johnson, February 9, 1967, LBJL, National Security Files, Name File, Box 7, Folder "Rostow Memos."

16 Cairo to the Foreign Office, February 23, 1967, The British National Archives (hereafter UKNA), FCO 39/245.

17 President Nasser's Speech at Cairo University on February 22, UKNA, FCO 39/245.

18 *Al-Ahram*, February 23, 1967, in Fuad A. Jabber, ed. *International Documents on Palestine, 1967* (Beirut: Institute For Palestine Studies, 1970), p. 496.

19 Letter, Fletcher to Unwin, No. 1036/67, March 2, 1967, UKNA, FCO 39/245.

20 Minute by D. J. Speares, February 24, 1967, UKNA, FCO 39/245.
21 *Al Ahram*, February 23, 1967, in Jabber, *International Documents on Palestine*, p. 495.
22 Ibid., p. 500.
23 Ibid., p. 495.
24 Daniel Dishon, ed. *Middle East Record, 1967* (Jerusalem: Israel Universities Press, 1971), p. 547.
25 Ibid., p. 550.
26 *Jumhūriyya*, January 1, 1967 in Dishon, *Middle East Record, 1967*, p. 538.
27 *Jumhūriyya*, April 28, 1967 in Dishon, *Middle East Record, 1967*, p. 538.
28 Dishon, *Middle East Record, 1967*, p. 551.
29 Telegram 4763, Cairo to State, February 23, 1967, LBJL, NSF/UAR/160/5.
30 See Letter, Saunders to Battle, February 3, 1967, LBJL, NSF/Saunders/32.

21 Cold Shoulders

1 Telegram, Cairo to State, February 24, 1967, *FRUS 1964–1968*, Vol. XVIII, doc. 392.
2 Telegram, Cairo to State, March 4, 1967, *FRUS 1964–1968*, Vol. XVIII, doc. 393.
3 Telegram 5031, Cairo to State, March 4, 1967, LBJL, NSF/UAR/160/5.
4 Telegram 5036, Cairo to State, March 5, 1967, LBJL, NSF/UAR/160/5.
5 Telegram, Cairo to State, March 4, 1967, *FRUS 1964–1968*, Vol. XVIII, doc. 393.
6 Hasanayn Haykal, "We and the US," *Al-Ahram*, February 24, March 3, 10, 17, and May 5, 12, 1967, in Dishon, *Middle East Record, 1967*, pp. 49–50.
7 *Al-Ahram*, March 17, 1967, in Dishon, *Middle East Record, 1967*, p. 51.
8 Rostow to Johnson (at the LBJ Ranch), March 4, 1967, LBJL, NSF/UAR/160/5; Telegram 8693, Cairo to the White House, "Eyes Only for Walt Rostow and Howard Wriggins," undated, LBJL, NSF/UAR/160/5. Saunders recommended that Johnson meet with Nasser, which Rostow dismissed with: "Perhaps a letter from you could do the job."
9 Memorandum, Bergus to Battle, March 16, 1967, *FRUS 1964–1968*, Vol. XVIII, doc. 396.
10 Telegram 149868, State to Cairo, March 6, 1967, LBJL, NSF/UAR/160/5.
11 Telegram 5036, Cairo to State, March 5, 1967, LBJL, NSF/UAR/160/5.

22 US-Egypt Relations Unbound

1 Resolutions Adopted by the Arab League Council at Its Forty-Seventh Ordinary Meeting, Cairo, March 18, 1967, in Jabber, *International Documents on Palestine*, p. 511.
2 Cairo Domestic Service, April 11, 1967, FBIS, April 11, 1967, B1.
3 See Dishon, *Middle East Record 1967*, p. 54; Saunders to Rostow, April 26, 1967, LBJL, NSF/Saunders/32; Draft Memorandum for Johnson, "What is Nasser up to in Yemen," May 3, 1967, LBJL, NSF/Saunders/32. According to Saunders, junior officials at the Egyptian camp "dropped their guard," were attacked by "local tribesmen" who killed "nine Egyptians," and therefore "the only way the juniors saw to shift blame from themselves was to pin the attack on us." See Memorandum, Saunders for Rostow, "An Arab Interpretation of Nasser's Policy," May 10, 1967, LBJL, NSF/Saunders/32.

4 Memorandum, Rostow for Johnson, "Our Latest Brush with Nasser," May 10, 1967, LBJL, NSF/Saunders/32.

5 Cairo Press Review, May 3, 1967, UKNA, FCO 39/245.

6 Sana Domestic Service, May 8, 1967, FBIS, May 9, 1967, E1. According to the Syrian Charge in Washington, in a conversation with Saunders, "Yemen is the opening gun in a campaign to show us [the United States] how much he [Nasser] can do if we don't provide food aid." See Memorandum, Saunders for Rostow, "An Arab Interpretation of Nasser's Policy," May 10, 1967, LBJL, NSF/Saunders/32. Saunders dismissed the theory of Nasser having a "master plan for driving us out of the Middle East."

7 Speech of UAR President Nasir on Labour Day, May 2, 1967, *Al-Ahram*, May 3, 1967, in Jabber, *International Documents on Palestine*, p. 525.

8 Radio Cairo, May 17, 1967, FBIS, May 18, 1967, B4.

9 Radio Cairo, May 21, 1967, FBIS, May 22, 1967, B1.

10 Radio Cairo, May 23, 1967, FBIS, May 23, 1967, B4.

11 Radio Cairo, May 23, 1967, FBIS, May 24, 1967, B4.

12 Radio Cairo, May 23, 1967, FBIS, May 24, 1967, B5.

13 Radio Cairo, May 24, 1967, FBIS, May 24, 1967, B6.

14 Radio Cairo, May 24, 1967, FBIS, May 24, 1967, B7.

15 Radio Cairo, May 26, 1967, FBIS, May 26, 1967, B1.

16 Radio Cairo, May 26, 1967, FBIS, May 26, 1967, B2.

17 Memorandum of Conversation, "Farewell Call on Foreign Minister Riad," June 3 1967, US National Archives at College Park (hereafter USNA), RG 59, Middle East Crisis Files 1967, Box 2.

18 Telegram 8485, Cairo to State, June 4, 1967, USNA, RG 59, Middle East Crisis Files 1967, Box 4.

19 Malcolm Kerr, *The Arab Cold War, 1958–1967: A Study of Ideology in Politics* (Oxford: Royal Institute of International Affairs, 1967).

20 "Interview Granted by Saudi King Faysal to a Correspondent of American Television," *Al-Bilal*, May 31, 1967, in Jabber, *International Documents on Palestine*, p. 570.

21 Memorandum, Rostow for Johnson, May 26, 1967, USNA, Middle East Crisis Files, 1967, Box 2.

22 See Gamal Abdel Nasser, *On Non-Alignment* (Cairo: UAR Information Administration, date unknown).

23 See Nasser, *The Philosophy of the Revolution*.

24 Speech of UAR President Nasir to Members of the National Assembly, May 29, 1967, in Jabber, *International Documents on Palestine*, p. 564.

23 Conclusion: Applied History

1 Graham Allison and Niall Ferguson, "Why the U.S. President Needs a Council of Historians," *The Atlantic* (September 2016); Richard Neustadt and Ernest May, *Thinking in Time: The Uses of History for Decision Makers* (New York: The Free Press, 1986); William H. McNeill, "Why Study History?" *American Historical Association* (1985).

2 Richard Parker, ed., *The Six-Day War: A Retrospective* (Gainesville: University Press of Florida, 1996), p. 196.

3 For a president who spent much of his time on the phone, Johnson spoke very rarely about Nasser during his five years in office.

4 Parker, *The Six-Day War*, p. 229.

5 Memorandum of Conversation by Rostow, May 22, 1967, LBJL, NSF/Saunders/32; Saunders Memorandum for Rostow, "Kamel's Conversation with the President," May 24, 1967, LBJL, NSF/Saunders/32.

6 Parker, *The Six-Day War*, p. 213.

7 Niall Ferguson, *Kissinger*, vol. I: *1923–1968 – The Idealist* (London and New York: Allen Lane/Penguin Press, 2008), p. 805.

8 Bayly, *The Birth of the Modern World*, p. 88.

Bibliography

Unpublished Documents

Liddell Hart Centre for Military Archives, King's College London (LHCMA)
   Transcripts of interviews for *The Fifty Years War: Israel and the Arabs*
Lyndon Baines Johnson Presidential Library, Austin, Texas (LBJL)
   National Security Files, Committee Files, Committee on Nuclear Proliferation, Cairo Resolutions
   National Security Files, Country Files, Middle East
   National Security Files, Country Files, Middle East Crisis
   National Security Files, Country Files, United Arab Republic
   National Security Files, Files of Harold H. Saunders
   National Security Files, Files of Howard Wriggins
   National Security Files, Files of McGeorge Bundy, Miscellaneous Meetings, Vol. 1
   National Security Files, Files of Robert W. Komer
   National Security Files, Files of the Special Committee of the NSC, 1967 Middle East Crisis
   National Security Files, Files of Walt W. Rostow, Middle East
   National Security Files, Memos to the President
   National Security Files, Name Files, Komer Memos, Vol. 1
   National Security Files, Name Files, Komer Memos, Vol. 2
   National Security Files, Name Files, Rostow Memos
   National Security Files, Name Files, Saunders Memos
   National Security Files, Name Files, Wriggins Memos, 1966
   National Security Files, Name Files, Wriggins Memos, 1967
   National Security Files, National Security Action Memoranda
   Oral History Collection
   President's Daily Diary
   White House Central Files, Subject File, Countries, United Arab Republic
   White House Confidential Files, United Arab Republic
The National Archives, Kew, London (UKNA)
   CAB: Cabinet Office
   FCO: Foreign and Commonwealth Office
   FO: Foreign Office
   PREM: Records of the British Prime Minister's Office
United States National Archives, College Park, Maryland (USNA)
   RG 59: Central Foreign Policy Files, 1967–1969
   RG 59: Middle East Crisis Files, 1967
   RG 59: Records for the Middle East Crisis
   CIA Records Search Tool (CREST)

Published Documents

Diab, Zuhair, ed. *International Documents on Palestine, 1968*. Beirut: Institute for Palestine Studies and the University of Kuwait, 1971.

Dishon, Daniel, ed. *Middle East Record, Volume 3, 1967*. Jerusalem: Israel Universities Press, 1971.

Dishon, Daniel. *Middle East Record, Volume 4, 1968*. Jerusalem: Israel Universities Press and John Wiley, 1973.

Jabber, Fuad A., ed. *International Documents on Palestine, 1967*. Beirut: Institute for Palestine Studies, 1970.

Ministere Des Affaires Etrangeres (Commission Des Archives Diplomatiques). *Documents Diplomatiques Francais: 1967: Tome 1: 1er Janvier–1er Juillet*. Brussels: P.I.E. Peter Lang, 2008.

Ministere Des Affaires Etrangeres (Commission Des Archives Diplomatiques). *Documents Diplomatiques Francais: 1967: Tome 2: 1er Juillet–29 Decembre*. Brussels: P.I.E. Peter Lang, 2008.

Naumkin, Vitaly, ed. *Blizhnvostochnyi Konflict: Iz Dokumentov Arkhiva Vnyeshney Politiki Rossiyskoy Federatsii: Tom 2: 1957–1967*. Moscow: Materik, 2003.

Oron, Yitzhak, ed. *Middle East Record Volume 1, 1960*. Jerusalem: Weidenfeld and Nicolson, 1965.

Oron, Yitzhak, ed. *Middle East Record Volume 2, 1961*. Jerusalem: Israel Program for Scientific Translations, 1966.

Online Documents

Association for Diplomatic Studies and Training (adst.org)
Oral Histories
Board of Governors of the Federal Reserve System (search.newyorkfed.org)
CIA Freedom of Information Act (CIA FOIA) Electronic Reading Room (foia.cia.gov)
    The Arab-Israeli Handbook
    Central Intelligence Bulletin
    Intelligence Memorandum
    Intelligence Report
    National Intelligence Estimate
    Special Series Crisis Collection
    Studies in Intelligence
    The President's Daily Brief
Foreign Broadcast Information Service (FBIS) Daily Reports, 1941–1996 (readex.com)
Foreign Relations of the United States (FRUS), Office of the Historian (history.state. gov)
    1952–1954, Vol. IX, Part 1, Near and Middle East
    1952–1954, Vol. IX, Part 2, Near and Middle East
    1958–1960, Vol. IV, Foreign Economic Policy
    1958–1960, Vol. XIII, Arab-Israeli Dispute; United Arab Republic; North Africa
    1961–1963, Vol. XVII, Near East, 1961–1962
    1961–1963, Vol. XVIII, Near East, 1962–1963

1964–1968, Vol. VIII, International Monetary and Trade Policy

1964–1968, Vol. IX, International Development and Economic Defense Policy; Commodities

1964–1968, Vol. X, National Security Policy

1964–1968, Vol. XIV, Soviet Union

1964–1968, Vol. XVI, Cyprus; Greece; Turkey

1964–1968, Vol. XVIII, Arab-Israeli Dispute, 1964–1967

1964–1968, Vol. XIX, Arab-Israeli Crisis and War, 1967

1964–1968, Vol. XX, Arab-Israeli Dispute, 1967–1968

1964–1968, Vol. XXI, Near East Region; Arabian Peninsula

1964–1968, Vol. XXXIII, Organization and Management of Foreign Policy; United Nations

1964–1968, Vol. XXXIV, Energy Diplomacy and Global Issues

Miller Center, University of Virginia (millercenter.org)

The Secret White House Tapes

Presidential Speeches

The American Presidency Project, University of California, Santa Barbara (presidency.ucsb.edu)

US Government Accountability Office (GAO) Electronic Records Archive (gao.gov)

Public Law

Report to Congress

US Government Printing Office (GPO) Senate Prints (gpo.gov)

Executive Sessions of the Senate Foreign Relations Committee Together with Joint Sessions with the Senate Armed Services Committee (Historical Series)

Rand Corporation (rand.org)

United States Air Force Project

United Nations (UN Docs), Officials Documents of the United Nations (documents.un.org)

United States Agency for International Development (USAID), Development Experience Clearinghouse (dec.usaid.gov)

Wilson Center (wilsoncenter.org)

Nuclear Proliferation International History Project

Newspapers, Magazines, and News Agencies (Print and Online)

Al-Ahram

Associated Press (AP)

Chicago Tribune

Jewish Telegraphic Agency

Haaretz

Independent

New Yorker

New York Times

Reuter

Time

United Press International (UPI)
Wall Street Journal
Washington Post

Memoirs and Autobiographies

El-Sadat, Anwar. *In Search of Identity: An Autobiography.* New York: Harper & Row, 1978.

Fawzi, Mohamed (General). *The Three Years War, 1967–1970: The Memoir of General Mohamed Fawzi, the Former War Minister.* Cairo: Dar al-Mustaqabal Printing, 1990 (5th ed.). Translated and annotated by Aboul-Enein, Youssef H., ed. *Reconstructing a Shattered Egyptian Army.* Annapolis: Naval Institute Press, 2014.

Heikal, Mohamed. *Nasser: The Cairo Documents: The Private Papers of Nasser.* London: New English Library, 1972.

Heikal, Mohamed. *Sphinx and Commisar: The Rise and Fall of Soviet Influence in the Arab World.* London: Collins, 1978.

Riad, Mahmoud. *The Struggle for Peace in the Middle East.* London: Quartet Books, 1981.

Pamphlets and Working Papers

Kadi, Leila S. *Arab Summit Conferences and the Palestine Problem 1936–1950, 1964–1966.* Beirut: Palestine Liberation Organisation Research Centre, 1966.

Kerr, Malcolm. *The Arab Cold War, 1958–1967: A Study of Ideology in Politics.* Oxford: Royal Institute of International Affairs, 1967.

Komer, Robert. "Organization and Management of the 'New Model' Pacification Program—1966–1969." Rand Corporation, May 7, 1970.

Lowdermilk, Walter Clay. "Palestine Prospects and the Jordan Valley Plan." In *Palestine Can Take Millions.* Jerusalem: Hamadpis Lipshitz Press, 1944.

Lowdermilk, Walter Clay. *The Untried Approach to the Palestine Problem.* New York: American Christian Palestine Committee, 1948.

Nakhleh, Issa. *The Diversion of Waters from the International Water System of the Jordan Valley by Zionist Authorities in Occupied Palestine Is a Violation of International Law and Constitutes an Aggression Against the Arab States: Memorandum Submitted by the Arab Higher Committee for Palestine to The Ministries of Foreign Affairs of Member States of the United Nations.* New York: The Palestine Arab Delegation, January 1964.

Nasser, Gamal Abdel. *The Philosophy of the Revolution: Book 1.* Cairo: Mondiale Press, date unknown.

Nasser, Gamal Abdel. *On Non-Alignment.* Cairo: UAR Information Administration, date unknown.

Srivastava, Uma K. *Impact of P.L. 480 Aid on India's Money Supply and External Debt-Service Obligations: A Look Ahead* (Card Report 44). Ames: The Center for Agricultural and Rural Development, 1972.

United Arab Republic. *Address by President Gamal Abdel Nasser at the Meeting of the National Assembly's Ordinary Session, Cairo, March 26, 1964.* Cairo: Information Department, undated.

United Arab Republic. *The River Jordan and the Zionist Conspiracy.* Cairo: UAR Information Department, 1965.

Articles

Bunch, Clea Lutz. "Strike at Samu: Jordan, Israel, the United States, and the Origins of the Six Day War." *Diplomatic History* 32, no. 1 (January 2008): 55–76.

Cohen, Raymond. "Intercultural Communication between Israel and Egypt: Deterrence Failure before the Six-Day War." *Review of International Studies* 14, no. 1 (January 1988): 1–16.

Dawn, Ernest C. "The Egyptian Remilitarization of Sinai, May 1967." *Journal of Contemporary History* 3, no. 3 (July 1968): 201–24.

Epstein, Charlotte. "Theorizing Agency in Hobbes's Wake: The Rational Actor, the Self, or the Speaking Subject?" *International Organization* 67, no. 2 (April 2013): 287–316.

Ferris, Jesse. "Soviet Support for Egypt's Intervention in Yemen, 1962–1963." *Journal of Cold War Studies* 10, no. 4 (Fall 2008): 5–36.

Fromkin, David. "Lyndon Johnson and Foreign Policy: What the New Documents Show." *Foreign Affairs* (January/February 1995).

Kear, Simon. "Diplomatic Innovation: Nasser and the Origins of the Interests Section." *Diplomacy and Statecraft* 12, no. 3 (September 2001): 65–86.

Little, Douglas.. "David or Goliath? The Israel Lobby and Its Critics." *Political Science Quarterly* 123, no. 1 (Spring 2008): 151–6.

Little, Douglas. "The Making of a Special Relationship: The United States and Israel, 1957–68." *International Journal of Middle East Studies* 25, no. 4 (November 1993): 563–85.

Mawby, Spencer. "Britain's Last Imperial Frontier: The Aden Protectorates, 1952–1959." *Journal of Imperial and Commonwealth History* 29, no. 2 (May 2001): 75–100.

McNamara, Robert. "Britain, Nasser and the Outbreak of the Six Day War." *Journal of Contemporary History* 35, no. 4 (October 2000): 619–39.

Miller, Rory. "Bible and Soil: Walter Clay Lowdermilk, the Jordan Valley Project and the Palestine Debate." *Middle Eastern Studies* 39, no. 2 (April 2003): 55–81.

Nasser, Gamal Abdel. "The Egyptian Revolution." *Foreign Affairs* 33, no. 2 (January 1955): 199–211.

Neff, Donald. "Conflict at the Jordan River, 1949–1967." *Journal of Palestine Studies* 23, no. 4 (Summer 1994): 26–40.

Paterson, Thomas G. "The Historian as Detective: Senator Kenneth Keating, the Missiles in Cuba, and His Mysterious Sources." *Diplomatic History* 11, no. 1 (January 1987): 67–70.

Sadat, Anwar el. "Where Egypt Stands." *Foreign Affairs* 51, no. 1 (October 1972): 114–23.

Books and Monographs

Abo-el-Einen, Mohammed Mahmoud. *Foreign Aid and Dependency: United States Food Aid to Egypt, 1954–1980.* Madison: University of Wisconsin-Madison, 1983.

Aburish, Said K. *Nasser: The Last Arab.* New York: Thomas Dunn Books, 2004.

Ahlberg, Kristin L. *Transplanting the Great Society: Lyndon Johnson and Food for Peace.* Columbia: University of Missouri Press, 2008.

Ajami, Fouad. *The Arab Predicament: Arab Political Thought and Practice Since 1967.* Cambridge: Cambridge University Press, 1999 (originally published 1981).

Amin, Galal A. *Egypt's Economic Predicament: A Study in the Interaction of External Pressure, Political Folly, and Social Tension in Egypt, 1960–1990.* Leiden: E.J. Brill, 1995.

Ashton, Nigel. J., ed. *The Cold War in the Middle East: Regional Conflict and the Superpowers, 1967–1973*. London: Routledge, 2007.

Bacchus, William I. *Foreign Policy and the Bureaucratic Process: The State Department's Country Director System*. Princeton: Princeton University Press, 1974.

Barrett, Roby C. *The Greater Middle East and the Cold War: US Foreign Policy under Eisenhower and Kennedy*. London: I.B. Tauris, 2007.

Bass, Warren. *Support Any Friend: Kennedy's Middle East and the Making of the US-Israel Alliance*. Oxford: Oxford University Press, 2003.

Bayly, C. A. *The Birth of the Modern World: 1780–1914*. Oxford: Blackwell Publishing, 2004.

Berlin, Isaiah. *The Hedgehog and the Fox: An Essay on Tolstoy's View of History*. New York: Simon and Schuster, 1953.

Brands, H. W., ed. *The Foreign Policies of Lyndon Johnson: Beyond Vietnam*. College Station: Texas A&M University Press, 1999.

Burns, William Joseph. *Economic Aid and American Policy toward Egypt, 1955–1981*. Albany: State University of New York Press, 1985.

Caro, Robert A. *Means of Ascent*. New York: Vintage Books, 1990.

Cohen, Avner. *Israel and the Bomb*. New York: Columbia University Press, 1998.

Cohen, Warren I., and Nancy Bernkopf Tucker, eds. *Lyndon Johnson Confronts the World: American Foreign Policy, 1963–1968*. Cambridge: Cambridge University Press, 1994.

Coleman, David. *The Fourteenth Day: JFK and the Aftermath of the Cuban Missile Crisis*. New York: W.W. Norton, 2012.

Copeland, Miles. *The Game of Nations: The Amorality of Power Politics*. New York: Simon and Schuster, 1969.

Doran, Michael Scott. *Ike's Gamble: America's Rise to Dominance in the Middle East*. New York: Free Press, 2016.

Dumbrell, Josh. *President Lyndon Johnson and Soviet Communism*. Manchester: Manchester University Press, 2004.

Ferguson, Niall. *Kissinger*, vol. I: *1923–1968 – The Idealist*. London and New York: Allen Lane/Penguin Press, 2015.

Ferris, Jesse. *Nasser's Gamble: How Intervention in Yemen Caused the Six-Day War and the Decline of Egyptian Power*. Princeton: Princeton University Press, 2013.

Gaddis, John Lewis. *On Grand Strategy*. New York: Penguin Press, 2018.

Gaddis, John Lewis. *Strategies of Containment: A Critical Appraisal of American National Security Policy during the Cold War*. Oxford: Oxford University Press, 2005. Revised and Expanded Edition.

Gat, Moshe. *Britain and the Conflict in the Middle East, 1964–1967: The Coming of the Six-Day War*. Westport: Praeger, 2003.

Gerges, Fawaz A. *The Superpowers and the Middle East: Regional and International Politics, 1955–1967*. Boulder: Westview Press, 1994.

Gibson, Bryan R. *Sold Out? US Foreign Policy, Iraq, the Kurds, and the Cold War*. New York: Palgrave MacMillan, 2015.

Guess, George M. *The Politics of United States Foreign Aid, Volume 7*. London: Routledge, 1987.

Halberstam, David. *The Best and the Brightest*. New York: The Modern Library, 1972.

Hart, Parker T. *Saudi Arabia and the United States: Birth of a Security Partnership*. Bloomington: Indiana University Press, 1998.

Hatzivassilou, Evanathis. *Greece and the Cold War: Front Line State, 1952–1967*. London: Routledge, 2006.

Hofstadter, Richard. *Anti-Intellectualism in American Life*. New York: Vintage Books, 1962.

Hogan, Michael J. *America in the World: The Historiography of US Foreign Relations Since 1941*. Cambridge: Cambridge University Press, 1995.

Hourani, Albert. *A History of the Arab Peoples*. Cambridge: Harvard University Press, 2002 (originally published 1991).

Ions, Edmund S. *The Politics of John F. Kennedy*. London: Routledge, 1967.

Jacobs, Matthew F. *Imagining the Middle East: The Building of an American Foreign Policy, 1918–1967*. Chapel Hill: The University of North Carolina Press, 2011.

Jankowski, James P. *Nasser's Egypt, Arab Nationalism, and the United Arab Republic*. Boulder: Lynne Rienner Publishers, 2002.

Jones, Frank Leith. *Blowtorch: Robert Komer, Vietnam, and American Cold War Strategy*. Annapolis: Naval Institute Press, 2013.

Kandil, Hazem. *Soldiers, Spies, and Statesmen: Egypt's Road to Revolt*. London: Verso, 2012.

Karsh, Efraim. *Islamic Imperialism: A History*. New Haven: Yale University Press, 2006.

Kerr, Malcolm H. *The Arab Cold War: Gamal Abd al-Nasir and His Rivals, 1958–70*. London: Oxford University Press, 1971.

Kerr, Malcolm H. *Egypt under Nasser*. New York: Foreign Policy Association, 1963.

Kerr, Malcolm H. *Rich and Poor States in the Middle East: Egypt and the New Arab Order*. Boulder: Westview Press, 1982.

Klinghoffer, Judith A. *Vietnam, Jews and the Middle East: Unintended Consequences*. New York: St. Martin's Press, 1999.

Kunz, Diane B., ed. *The Diplomacy of the Crucial Decade: American Foreign Relations During the 1960s*. New York: Columbia University Press 1994.

Laqueur, Walter. *The Struggle for the Middle East: The Soviet Union and the Middle East, 1958–1968*. London: Routledge, 1969.

Little, Douglas. *American Orientalism: The United States and the Middle East since 1945*. Chapel Hill: University of North Carolina Press, 2009.

Louis, Roger Wm. and Avi Shlaim, eds. *The 1967 Arab-Israeli War: Origins and Consequences*. Cambridge: Cambridge University Press, 2012.

Mawby, Spencer. *British Policy in Aden and the Protectorates, 1955–1967: Last Outpost of a Middle Eastern Empire*. London: Routledge, 2006.

Milne, David. *America's Rasputin: Walt Rostow and the Vietnam War*. New York: Hill and Wang, 2008.

Mortimer, Rex. *Indonesian Communism under Sukarno: Ideology and Politics, 1959–1965*. Ithaca: Cornell University Press, 1974.

Neustadt, Richard and Ernest May. *Thinking in Time: The Uses of History for Decision Makers*. New York: The Free Press, 1986.

Parker, Richard B., ed. *The Six Day War: A Retrospective*. Gainesville: University Press of Florida, 1996.

Perlmutter, Amos. *Egypt: The Praetorian State*. New Brunswick: Transaction Books, 1974.

Preston, Andrew. *The War Council: McGeorge Bundy, the NSC, and Vietnam*. Cambridge: Harvard University Press, 2010.

Prins, Nomi. *All the President's Bankers: The Hidden Alliances that Drive American Power*. New York: Nation Books, 2014.

Quandt, William B. *Decade of Decisions: American Policy toward the Arab-Israeli Conflict, 1967–1976*. Berkeley: University of California Press, 1974.

Rakove, Robert R. *Kennedy, Johnson, and the Nonaligned World*. New York: Cambridge University Press, 2013.

Rostow, W. *The Stages of Economic Growth: A Non-Communist Manifesto*. Cambridge: Cambridge University Press, 1960.

Safran, Nadav. *Saudi Arabia: The Ceaseless Quest for Security*. Ithaca: Cornell University Press, 1988.

Savage, Sean J. *JFK, LBJ, and the Democratic Party*. Albany: State University of New York Press, 2004.

Schake, Kori. *Safe Passage: The Transition from British to American Hegemony*. Cambridge: Harvard University Press, 2017.

Shalom, Zaki. *The Role of US Diplomacy in the Lead-Up to the Six Day War: Balancing Moral Commitments and National Interests*. Eastbourne: Sussex Academic Press, 2012.

Sharnoff, Michael. *Nasser's Peace: Egypt's Response to the 1967 War with Israel*. London: Routledge, 2017.

Sirrs, Owen L. *Nasser and the Missile Age in the Middle East*. London: Routledge, 2006.

Spiegel, Steven L. *The Other Arab-Israeli Conflict: Making America's Middle East Policy, from Truman to Reagan*. Chicago: The University of Chicago Press, 1985.

Strassler, Robert B., ed. *The Landmark Herodotus: The Histories*. New York: Anchor Books, 2007.

Summitt, April R. *John F. Kennedy and US-Middle East Relations: A History of American Foreign Policy in the 1960s*. New York: Edwin Mellen Press, 2008.

Walt, Stephen M. *The Origins of Alliances*. Ithaca: Cornell University Press, 1987.

Waterbury, John. *The Egypt of Nasser and Sadat*. Princeton: Princeton University Press, 1983.

Weinbaum, Marvin G. *Egypt and the Politics of US Economic Aid*. Boulder: Westview Press, 1986.

Weiner, Tim. *Legacy of Ashes: The History of the CIA*. New York: Anchor Books, 2007.

Wendt, Alexander. *Social Theory of International Politics*. Cambridge: Cambridge University Press, 1999.

Westad, Odd Arne. *The Cold War: A World History*. New York: Basic Books, 2017.

Winrow, Gareth. *The Foreign Policy of the GDR in Africa*. Cambridge: Cambridge University Press, 2009.

Zvi, Abraham Ben. *Lyndon B. Johnson and the Politics of Arms Sales to Israel: In the Shadow of the Hawk*. London: Frank Cass, 2004.

Index